W9-BWU-103

Sociology of "Developing Societies"
Latin America

Sociology of "Developing Societies"

General Editor: Teodor Shanin

THEMATIC VOLUMES

INTRODUCTION TO THE SOCIOLOGY OF
"DEVELOPING SOCIETIES"
Hamza Alavi and Teodor Shanin

SOCIALIST "DEVELOPING SOCIETIES"?
(in preparation)

THEORIES OF SOCIAL TRANSFORMATION
(in preparation)

REGIONAL VOLUMES

SUB-SAHARAN AFRICA
Chris Allen and Gavin Williams

SOUTH ASIA
John Harriss and Hamza Alavi (forthcoming)

LATIN AMERICA
Eduardo P. Archetti, Paul Cammack and Bryan Roberts

THE MIDDLE EAST
Talal Asad and Roger Owen

SOUTH-EAST ASIA
John Taylor and Andrew Turton (forthcoming)

CENTRAL AMERICA AND THE CARIBBEAN
(in preparation)

170873

11.00
GoP

Latin America

**edited by Eduardo P. Archetti,
Paul Cammack and Bryan Roberts**

980
L357a

**Monthly Review Press
New York and London**

Alverno College
Library Media Center
Milwaukee, Wisconsin

Selection, editorial matter and Introduction © Eduardo P. Archetti,
Paul Cammack, Bryan Roberts 1987

All rights reserved. No reproduction, copy or transmission
of this publication may be made without written permission.

Library of Congress Cataloging-in-Publication Data

Latin America.

Bibliography: p.
1. Latin America. 2. Latin America–Social
conditions.   3. Latin America–Economic conditions.
I. Archetti, Eduardo P.   II. Cammack, Paul.
Roberts, Bryan R., 1939–
F1408.L384 1987   980   86–8456
ISBN 0–85345–685–2
ISBN 0–85345–686–0 (pbk.)

Monthly Review Press
155 West 23rd Street
New York, N.Y. 10011

Printed in Hong Kong

10 9 8 7 6 5 4 3 2 1

Contents

Series Preface

The question of the so-called "developing societies" lies at the very heart of the political, the economic and the moral crises of the contemporary global society. It is central to the relations of power, diplomacy and war of the world we live in. It is decisive when the material well-being of humanity is concerned; that is, the ways some people make a living and the ways some people hunger. It presents a fundamental dimension of social inequality and of struggles for social justice. During the last generation it has also become a main challenge to scholarship, a field where the perplexity is deeper, the argument sharper and the potential for new illuminations more profound. That challenge reflects the outstanding social relevance of this problem. It reflects, too, an essential ethnocentrism that weighs heavily on the contemporary social sciences. The very terminology which designates "developing" or "underdeveloping" or "emerging" societies is impregnated with teleology which identifies parts of Europe and the USA as "developed". Images of the world at large as a unilinear rise from barbarity to modernity (or vice versa as a descent to hell) have often substituted for the analysis of actuality, as simplistic metaphors often do. To come to grips with a social reality, which is systematically different from that of one's own, and to explain its specific logic and momentum, is a most difficult conceptual and pedagogic task. It is the more so, for the fundamental questions of the "developing societies" are not of difference only but of relationships past and present with the countries of advanced capitalism and industrialization. It is in that light that we encounter as analysts and teachers not only a challenge to "sociology of development", but also a major challenge to radical scholarship itself.

The Sociology of "Developing Societies" series aims to offer a systematically linked set of texts for use as a major teaching aid at university level. It is being produced by a group of teachers and scholars related by common interest, general outlook and commitment sufficient to provide an overall coherence but by no means a single monolithic view. The object is, on the one hand, to bring relevant questions into focus and, on the other hand, to teach through debate. We think that at the current stage "a textbook" would necessarily gloss over the very diversity, contradictions and inadequacies of our thought. On the other hand, collections of articles are often rather accidental in content. The format of a conceptually structured set of readers was chosen, sufficiently open to accommodate variability of views within a coherent system of presentation. They bring together works by sociologists, social anthropologists, historians, political scientists, economists, literary critics and novelists in an intended disregard of the formal disciplinary divisions of the academic enterprise.

Three major alternatives of presentation stand out: first, a comparative discussion of the social structures within the "developing societies", focusing on the generic within them; second, the exploration of the distinct character of the main regions of the "developing societies"; third, consideration of context and content of the theories of social transformation and change. Accordingly, our *Introduction* to the series deals with the general issues of comparative study, other books cover different regions, while a final volume is devoted to an examination of basic paradigms of the theories of social transformation. They therefore represent the three main dimensions of the problem area, leaving it to each teacher and student to choose from them and to compose their own course.

The topic is ideologically charged, relating directly to the outlook and the ideals of everyone. The editors and many of the contributors share a broad sense of common commitment, though there is among them a considerable diversity of political viewpoint and theoretical approach. The common ground may be best indicated as three fundamental negations. First, there is an implacable opposition to every social system of oppression of humans by other humans. That entails also the rejection of scholastic apologia of every such system, be it imperialism, class oppression, elitism, sexism or the like. Second, there is the rejection of "preaching down" easy solutions from the comfort of air-conditioned offices and campuses, whether in the "West" or in "developing societies" themselves, and of the tacit assumption of our privileged wisdom that has little to learn from the common people in the "developing societies". Third, there is the rejection of the notion of scholastic detachment from social commitments as a pedagogy and as a way of life. True scholarship is not a propaganda exercise even of the most sacred values. Nor is it without social consequences, however conceived. There are students and teachers alike who think that indifference improves vision. We believe the opposite to be true.

TEODOR SHANIN

Acknowledgements

The editors and publishers wish to thank those who have kindly given permission for the use of copyright material:

Cardoso and Falleto: Multiple Paths, by Ian Roxborough, from "Historical Unity and Diversity in Latin America", *Journal of Latin American Studies*, 16, 1, 1984.

Dependency Revisited, by Philip O'Brien from article of same name in C. Abel and C. Lewis, eds, *Latin America, Economic Imperialism and the State: the Political Economy of the External Connexion from Independence to the Present*. Athlone Press, 1984.

The Dependency Perspective, by Fernando Henrique Cardoso, from "The Consumption of Dependency Theory in the United States", *Latin American Research Review*, 12, 3, 1977.

The Spatial Organisation of the Colonial Economy, by Carlos Sempat Assadourian, in *El sistema de la economia colonial*, IEP, Lima, 1982.

Forced and Free Labour in Late Colonial Potosi by Enrique Tandeter, from article of the same name in *Past and Present*, 93, 1981.

The Struggle for Solidarity: Class, Culture and Community in Highland Indian America by Steve J. Stern from article of same name in *Radical History Review*, 27, 1983.

Slavery and Resistance in the Colombian Chocó by William F. Sharp, from "Manumission, Libres and Black Resistance, The Colombian Chocó, 1680–1810" in Robert Brent Toplin, ed., *Slavery and Race Relations in Latin America*, Greenwood Press, 1974.

Political Elites and State Building: Brazil in Comparative Perspective, by José Murilo de Carvalho from 'Political Elites and State Building: the Case of Nineteenth Century Brazil", *Comparative Studies in Society and History*, 21, 3, 1982.

Bases of Political Alignment in Early Republican Spanish America, by Frank Safford, from article of same name in Richard Graham and Peter Smith, eds, *New Approaches to Latin American History*, University of Texas Press, 1974.

Rural Workers in Spanish America: Problems of Peonage and Oppression by Arnold J. Bauer, from article of the same name in *Hispanic American Historical Review*, 59, 1, 1979.

The Introduction of Free Labour on São Paolo Coffee Plantations, by Verena Stolcke and Michael M. Hall, from article of the same name in *Journal of Peasant Studies*, 10, 2–3, 1983.

The Working Class and the Mexican Revolution, by Alan Knight, from "The Working Class and the Mexican Revolution c. 1900–1920". *Journal of Latin American Studies*, 16, 1, 1984.

The Development of a Revolutionary Labour Movement in Chile, by Peter DeShazo, from "The Valparaíso Maritime Strike of 1903 and the development of a Revolutionary Labor Movement in Chile", *Journal of Latin American Studies*, 11, 1, 1979.

Latin American Populism by Ian Roxborough, from "Historical Unity and Diversity in Latin America", Journal of Latin American Studies, 16, 1, 1984.

Populism and Social Control, by Steve Stein, from *Populism in Peru*, University of Wisconsin Press, 1980.

Peronism in Historical and Comparative Perspective, by Ernesto Laclau, from "Towards a Theory of Populism" in *Politics and Ideology in Marxist Theory*, Verso, 1977.

Velasquismo: An Interpretation, by Agustin Cueva, from monograph of the same name in *The Process of Political Domination in Ecuador*, Transaction Books, 1982.

Paths of Transition, by David Goodman and Michael Redclift, in *From Peasant to Proletarian: Capitalist Development and Agrarian Transitions*, Blackwell, 1981.

Capitalist Development and Agrarian Structure in Brazil, by Juarez Rubens Brandão Lopes, from article of the same name in *International Journal of Urban and Regional Research*, 2, 1, 1978.

Rural Bourgeoisie and Peasantry in the Highlands of Ecuador, by Eduardo Archetti and Kristi Anne Stölen, from "Burguesia rural y campesinado en la sierra ecuatoriana", *Caravelles*, 34, 1980.

Achievements and Contradictions of the Peruvian Land Reform, by Cristobal Kay, from article of the same name in *Journal of Development Studies*, 18, 2, 1982.

The Division of Labor by Sex in Agriculture: A Peruvian Case Study, by Carmen Diana Deere in *Economic Development and Cultural Change*, 30, 4, 1982.

Peasant Production and Population in Mexico, by Arturo Warman, from article of the same name in Joan Mencher, ed., *Social Anthropology of Peasantry*, Somaiya, 1983.

The Logic of Disorder, by Lucio Kowarick, from paper of the same name, Discussion Paper 102, IDS, University of Sussex.

Urban Transport and Popular Violence in Brazil, by José Alvaro Moises and Verena Stolcke, *Past and Present*, 86, 1980.

Unequal Exchange in the Urban Informal System, by Alejandro Portes, from A. Portes, and J. Walton, *Labor, Class and the Industrial System*, Academic Press, 1981.

Urban Careers and the Strategies of the Poor, by Bryan R. Roberts, from *Organizing Strangers*, University of Texas Press, 1973.

Confederations of Households: Extended Domestic Enterprises in City and Country, by Gavin A. Smith, from N. Long and B. Roberts, eds, *Miners Peasants and Entrepreneurs*, Cambridge University Press, 1984.

Networks and Social Marginality, by Larissa Lomnitz, from book of the same name, Academic Press, 1977.

The Soldier as Politician, by Alan Angell, from article of the same name in D. Kavanagh and G. Peele, eds, *Comparative Government and Politics* Heinemann, 1984.

The New Union Labour Movement in Brazil, by Maria Helena Moreira Alves, from article in *Latin American Perspective*, 11, 1, 1984.

The Experience of Poor Women in Guayaquil, by Caroline Moser, from "Residential Struggle and Consciousness: The Experiences of Poor Women in Guayaquil, Ecuador", DPU Gender and Planning Working Paper No 1, Development Planning Unit, London.

Westernization and the Bari of Colombia, by Elena Buenaventura-Posso and Susan Brown, from M. Etienne and E. Leacock, eds, *Women and Colonization*, Praeger, 1977.

TNCs, The State and Latin American Industrialization, by Rhys Jenkins, from *Transnational Corporations and Industrial Transformation in Latin America*, Macmillan, 1984.

Boom, Yes; New Novel, No, by Gerald Martin, *Bulletin of Latin American Research*, 3, 2, 1984.

Introduction

The justification for the isolation of Latin America as an object of study lies in specific features of its history which give it a distinctive character, and a distinctive place in the emergence of the modern world. First of all, colonization by Spain and Portugal provided a degree of homogeneity which was both linguistic (with Portuguese spoken in Brazil and Spanish elsewhere) and cultural. The sense of a cultural community embracing the whole of Latin America owes much to the dominant role played since the arrival of the Spanish and Portuguese by the Catholic Church, and the impact – enduring long after independence – of social practices and modes of thought established over three centuries of colonial rule. After independence, as the new states of the region were eventually drawn more tightly into the commercial orbit of the advancing industrial nations, a common sense of grievance over the subordination of local economics to those of the leading capitalist powers bred a new spirit of economic nationalism, but this was delayed and weakened for two reasons. First, the burst of export-led expansion which came after the middle of the nineteenth century produced a degree of stability and prosperity which persuaded many that closer links with the dynamic industrial economies spelt salvation rather than doom. Second, a powerful current of thought, with its roots deep in the colonial period, blamed the backwardness of Latin America on the colonial powers, and admired and sought to emulate the thrusting dynamism of Britain, and later of the United States. The significance of colonial rule and post-colonial export-led development could be variously interpreted and, as we will see, this fact is reflected in contemporary theories of Latin American development.

We need to turn directly to the political and economic history of the area, particularly from the nineteenth century on, to understand the central legacy of colonization. By the end of the colonial period, Latin America was set firmly on an economic path it would follow, if with difficulty at first, for a hundred years. It would supply Europe, and increasingly the United States, with its precious metals, minerals, and agricultural and pastoral products, in return for other primary commodities and the growing range of manufactures produced in the workshops of the world. From the very first, Latin

America had exported to Europe, and played its part in the genesis and consolidation of the capitalist world economy of today. The extraction of precious metals from Mexico and Peru (and in the eighteenth century from Brazil), sugar, cocoa, animal hides and various other goods was based on a thoroughgoing transformation of indigenous societies, leading to the breakup of existing patterns of social organization and the imposition of settlement patterns that facilitated the provision of labour for the new enterprises and the supply of foodstuffs for the mining and administrative towns. Where there was no available indigenous population, as in the case of Brazil, then slaves were imported from overseas.

The new settlement patterns were composed of a complex set of linkages: the administrative cities in which were located the colonial authorities, their garrisons and merchant communities; the mining towns and plantations which sent their export products along trade routes guarded and organized through the cities, and the large estates (*haciendas, latifundia*) and peasant communities that supplied the foodstuffs for the urban markets. The peasant community, indeed, sustained much of this complex edifice, supplying not only foodstuffs, but labour to the other enterprises and a fund of agricultural products and techniques that were to be adapted by the commercial enterprises and, in turn, exported to enrich the diet and agriculture of Europe. This pattern of linkages, the trade flows that resulted from it and the systems of production it sustained configured Latin American space in new ways, creating regional identities that were often based on a dominant city and the trade routes and production systems it and its élites controlled. Indeed, these "city states" often became the basis for the new Republics that emerged, with independence, in Spanish America.

These patterns of settlement, trade and production would later provide the basis for a dramatic response to the new and greatly multiplied demands created as the industrial revolution, and the urbanization in Europe and the United States that accompanied it, massively expanded markets for inputs to industrial processes, and for consumption goods. One particular factor deserves mention here: the colonial pattern of settlement and the export-orientation of the colonial economy gave especial prominence to the major cities of the continent, laying the basis for their rapid growth and the population and economic concentration in them of subsequent periods.

Of equal importance is the fact that the failing power of Spain and Portugal within Europe, dramatically revealed in the period of the Napoleonic Wars, led them to lose their grip on all the mainland

Latin American colonies in the first decades of the nineteenth century. Just as the industrial revolution was gathering pace in Europe, a new group of distant and relatively impoverished and underdeveloped states came into being across the Atlantic. The wars of independence disrupted colonial patterns of production and trade, and 50 years would pass before the majority of them found any secure footing in the new world economy. It was the way in which this footing was achieved throughout Latin America which provides the single most important common characteristic of the area, and makes it a coherent object of study.

First of all, the countries of the region were drawn into the new international economy forged by the industrial revolution as producers on a considerably expanded scale of primary export commodities; this had radical consequences as regards the social constitution of the new ruling élites, and the relations between different classes. The interests of the élites were based squarely on the export relationship, making them natural collaborators with foreign merchant interests and, on the whole, uninterested in the development of a local industrial base since they also profited from the import of cheap manufactures. There was little basis, then, for the development of an industrial bourgeoisie or of an urban working-class. The mines would be worked by labour that was drawn from the rural areas and which returned to the villages after a period of years. The plantations were also rural institutions worked mainly by seasonal migrants from peasant communities or – in the case of the coffee plantations of São Paulo – by successive waves of immigrants who, in the face of low wages, moved on to other rural areas or to the towns.

Second, they did so as politically independent units recently emerged from the tutelage of once dominant but latterly weak mercantile European powers, Spain and Portugal. The new nations had little internal coherence and their governments had relatively little control over the regions and the classes that dominated in them. Poor communications and a weak fiscal base weakened central government in the new Republics and, consequently, its ability to resist the encroachment of foreign interests. In many of the Republics, in the early nineteenth century, foreign merchants and diplomats bypassed central governments and negotiated directly with regional élites, at times even fomenting rebellions against the government of the day.

It is this virtually unique combination in the nineteenth century of political independence and primary commodity-led incorporation into the international capitalist economy which provides the starting point for an understanding of Latin American society and politics from independence to the present day. It was, however, part of a single global process dominated successively by the rise to industrial pre-eminence of Great Britain, rivalry between the leading capitalist economies from the late nineteenth century on, two World Wars centred on Europe, and the subsequent emergence of the United States in a position of unrivalled supremacy within the capitalist world. No understanding of Latin America can be gained outside the context of that global process. But at the same time it has to be understood that the factors which make the Latin American experience comprehensible are highly specific to the region.

It is as foolish to assume that the nations of Latin America have been following independently, if belatedly, the same path to industrial maturity as has been traced out by the first industrial nations (as some of the simpler exponents of modernisation theory would have us believe) as it is to claim that the role of primary producers is one forced upon an unwilling sub-continent by scheming European powers, and bound to endure for as long as the sub-continent remains within their commercial and political orbit (as the crudest dependency theorists would seem to believe). The truth is that the development of Latin America has been complementary to that of the most advanced industrial nations, and is hence incomprehensible except within that broader global picture, but that at the same time it has had its own complex internal dynamic, varying from region to region, arising primarily out of the secular struggle between the different class forces spawned by that complementary pattern of development.

The industrial revolution in Western Europe meant the rise to political prominence of the bourgeoisie, and the subordination to its interests and to its command, to one extent or another, of the formerly dominant landowning élite. This does not mean, of course, that the bourgeoisie ruled alone. As the histories of Britain, France, Germany and Italy show, a variety of complex class alliances were possible, each with different consequences for the evolution of political regimes and the role played by the state itself. But, in each case, the pivotal role in the formation of alliances and the constitution of the regime was played by the bourgeoisie, and particularly by the industrial bourgeoisie; other social classes took up their positions, either within the circle of power or outside it, with reference to this class. In Latin America, as we have seen, the counterpart of industrial development in Europe was export-led development, based upon the land, or upon the exploitation of mineral resources. This meant that throughout Latin America the landed class played the role played in many parts of Europe by the urban bourgeoisie. Whereas in Europe, then, the industrial revolution often meant the displacement of the landed élite from political power, in Latin America it meant that the hold of this class on power and on the state was strengthened. Of course, the landed élite was substantially transformed in the process. Equally, it did not rule alone, any more than the European bourgeoisies were able to do. But it played the crucial pivotal role, and it is in its fortunes and changing strategies, as the countries of the region turn from the mid-nineteenth century on to expanded export-led development, that we find the secret of the array of social forces within the political and economic regimes of the period.

It is in this context that the significance of the political independence gained across Central and South America in the early decades of the nineteenth century becomes apparent. When it came to restoring order and stability, and securing political arrangements which would allow a sustained response to the new opportunities created by the industrial revolution, the new élites of Latin America were left to work out their own salvation. The twin process of restoring political and social order, and organizing production and commercialization, absorbed the energies of successive generations of élites. In the course of the process, alliances were made, and patterns of production established, which would leave their mark long after the first World War and the crash of 1929 had put an end to the period of export-led development across the region. Without anticipating in detail the general consequences of this common and unique set of circumstances, we may say that the massive expansion of primary production for export in Latin America from the mid nineteenth century, on which was based Latin America's own contribution to the industrial revolution, transformed and strengthened the landed élites of the region, while the late, secondary and relatively feeble development of industrial production made for a weak, dependent and subordinate bourgeoisie. At the same time, the weakness of industry and the central importance of the production of primary commodities for export meant that relations of production in the leading sector of the economy were not rapidly transformed into pure wage-labour.

Entrepreneurs faced two major problems in obtaining the labour that they needed. First, the highly labour-intensive nature of primary production made it necessary to keep wages as low as possible to ensure profits. In the case of these export enterprises in which labour demand was seasonal – as in the case of most plantation crops – entrepreneurs did not need a permanent labour force.

Second, much of the available labour in Latin America was embedded in peasant communities and semi-subsistence farming and these
farmers were reluctant to sell their labour on a full-time basis. These
two factors reinforced each other: low wages were insufficient to
maintain a whole family, but the village economy provided a subsistence base which would permit the labour migration, for varying
periods, of males – and, as in the case of Peruvian cotton production, females.

Even so, entrepreneurs initially had to resort to a variety of
devices to secure their labour supply, of which debt peonage was one
strategy. In those regions such as Argentina and Southern Brazil in
which there was no available labour force, workers were imported in
their millions from Europe. Even in these cases, however, wage
labour was rarely "pure". In Argentina, the wheat of the Pampas
was harvested through complex tenantry arrangements and in São
Paulo's coffee plantations workers, though paid a wage, were
granted land to cultivate for their subsistence. Given the division of
labour which emerged internationally, Latin America's insertion
into the capitalist world economy thus did not mean the inevitable
spread of wage-labour throughout its national economies. At the
same time, late and limited industrialization produced only a small
modern working-class in the cities, heavily outnumbered by artisan
producers who retained some access to the means of production.
Whether in the countryside or the town, the proletariat proper was
small. Even today, the consequences of this pattern of development
have yet fully to work themselves out.

It is the specificity of Latin American political and economic
development within the global process of the emergence of an
international capitalist economy over the last five centuries which
makes it a suitable object of study. The study of the region from this
perspective is justified by the crucial part it has played in the
emergence of the contemporary world economy, not simply through
its early exports of bullion, but as a provider of essential and cheap
raw materials and, latterly, as a market for the technology of the
advanced industrial countries. The Latin American development
experience illuminates aspects of the nature and impact of this world
economy, particularly the enduring structures of inequality that it
has created. This spatial structure of inequality with its implications
for the poverty and political and economic backwardness of the
underdeveloped world deserves as much recognition as an integral
part of the process of global capitalist development as do Western
democracy, world war, and the welfare state.

Latin America: Uniformity and Diversity

Thus far we have sought to draw attention to the common characteristics of the Latin American nations. These common characteristics, however, only provide a common framework within which the history and experience of each particular nation can be approached. It does not follow from what we have said that we should expect each Latin American nation to have followed a similar evolution, any more than we should expect to find identical patterns of political development among the advanced industrial nations. It is only when we move from the abstract to the specific, and examine the manner in which the different factors identified interact with each other in particular cases, that we are able to trace the implications of the general argument sketched out above.

Material resource endowments vary widely across Latin America, as did the density and level of development of indigenous populations and civilizations at the time of colonization. Spanish and Portuguese needs and practices varied, as did their intentions and their ability to promote them within the vast territories to which they laid claim. Contrasts arising out of the degree and nature of development experienced under colonial rule may have been modified or further reinforced in the early independence period, depending upon the degree of disruption caused by the transition to independence, and the re-establishment of order thereafter. The ability of local élites to respond to the new opportunities created by the industrial revolution in Europe varied in accordance with all these factors. Above and beyond all this, though, what was most decisive in setting the different Latin American nations on different political and economic trajectories in this period was the combined effect of the class and regional nature of the political alliances under which export-led development was pursued, and of the manner in which the problems of organizing production were resolved. Nations such as Peru and Bolivia thus developed through the exploitation of mining and plantation enclaves or the export of other primary products in which foreign interests gained substantial control in alliance with national entrepreneurs, while urban industrial development was slow to begin. In contrast, Brazilian landowners controlled the coffee production of São Paulo, and imported labour from Europe, and both their profits and their workers helped stimulate the rise of São Paulo as Latin America's first industrial metropolis.

As patterns of class alliance and class conflict varied from nation to nation, so did the types and sequences of political regimes which were created. Even regimes that have been categorized in similar ways, such as the "populist" governments of Vargas in Brazil and of Perón in Argentina, show significant differences, the former based on regional and class alliances in which the industrial working class was a subordinate actor and the latter permitting more independent power to organized labour. The inevitable consequence of this was that the successive "external shocks" felt by the region as a whole at irregular intervals – the first and second World Wars and depression which came between them; the Cold War; the oil price rises of the 1970s, the recession and debt crisis of the 1980s – provoked not *uniform* responses, but varied and sometimes diametrically opposed consequences. The record which has to be explained is one of *diversity*. The commonalities described above form an essential part of the explanation, but they provide only the starting-point for detailed and systematic explorations of distinct national trajectories.

This is nowhere more clearly seen than in relation to the record of liberal democracy in Latin America. Theorists of political develop-ment in the area have tended to draw conclusions with regard to the viability of democracy which they apply uniformly to Latin America as a whole. However, the most striking characteristic of the area is that of sharp contrast between types of regimes at any one time, and over time. Some nations experience general instability, with alter-nating short periods of democracy and dictatorship; some enjoy relatively long periods of stable democratic rule, only to collapse, at fairly high points of economic development, into dictatorship; some move from extended democracy to extended dictatorship, or from instability to stability, at the very moment when others are moving just as firmly in the opposite direction. Others again achieve stab-ility over long periods of time not under regimes of competitive democracy, but under dominant or single parties closely associated with the state. The very least we might ask of an approach to the sociology of Latin American development is that it offer some hope of explaining this diversity.

A starting point is the substantial transformation of Latin Ameri-can societies during this century. At the beginning of the century, all Latin American countries were predominantly rural in the settle-ment of their population and most of their populations were engaged in agriculture. By the 1980s, Latin America was predominantly urban with almost half the population living in cities of over 100 000 people. In only a few countries, such as Honduras, Guatemala and Ecuador, were more than half the economically active population working in agriculture: the services, construction and manufactur-ing industry are now the occupations of the majority of the area's

people. This transformation did not occur at the same pace or at the
same time throughout the region. Nor did the transformation occur
in the same way: contrast, for example, the large-scale migration of
Europeans into Argentina and Brazil that populated their cities
with the rural–urban migrations that fed those of other countries.
Moreover, the fit between urbanization and industrialization differed depending both on the timing and scale of rural modernization
that ejected the peasant populations and the timing and scale of the
industrial development that provided work for part, at least, of the
rural exodus. Some countries, notably Brazil and Mexico, have in
recent decades been relatively successful in expanding employment
opportunities in the cities; others, such as Peru or Ecuador, have
been notably less successful.

It is this pattern of economic growth, and its diversity, that
explains much of the political volatility and the distinct patterns of
political development in Latin America. Though there are few
examples of successful political organization among the peasants
and working-classes of Latin America, there has, in this century,
been a mobilization of both rural and urban populations that has
made them political factors, though also pawns in the political
game. The old structures of control have disappeared in the face of
economic and political centralization, based on landholding, vertical relationships of dependence and poor communications. An early
example of the consequences of the undermining of existing power
structures by capitalist development was the peasant rebellions of
Mexico at the beginning of the twentieth century. In the north and
centre of the country, peasants reacted violently to their ejection from
land or to being forced to produce under increasingly arduous and
insecure conditions, as capitalist enterprises expanded and disrupted traditional strategies of survival. Though these peasant
rebellions only marginally affected the outcome of the Mexican
Revolution, they were the spark that allowed new political structures of control to emerge, in particular Mexico's dominant party,
the PRI.

Also, as we noted above, capitalist development in the various
countries of Latin America has differed in the extent to which a
permanent wage-labour force exists and thus provides the basis for
the emergence of trade unions or political parties that are committed
to advance the interests of the working-class. Nor, for that matter,
has economic development produced a substantial "middling" class
in all Latin American countries, whose interests differ from both rich
and poor. Contrast, for example, the relatively polarized-class
structures of the Central American Republics with the differentiated

ones of Brazil, Argentina or Mexico. Furthermore, even in those countries where class-based political organizations have emerged, they vary in the extent to which they include all the working population. The so-called "marginal populations" of the cities are, for example, rarely given institutional representation in any political organization.

There is, in general, only a weak development of political institutions in Latin America which represent, in a stable fashion, the interests of different classes of the population. Instead, urban and rural populations are, in varying degrees, available to the various political parties or interest groups that compete for their allegiance. The stability or instability of government in Latin America, and the extent to which it permits popular participation must, then, be analysed in terms of the flexibility of national political institutions in responding to and co-opting the diverse interests that urban–industrial development has created. Equally important, however, are the specific social and economic pressures present at a given stage of a country's development.

There is one last issue which we must briefly cover since it has been central to the debates over Latin American development. Latin America is classed among the underdeveloped regions of the world, but there remains considerable controversy over whether or not some or all of the countries of the region will become developed. The theorists of modernization, in the 1950s, saw this as primarily a problem of economic and social engineering, ensuring the right mix of investment, appropriate educational systems and efficient state institutions. Subsequently, early theorists of dependency, such as Andre Gunder Frank, demonstrated the mechanisms through which the underdevelopment of Latin America was both produced and maintained by its exchanges with the core capitalist countries. Neither position now seems correct. Modernization theorists were over-optimistic with respect the benevolent intentions of the developed world and its corporations toward the development of the underdeveloped world and, for that matter, overestimated the interest and capacity of entrepreneurs and governments in underdeveloped countries to devote resources to economic take-off. Yet much dependency theory ignored both the real economic growth that had taken place in the region, and the diversity of patterns of growth.

Until the debt crisis of the 1980s, there seemed a good prospect that countries such as Brazil and Mexico would continue to grow rapidly and approach some of the poorer developed countries in terms of their Gross National Product *per capita*. Also, this economic growth was accompanied by some indications of a rise in the living standards of the population as a whole. Surveys of the urban poor showed that most informants saw their position as having improved over that of their parents, and they had similar expectations for their children. The range of consumer goods present even in urban slums indicated a general "trickle down" effect of economic growth. Recently, extensive public welfare systems have begun to emerge in such countries as Brazil which cater for both urban and rural poor. It remains, however, an open question whether these indicators of increasing wealth represent a genuine improvement in the life conditions of the bulk of the region's population. The increasing overcrowding and poor infrastructure of Latin America's great cities can imply a relative deterioration in standard of life, even when compared with the impoverished rural areas from which many of the population have come.

This debate draws attention to one fact of Latin American development and that is the diversity of development experiences. The contribution of Fernando Henrique Cardoso and his colleagues to the sociology of development lies precisely in their analysis of the different types of dependency situation created historically in Latin America. He also stresses, as we will see, that these situations are constantly changing and evolving. The poor, agriculturally-based countries of Central America are quite different in their dependency situation to the industrial giants such as Brazil and Mexico. This diversity, and the economic and class forces that have shaped it, based as it is on a historically specific evolution, requires attention if we are to speak with any confidence about development or underdevelopment in Latin America.

The selections in this volume are either extracts from longer works, or substantially edited down from original articles. We are grateful to the authors concerned for their tolerance and cooperation. In particular, it should be noted that much supporting evidence relating to sources has necessarily been omitted. Readers are therefore referred to the original books and articles, all of which are listed in the concluding bibliography.

Part 1
The "Dependency" Perspective

Introduction

The most satisfactory overall account of social change in Latin America remains Cardoso and Faletto (1969), published in Spanish in 1969, and available in translation in English (in an amended and expanded form) since 1979. A subsequent article by Cardoso (1972) is included in the introductory volume to this series, and makes a good starting point. In the period since the "dependency" perspective was first formulated a substantial debate has taken place, and a considerable body of empirical work has accumulated. As an introduction to these developments, and to current attitudes, we reproduce here two short critical accounts of the original essay, both dating from 1984, and an earlier discussion by Cardoso himself of the context in which it emerged, and the intentions behind it.

Roxborough, below, points to a growing body of empirical evidence which suggests that the accounts on which Cardoso and Faletto initially drew are deficient, and both he and *O'Brien*, below, argue that weaknesses also arise from a failure to consider subordinate classes, specific forms of production, and their consequences. However, *Cardoso's* own account shows that the original intention, however imperfectly realised, was to grasp the specificity and variety of the forms of development experienced in Latin America. On this particular point, Roxborough and O'Brien are at one in endorsing, in broad terms, the methodology adopted by Cardoso and Faletto, and in finding that despite its weaknesses the text has proved singularly fruitful in orienting debate, and remains of significance and value.

For further reading, Abel and Lewis (1984) makes a good starting point for current attitudes to the dependency debate. It includes the full version of *O'Brien*, below. In addition, Munck (1984) and Skidmore and Smith (1984) offer complementary perspectives. *Roxborough* (1984), from which the selection below is taken, sets the dependency perspective in comparative context, as do Martz and Myers (1983) and Smith (1985). Other useful critical perspectives are provided by O'Brien (1975), *Latin American Perspectives* (1974,

1

1981), Boron (1979, 1982), and Therborn (1979). Anglade and Fortin (1985) offer excellent country studies. Case studies hostile to dependency theory generally offer such weak versions that they fall short of their objectives, but often provide rich and valuable accounts at the same time. For an example of such work see Becker (1983, 1984). For useful broad appraisals of dependency theory, see *Cardoso* (1977), from which the excerpt below is taken, and Palma (1978).

Dependency and Development

Cardoso and Faletto: Multiple Paths

Ian Roxborough

In 1969 Fernando Henrique Cardoso and Enzo Faletto published a short interpretative account of Latin American history (Cardoso and Faletto, 1969). It should be noted that it is by no means clear whether the authors intend to develop a general theoretical model of Latin American development, or whether they are merely applying a particular kind of methodology to a series of concrete historical cases without any attempt to develop such a general theory. At the very minimum, however, *Dependency and Development* indicates the key variables which, according to the authors, enable the analyst to make sense of the multiplicity of developmental paths followed by Latin American countries. Their starting point is a differentiation of types of export economics in the nineteenth century into two basic types: (1) enclave economies and (2) economies with national control of the productive system. The enclaves which Cardoso and Faletto have in mind are mining or plantation enclaves. Although the image conjured up by the notion of an enclave is of a geographically separate entity, the key feature for these authors appears to be not the geographical situation of the productive enterprise but rather whether ownership is foreign or domestic. Now it is certainly the case that most plantations and mining concerns in Latin America have been owned by foreign interests, and that agricultural activities which have been more widely diffused across the national territory have generally been owned by nationals. Nevertheless, it is important for the logic of the explanation not to conflate the locational characteristics of the enterprise with the nationality of its owners.

This said, Cardoso and Faletto claim that this difference in the structure of the export sectors led to different trajectories for these two groups of countries. The key question facing Latin American states in the early twentieth century was how the middle classes were to be incorporated politically. In the enclave economies the state was under the exclusive domination of the oligarchy. As a consequence, the incorporation of the middle classes could proceed either by a breakdown of the oligarchic order, as in the Mexican

3

revolution, or as a result of conflicts among the dominant classes, enabling a middle class challenge to succeed. In this path, characteristic of Chile, the role of the state was a key to the success or otherwise of this project.

In the societies where there was national control of the productive system, the state reflected a co-existence of the oligarchy and the bourgeoisie. Here also there were two possible routes to the incorporation of the middle classes. Where there was a substantial degree of unity among the dominant classes, the incorporation of the middle classes would occur under the hegemony of the bourgeoisie. According to Cardoso and Faletto, Argentina illustrates this case. In countries where the dominant classes were fragmented, such as Brazil, there was only a partial incorporation of the middle classes. In both enclave and nationally owned export sector situations, middle class challenges to the system of oligarchic domination might fail, due to the resistance of the oligarchy and/or the weakness of the middle classes. Such was the case in Peru and Colombia.

Such, in brief, is the basic schema outlined by Cardoso and Faletto. Variations in the structure of the dominant class are used to explain differing political outcomes, defined in terms of the varying modes of incorporation of the middle classes. Condensing the account presented in *Dependency and Development* in this manner naturally runs the risk of doing serious injustice to the complexities and richness of their historical account. This difficulty is doubly compounded by the fact that Cardoso and Faletto have written a text

Table 1   *The Cardoso–Faletto scheme*

Type of dependent economy	Middle-class challenge	Outcome
Enclave economies		
	Successful middle-class challenge	Breakdown in oligarchic domination (Mexico, Bolivia, Venezuela) Middle-class access to oligarchic bourgeois domination (Chile)
	Unsuccessful middle-class challenge	Maintenance of oligarchic domination (Peru)
Nationally-owned export sector economies	Successful middle-class challenge (dominant-class unity)	Middle-class incorporation under bourgeois hegemony (Argentina)
	Successful middle-class challenge (dominant-class divided)	Partial incorporation of middle-class (Brazil)
	Unsuccessful middle-class challenge	Maintenance of oligarchic domination (Colombia)

which, in many places, is elliptical to the point of opacity. As I shall attempt to demonstrate below, their account is open to a number of objections.

Throughout their account the key terms "middle classes", "bourgeoisie" and "oligarchy" are left undefined and often without any clear empirical referent. The result is a rather shadowy portrayal of socio-economic conflict in which individuals, governments, policies or political parties are held to "represent" the class forces supposedly in conflict. The existence of these class forces, and of the conflicts of interest among them, is asserted or inferred rather than demonstrated empirically. This is particularly crucial since the key issues in the model presented by the authors revolve around the degree of unity or disunity of the dominant classes and the relationship between dominant classes and the state. If there is no independent measure of these variables, then we are likely to be presented with an analysis which is both reductionist and tautological: reductionist because political forces are taken to indicate the presence of social classes; tautological because the evidence for the existence of classes is the existence of political actors.

The signal advance of the Cardoso–Faletto model over both the essentialist theories and the modal pattern model is that, on the basis of two dichotomous variables (national *v.* foreign ownership of export sectors, and degree of dominant class unity), a number of *different* political paths can be traced.

The Cardoso–Faletto model is based on the interaction of previously specified theoretical variables which in turn specify alternative paths. In addition, the Cardoso–Faletto model has the advantage of being a social action approach: as an integral part of the theory, social actors are faced with real choices, and hence outcomes are not deterministic. This feature of the model also moves the analyst toward a consideration of multiple paths. The Cardoso–Faletto model, then, offers a theoretically satisfactory account of the diverse political trajectories of the nations of Latin America. However, as we shall see, while the Cardoso–Faletto methodology might be acceptable, their empirical analysis suffers from a number of serious problems.

Clearly Cardoso and Faletto had a certain body of empirical material in mind when in the mid-sixties they wrote their short book. There is, indeed, evidence concerning the structure of dominant classes in Latin America, and this can be brought to bear on the propositions advanced by Cardoso and Faletto. Interestingly, such evidence as is presently available suggests that many of the claims and assumptions concerning the nature of dominant classes put forward in *Dependency and Development* are mistaken. (The evidence on this topic is, it must be noted, both sparse and replete with methodological problems. Until further studies are published, however, we have no choice but to work on the basis of the existing material.)

In Argentina, Cardoso and Faletto refer to "class unity". While Cardoso and Faletto note the existence of a variety of fractions of the dominant classes in Argentina, they assert that "the agro–livestock-exporting sector" constituted a hegemonic dominant class. The work of Peter Smith and of Miguel Murmis and Juan Carlos Portantiero, however, suggests that the dominant classes in Argentina were sharply divided. In the agrarian sector, there was a division between the breeders of the interior provinces and the fatteners of the pampa near Buenos Aires. Similarly, Argentine industrialists were divided into those closely linked to foreign enterprises and those concerned primarily with the domestic market (Smith, 1969; Murmis and Portantiero, 1971).

In their remarks on Brazil, Cardoso and Faletto make the claim that the division within the ranks of the dominant classes was one between the coffee oligarchy and the industrialists. They also assert that there was considerable state autonomy with regard to the industrialization programme. With regard to the first claim about the disunity of the Brazilian dominant class, it does, indeed, appear to be the case that there was considerable fragmentation and conflict among dominant classes. The conflict, however, was not between the coffee oligarchy and industrialists. As the work of Warren Dean indicates (Dean, 1969), Brazilian industrialists came from the ranks of the coffee planters, particularly in the state of São Paulo, and retained close ties with them. Moreover, it is difficult to point to sectoral clashes between coffee exporters and industrialists during this period.

Rather than a sectoral division, the Brazilian dominant classes were divided along regional lines. This had its origins in the changing pattern of Brazil's exports, the historical development of which meant that regions and with them, regional oligarchies rose and fell as their exports prospered and declined in the world market. The conflicts within the dominant classes in Brazil in the early twentieth century were between the oligarchies of São Paulo and Minas Gerais (the famous *cafe com leite* alliance) and the weaker oligarchies of Rio de Janeiro, Rio Grande do Sul, and the states of the north-east. It was conflicts among these states which explain Vargas' assumption of power in 1930 and the subsequent Paulista Civil War of 1932, alliances and conflicts which cannot easily be described in sectoral terms.

As to the question of the relative autonomy of the state under Getúlio Vargas (1930–45), this is a matter of some controversy, and it is somewhat premature to pronounce a judgement on the ongoing debate on this topic. However, it cannot be disputed that the claim that this was a period of relative autonomy for the state has been subjected to sustained attack.

In the case of Chile, Cardoso and Faletto, following the widely known analysis of Claudio Véliz, assert that conflicts among dominant groups were responsible for the particular pattern of development followed in that country. However, the bulk of recent empirical evidence suggests that the dominant class in Chile was remarkably homogeneous. As both Zeitlin and his associates (Zeitlin and Ratcliff, 1975; Zeitlin *et al*; 1976) and Kirsch (1977) demonstrate, there were considerable ties of ownership between bankers, merchants, industrialists and landowners. As Zeitlin and Ratcliff (1975, p. 59) note:

> The contradictions between agrarian and industrial capital, and the clashes over state policies affecting them . . . did not arise between ontologically "real" class segments of large landowners and capitalists. For *contradictory interests* and *social cleavages* within the dominant class did *not* coincide; rather, the dominant agrarian and industrial elements were internally related, if not "fused", in so complex a pattern that *neither of them possessed specific autonomy or distinctive social identity* [emphasis in original].

Thus, while there is a great deal to commend the Cardoso–Faletto model on methodological grounds, in the key countries of Chile, Brazil and Argentina, and on the key question of the unity/fragmentation of the dominant classes, it must be found lacking both in its empirical assertions and in the lack of conceptual clarity in the definition of key terms. The central division made by the authors between enclave economies and nationally owned productive systems obscures what is, in fact, the key variable: foreign *v.* national control of the export sector; and the values assigned to the second key variable (unity/disunity of the dominant classes) are, in a number of instances, empirically incorrect.

The key variables of the Cardoso–Faletto model had to do with the structure of the dominant classes. This derived from the nature of the productive system, in particular, from the organization of the export sectors and their linkages with the world market. This seems an indispensable starting point. It enables the analyst to incorporate into a single theoretical framework both a concern for situations of external dependency and a focus on the productive structure of the particular Latin American country. This means that it is not necessary to treat the Latin American economies as simple adjuncts or reflexes of the metropolitan economies, as was done with some of the earlier and less sophisticated writing on dependency.

However, this model needs to be complemented with variables relating to the structure of subordinate classes. As Colin Henfrey (1981) has noted, with its exclusive focus on dominant classes, the Cardoso–Faletto model is in danger of becoming a one-class model of history. On the contrary, social change is better analyzed in terms of conflicts, tensions, and accommodations between and within both dominant and subordinate classes (and strata, quasi-classes, etc.). Even in those situations where subordinate classes appear to have little or no political input and where politics appears to be entirely an intra-élite affair, a two-class model is still called for. The passivity or quiescence of subordinate classes and strata is something which requires explanation. The model, then, calls for two key variables (or sets of variables) defining the structure of both dominant *and* subordinate classes.

Dependency Revisited

Philip O'Brien

The Classic Text: Theory and Concepts

As an interpretative text, in terms both of the formulation of the concept and of the analysis of concrete situations, *Dependency and Development in Latin America* has not been superseded. Serious students of dependency situations therefore have to return to this classic work. The original is still best.

What then is the object of analysis, the methodology, theory and concepts employed by Cardoso and Faletto to analyze the concrete realities of Latin America? There has, of course, been an evolution in the thinking of Cardoso and Faletto, with respect to their original draft. The preface to the English edition of their book is much more explicit about their proposed object of analysis and methodology than the earlier Spanish editions. It could be argued that what is explicit in 1979 was only partially so in 1969. But it is surely unfair to restrict criticisms to an initial position (as so many critics do with A. G. Frank, and thus ignore his later, and improved, writings). So this critique and appreciation will concentrate on the English edition of *Dependency and Development in Latin America* (1979).

The object of analysis, methodology, theory and concepts here proposed all place strong emphasis on the problem of the need to attain a dialectical, global and dynamic understanding of social structures in Latin America. Yet invariably in the sentence following such an emphasis Cardoso and Faletto stress that the basic aspect of such a task is to determine what forms the structures of domination will adopt. This changing focus is important because, although Cardoso and Faletto state that they are analyzing "how social, political, and economic development are related in Latin America", (1979, p. vii) explaining "exploitative processes" and "the system of production and the institutions of appropriation" and "the possibilities for change", in practice all this is equated with analyzing the "processes of domination through which existing structures are maintained"(1979, p. x). This is an important shift, and one which dominates the substantive analysis of the concrete situations.

In view of ECLA's own exclusive emphasis on economics, there may have been a case for bending the stick in the direction of the political; after all, as Cardoso and Faletto point out, ECLA's critical view of comparative advantage managed to avoid an analysis of social processes, imperialism and classes. But for the political economy tradition which Cardoso and Faletto claim to represent, an exclusive emphasis on domination is strange and somewhat paradoxical.

It is somewhat paradoxical given that their key concept, dependency, is meant to help explain class formations and domination. Cardoso and Faletto define dependency thus: "a system is dependent when the accumulation and expansion of capital cannot find its essential dynamic component inside the system" (1979, p. xx). In a later article Cardoso explained this as follows: "the production goods sector (Department I) which is the centre pin of accumulation in a central economy does not develop fully" (1977, p. 90). Thus though all economies nowadays are highly "interdependent", this interdependency is not equal, for peripheral economies do not have capital goods sectors strong enough to ensure continuous advance, in financial, technological and organizational terms, so they have to obtain them elsewhere and face rules of domination. Whereas developed capitalist countries face rules of competition, underdeveloped countries face, and have always faced, rules of domination. Dependency therefore is introduced to emphasize the difference between a developed capitalist nation and an underdeveloped one, and hence, presumably, the way in which internal relations of dominance express themselves differently in each case.

Both Cardoso and Faletto emphasize that they are not proposing "a theory of dependent capitalism" because by definition there cannot be such a theory without some treatment of the global dynamics of capitalism. They are, they state, referring to "situations of dependency". This is a valid point if they wish to emphasize that there is no simple unilinear theory applicable spatially and temporally, and that what are important are "concrete analyses of concrete situations" (Lenin). But Cardoso and Faletto are being excessively evasive – the frequent criticisms made of their open-endedness, a virtue, can justifiably be made of a certain evasiveness and even slipperiness in their writing – in maintaining that all they are doing is proposing a series of empirical analyses giving specificity and bringing up to date "the analysis of a general economic theory of capitalism". For the very concept of dependency must cast doubt on that general economic theory as it has usually been propounded. The concept of dependency was introduced precisely because the theories of imperialism were considered inadequate. For these theories not only failed in their explanation of the dynamics of capitalist expansion (for instance, Lenin's "last stage of capitalism", "overripeness"), but also, and more crucially for dependency writers, they failed in their analysis of both the political and economic consequences of the expansion of capitalism in imperialized countries.

There is of course no pre-ordained reason why a developed capitalist country cannot slip into the category of underdeveloped nor an underdeveloped one become developed. What is unlikely, however, is a process of convergence, a global shift in economic power to the LDCs as a whole, which is Warren's thesis. There may be conjunctural shifts for a whole group because of favourable monopoly prices, for example in the case of the oil-exporting countries–conjunctures not unknown in the history of LDCs. But evidence of a structural shift even among the newly industrializing LDCs remains unconvincing.

This is really the heart of the argument. One could well argue that the rules of capital accumulation which have prevailed in developed capitalist countries are now in the process of breaking down. Nevertheless, since the end of the Second World War the process of capital accumulation, the totality of the social circuit of capital in developed capitalist countries as a whole, has operated within a pattern which some French Marxists have called "central Fordism", by which they mean two interlinked phenomena: first, a mode of capital accumulation, a system of intensive accumulation combining a rise in labour productivity with an increase in *per capita* fixed capital (the technical composition of capital), and second, a continual adjustment of mass consumption to this increased productivity so that wage-earners, and through them virtually the whole of society, were integrated into the process of capital accumulation. Naturally, central Fordism, Keynesianism and the social democratization of all workers' parties went together.

It is this pattern which many people mean when they talk about industrialization or even development. And this was clearly behind ECLA's views of the potential role of industrialization in Latin America. It would be dangerous to idealize a package with such a brutal exploitative underbelly. Nevertheless as a process, and particularly when compared to the real experiences of the USSR and Comecon countries, it had its attractions.

The question remained: could such a "central Fordist" package be exported to the Third World or even, if this was unrealistic, could the processes of establishing such a package be exported? Contrary to Warren, it seems this was never exported as a package to underdeveloped capitalist countries. Their lack of a Department I meant that their integration into the social circuit of capital was only partial, and they were unable to integrate mass consumption into their internal social circuit even when, as in Brazil, intensive accumulation did lead to the mass production of technically sophisticated goods for the internal market. Capital, therefore, has never been constantly expanding value internally in the Third World. This is not to deny the rapid growth of local capitalism in some LDCs. Such a growth, largely financed through foreign debt, has indeed taken place and has dramatically altered the political, social and economic situation in these countries. It is precisely on the analysis of these situations that the "new dependency" theory has focused – for this pattern of accumulation, this rapid development of the forces of production, does not imitate the patterns of the centre. Both the dissolution of the old and the reconstruction of the new in the periphery remain highly fragmented. Hence, to return to Cardoso's and Faletto's concern, the internal relations of dominance are different.

But having reached the nub of the problem, and having indicated its essence, Cardoso and Faletto back away from analyzing in depth the ways in which the rules of domination have operated, and the whys and wherefores of their changes in relation to the key concept of dependency. For having defined dependency, Cardoso and Faletto then correctly observe that, for rules of domination to operate effectively, internal allies are needed to operate them. Thus any analysis of dependency situations requires a dialectical analysis of the relationship between the internal and the external. "We conceive the relationship between external and internal forces as forming a complex whole whose structural links are not based on mere external forms of exploitation and coercion but are rooted in coincidences of interests between the local dominant classes and on the other side are challenged by local dominated groups and classes" (1979, p. xvi). Thus there is a need to "elaborate concepts and explanations able to show how general trends of capitalist expansion turn into concrete relations among men, classes and states in the periphery" (1979, p. xviii), that is, a methodological movement from an abstract style of analysis into a concrete form of historical knowledge. This indeed is an admirable statement. But in practice Cardoso and Faletto apply neither their key concept of dependency, nor the general methodology proposed, to their analysis of the general social formations of Latin America. For the nature of Department I goods in the world system, and in turn the lack of them, has consequences for the rules of domination both internally and externally.

One would thus have expected Cardoso and Faletto to analyze these changes in relation to different periods in the social formations of Latin America. Instead they return to domination as being political, and concentrate on groups and classes and their factions in the pact of domination at the level of the state, linking this to changes in some characteristics of the system of production.

There is nothing wrong with focusing on the political level nor, indeed, particularly given the history of Latin America, with concentrating on the concrete processes of domination. Such a concentration could still have used "dependency" to bring out empirically the specificity of "the connection of the social and political structure with production", as Marx argued, and to give a "global and dynamic understanding of social structures". But in Cardoso and Faletto the dialectical and contradictory process becomes too one-sided, and the specificity of changing class structures in Latin America becomes in practice varieties of ruling-class domination – leading to a focus not on class relations, but on the internal structures of the ruling class.

The Dependency Perspective

Fernando Henrique Cardoso

Studies of dependency, constitute part of a constantly renewed effort to re-establish a tradition of analysis of economic structures and structures of domination; one that would not suffocate the historical process by removing from it the movement which results from the permanent struggle among groups and classes. Instead of accepting the existence of a determined course in history, there is a return to conceiving of it as an open-ended process. Thus, if structures delimit the range of oscillation, the actions of humans, as well as their imagination, revive and transfigure these structures and may even replace them with others that are not predetermined. These studies also had a peculiarity within this tradition of criticism: instead of limiting themselves to the theoretical–abstract plane, they sought to utilize the historical–structural, "non-vulgar" method to analyze concrete situations. And instead of limiting their studies to the analysis of circumscribed problems, they sought (returning to the theme of development) to define questions relevant to national politics and to the relations between the central capitalist economies and the dependent and non-industrialized periphery, following in this respect the tradition of the ECLA perspective. It did not interest them merely to describe abstractly the consequences of the accumulation of capital and of its expansion at the global level; they also posed questions arising from the historically determined point of view of dependent societies: What are the forces that operate in them, and what are their objectives? How and under what conditions is it possible to overcome a given situation of dependency?

The central question in Brazilian discussions concerning the past nature of social relations in rural areas and their specific weight in determining a certain type of socio-historical formation was not a debate between the partisans of the existence of a feudal structure and those who believed that "since colonial times" the concept of capitalism best described the existing social relations and forms of production. Nor was it a debate between pre-capitalism and capitalism *tout court* (although this discussion was more common). These propositions lost their force when confronted with the concern of those who tried to characterize the mode of production that prevailed in the past by taking colonial slaveholding into account. Except for the crudest of the evolutionist Marxists (who really did see "feudalism" as an important characteristic of Brazilian society), the discussion had for a long while centered on slaveholding colonial production and on the specific nature of a social formation which, although created by the expansion of mercantile capitalism, was based on slave-labor relations and reserved the most dynamic part of its output for the international market.

Gunder Frank simplified the debate, disdained the specificity of the situation (a procedure contrary to that of the dependentistas), and failed to attempt any sort of theoretical scheme of a dialectical type that might draw together the general and the particular in a specific whole. With the masterful polemics that are his special skill, he mortally wounded the dualists and blamed the confusion, sometimes correctly and sometimes not, on Marxists and ECLA theorists.

Nevertheless, the paradigm of dependency is consumed in the US as though its contribution to the historical debate had been centered on a critique of Latin American feudalism. That is, some of Gunder Frank's works are taken to mark the beginning of a "new" perspective in Latin America. Bagu, Caio Prado, Simonsen, Celso Furtado, Florestan Fernandes, Alonso Aguilar, and many others, had already written on the colonial period or on the structure of agricultural production for export, basing their analyses on considerably more complex themes than the simple duality between feudalism and capitalism.

The second distortion produced in the consumption of dependency theories concerns the relationship between the social, economic, and political structures of the dependent countries and the international capitalist system. Dependency analyses in the years 1965–8 were pre-occupied much less with the external conditioning of the Latin American economies, which was taken for granted, than with the development of a type of analysis that could grasp the political alliances, the ideologies, and the movement of structures within the dependent countries. How was this to be done? The "vulgar" current was predominant in analyses that regarded imperialism and external economic conditioning as the substantive and omnipresent explanation of every social or ideological process that occurred. Certain political forces endorsed that formulation for tactical reasons. Clearly the target of the struggle was evident – North American imperialism; and the allied camp was also clearly defined – everyone, except the agro-exporting latifundists linked to imperialism.

The dependentistas put the question the other way around: social movement cannot be theoretically represented by means of a "mechanical" opposition between the internal and the external, in which the latter cancels out the existence of the former. The approach ought to be historical, and it therefore starts from the emergence of social formations. Underdevelopment then comes to be seen not merely as a process which is a concomitant of the expansion of mercantile capitalism and recurs under industrial capitalism, but as one which is actually generated by them. The approach ought also to emphasize the *specificity* of dependency situations, as against societies in countries of the economic center. In other words, although the social formation underlying situations of dependency is the product of the expansion of capitalism, it is distinguishable from the classical pattern to the extent that "slaveholding colonialism," or some other form of colonial exploitation, is present as the basis of the articulation between dependent and dominant societies. On the other hand, after the passage from the colonial situation to situations of dependency of national states, it is observed that: (a) the passage implies the creation of states in answer to the interests of local property-owning classes; (b) these, however, have their structural situation defined within the larger framework of the international capitalist system and are thus connected and subordinated to the conquering bourgeoisies of the western world and to those classes which succeed them; in this way alliances are established *within the country*, even though in contradictory form, to unify external interests with those of the local dominant groups; and (c) as a consequence, the local dominated classes suffer a kind of double exploitation.

The "movement" that had to be understood, then, was that deriving from the contradictions between the external and the internal, viewed in this complex fashion and summed up in the expression "structural dependency." If imperialism was embodied in the penetration of foreign capital (invasions by Americans in the Caribbean, by the English in South America, etc.), it also implied a structural pattern of relations that "internalized" the external and created a state which was formally sovereign and ready to be an answer to the interests of the "nation," but which was simultaneously and contradictorily the instrument of international economic domination. Certainly, the phases and forms of capitalist expansion (colonial–mercantile, mercantile–financial and industrial–financial capitalism, oligopolist forms of "multinationalized" capitalism, etc.) are constituent parts of dependency situations, but the latter are explicable only when those forms cease to be taken as an entelechy or as an abstract and general conditioning factor, and reappear concretely in the analysis of their articulation in each local economy at different moments of time. This process was to be explained not as the "abstract" unreeling of forms of accumulation, but as a historico-social process through which certain classes impose their domination over others, certain factions of classes ally or oppose themselves to others in political struggles. In this struggle, what appears at first as inevitable because of the "logic of capitalism" is revealed without disguise: one side wins or loses, one form or another of dependency is maintained or makes way for another, the general conditions for capitalist development are sustained or reach their limits, and other forms of social organization are foreseen as a historical possibility.

Thus, right from the initial propositions, dialectical analysis was the point of departure. What was significant was the "movement," the class struggles, the redefinitions of interest, the political alliances that maintained the structures while at the same time opening the possibility of their transformation. The structures were regarded as relations of contradiction, and therefore dynamic.

However, if there have been so many distortions in the consumption, it is because the original production was not clear regarding several of these points, and may even have included, in latent form, much that later appeared as simplification and inconsistency. I shall not repeat here what I have already said in previous works. I want merely to emphasize that, if it is to be judged on the basis of its own assumptions, the point of view of dependency ought to be confronted with at least three types of question:

1. Have dependency studies been able to whet the imagination so that discussion is opened on themes and forms of comprehending reality which are compatible with the contemporary historical process?
2. Does the theoretical representation of the dynamic of this process proposed by dependency studies permit us to comprehend the forms of capitalist expansion on the periphery and realistically to make out the alternatives to it?
3. Do the studies enable us to define the classes and groups that give life to dependent structures through their political struggles? Do they make it possible to go beyond the structural frame of reference in order to clarify the relations between ideologies and social and political movements in specific political conjunctures, so as to assist action to transform reality?

As for the first question, if the initial studies of dependency possessed any novelty, it certainly was not the affirmation that dependency exists, but it was rather the characterization and the search for an explanation of *emerging forms of dependency*. The studies sought to show the meaning of the industrialization of the periphery (and thus the formation of an internal market, since in Latin America this process did not involve the construction of mere export–manufacturing enclaves), under the control of what later came to be called "multinational corporations." The recognition of the effects of this process – the "new dependency" – was the point of departure for reflection on this theme. Today, this appears to constitute another banality. Nevertheless, in Latin America up to the end of the decade of the 1950s there was a deeply rooted conception that the international economic trusts were not interested in the industrialization of the periphery, since they exported finished goods there; their fundamental interest was the control and exploitation of primary agricultural and mineral products. The theory of imperialism reinforced this point of view, which was moreover consistent, at least in part, with what happened up to that point. The anti-imperialist struggles were at the same time struggles for industrialization. The local states and national bourgeoisie seemed to be the potential historical agents for capitalist economic development, which in turn was looked upon as a "necessary stage" by a considerable part of critical opinion.

The dependentistas showed that a kind of industrialization was occurring under the control of the multinationals, and they drew certain conclusions from it. There was even an attempt to propose a more general model of the process, to characterize a "transnational capitalism" and to estimate its effects, not only on the periphery, but also on the very center of the capitalist economies.

The revision proposed on the basis of these perspectives – that of the industrialization of the periphery and the internationalization of internal markets – made it possible to generalize the criticisms of the theory that the national bourgeoisies could repeat the function they served in the center as the leaders of the capitalist process in underdeveloped countries. It also displayed the insufficiencies of the theory of modernization and the expectation that there would be stages of development identical to and in the same sequence as those in Europe. From that point on, the question of the state came to be reformulated, and the role of the bureaucracy (and what later on I called the "state bourgeoisies") came to be discussed in greater depth. On the other hand, thanks to the characterization of the specific form of capitalist industrial development on the periphery – where what dominated was oligopolistic–corporative production oriented toward consumption by the high-income classes – numerous hypotheses were advanced and some studies were made on the theme of marginality and of the formation and behavior of the working-class.

On balance, the effect of dependency theories on the sociological imagination seems to me to have been positive. Thanks to these theories (but not exclusively so, since the ECLA group had already pointed in that direction), attention was called to a thematic frame that ceased to see capitalist development on the periphery as a mere "consequence" of accumulation of capital in the center, and began dealing with the historical form that this process acquired in dependent societies.

Part II

The Colonial Experience and Independence

Introduction

In Part II, *Assadourian* explains the main consequences of colonial domination in Latin America: the incorporation of the region into the world economy through mining production, the disarticulation of indigenous systems of production and exchange, the expansion of the internal market and the gradual consolidation of the monetary economy. This process provoked a rapid change in the agrarian structure with the growth of commercial units of production under European control and the marginalization of the peasant economy condemned to subsistence production. According to *Tandeter*, the expansion of mining was related to the exploitation of forced rural migrants. The labour force used in the mines was in part reproduced by the rural communities because the miners took with them the supplies and clothing needed during the period of absence. He clearly demonstrates that even in the eighteenth century the supply of free labour was not abundant.

Stern analyses the consequences of colonialism in the creation of different ethnic groups separated by history, language and culture, a heritage that is still present today in many areas of Latin America. Colonialism favoured the internal differentiation of Indian society, creating a kind of Indian élite which embraced values and followed strategies determined by the power of the colonists. This process on the one hand reinforced the internal solidarity of the indigenous population, creating the closed corporate community, and on the other consolidated a group of wealthy Indians.

Concomitantly with this process the expansion of the plantations producing for the world market was only possible through the massive import of African slaves. The black population resisted slavery in a number of different ways. *Sharp's* article is an illustration of the kind of revolt that occurred in many places during the seventeenth and eighteenth centuries.

The colonial heritage conditioned the economy and society of the Latin American countries during the process of acquisition of

19

political independence in the nineteenth century. The articles by *Carvalho* and *Safford* are focussed on political developments, showing the variations observed in Spanish and Portuguese colonies, documenting the emergence of a "state" interest, and detailing the lines of political cleavage which emerged.

The best starting-point for an understanding of the colonial period in Latin America is the wide-ranging and authoritative *Cambridge History of Latin America* (vols I-III – Bethell (1984)). Each volume contains a set of detailed bibliographical essays. A useful introductory survey is Lockhart and Schwartz (1983). A more radical account, of enduring value, is Stein and Stein (1970). The most accessible general survey of Spanish rule is Gibson (1966); for Mexico, Peru and Brazil respectively it may be supplemented by Gibson (1964), Lockhart (1968), and Boxer (1969). For the impact of colonilization upon indigenous societies, see Leon-Portilla (1962), Wachtel (1977), and Hemming (1978). Spalding (1983), and Stern (1982) are valuable case studies. Schwartz (1973) is a good general account. On slavery, Sharp (1976) is recommended. For rural issues, Keith (1977) is a useful collection. On the role of women in the colonial period, consult Lavrin (1978), and Etienne and Leacock (1977).

The Colonial Economy and Society

The Spatial Organisation of the Colonial Economy

Carlos Sempat Assadourian

This essay describes in outline the colonial economic system and its spatial organization, taking as examples the two great silver-producing complexes, the viceroyalties of New Spain and Peru.

The Circulation Cycle of Mining Capital

To my mind, the adequacy of a model of the colonial economic system and its spatial organization depends essentially upon the manner in which it conceives of both the form and the predominant functions of mineral production within that system. With regard to this central issue a number of misapprehensions still prevail. This is partly because the colonial production of silver was an important element in the dynamic of the European economy and in the formation of the world market. As a consequence, analyses have tended to concentrate exclusively upon the articulation and the external effects of that colonial export economy, and to neglect the empirical and theoretical investigation of the process of production of silver itself, and its effects in the region of production. The emphasis placed upon the external effects of silver, and the state of ignorance regarding the internal processes which its production set in train, have led to false perceptions of the nature and functions of the colonial system. This approach, common to liberal and marxist historiography, has been reinforced in recent years by the theory of dependency, which defines the mineral export economies as *enclaves*, better integrated into the world outside than into the economy of the territory in which they are located.

Taking as a starting point the model provided by Elhuyar in 1825, I shall attempt to provide a new synthesis of the constitution of the colonial economy. The prior requisite, the point of departure for the formation of the system, is mineral production, the final product of which (the commodity money) has the capacity of being immediately realizable internationally. This production, on account of the

21

very nature of its final product, and "the complexity of the operations and processes which its pursuit requires" (Elhuyar, 1825 p. 3), creates its own market, within which agrarian products are converted into commodities, while at the same time it promotes new types of production which are based from the very start upon exchange with the mineral market. The result of this process is the constitution of a mercantile economic system, with commerce developed to a certain degree and the consequent circulation of money within certain limits. We witness the creation of an economic space integrated and held together by mercantile interchange: "from all that there resulted the variety of exchanges of goods and produce, an active reciprocal commerce between the provinces of different temperaments and dispositions" (Elhuyar, 1825 p. 20). The discovery of the mineral resources in zones situated outside the domain of the great indigenous states set in motion an intensive process, stretching over half a century, of territorial expansion and occupation of the land. The location of the site of the dominant form of economic production meant, as a result, that there took shape a completely new territorial organization of the process of production, original in relation to the spatial forms of occupation proper to the structures of the primitive indigenous system.

From the 1560s and 1570s on – these being the periods in which the technique of processing the silver ores by amalgamation with mercury was introduced in New Spain and in Peru – the colonial production of silver constituted one of the sectors with the largest scale of production and the most intensive use of capital in the world economy of those times.

Mining retained its dominant position within the system, by virtue of its double function as the principal element of articulation with the exterior and the element which determined the course of the whole of the process of production within the colony. This thesis is of the greatest importance. On the one hand it implies that the world market continued to condition the colonial economic system (and its territorial organization) through the specific demand for the commodity silver. Therefore external factors, by not creating new zones with production realised internationally, contributed to the reproduction of the essential patterns of territorial–economic organization established during the process of the formation of the colonial system.

If our understanding that the geographic division of labour in Peru and in New Spain was to all intents and purposes established in the second half of the sixteenth century is correct, then the analysis of this problem in the seventeenth and eighteenth centuries is limited to readjustments, modifications of degree in the territorial organization of production. All of this is determined, in large part, by the major trends in the colonial economy, by those secular movements of general stagnation and growth, equally general, of mercantile production.

Indigenous Territory in the Colonial Agrarian System

In the Andean region the true process of the formation of an agrarian structure of the colonial type took place over the last quarter of the sixteenth century and the first years of the seventeenth. It is worth noting, therefore, the principal changes which had taken place over the previous period, of some fifty years in length. Between 1530 and 1550, in the first decades following the violent invasion of the Spanish forces, the imperial Inca state was destroyed and the structure and demographic dynamic of the indigenous society were shattered. In this brief period, which could be extended five years more if we were to include the war of dynastic succession following upon the death of Wayna Qhapaq, the collapse of the indigenous population ran its course.

The transition began with a radical transformation in the agrarian landscape: the sudden collapse of the population brought about a sharp reduction in the area of land under cultivation, after demographic pressure in previous years had extended it to embrace land less than ideal for the raising of crops.

Along the extensive Peruvian littoral, the shortage of manpower led to the rapid deterioration and abandonment of the intervalline irrigation canals, which formed a genuine hydraulic system: whole areas of intensive irrigated cultivation returned to sand. In the sierra, where the terraces were the greatest technical achievement in the development of highly productive agriculture, there are numerous signs of the abandonment of some of these areas of intensive cultivation.

The second phase of the transition covers more or less the following quarter century, from 1550 to 1575. In theoretical terms, I am inclined to define it as the phase of the formal subordination of the primitive system. In fact, one of the dominant characteristics of this phase is given by the normative order which the colonial state imposes upon the encomienda system, an order which tends to transform it completely into a rent in goods, eliminating personal service (rent in labour). Although encomienda rent differs in some ways from those rents derived from the Inca *mita*, the colonial norms set out expressly to reproduce within it various conditions and forms of the immediate process of production which were characteristic of the indigenous system. For example, the territorial registration of each ethnic group was maintained, orders were issued that the products of the tribute should be the same use values traditional in village production, and the apparatuses of indigenous power retained control over the process of production of the surplus, a process which took place, in addition, in accordance with existing techniques and conditions of social organization.

The Andean formation prior to the Spanish invasion, in which production for one's own subsistence predominated, functioned through an intensive exchange of goods ("there are very few lands, or none in the sierra, where the Indians can manage without going to others for their needs", says Polo de Ondegardo), but through forms prior to those of mercantile exchange. In my view there were three principal forms: (a) Circulation controlled by the state, a "system of reciprocity and redistribution", of whose scope and function we have as yet no certain knowledge; (b) The circulation of use values within the single spatial organization of each ethnic group, or in other words that Andean pattern which Murra has studied and called "the vertical control of a maximum number of ecological levels" (Murra, 1972); and (c) Exchange between different ethnic groups, controlled by the groups themselves.

Thus we have a mode of production in which a great part of production never enters into circulation, and is the object neither of exchange nor of barter, and in which another part enters into circulation but is neither produced as a commodity nor converted into a commodity. We should note here the ruptures that the process of transition introduces. The Spanish invasion, by destroying the imperial Inca state, provokes the disappearance of the first form, circulation under state control. Equally, the demographic collapse and the distribution of encomiendas among the Spanish disturbs the functioning of the second form, the circulation of goods between the different ecological levels which made up the territorial unit of each ethnic group. Leaving untouched the direct exchange of goods between the territories of the different ethnic groups, European domination began to impose a new form, which the indigenous population encountered for the first time: the transformation of use values into commodities, and the realization of these in money. From the perspective of the formation of the internal market, and the running of a mercantile system, the mineral market of Potosí, situated at more than 4 000 metres above sea·level, takes on the character of a dominant zone, articulating the colonial Andean economic space.

Let us see, then, how the new agrarian structure of the Andean region took shape in the last quarter of the sixteenth century.

In general terms, we may say that the project entrusted to Viceroy Toledo, which consisted of maximizing the remittances of the commodity money from the colony to the metropolis, could not be carried out as a process localized in the mining zone alone, simply through the introduction of modifications to the technical processes of silver production. The changes imposed in Potosí, along with the development of Huancavelica, irradiated throughout the whole of the Andean region, and meant the constitution of a new economic system founded upon the production of the maximum quantity of silver. For the agrarian structure this implied a radical re-ordering of both the forms of access to the land and the forms of exploitation of the mass of peasant energy.

Let us look, then, at the policy pursued by Toledo on each issue. Between 1572 and 1576 the Viceroy changed the nature of the encomienda system, by converting the tribute in goods into a rent in which payment in silver played the greater part. This change had clear significance for the development of the new economy, as the monetization of agrarian rent is the key mechanism, applied by the state, which obliges the indigenous peasants to work under the direct control of the Spanish, in the towns, in the mining centres, and in agrarian enterprises. It should be noted that the latter experienced a double stimulus to their expansion: the increased demand from the mining industry, and the seasonal "supply" of indigenous workers generated by the state through the monetization of encomienda rents.

Along with increases in the production of silver and the intensification of the process of monetization of encomienda rents, the state prompted a profound reorganization of the occupation of the land, redistributing the indigenous population and allowing the Spaniards to occupy the vacant lands. It was Viceroy Toledo himself, of course, who carried out the policy of reductions, obliging the total numbers of each ethnic group, divided between twenty, eighty, or a hundred and more villages, to come together into two or three large towns. There is no doubt that the colonial state, with this vast compulsory redistribution of the indigenous population, was forcing along the process of transition to a new economy.

Let us present in synthesis, then, the principal characteristics of this new agrarian organization. Its basic characteristic is the existence of two territories with differentiated populations and functions linked to each other through relations regulated and controlled by the state itself. The indigenous territory, relocated and reduced in size as we have seen, loses its character as the principal source of mercantile surplus which it had had during the earlier phase of *transition*, and becomes practically an area reserved for the peasant subsistence economy. In accordance with the project of the crown, the granting of plots to each indigenous family unit would retain this population in the new towns and ensure in addition the process of reproduction of the peasant energy destined to be employed seasonally in every sector of the new economy (mining, Spanish towns, agrarian enterprises, transport). The Spanish territory, the rapid expansion of which was legitimated by the royal decree of 1591, became the area in which the production of the mercantile surplus was concentrated, in which new sectors of production were developed: European cattle and poultry, crops such as grapes, olives, sugar cane and cereals, and textile manufacture on the basis of European techniques. Once they were directly in control of mercantile production the Spanish organized it in accordance with their own economic principles, with regard to technical conditions and to the rhythm of work and forms of labour co-operation. All these changes in the form of production of the mercantile surplus were subject, to a large extent, to the numbers of indigenous peasants who could circulate between the indigenous territory and the Spanish. This fundamental relation – the supply of the factor labour from one territory to the other – remained under the control of the state. This arrogated to itself the function of regulating the number of indigenes which should migrate for seasonal work to the Spanish territory, establishing the proportion of them which should be distributed to each sector of production and to each enterprise in particular, and setting the price which the Spanish should pay for this labour force.

Forced and Free Labour in Late Colonial Potosí

Enrique Tandeter

The annual forced migration to the mines of Potosí (the *mita*) was an extreme case in which, despite the payment of wages on the part of the mining entrepreneur, almost the entire reconstitution of immediate labour-power was the responsibility of the community to which the migrant worker belonged. In the appropriation of this labour rent on the part of the entrepreneur, the object of exploitation was not the individual migrant worker but his entire community. Thus the communities were transferring part of their communal surplus labour to the sphere of production of the mines of Potosí, a process which affected their own accumulation and reproduction. Our hypothesis in this article, which will be restricted chronologically to the second half of the eighteenth century, is that this transfer of value was crucial to the mining industry of Potosí and that without it the latter would hardly have been able to survive. At the same time, considerable attention will be paid to the role of free labour within the mining industry of Potosí in an attempt to explain the circumstances which determined the co-existence and interaction of free and forced labour.

Around 1790, the Potosí mining industry presented a tripartite structure of *rentier* owners, tenant entrepreneurs and workers. The entrepreneurs rented a number of mines, an ore refinery and the right to a certain number of forced labourers. They paid a fixed sum each week to the owner who sometimes lived in the same town, or in Lima, Buenos Aires, La Plata (nowadays known as Sucre), or even in Spain. The tenants were generally immigrants who arrived from Spain without capital. In order to exploit the plant and its mines they relied on the free credit which the Real Banco de San Carlos made available to them. This was a state institution which enjoyed the monopoly of the purchase of silver production. The price that the bank paid to the entrepreneurs was the value of the silver at the mint less a tax of 10 per cent which was levied upon mining production. We have calculated that of the surplus generated from mining in Potosí, 20 per cent corresponded to the profits of the tenant, 37 per cent to the rent paid to the owner and 43 per cent to the crown.

There were almost 5 000 workers in the industry, divided into free and forced labourers (see Table 1). This division broadly corresponded to that existing between skilled and unskilled workers. In fact, the forced labourers were part of an annual migration, and as they lacked previous training in mining they were only able to carry out the most simple of tasks.

Since the original organization of the *mita* system in the 1570s there had existed an elaborate legal framework to guide its functioning. The migrants were forced to work for a particular mining entrepreneur for one out of every three weeks during the year of their stay in Potosí. Regulations fixed the salaries which the workers received during this week; these were much lower than those prevalent in the free labour market which existed in Potosí from the very beginning of its exploitation in the 1540s. The regulations also specified a maximum working day for the forced labourers.

The entrepreneur had few incentives to protect his work-force: as

Table 1   *The mine workers of Potosí (c. 1790)*

Place of work and work description	Forced labourers	Free labourers	Total
Mines			
Ore carriers	1 509	402	
Pick-men	—	517	
Others	—	625	
Mills:			
Grinders	867	—	
Others	—	1 039	
Totals	2 376	2 583	5959

Table 2   *Annual total of forced migrants drafted to Potosí (1692–1801)*

Province of origin	Total fixed by viceregal resolution		Effective total		
	1692	1736	1740	1754	1801
Porco	447	418	281	312	323
Chucuito	535	334	423	462	371
Canas, Canchis and Tinta	453	318	228	180	204
Sicasica	120	117	120	124	119
Carangas	306	154	223	199	190
Quispicanchis	111	38	43	34	—
Azángaro	240	120	150	150	103
Paria	302	186	154	211	222
Lampa	266	332	141	210	266
Paucarcolla	84 ⎫		34	34	67
Pacajes	304 ⎭	205	308	316	298
Chayanta	674	674	457	453	477
Omasuyos	159	159	129	111	103
Cochabamba	48	48	48	48	41
Tarija	96	96	78	75	25
Totals	4 145	3 199	2 817	2 919	2 809

the draft labourer was not recruited from a free market, the prevailing conditions in a production unit could not deter potential workers. The forced labourer could not choose to abandon the works to which he had been sent unless he fled, in which case he ran the risk of various losses while the entrepreneur, as we will see, could receive pecuniary compensation for his absence. From the other end of the spectrum, the forced labourer was not a slave and his exploitation did not place any investment at risk; nor did the entrepreneur have to concern himself with the reproduction or even the reconstitution of labour-power, as these depended upon an economy totally separate from his sphere of production, in which respect the system differed radically from feudal serfdom. In short, immediate profitability was the overriding consideration of the entrepreneur in his relations with the forced labourers.

The result was a change in the pattern of work and rest which had been established around 1570. Night work was established soon after. Later on, around 1606, the forced labourer had to stay on the mountain where the mines were located (the *cerro*) for an entire week. Even more important, some entrepreneurs replaced the concept of a working day of a certain number of hours with that of a set amount of work or fixed quota (*tarea*) measured in units of weight which the labourer had to extract from the mine. This practice was probably already in existence during the early years of the *mita* system, as it was prohibited in 1574, when it was laid down that during the working day the Indians "should do as much as they can to the best of their ability, as it is decreed". The prohibition of fixed quotas was reiterated without having any effect.

While in the 1750s the forced labourer was required to extract five sets of loads (each set being the equivalent to fifteen loads) during five nights work in the mines, around 1767 each set was the equivalent of thirty loads. During 1786–7 each set was approximately the equivalent of twenty-five loads. The records of the three official inspections of the mines carried out by Intendant Sanz in 1790, 1792 and 1793 present a varied picture but essentially confirm a process of increasing quotas.

On average, the forced labourers of the mines and plants of Potosí worked more than forty-six weeks during the year which they spent in the city. In other words, the obligatory period of seventeen weeks was increased by 167 per cent.

To sum up, if the number of working weeks per year exceeded by 167 per cent those established by law, or even more, by an excess of 285 per cent if measured in working shifts, the annual wages paid exceeded those fixed by law by only 41 per cent. Historiography has referred time and time again to the "abuses" committed by the mining entrepreneurs of Potosí against their forced labourers, but the difference between law and social reality, as we have seen, is of such a magnitude that the word "abuse" is meaningless. Contemporaries of the eighteenth century in Potosí knew better, so they used a neutrally descriptive term (*entable*) when referring to the actual pattern of forced labour. Our conclusion is that we are faced with a specific relation of production, which we call *mita* rent, in respect of which the state institution of the *mita* only provided one of the conditions of existence.

Our own conclusion is that the *mita* rent was the dominant relation of production in the mining industry of Potosí during the eighteenth century, in as much as the very survival of the industry depended upon its reproduction.

If quotas and domestic service dominated the labour process they were not the only burdens weighing upon the migrant worker. As well as their usual tasks, the forced labourers had to undertake super-derogatory work known as *faenas*.

As we have already stated, the families of the migrant workers took part in mining work to complete the unending burden of fixed quotas. We also cited evidence showing that the forced labourers sought the assistance of a significant number of relatives to deal with this work.

As we have mentioned above, the *mita* constitutes a peculiar example of labour rent, by which not only the maintenance and reproduction of the labour force but even the immediate labour-power reconstitution were the responsibility of the communities from which they originated. This was carried out through the migrants' transporting to Potosí the supplies and clothing needed during their absence, which would sustain them for twelve to fourteen months according to the distance between their villages and the city. In some cases, when distances allowed them to do so, groups of draft labourers absented themselves from Potosí during the middle of the year and returned to their villages in search of extra supplies.

The greater part of the wages of the forced labourers were already committed to the payment of the supplies advanced by the mill's general store. This stocked coca leaves and alcoholic beverages (*chicha, aguardiente*), which were sold to them at prices double those prevalent in the city, and these were already high. The low wages meant that the forced labourer depended on the general store to advance him goods. The entrepreneur did not manage the general store but rented out to the mining supervisors the right to install one. The latter, being responsible for the recruitment of the free workers and the payment of weekly wages to both free and forced labourers, were thus able to achieve maximum profits from the store.

Faced with the situation that we have described, it is little wonder that the Indians drafted for the *mita* attempted to evade working in

Potosí. The most general and well-known result of this was the exodus to villages that were exempt from the *mita* obligation. Even those who did not choose such a radical alternative had the choice of other possible options. A monetary payment to the local Indian chieftain who compiled a list of future migrants could result in exemption from the obligation. This method seems to have consolidated into a kind of annual tax *sui generis*, which the most affluent of the Indians paid the local chieftain year after year. This method was already in operation by the end of the seventeenth century, and was to continue until the final days of the *mita* system.

Looking at the problem from the point of view of the draft labourer, flight presented the same disadvantages as the definitive abandonment of his community of origin, for in both cases he would lose his rights in the community. In practice, however, the situations were more complicated and a link was established between commutations, flights and absenteeism.

Whether the escaped forced labourers returned to their villages or not, the entrepreneurs, with the support of the authorities, claimed compensatory payments from the local magistrates of those villages who, in turn, would have to obtain them from the Indian chieftains. It seems that they were not very successful in these negotiations repeated year after year. In spite of the fact that the law demanded that a draft labourer should be replaced by another worker and not through payment, the entrepreneurs imposed the idea that only monetary payment was adequate compensation for the absence of a forced labourer.

As during the 1570s the *mita* system was institutionalized, from then onwards the division between skilled and unskilled mining labour corresponded in general terms to that existing between free and forced labour. During the second half of the eighteenth century this distinction still prevailed, although certain marginal works which were not allocated forced labour had to turn to the free labour market even to hire their less skilled workers.

The supply of free labour was not abundant at any time during the eighteenth century. We should recall that the indigenous population of upper Peru continued to fall in absolute numbers until 1750, and even afterwards its recuperation was slow and uneven.

A crucial problem here was that some of the migrant families who had arrived to undertake their annual obligation sought to settle in Potosí. Specific legal regulations aiming to protect the regular working of the *mita* and also the reproduction of the Indian communities prohibited permanent settlement. But the scarcity of free labourers led the authorities of the city to conceal the violation of the law, their only concern being that the new inhabitants should not avoid the payment of taxes through having changed their place of residence.

The problem of the shortage of free labourers manifested itself in different ways according to the level of experience required from the worker. Those without any training at all who undertook similar duties to those of forced labourers, for the entrepreneurs without access to such labourers, or those who mixed the amalgamated pile of ores and mercury with their feet (known as *repasiris*), were easier to attract and retain. They were generally hired through an advance payment of part of their weekly wage. The obligation to pay the annual tribute to the crown also served to facilitate the recruitment of these unskilled workers. In some works they were hidden from the tax collector, whilst in some cases the latter acted as intermediary on behalf of the mining entrepreneur in hiring Indians who were in arrears with their taxes.

Debts with the general store of the works was a method used to retain free labourers, but in the face of a constant excess of demand over supply of labour it does not seem that indebtedness impeded mobility between works or prevented departure from the city. Even more important to retain the workers was the survival of their customary working practices, a source of permanent dissatisfaction on the part of the entrepreneur. The latter complained of the "laziness of the pick-men", of their "neglect", of their "fickleness". The devotion to traditional working practices led the free labourers in 1792 to boycott a plant in which new refining machinery was being tried and which would have resulted, if successful, in a reduction in the labour force required.

The entrepreneurs had difficulty in imposing their ideas of work discipline even on the less skilled free labourers, who undertook the same work as the forced labourers of the mines and works.

In absolute contrast to the apparently unlimited submission of the forced labourers with whom they co-existed in the same works, the free labourers were by then very undisciplined. More than the scarcity already mentioned, another factor which explains this situation was the very fact that the *mita* rent was the dominant relation of production in the industry. As we have seen, the work process and wage remuneration of the forced labour group were structured through the system of fixed quotas to be accomplished. It has also been seen that in this way the costs of eventual supervision were reduced and the output of the forced labourer in each shift was not the basic preoccupation of the entrepreneur. Supervision the weakened, to the point where nights and days would pass without the supervisor going up to the mine, and the free workers therefore did as they pleased.

Faced with the world price of silver fixed essentially in relation to the yield of the Mexican mines, the massive and regular exploitation of the Potosí mines could survive only as a result of this specific and distinctive relation of production. The *mita* institution, established, regulated and organized year after year by the Spanish colonial state, was only one of the conditions of existence of the *mita* rent. The organization of the labour process and the criteria and levels of wage remuneration of the migrants developed independently of and in contradiction to that institution and its legal regulations. The mining entrepreneurs could thus maximize the transference of value from the Indian communities to their own sphere of production. As for workers contracted in the free labour market, they presented a very imperfect level of proletarianization. Their recruitment was difficult and irregular, and their labour discipline highly unsatisfactory to the mining entrepreneurs. Apart from their links with the peasant economy, they developed a special productive sphere in the mining of Potosí itself and this explains their limited dependence on the wage relation.

The Struggle for Solidarity: Class, Culture and Community in Highland Indian America

Steve J. Stern

The Problem and its Implications

Colonialism implies the rule of one people by another. The dominant image is that of a clash between two vastly different "worlds" – two peoples separated by history, language, culture. The result subjugates a colonized race or people, defined as degraded and inferior, to the economic, political, and cultural forces of an expansionist, imperial people. The legacy of this process is dramatic in Latin America. Where there once flourished great indigenous civilizations – the highlands of southern Mexico, Guatemala, Ecuador, Peru, Bolivia – today resides an impoverished and oppressed Indian peasantry. One people or "world" now defined as "nationals" of white or mixed racial ancestry, continues to rule another. Within the society of "nationals" the dominant class and the state promulgate models of "progress" which reproduce the oppression of Indians, or provide assimilation ("integration") as an alternative.

The misleading element in this image is the way it homogenizes colonized peoples, placing them into a single social category, and thereby overlooks one of their most important struggles – the building of solidarity and unity against the forces of fragmentation. Even within a single culture area the conquered peoples of Latin America held diverse ethnic indentifications. "Indian " was, after all, a name imposed by colonizers. Moreover, the ability of the invaders to weaken traditional lines of internal solidarity was a key force sustaining colonial rule. Three centuries of Spanish rule (1520–1820) remolded the colonized community, fragmented it in new ways, and integrated a divided people into the structure of colonial power. A striking dimension of these changes was the emergence of "successful Indians" – natives who escaped severe economic burdens imposed upon the majority, in some cases climbed the social ladders, and accumulated considerable wealth. Colonialism unleashed new class forces within village or provincial society, and under certain conditions encouraged differentiation into rich and poor.

In this essay, I wish to explore the process of class differentiation and its social consequences among colonized native peoples. I will focus on the sub-imperial, provincial level of indigenous society rather than on the Aztec and Inca peoples who ruled vast pre-Columbian empires. Much of the data will be drawn from a case study of Huamanga, a southern Peruvian region whose mercury and silver mines, strategic commercial location, and large Indian laboring populations brought prosperity to entrepreneurs of the late sixteenth and early seventeenth centuries. I will refer to research on other regions and time periods, however, to illustrate the ways in which patterns found in early colonial Huamanga reflected a broader process affecting large portions of the Andean and Mesoamerican highlands.

The Indian peasantry's defense of internal solidarity and cohesion, I will suggest, illuminates the historical forces that gave rise to "closed corporate communities" in highland Indian America. These peasant communities, although never fully "closed" to outsiders, and possibly experiencing decisive erosion and transformation during the past twenty years, have been encountered repeatedly by anthropologists throughout much of the Andean and Mesoamerican highlands in the twentieth century. Such communities maintained a resilient complex of institutions and social pressures which, on the one hand, drew members inward, binding them to the life and needs of the collective group, and on the other, erected barriers to penetration by "outsiders" defining sharp limits beyond which intrusions normally could not advance. Community sanction limited individual freedom to sell property to outsiders, or to look beyond the community for marriage partners. Outsiders often contended with hostility, indifference, or feigned ignorance in their relations with such communities; the outsiders' motives and interests were held suspect unless proved otherwise. Within the community, male heads of household participated in an elaborate structure of civil and religious offices (the famed "cargo systems"), thereby earning prestige and membership in the community. Climbing the ladder of "cargos" (civil and religious posts) brought increasing prestige but required also that a man and his relatives underwrite increasingly burdensome community fiestas and expenses. Widespread participation in the cargo system and other community institutions destroying or redistributing accumulated wealth did not create a uniformly poor, egalitarian community. But such institutions did place sharp constraints on individual accumulations of wealth, and on the conversion of such wealth into investment capital, within the participant community. Religious cargos often left their sponsors heavily in debt and, significantly, intense social pressure often proved necessary to "convince" a sponsor whose turn had arrived to accept his obligation to the community. The individuals charged with such persuasion commonly tried to ease their task by getting the reluctant sponsor drunk.

A widespread, important, and apparently long-established feature of indigenous highland life, the closed corporate community has provoked several scholarly explanations of its historic origins, structural principles, and social functions. One line of argument has viewed civil–religious cargo systems as a pre-Columbian community structure adapted and remolded under colonial rule. Another argument has noted the usefulness of closed corporate communities to outsiders, and seen it as a colonial institution designed to benefit the oppressors of the indigenous peasantry. Yet another approach has suggested that the closed corporate communities began to take familiar shape in the mid-to-late seventeenth century. On this view, the poor, but relatively egalitarian, closed corporate community was a defensive response to the outside world, one constructed under very particular historical conditions, but whose resilience would endure for centuries. These lines of argument are not mutually exclusive, nor entirely incompatible with the hypothesis proposed in this essay. But all neglect analysis of the forces and conflicts *within* colonized indigenous life that may have pushed toward – rather than against – the constellation of institutions, norms, and pressures associated with the closed corporate community.

This essay will suggest that the historical origins, functions, and resilience of closed corporate communities had as much to do with internal struggles among natives as they did with the survival of tradition, the desires of exploiters, or the defenses of impoverished Indians against non-indigenous outsiders. These intra-native struggles were linked to new class forces unleased by colonial rule, to the threat that these forces posed to native solidarity and resistance, and to the response of poor peasants to the threat of "class fragmentation." Let us turn, then, to the stimulus given to internal differentiation by European conquest.

Internal Differentiation

Spanish colonialism subjected the indigenous peasantries of America to the demands of an emerging international market. With the discovery of important silver mines in Mexico and greater Peru, commercial prosperity could take on impressive dimensions. Wealthy mining centers created markets for a large variety of goods and services; food, drink, coca leaf, textiles, crafts, candles, transport, entertainment, European imports. The silver city of Potosi (in modern Bolivia) was, by 1611, one of the great cities of the European world – a concentration of 160 000 people, a center of fabulous wealth based on the labors of tens of thousands of Indians. Huamanga lay directly along the route linking Potosi and Lima, the capital city of the Pacific coast which controlled commercial connections to Europe. Furthermore, the region included mercury and silver mines which gave rise to two urban centers. Huancavelica and Castrovirreyna, in addition to the city of Huamanga. By the last decades of the sixteenth century the region enjoyed a heady wave of commercial prosperity and expansion. Its colonial elite of aristocrat entrepreneurs had overcome local resistance and accumulated fortunes in mining, textile manufactures, commercial agriculture and ranching, and trade.

For the native peasantry, Huamanga's boom imposed intense economic pressures. The peasants supplied the drafts (mitas) of cheap laborers who worked Huamanga's mines, primitive textile factories and workshops (obrajes), landed estates and plantations. Their communities or ethnic groups delivered the tributes in money and in kind which supplied revenue and commodities for investment and trade. Their ayllus (subethnic lineages or kin groups, the "building blocks" of a community or ethnic group) suffered the expropriation of lands, waters, and resources attractive for commercial agriculture, ranching, mining, and other enterprises. By the early seventeenth century, the colonial regime had reduced Huamanga's natives to a pauperized existence. A shrinking population, buffeted by European epidemics as well as abuse and overwork, retained access to some means of production. But, significantly, it could no longer provide consistently or entirely for its necessities on the basis of subsistence production. Monetary needs and obligations, local circulation of commodities including foodstuffs and land, subsistence shortfalls and debt, voluntary labor contracting – all emerged as important forces in seventeenth century rural life. The burdens of community life weighed so heavily that a certain proportion of Indians fled outright. The runaways, known as *forasteros*, sought new lives as peons on landed estates, day laborers, petty producers, émigrés integrated into new Indian communities, and the like.

Despite conditions which impoverished most natives, however, a minority managed to accumulate significant wealth. Some, for example, bought or rented lands and homesteads for sums far beyond the economic horizons of most natives. Even as monetary obligations and debt became increasingly oppressive forces in the lives of poor Indians, an emerging sector of natives accumulated enough liquid wealth to become creditors. Not all their loans were petty, and even Spaniards turned to wealthy Indians for credit on occasion.

A highly commercialized regional economy, sustained by massive expropriations of native labor and resources, had despoiled most peasants of their capacity to produce and market a surplus – let alone provide for a regular subsistence. But it had also created conditions by which an Indian minority could differentiate itself from the majority and accumulate considerable wealth. Commercial prosperity, in an economy whose technology relied heavily on artisanal or craft skills, provided opportunities to those who could market special skills or services. Skilled mine workers, in high demand partly because of the effects of peasant resistance against forced labor drafts, commanded handsome wages in the seventeenth century. The numerous Indian *arrieros* (muleteers, drivers of animal trains) and artisans of Huamanga could earn several hundred pesos a year – a respectable, though not dazzling, sum by Hispanic standards, and certainly far beyond the means of most peasants. More generally, Indians who engaged in substantial trade or commercial production on "private" property might accumulate significant wealth in times of economic prosperity. Indian *arrieros*, merchants, and artisans speculated in commodities. "Successful"

Indians carved out private landholdings for commercial production of coca leaf, wine, maize, wheat, vegetables, wool, meat, hides, and cheese. Like their Spanish counterparts, Indian entrepreneurs tended to concentrate their landholdings in zones whose fertility, special ecological features, or location near cities or commercial routes made them particularly promising for commercial agriculture and ranching.

Marketable skills and services, commercial production, and trade itself earned Indians considerable revenues, but they do not explain how a successful minority protected its wealth from expropriation. The economic function of the colonial power structure was, after all, to usurp Indian resources and to siphon the surplus of a native society reduced to bare subsistence. Moreover, native traditions – communal property rights, reciprocal exchange of services, redistributive obligations of chiefs to commoners – limited the capacity of natives to accumulate personal wealth while less fortunate kinfolk slid deeper into poverty. Under these circumstances, earning a respectable income did not, by itself, insure one against impoverishment. Indians could achieve lasting economic success only if their socio-economic "strategy" shielded them – in part, at least – from colonial expropriations and from redistributive obligations to poorer Indians.

The shielding process took various forms. One method involved "privatizing" property rights. *Ayllu* or community land tenure was a precarious proposition in colonial Huamanga. From the 1590s on, the state periodically raised revenue by inspecting and regularizing colonial land titles. Legally, the judges could sell "surplus" lands of native communities to petitioners for private title. The inspections however, also allowed wealthy Indians to compete with Spaniards for the auctioned lands, and permitted *kurakas* (chiefs) to "privaize" their traditional land-use rights. Individual title to land gave an Indian a powerful weapon against the state's legal confiscations, and against the overlapping or competing claims of *ayllus* and ethnic groups. During the state's first general land inspection, in 1594, some of Huamanga's *kurakas* secured private title to extensive land use rights traditionally accorded them by *ayllus*. One lord gained title to over seventy sites, totalling thousands of hectares, which he had, "always possessed since [his] ancestors". A *kuraka* who wished to protect his prestige, or to work the lands by calling upon traditional relations of reciprocity and redistribution, probably could not alienate such lands from collective claims in an absolute sense. But we know that *kurakas* sold or rented some of these lands to outsiders, and that in later generations the heirs of deceased chiefs defended their private holdings against the claims of Indian relatives. Moreover, chiefs held authority to sell community lands in order to pay tributes or to hire substitutes for the *mita* labor drafts. Fertile lands once held by *ayllus* circulated as commodities on a surprising scale in the seventeenth century, especially in dynamic zones attractive for commercial agriculture. And the buyers of valuable property, now alienated from ethnic and *ayllu* domains, included Indians as well as Spaniards and mixed-bloods.

Another shielding method relied on building privileged relations with the colonial power structure. For some, privilege meant simply escape from standard tribute and labor obligations. The colonial regime exempted certain natives from *mita* and tribute, and failed to incorporate systematically the large sector of runaway Indians, *forasteros*, until the eighteenth century. Widows and other independent women, heads of households, *forasteros*, and artisans – all exempt from standard tributary status – assumed a conspicuous role in private accumulations of property.

Thus colonial conditions not only expropriated the labors and resources of native society, but also stimulated internal differentiation into rich and poor. This process, in part, built upon pre-existing potentials. Given an unequal distribution of power, resources and burdens in pre-Hispanic native society, we should hardly be surprised to find that colonial burdens and rewards were not spread evenly. Nonetheless, internal differentiation reflected new political and economic forces, and represented a sharp departure from the structure of community rights over property and revenue prevalent in pre-Hispanic Huamanga. Traditionally, the privileges, influence, and legitimacy of local chiefs derived from bonds of mutual obligation which redistributed accumulated goods and maintained overlapping, collective claims to society's productive resources. Colonial conditions weakened these and other constraints guaranteeing broad and effective subsistence rights to even less powerful households, *ayllus*, and ethnic groups. The process of differentiation under colonial rule was, by modern standards, incomplete, since the poorest *ayllu* peasant almost invariably retained access to some land, labor, and redistributive rights. Moreover, those who earned relatively high incomes did not necessarily shield "private" resources from overlapping or redistributive claims by poorer relatives. In some cases, at least, continuing ties of kinship and mutual obligation meant that apparently "private" resources helped, in fact, to shore up the faltering economic base of poorer kinfolk. In these cases, "success' was less individualized, more subject to a web of overlapping rights which redistributed accumulations.

By the seventeenth century, however, an emerging stratum of ambitious Indians superseded such obstacles and accumulated impressive personal wealth. A small minority had freed itself from constraints that bound most peasants to utter poverty. Significantly, land itself had begun to circulate as a commodity even among Indians. As commodity circulation penetrated local life and, to a limited extent, means of production, those with political or economic advantages gained, while others floundered in a sea of tributes, corvées, debts, and subsistence problems.

Few studies have explored directly and in detail the process of internal differentiation, but the evidence suggests that patterns evident in early colonial Huamanga did not distinguish it from other Andean highlands regions. What may have been unusual in post-conquest Huamanga was the rapid development of the process and some of its particular characteristics. The economic conjuncture in early colonial Huamanga – a region which included important mines and cities – imposed severe burdens *and* created significant opportunities.

For the Mesoamerican highlands, the evidence is less clear. Research on the sub-imperial, provincial level of Indian society has emphasized the decline of the native aristocracy. Colonial pressures, in general, undermined maintenance of complex pre-Hispanic stratification systems. Over time, the net result tended to reduce all natives to the lot of the peasantry. Recent research also indicates, however, that the levelling process was neither universal nor total in its effect. Indeed, some evidence suggests a counter-tendency similar to forces observed in the Andes. In both Mexico and Central America, a minority of Indians became landowners whose holdings and labor relations resembled those of Spanish *hacendados* (owners of landed estates mixing ranching and farming). One way or another, these figures had escaped the pressures subjecting most natives to the equality of poverty.

Indian Hispanism: Material and Symbolic Dimensions

Individual advancement, under colonial rule, rested above all else upon one's capacity to imitate Hispanic strategies of accumulation, or to develop close ties with Hispanic *mestizo* society. (*Mestizos* were the offspring of mixed native–white ancestry). The successful Indians of seventeenth-century Huamanga were independent producers and merchants who owned private property and invested in trade; artisans and others whose special skills earned them decent incomes, sufficient to purchase property or engage in commerce;

political and religious functionaries of native villages who held exemptions from tribute–labor obligations, and who profited from their position in the colonial power structure. The material wellbeing of these Indians no longer depended, as it had for their ancestors, on their ability to mobilize traditional forms of property, reciprocity obligations, and loyalty within an ancient community of *ayllu* and ethnic "kin". Their economic welfare came to depend primarily upon their capacity to privatize interests in a commercial setting – to accumulate private property, exploit commercial opportunities, convert political influence, service, or privilege into liquid wealth.

A certain Hispanization of property and relationships thus began to remold the internal structure of Indian society in Huamanga. The process of Hispanization was only partial or incomplete. The traditional reciprocities and property rights of *ayllu* life still constituted an important resource for many, including relatively wealthy natives. But those who depended exclusively upon "traditional" rights were condemned to poverty, and relations between rich and poor Indians began to take on a more "Hispanic" tonality. Wealthy Indians no longer depended upon the collective claims of *ayllus* and ethnic groups for access to property: they acquired private title to the best Indian lands, both in their original homelands and among ethnically foreign natives.

The emerging Indian élite thus embraced strategies and relationships drawn from the dominant, exploiting sector of society. Increasingly, in both Mesoamerica and the Andes, Hispanic models of advancement offered the only way out of shackles dooming most Indians to poverty. Not surprisingly, the material culture and technology of Indian production bore witness to the Hispanization of economic life. Artisans used Spanish tools and materials in their shops; ranchers raised herds of cows and sheep; farmers harnessed plows to oxen to till wheat fields.

But Indian Hispanism, in Huamanga and elsewhere, represented more than an economic response to the pressures of colonialism; it constituted a powerful new cultural force reshaping native lifeways, values, and prestige symbols from within. Wealthy Indians acquired the trappings of cultured Spanish folk. They wore fine imported clothes; travelled on horse and saddle; bought furniture, jewellery and trinkets for their homes; enjoyed wine with meals; owned Spanish firearms and swords. Some even owned African slaves. The successful and the pretentious used the Spanish Don/Doña before their names and acquired urban predilections. Even if their livelihood rooted them in the countryside much of the time, wealthy

Indians established second homes to live and do business in cities. A few cultured natives even read and wrote Spanish. In short, economic success helped transform natives, culturally, into *ladinos* – people of Indian parentage whose material culture, demeanor, and life-styles took on a more *mestizo* or even Spanish cast. They knew the ways of Spanish–*mestizo* society, dressed in non-traditional garb, understood and spoke Spanish, and in some cases cut their hair. In cities and mining centres especially, *ladino* traits characterized an Indian population far greater than successful, prospering élites. But the most "Hispanic" – least "*mestizo*" or "Indian" – of the *ladinos* were those whose socio-economic stature allowed them to buy fine clothes, mix in Spanish circles, get an education, and the like. Not all *ladinos*, for example, could support the tastes of a Don Fernando Ataurimachi of Huamanguilla (a village in northern Huamanga). Ataurimachi – descendant of Inca nobles, related by kinship to Spaniards, owner of urban property and irrigated maize land – collected Spanish guns, lances, halberds, and swords. The proud Indian made a point of showing off his collection at great public festivals.

Some of the Hispanizing Indians took Christian religion quite seriously. All Indians, of course, needed to avoid the wrath, or cultivate the goodwill, of powerful Christian gods and priests. Soon after Spanish conquest, Indian peasants generally submitted to a thin overlay of Catholic ritual and worship. This tendency was reinforced, in the Andes, by repression of an anti-Christian millenarian movement in the 1560s. By the late colonial period, the ultimate outcome of such an adaptation was clear: a syncretic religious culture in which Christian symbols (such as the Virgin of Guadaloupe in Mexico) could play an important role. But in the early colonial period, when the Christian overlay was more superficial and beset by nativist hostility, Indian, Catholicism had a narrower and more fragile social base. It is in this context that the apparent enthusiasm of a wealthy minority of "Christian" natives takes on significance. In seventeenth-century Huamanga, they led the native *cofradías* (Catholic lay associations); donated private and community resources to the church; sought Christian burials in honored spots ("inside the church next to the pulpit"); and set up ecclesiastical benefices to look after their souls. Some, of course, had climbed the social ladder by serving as lay assistants of Catholic priests.

In societies where the "cultural" and "economic" dimensions of life interpenetrated one another deeply, Indian Hispanism had profound symbolic importance. Andean culture, for example, esteemed cloth highly as a ritual article, and as an emblem of ethnic affiliation and social position. In this context, natives who wore fine Hispanic clothes not only displayed superior wealth. They also expressed an aspiration to move beyond a condemned Indian past and merge into the upper strata of colonial society. Most native cultures in Mesoamerica and the Andes interpreted "religious" relationships as an exchange of services which brought material reward or protection to those serving the gods. In the early colonial context, Christian devotion by wealthy Indians symbolized their attempt to nurture a mutually beneficial interchange with the Hispanic world, its deities as well as its people. Symbolically, then, cultural Hispanism expressed a new socio-economic fact of life: the rise of Indians whose acquisition of private property, social relationships, and commercial gains tended to differentiate them from the native peasantry, and to assimilate them to the world of colonial artistocrat–entrepreneurs.

At its highest levels, Indian Hispanism signified the emergence of colonial-style class relationships within the colonized society. The achievements of a minority furthered the shrinkage of traditional resources, prerogatives, and relationships sustaining the indigenous peasantry. And the forces fragmenting a colonized people could take on a starkly symbolic character. In Huamanga, if one saw a gallant figure dressed in rose velvet breeches with fine gold trim, bright doublet beneath a dark velveteen cape from Segovia, broad felt hat, and a pair of good shoes, one probably expected to see the face of a wealthy colonial , or perhaps a *mestizo*. Sometimes, however, the face belonged to an Indian. Over time, the cultural dimensions of class differentiation created stratum of "Europeans" with native skin and faces. Materially and culturally, the prosperous tended to become foreigners – people whose economic relations, social bonds, and cultural symbols distinguished them from poorer, more "Indian" counterparts, and imparted a Hispanic–*mestizo* dimension to their identities. Taken to its extreme, the process could transform "insiders" into alien "outsiders". A Hispanized Indian chief of highland Chiapas (Mexico) requested government protection when he returned to visit his village in 1716. The precaution may have been wise, for as we shall see, the new class forces generated considerable tension between Indian rich and poor.

Conflict and Solidarity

In some cases, class tensions flared into open conflict over land, labor, revenues, or power. In a society where ethnic loyalties continued to set Indian communities against one another, a wealthy "outsider" who intruded on traditional community domains risked considerable hostility. Tension between rich and poor also conditioned life *within* a community or ethnic group. In early colonial Peru, the Indian chronicler Félipe Guaman Poma de Ayala observed the development of more precarious, strained relationships between chiefs and "their" people. Social climbers who had usurped chieftainship from rightful heirs, and chiefs whose social and economic activities allied them with hated colonials "are no longer obeyed nor respected". At times, loss of confidence in the reciprocal exchanges that traditionally legitimated the moral authority of chiefs erupted in outright refusals to obey an "illegitimate" request. At one point (during the years 1601–6), for example, some Papres and Chilques *kurakas* of Huamanga decided, with local Spanish priests, that *ayllus* ought to plant nearly three hundred hectares of wheat to earn funds for local churches and *cofradias* (lay associations). When the peasants discovered that they were not to be paid for the work, resistance grew so fierce that the project had to abandoned.

By the late colonial period, the revamped structure of Indian life gave rise to dramatic – and ironic – events, in Mexico, hacienda-community conflicts over land sometimes pitted chiefs, as private landholders, against their communities. In some villages, Indian officials carried pistols on their persons.

Yet despite the evidence of internal differentiation and its attendant tensions, instances of overt conflict between Indian rich and poor are not particularly frequent in the historical literature. This is especially the case when one considers the early colonial period (1520–1650), or when one considers natives of the same community or ethnic group. The scarcity of evidence may, of course, simply reflect deficiencies of the extant documentation, or neglect by historians preoccupied by other issues.

But I would suggest that the explanation lies elsewhere. In the late sixteenth and early seventeenth centuries especially, when new economic patterns were relatively recent and had not yet "hardened", class tensions within the community may often have sparked not open conflict over economic or political issues, but more subtle forms of social pressure. My hypothesis is that peasants exerted day-to-day pressure on their wealthier and more acculturated counterparts to demonstrate their loyalties to the people to whom they "belonged". By serving the community or ethnic group, "successful" Indians could avoid social ostracism, and even earn prestige and respect. Such services included functioning as protective "brokers" defending community interests against the "outside" world of

Hispanic-*mestizo* exploiters; submitting, at least in part, to rules of "generosity" and community responsibility which redistributed wealth to poorer peasants; and joining in symbolic expressions of solidarity with native society. Significantly, such services limited the degree to which an Indian élite could privatize economic resources or function effectively as reliable partners of colonial exploitation. To the extent that Indian élites submitted to community pressures, they were caught in a "double bind" that constrained private gain. The threat of social alienation might *limit* the process of internal differentiation and redefine the local balance of class forces.

What is also clear from the investigations, however, is that at certain moments, tensions related to Indian Hispanism exploded in nativist outbursts seeking to purge Indian society of Hispanic–Christian influence. The Jesuits recorded one such instance when an epidemic swept western Huamanga in 1613. In this case, at least, nativist "idolatry" mobilized fierce loyalties and even violence. Indians killed not only two Catholic priests, but also, as we shall see, one of their own chiefs! The Andean gods had appeared to large numbers of people in visions and dreams, and issued a series of "commandments". The Indians should refuse to recognize Christian gods, believe Christian teachings, or collaborate with Spaniards. They should not serve or even communicate with Spaniards "unless forced to" but should close ranks around a purifying hatred of colonials and Christian influence. "The day that a cleric or priest leaves town" ordered the gods, "[the Indians] should catch an all-black dog and drag him along all the streets and spot where the priest had walked". Afterwards, the natives should kill the animal at a river, "and where [the river parts into] two branches they should throw in [the body], in order that . . . they purify the place walked by the priest". In Andean culture, the juncture of two streams had special ritual significance as a symbol of perfection, purification, and cosmic "balance".

Religious convulsions such as these responded to internal crisis which was both cultural and economic. The cultural trappings of Hispanized Indians symbolized the conversion, real or potential, of Indian society's foremost figures into partners of colonial rule and exploitation – a widening split of interests, loyalties, and orientations that accompanied differentiation into rich and poor. Indian Hispanism symbolized, too, a loss of "confidence" which touched all sectors of Andean society. Poor peasants understood too well the temptation to escape or soften burdens by allying with the world of the colonials, in a search for personal gain which weakened community solidarity. At bottom, nativist currents and outbursts represented a protest against internal trends that sapped the strength and unity of Andean society. The message of anti-Hispanism, we ought to remember, was directed at Indians, not Spaniards. The Andean gods called upon all natives to reject the temptation to forsake the Andean for the Hispanic, but the most pointed targets of such commands were those who had already made such a choice. Those who rejected the call to affirm their solidarity with native gods and peoples risked extreme alienation and even violence. In the 1613 mobilization, nativists turned against ethnic élites who shied away from religious purification and in one case poisoned " a *kuraka* of theirs, a good Christian, for not coming to their rites nor wanting to worship their idols". Murder remained the exception rather than the rule, however; a good many élites responded to the pressure of local sentiment by joining in the condemnation of their Hispanic–Christian ways! Why an important fraction of the colonial Indian élite, especially its poorer and more rural segments, may have been vulnerable to the pressure of social ostracism lies beyond the scope of this chapter. But some clearly sought social esteem among Indians, even in the absence of nativist mobilization, and even at the risk of jeopardizing successful individual adaptations to colonial rule.

Thus the new class forces remolding Indian society from within generated at least two levels of conflict. One was open confrontation over lands, revenues, labor, and power. Such conflicts hardened antagonisms and defined class enemies. They were probably more common in the late colonial period, and in cases where ethnic distinctions coincided with class divisions. Another response, however, was more covert and indirect. It involved a struggle to assert internal solidarities which might block the forces of class fragmentation. Seventeenth-century native religion, I suspect, played a key role both as an arena of conflict and of reconciliation. Those who submitted to such pressures joined in the creation of more cohesive, inward-oriented Indian communities – shielded by social "barriers" discouraging penetration by outsiders, sustained by community ceremonies and traditions redistributing or destroying accumulated wealth, strengthened by ritual reaffirmations of loyalty and service to the community or ethnic group.

The struggle for solidarity probably provoked two apparently contradictory tendencies. One was the rise of the "closed corporate community" structures still evident in much of highland Indian America in the twentieth century. Community members participated in a syncretic culture, "indigenous" in many of its traditions, characterized by strong nativist (anti-colonial) undercurrents, re-distributive and ritual responsibilities to the group, protection of community property, and a "closed" or defensive posture toward the outside world. It is striking that an Indian region such as Huamanga, whose sixteenth-century posture toward European colonials was "open" and flexible, later became a classic setting for the "closed corporate community". The demands for internal purification and pro-Andean loyalties during the nativist upheaval of 1613 constituted an early, tentative step, towards this transition. In Huamanga as elsewhere, the consolidation of resilient, inward-looking institutions and norms familiar to anthropologists probably occurred in the late seventeenth century. It is striking, too, that the colonized community's civil and religious posts, once a source of privilege facilitating individual advancement and internal differentiation, became eventually *the* classic means by which communal obligation destroyed or redistributed individual wealth. By the eighteenth century, widespread participation in an expanded structure of civil–religious cargos was common in both Andean and Mesoamerican highland communities.

The other tendency was a sharper distinction between loyal "insider" and alien "outsider", regardless of the latter's racial or ethnic origin, or geographical residence. The differentiation of a minority of relatively wealthy, Hispanized Indians from the peasant majority could not be stopped. But those whose success violated community norms, or who failed to demonstrate loyalties to natives rather than colonials, would suffer an awkward, alienated relation-ship – governed by colonial rules of coercion and economic domina-tion – with Indian peasants.

The first tendency turned an important proportion of Indian society inward in the seventeenth century, blocking further economic differentiation and redistributing at least some accumulated wealth. The second tendency made the class structure of Indian society more brittle and vulnerable to conflict, since a minority of Indians continued to accumulate private wealth, to adopt Hispanic patterns of economy and culture, and to co-operate with colonial power networks exploiting the peasantry.

Conclusions

Spanish colonialism had as one of its consequences the "class fragmentation" of colonized peoples in Mesoamerica and Andean South America. An important aspect of peasant resistance against colonial abuse, therefore, was the struggle to assert solidarities which strengthened defenses, and imposed pressures on privileged Indians to remain loyal to "their" people. The effort to build unity against the forces of fragmentation was only partially successful. No community or ethnic group could "close" itself fully from colonial society or control completely the economic options of its people. Economic and demographic pressures, as well as political coercion, forced or lured natives into Hispanized sectors of the economy, and Indian migration, temporary and permanent, was common under colonial rule. Moreover, in a society already divided by ethnic and community rivalries, building solidarities by turning inward may have made inter-ethnic or inter-community loyalty and collaboration even more difficult. Indeed, one can argue that militant religious mobilizations such as the "idolatry" of 1613 tried to supersede *both* ethnic and class divisions in order to forge a more unified Indian front.

The form that such struggles took indicated the close interplay of class, culture, and community in highland Indian America. Anti-colonial cultural symbols could play an important role in the effort to redefine internal class forces precisely *because* the economic accumulations of a privileged Indian minority were so closely associated with their cultural Hispanism. Appealing to community identification and sanction protected the peasants' class interests precisely *because* internal differentiation was predicated upon violating the constraints of communal or ethnic tradition. The building of cohesive community defenses met, as we have seen, with limited success, and may even have impeded the kind of inter-community organization necessary for a wider defense of indigenous peasantry's class interests. But the "closed corporate community" which took shape by the late colonial period, although it incorporated pre-Columbian traditions and sensibilities, did not represent simply the stubborn survival of archaic ethnic and community identifications under colonial rule. Nor did it represent simply a defense against external threats. The strengthened structure of community life represented, too, a practical response to dangerous class forces that had emerged in the very heart of colonized native America.   □

Slavery

Slavery and Resistance in the Colombian Chocó

William F. Sharp

For almost a century and a half during the colonial period – 1680–1810 – the Colombian Chocó became an important source of gold in the Spanish empire. But guarded by towering mountains and dense tropical rain forests, the Chocó is an area of heat, humidity, jungle, rivers, and rainfall. Because of geography and climate the Spanish themselves rarely attempted colonization, although those who came succeeded in extracting millions of pesos' worth of precious yellow metal. These same Spanish officials and mine owners constituted a ruling elite exhibiting little interest in anything other than accumulating wealth. Laws were violated, Indians and blacks mistreated, and bullion was produced in large quantities.

The profitable economic monoculture of mining, however, meant that Spaniards concentrated their efforts almost entirely on extracting gold from the placer mines. In doing so, they were at times almost impervious to the manner in which they exploited their surroundings. Indians died by the thousands and even slaves starved because their masters, intent on amassing fortunes, failed to establish proper supply lines or food sources. Often mistreated and limited in position, opportunity, and education, blacks had ample reason to rebel. That slaves resented their captivity is obvious from their numerous acts of resistance. But the Chocó's placer mines also presented an avenue of escape from slavery for many blacks. As Frank Tannenbaum noted so succinctly almost 30 years ago, manumission was an integral part of the Spanish slave system. Blacks could always buy their own freedom, provided they had the money to do so. In many regions of Latin America where slaves were employed in plantation agriculture, it was difficult for slaves to earn much extra cash, and they depended on the goodwill of their masters while seeking freedom. In the Chocó gold fields, however, an accessible cash crop existed that they were able to exploit during their own time, thereby accruing funds that could be used to purchase extra provisions and even freedom itself. The incidence of violence would perhaps have been much greater in the region had this safety valve of manumission not been present and effective. It is significant to note, however, that once freed, many *libres* rejected co-existence with the whites, instead seeking freedom from Spanish domination by moving to isolated jungle homes. The advantages of greater self-determination apparently outweighed all other considerations. Their chances of success by monetary or political standards were few as a result of this chosen seclusion, but in fact they were restricted in their opportunities for jobs, education, or authority even if they remained in the Spanish communities.

In at least one significant aspect Spanish societal mores with regard to slavery in the Chocó seem to have worked to the advantage of the slaves. Manumission in the Chocó was not only possible, but frequent. By the year 1782, over one-third of the black population (3 899 out of 10 987) was free. Any Spaniard could free his slaves either during his lifetime, or in his will without restrictions, and a number doubtless did so. The most common means of manumission in the Chocó, however, was the system whereby a slave purchased his own freedom. The value of a slave was legally established by one of the Spanish officials in the region (usually the lieutenant governor), and the owner had to accept this price. Slaves could work on their "free time," including religious holidays, and keep what they earned. Owners hoped slaves would use this money to buy extra food, tobacco, and liquor, which they sold to their slaves at high prices. But with luck and hard work slaves working in the placer mines could save enough to buy their own freedom. Because notary records no longer exist for the Chocó during the colonial period, it is impossible even to estimate the number of slaves who were able to purchase liberty, but the number was clearly substantial. Apparently many owners agreed to this "self-purchase," and at least by the nineteenth century some slaves had even made arrangements to pay for their manumission in instalments. These slaves were freed from service to their masters once they had submitted a specified part of their value (the amount varied from 10 to 50 per cent), but they were, of course, expected to continue payments. Thus, following a down payment, some slaves were free to seek their own employment and work full-time on their own accounts.

Freed blacks and mulattoes in the Chocó did acquire a greater degree of protection before the law than their slave brethren elsewhere, but very few *libres* seem to have taken advantage of this — probably because they did not know their legal rights or were too intimidated to use them.

Although black *libres* had a slightly higher legal and social standing than slaves, many of the regulations that applied to the slave also applied to them. Legally they could not bear arms or hold any political or military office without special crown approval; they could not live among the Indians or hold Indian servants; nor could they use such prestige symbols as a walking cane.

Jobs were available in the mines and wages were often as much as a peso a day, but few free blacks showed any desire to work in the mines of their former owners. Although *libres* did do some mining, few qualified as *masamorreros* (independent prospectors). The term was usually used for those full-time prospectors who worked their own claims. In the province of Citará (one of the two Chocó provinces), which contained 814 *libre* males in 1782, there were only 188 *masamorreros* and some of these doubtless were Spaniards. Some *libres* attempted commercial agriculture, living near the mines and villages and selling their corn and plantains to the overseers of the large slave gangs. Often, however, they were not welcomed near the Spanish communities and mines, because owners feared that the *libres* would be a corrupting influence on those who remained in bondage. Many of the *libres*, joined by runaway slaves (*cimarrones*) both from the Chocó and neighboring regions like the Cauca valley and Antioquia, retired to hard to reach spots in the mountains near the head waters of the numerous streams that meandered through the Chocó. There they produced their own food through primitive agriculture and mined just enough to supply themselves with basic necessities.

Certainly one of the most serious handicaps faced by the *libres* was the virtual impossibility of receiving any formal education. This doubtless prevented them from holding many positions that required some degree of literacy (overseers, clerks, and so on). It was not necessarily a deliberate policy on the part of the Spanish to withhold education from blacks (although that conclusion seems justified), because schools throughout Latin America were few in number.

One of the few prestigious occupations open to a free mulatto or black involved a position in the colonial militia. Blacks could join the militia in the eighteenth century with crown approval, but except in times of dire emergency they formed segregated regiments.

Census reports listed the Chocó's large number of *libres*, but they did not include the considerable number of *cimarrones*. Blacks often took advantage of revolts to escape bondage and congregated in places that were inaccessible to Spaniards intent upon their recapture. These runaway slaves posed a real threat to the prosperity of the region, since they returned to the Spanish mines and villages on raiding parties, looting and burning, stealing women, and sometimes raping and killing the inhabitants. Usually the *cimarrones* retreated before the forces sent to recapture them and were never really eliminated. In the beginning of the nineteenth century, for example, slaves from the Chocó, Barbacoas, and the Cauca valley formed a *palanque* (*cimarron* community) located just south of the Chocó. Expeditions sent against it found only deserted houses as the blacks slipped farther into the jungle. A foray led by the governor of Micay in 1819 finally succeeded in capturing a few of the *cimarrones* in this group and temporarily stopped raids on mines in the region. But the governor admitted that further problems would probably arise.

Certainly, purchasing freedom or fleeing from the forced labor of the slave gang were forms of black resistance, and they could cost the owner capital investment or future profits in his mine – but these problems were not what the Spanish feared the most. The real threat was that of black aggression. Docility is not a word that can be used accurately to describe the blacks in Latin America, and the Spanish knew, from experience virtually everywhere in the Americas, to expect physical opposition from their African bondsmen. Therefore the slave insurrections that erupted periodically in the Chocó were to be expected, but it is especially significant that they occurred in this particular region of the Spanish empire. Blacks everywhere resisted slavery, but rarely did they have the legal opportunities to escape bondage that were available in the Chocó. Hatred of slavery could be relieved by following legal channels, and those blacks who were the strongest, most aggressive (and therefore potentially the most dangerous) slaves could gain liberty by working for it. Opportunities to amass savings in the gold fields were ever present, and the safety valve of manumission doubtless let off tension. There was a steady stream of young able-bodied blacks who purchased their own freedom. Armed revolt, on the other hand, was a serious crime known to all, and any large rebellion was inevitably doomed to ultimate failure and perhaps death. The Spanish wanted the Chocó gold, and no slave, or group of slaves, could prevent the continued exploitation of men and metals. But significantly, confrontations did occur again and again and clearly demonstrated the frustrations and impatience of blacks at their captivity.

The first such altercation took place in 1684 when slaves who joined rebellious Chocó Indians were finally defeated by troops sent from the Cauca valley. The largest slave revolt to occur in the region took place in 1728 near the town of Tadó. Forty blacks who had been severely mistreated by a harsh overseer banded together and killed the offending Spaniard. Their hatred not satiated by this single act of vengeance, the blacks raided other isolated mines in the area, killing fourteen more Spaniards and enlisting other followers. The Spanish inhabitants of Tadó were terrified that the slaves would attack the town itself, and with only a handful of whites and a few weapons they thought themselves defenseless. But instead of making a direct assault on the town, the blacks scattered, attempting to get slaves from other *cuadrillas* in the Chocó to join them in a mass rebellion. The blacks, having few weapons, obviously believed that greater safety and effectiveness lay in numbers. But the tactic backfired as the savage initial outburst of the rebellion sputtered into inactivity, giving the Spaniards time to send reinforcements to the region. The governor of Popayán, afraid an organized slave revolt might spread into the Cauca valley, immediately sent an armed expedition to Tadó. Peace was restored to the area when the military commander of the Spanish expedition, Lieutenant Julian Tres Palacios Mier, tricked four of the rebel leaders into surrender and executed them. Lieutenant Tres Palacios had been correct in his solution to the rebellion. The remaining blacks, although a significant group, seemed lost and powerless without leadership, and the majority submissively returned to their owners. Some remained hidden as *cimarrones* along the jungle stream, but they posed no immediate threat to Spanish domination.

The 1728 rebellion, however, did provide slaves with an example of violent resistance. A number of slaves had firsthand experience as participants in an open rebellion against their masters, and *cuadrillas* throughout the Chocó had knowledge of the revolt.

Black freedmen also initiated several serious incidents in the Chocó, and the threat of their involvement in seditious acts increased with their numbers. Limited in their opportunities and often resentful of Spanish authority, the *libres* constituted a large, potentially disruptive group. In 1766 free mulattoes in the town of Bebará, disgusted with high prices for *aguardiente* (a liquor – literally firewater) and food, and with the Spanish officials in the Chocó, broke into the royal *aguardiente* warehouse in the town and stole all the liquor on hand. After consuming large quantities of the firewater they drunkenly marched to the *corregidor*'s house. Armed with stones, sticks, and a few knives, they raised their own flags and openly insulted the *corregidor*. The unruly mob then presented a list of grievances that began "long live the King and down with bad government". Although the blacks took no physical action at the time, they controlled the town and the *corregidor* was powerless to prevent their continued defiance of authority.

The absence of a major revolt during the last decades of the colonial period did not mean that conditions improved or that blacks were satisfied. The insubordination and unruliness described by Governor Ciaurriz in 1803 and 1806 are clear indications that life in the Chocó depended on forced alliances and was filled with tension and fear. Revolts failed, or perhaps were not even initiated, because many slaves concentrated their efforts on purchasing freedom rather than rebellion. But also the blacks' lack of success in insurrection proved the efficacious nature of the Spanish slave system. The white minority maintained, through the use of regimented authority and threats of armed reprisals, an uneasy but effective dominance over the colored majority. The slaves, who were born or raised in bondage, were carefully taught the dictates of their masters, and lessons in submission were repeatedly driven home by the end of a lash. Blacks learned to obey or expect punishment. Rebellion had virtually no chance of continued success, because blacks relied on quick, isolated acts of violence rather than prolonged, systematically organized campaigns. Weapons, education, and authority were a Spanish monopoly. Trained leadership within the black community was not encouraged and rarely tolerated. For the slave, the only acceptable avenue for personal initiative was hard work. This might bring him increased personal comforts, food, liquor, clothing, or, if he was diligent and lucky, enough money to purchase freedom. But under the Spanish even the *libre* still knew who was master. It would be extremely naive to expect white masters to accept former slaves as equals. Positions and opportunities were never equal, and acts of self-assertion were not permitted.

But despite the attempts on the part of the Spanish to destroy black pride and limit initiative, despite the overwhelming odds against them, slaves did rebel and they continued to seek and work for their freedom – not just freedom from slavery (this was done in many parts of the Americas), but also freedom from Spanish authority, domination, and law. This is doubtless the real reason so many free blacks, desiring to be free in spirit as well as legal status, left the Spanish settlements and retreated to inaccessible locations in the jungle. Whether they failed or succeeded in their rebellions is in reality not nearly as important as the fact that they resisted, and resisted in many ways.

Colonial Politics

Political Elites and State Building:
Brazil in Comparative Perspective

José Murilo de Carvalho

The most striking difference in the political evolution of the Spanish and the Portuguese colonial possessions is the well-known phenomenon of the Balkanization on the Spanish part, in contrast with the unified nation that emerged from the Portuguese domain. To put it in quantitative terms, at the beginning of the nineteenth century the Spanish colony was divided administratively into four viceroyalties, four captaincies-general, and thirteen high courts; by mid-century it was fragmented into seventeen different countries. In contrast, the Portuguese colony, of comparable size, which up to 1820 was still divided into eighteen captaincies-general, by 1825 had already been transformed into one independent nation.

Another important difference, although not as clear cut as the first, regards the nature of the two political systems. Brazil managed to maintain a reasonably stable constitutional monarchy, and this for 69 years, while most of the Spanish-speaking countries, Chile being the conspicuous exception, had to cope with constant political upheavals that ended frequently in civilian or military caudillistic types of government.

The political élites formed during the Spanish and Brazilian colonial periods confront us immediately with a major contrast. The great majority of the Brazilian élite at the time of independence and up to mid-century had three common characteristics: first, they were all trained in one university, Portugal's Coimbra; second, they were trained mostly in civil law; third, they were principally bureaucrats, especially magistrates or judges. Although there are, to my knowledge, no quantitative studies of the élites of the Spanish-speaking countries, from the evidence available it can be safely asserted that no group comparable to the Brazilian was present in any of them. Many élites were certainly highly educated, but not in one place and in one subject, and not with practical experience in matters of government.

This fact, I will argue, was due to a clear difference in the colonial

55

educational policies of Portugal and Spain. Portugal refused systematically to allow the organization of any institution of higher learning in her colonies, not considering as such the theological seminaries. Only after the arrival of the Portuguese court were two medical and two military academies allowed. The reason for this policy was clearly stated by the Conselho Ultramarino (Overseas Council) in 1768 when it denied a request by the still rich goldmining captaincy of Minas Gerais to build its own school of medicine. The Conselho answered that the question was a political one and that a favorable decision could lead to a further request for a law academy, and the whole process would end up in independence, since "one of the strongest unifying bonds that keeps the dependency of the colonies, is the need to come to Portugal for higher studies".

As a consequence of the refusal, Brazilian students had to go to Portugal for their training. From 1772 to 1872, a total of 1 242 of them, coming from all captaincies, were enrolled at Coimbra, of whom 80 per cent attended before 1828, when two Brazilian law schools were opened. As it turned out, a substantial part of the leadership involved in the independence movement at the national level, as well as the majority of the national political élite in the three decades that followed, was drawn from this group of university graduates. All of the university-educated cabinet ministers during the first decade of independence were trained in Portugal, and by mid-century almost half of the ministers still belonged to this Coimbra generation.

Nothing of the sort happened in the Spanish colony. It was the consistent policy of the colonial government to encourage the organization of universities under the aegis of the state or of the church. The royal universities were modeled after the University of Salamanca, the religious ones mostly after that of Alcalá. At the end of the colonial period, twenty-three (or twenty-five, according to some authors) universities had been created, the first ones, those of Peru and Mexico, as early as 1551. The geographical distribution of these universities presents a striking coincidence: there were universities in almost all of the regions that later became independent countries, except for some of the small Central American nations. The twenty-three universities were scattered in what eventually would become thirteen different countries.

My contention is that the phenomenon was no coincidence at all. The Spanish colonial universities made possible the creation of numerous local educated élites, with little if any contact with the mother country or with other neighboring colonial subdivisions.

When the struggle for independence began, few of these people had, as did the *libertadores*, the larger view of the whole colony in mind, the majority being limited by its parochial experience. But at the same moment, in the former Portuguese colony, there was a single élite, one which was, so to speak, a small club of friends and former classmates. Its members came from all parts of the huge colony, but they had got to know each other at Coimbra where they had an organization of their own. The absence of universities in the colony had also the consequence of holding the number of graduates to a small group. As mentioned, only slightly over a thousand Brazilian students were enrolled at Coimbra after 1772. In clear contrast, the Royal University of Mexico alone graduated around 39 000 before independence, and it has been calculated that the total number of graduates for the entire Spanish colony was 150 000. This greater diffusion of higher education also multiplied the chances for competing leaderships and for the spread of political conflict.

The ideological content of the education of the Spanish and Portuguese élites was another source of divergence. Since its beginning in 1290, the University of Coimbra had been under the intellectual influence of the University of Bologna, the major European center of study of Roman law at the time. Several of the Coimbra faculty had been trained at Bologna and were for this reason called "the *bolônios*".

The concentration of training in one place and in one discipline gave the élite a solid ideological homogeneity. The Romanist tradition was of particular importance. Although Roman law was used for various purposes after the revival of its study in Europe at the end of the eleventh century, in Portugal "the *bolônios*" had been using it consistently to help consolidate the power of the kings.

The absorption of a centralizing, post-classical version of the Roman tradition was instrumental in infusing the future Brazilian leaders with a strong statist orientation, a firm belief in the reasons of the state and in its supremacy over church and barons.

At the same time, Coimbra managed to isolate its students from the most dangerous aspects of the French Enlightenment, admitting only the reformist and Christian version of the *Lumières*. It is noteworthy that several Brazilian students who went to France or England, and even some priests trained in the colony, were more influenced by the subversive ideas of the time and more willing to put them into practice through political action than were their Coimbra fellows. It might not be an exaggeration to say that it was easier to have access to the *philosophes* in the captaincy of Minas Gerais, four hundred miles to the interior of Brazil, than at

Coimbra. The library of one priest who participated in a 1789 political rebellion which occurred in that captaincy was made the object of a study, the revealing title of which is "The Devil in the Canon's Library". The devil was *l'Encyclopédie*, Diderot, Voltaire, d'Alembert, Mably, and the like.

From the studies available on the élites of the Spanish-speaking countries, it can be concluded that no such ideological homogeneity existed among them. For one part, as already noted, the greater diffusion of higher education favored wider diffusion of ideas. For another, although Roman law was also very influential in Spain, most of the colonial universities were controlled by religious orders and dedicated to religious training. Jesuits, Franciscans, Dominicans, Augustinians competed for the control of higher education as a weapon of religious conquest. Even the state-controlled Royal University of Mexico put the emphasis of its training in theology, thus departing from its model, the University of Salamanca, where law had the upper hand. This type of education was less likely to convey a concern with and knowledge of state-building that was the training imparted at Coimbra.

The statist orientation of the Brazilian élite was further enhanced by the élite's third characteristic, its occupational composition. Up to 1853 the overwhelming majority of cabinet ministers were public employees. A similar picture can be obtained for senators and deputies. And among these public employees, the magistrates had a dominant position, be it among ministers, senators, councillors, or deputies, except during the first period when the military predominated among ministers.

Magistrates, as Stuart Schwartz (1973) has shown, were the backbone of the Portuguese state, over which they had made their influence felt since the fourteenth century. They were a surprisingly modern professional group with elaborate training and career patterns. They were made to circulate from colony to colony and from the colonies to the higher posts in Portugal. And since the exercise of judicial functions was always linked to public administration in general, the whole process transformed several of these magistrates into consummate statesmen. Another important point about this group, which was true also for the entire Portuguese bureaucracy, was that there was relatively little discrimination against Brazilian nationals. Brazilian judges served in different types of courts both in Portugal and in the colonies of Asia and America.

The Spanish bureaucracy was not very different from the Portuguese in terms of professionalization, and the magistrates – particularly the *oidores* of the *audiencias* – were its most important part.

The major difference here, and this has frequently been pointed out, was the much greater degree of exclusion of American-born Spaniards from the higher posts in the Spanish side. This fact has been singled out with reason as an important source of alienation of upper-class Creoles and of conflict with *peninsulares*. And it must be added that the exclusion had also the consequence of preventing the development of a sizable group of Creoles with practical experience in government matters at the highest levels of public administration, that is, of state-building proper. Participation in the *cabildos*, the local administrative bodies, was not likely to provide such experience.

In summary, I am arguing that the presence in Brazil by the time of independence of an élite that by the place and content of training, by career pattern and occupational experience, constituted a closely united group of people, ideologically homogenous, statist oriented, and practical in government matters, was a basic factor in the maintenance of the unity of the former colony and in the adoption of a centralized monarchical system. This could have been a not sufficient condition, but it seems to me that it was a necessary one. The great number of rebellions, some with secessionist tendencies, that took place in Brazil both before and after independence shows that the business of keeping the country together was a very difficult task indeed. Between 1831 and 1848 alone, more than twenty minor revolts and seven major ones broke out in different parts of the country. In three of the latter, the leaders proclaimed independent republican governments. Had there been numerous local and parochial élites, instead of a united national élite, the colony would most probably have broken apart into several different countries, just as happened on the Spanish side.

It is significant, for example, that very few of the graduates of Coimbra, or of the military trained at the College of the Nobles for that matter, took part in the rebellions. A look at the list of persons indicted for participation in three of the pre-independence rebellions shows that, aside from a few intellectuals trained in Europe outside of Portugal, the most conspicuous participants were priests and local lower-rank military. Priests, in fact, provided the clearest opposition to the magistrates among the educated élite. Most of the lower clergy had been educated in Brazil and were both more parochial, in the sense of lacking concern for maintaining the unity of the country, and more influenced by politically subversive ideas, such as popular sovereignty and republicanism. Two years after independence, a rebellion, led mostly by priests, went as far as to proclaim an independent republican government in the northeastern part of the country. By mid-century, when the rebellions had ended and the monarchy was solidly established, priests had been completely eliminated from the national political élite.

One alternative explanation that has been put forward for the difference in political behavior between magistrates and priests points in the direction of their different class origins, priests being recruited among the lower strata of the population. There may in fact have been some difference in social origin, in general, between the two groups. Only families of substance could afford to send their sons to Coimbra. But, on the other side, it is well known that to have a priest in the family was as prestigious as to have a magistrate or lawyer. It was also very convenient for rich families to have one of the sons become a priest since a non-inheriting male heir made it easier to keep the family estate intact. And the fact is that almost all priests who took part in the rebellions were rich and the offspring of wealthy families. Some priests were usurers, some landowners, some even plantation and slave owners. In terms of social origin, therefore, there seems to be little or no difference between the rebellious priests and the magistrates. The major difference was in their ideology and training.

As far as the military are concerned, their participation in the rebellions was limited to members of the lower ranks or to officers of the militia corps. Most of the higher ranking officers who appear among the national political élite during the first and second decades after independence were trained at Coimbra or at the College of the Nobles, and they did not differ very much in terms of political outlook from the magistrates, being also deeply involved in state affairs. Their number among the élite, particularly among senators and deputies, was progressively reduced in favor of magistrates and lawyers, reflecting the consolidation of the monarchical system. In the meantime, the training of the military took a more technical direction and was clearly separated from the training of the political élite. This fact, together with a change in the social composition of the officer corps and the influence of positivism, gradually helped to alienate them from the civilian élite and from the monarchy. They would come back to the national political scene at the end of the empire as allies of republican groups.

The absence of a radical break in the Brazilian process of independence made it possible for the national élite to replicate the policy that had produced it. Only two law schools were established during the empire, and the members of the élite, as previously shown, continued to be drawn from the graduates of these schools. An elaborate system of advancement in the political career was also developed: starting as a municipal judge, the politician would slowly proceed up to the highest posts of ministers and state councillors in a further reinforcement of the ideological unity, statist orientation, and familiarity with public office that were found among their Portuguese antecedents.

From the previous discussion it can be concluded that the presence of an élite such as the one found in Brazil at the end of the colonial period was no accident at all. It was the product of an explicit effort made by the Portuguese state. And this brings us to the problem of the nature of this state and of its relationships with society. The Portuguese state would and could train such an élite because it had itself benefitted from an early consolidation which dated from the accession to power of D. João I after his victory at the battle of Aljubarrota in 1385. D. João won with the support of the merchant class and this, according to Oliveira Martins, meant the end of the Middle Ages in Portugal, a final blow against the feudal barons, who were already weakened by the long struggle against the Moors. But, unlike the case in England, a modern market economy and a liberal society did not develop in Portugal at the same time that a modern state was being molded. With the overseas adventure, commercial capitalism developed under the protection of the crown, the king being the country's first and most powerful merchant. An independent bourgeoisie could not ascend to become a dominant social-class as in other European countries. As a consequence, there was a predominance of the state and a weakness of the institutions of political representation, one characteristic of which was the pervasive overrepresentation of public employees among the political élite.

In Brazil, this predominance – and that of the magistrates in particular – led eventually to a reaction. In 1855, a House bill was introduced in the Brazilian Congress intended to establish restrictions on the eligibility of magistrates and other public employees to serve as legislators. In the illuminating debate that followed, some deputies called attention to the consequences of the continued predominance of magistrates for the nature of political representation in Brazil. I quote one of them: "Can we say, Mr President, that a House represents faithfully the interests of all classes in society when 82 of its 113 members are legists [magistrates]? Where are, Gentlemen, the representatives of the industrial classes, of the landowners, of the capitalists, of the merchants?" Another had voiced a similar concern: "In this House there are no merchants, no farmers, all are public employees, so to speak". The role of the magistrates in politics was forcefully defended during the debate, but the fact remained that political representation was impaired by the overwhelming presence of government employees in the legislature.

In a parallel direction, there was a constant complaint against the excessive size and influence of the central bureaucracy. One of the most perceptive politicians and social reformers of the last years of the regime, Joaquim Nabuco, attributed this overgrown structure to slavery. In his view, the existence of slave labor prevented the majority of the free population from developing economic alternatives to public employment, to which the majority was forced to turn as a source of income; slavery made public employees, in his words, "the government's serfs". Nabuco was, of course, overstating the case. But public jobs were certainly the aspiration of many, and the bureaucracy weighed heavily on the state's budget. By the end of the empire, expenditures on personnel ate up 60 per cent of the central budget, and almost 70 per cent of the civil service was concentrated in the central government. This contributed to the high visibility of the national government, and the state in general, and led some observers to view the political system as stateful, and the state as a leviathan dominating an inert society. On the other side, those who stressed the existence of a powerful land- and slave-owning class, in control of the export-oriented economy, concluded that the government was simply the representative of the interests of this class. The present discussion of the political élite can help to reconcile such conflicting views.

The continuity that characterized the process of independence, and the centralized monarchical system that was established – in good part, as I have argued, because of the nature of the political élite – gave the state apparatus a significant weight of its own, and made the government a major actor in the life of the country, as had been the case in Portugal. It made possible the partial fusion of the bureaucracy and the political élite, giving at times the impression that it was the government and not social groups and classes that was represented in Congress. But, on the other side, unlike Portugal, Brazil had a strong landowning class highly dependent on slave labor. This class dominated the economy of the country, which was based mostly on exports of coffee, sugar, and tobacco. And the central government depended on the taxes levied on external trade, which amounted to 70 per cent of the budget. So the stability of the government required an alliance between the bureaucracy and the landed classes.

But this was an unstable alliance. Several observers besides Joaquim Nabuco have pointed out how the slave system restricted economic opportunities for elements of the middle sectors, both rural and urban. Moreover, the long-term stagnation of the sugar economy in the northern part of the country contributed to the unemployment of members of landed classes also. In addition, the near monopoly held by the foreigners on the commercial sector of the larger cities aggravated the situation. The bureaucracy became then one of the few alternatives for all those job seekers, and the scramble for public jobs was a widely recognized fact. Having been either expelled from the slave economy in its decadent sector, or denied channels of upward mobility by the general constraints of a slave society, many members of the bureaucracy had no strong commitment to maintain the slave system. They could support or even initiate social reforms once convinced that the fiscal basis of the state, that is, of their salaries, would not be threatened by such action. In fact, the major abolitionist law of 1871, that which declared free all children born thenceforward to slave mothers, was passed over the strong opposition of landowners, who bitterly attacked the government and the emperor. The approval of the law was made possible by the large number of public employees in the House.

This was a complex situation indeed. The élite, and the state itself, were dependent on the slave economy and were in some sense the supporters of the slave society. But they were also able to detach themselves from the interests of slavery and become an instrument of reform. This contradiction was perceived by Joaquim Nabuco when he observed that the state was at the same time a shadow of slavery and the only force capable of putting an end to it. This was also the reason why the regime was, on one side, able to survive for sixty-nine years, but, on the other, very vulnerable. One year after his daughter, then regent, was enthusiastically applauded in the streets of Rio for abolishing slavery, the aging emperor was quietly sent into exile after being overthrown in a bloodless coup d'état engineered by a sector of the bureaucracy he had always overlooked, the military, and by the republican landowners of the most prosperous coffee areas.

A unified élite was instrumental in consolidating the political power of the dominant classes by neutralizing the consequences of their internal divisions and by keeping at bay political mobilization from below. But in view of the very lack of cohesion within these classes, and as a consequence of its own training, the élite could achieve this goal only by building a national state apparatus, which then became a major political actor in its own right. Now, the major common interests between the state and the dominant classes were the maintenance of order and the control of political mobilization.

When it came to specific issues that affected differently the economic interests of various sectors of the dominant classes, the élite, and particularly its bureaucratic component, was able to play one sector against the other and implement important reforms, even at the cost of the political legitimacy of the regime. So, instead of a dichotomic division of state *v.* society, or of the mechanistic representation by the state of the interests of the landowners, Brazilian political reality looked more like a field of dialectical tensions which did not lead to radical ruptures, but was nonetheless dynamic enough to generate political and social changes.

Bases of Political Alignment in Early Republican Spanish America

Frank Safford

This discussion deals with some of the problems arising from attempts to describe the socio-economic bases of political alignments in Spanish America in the first half century of the republican period. As this was a time of beginnings, individuals in making their political commitments could not consult a well-established family tradition, as would be the case after the middle of nineteenth century. Thus the role that socio-economic factors may have played in shaping political choices is of particular interest. This essay refers solely to alignments among the political élite, the more or less visible elements in politics. The analysis uses the history of Colombia as its principal reference point but takes sidelong glances at Mexico, Venezuela, and other variants.

The parties that had emerged in even the most structured polities by the middle of the nineteenth century lacked many of the characteristics of parties as conceived in the twentieth century. Among other things they had no formal party organizations and mass bases. Before 1850 they generally did not have formally organized hierarchies or central directorates; nor were there party whips in the congresses. Even in the countries with relatively complex political parties, both personalism and factional flux continued to be evident, and individuals or factions of two opposing parties occasionally joined together to form a third force (as happens in modern parties). Finally, the political groups of the early nineteenth century were of course upper-class parties, in which the lower orders participated very little, except in time of civil war and then, one may assume, unwillingly in most cases.

The evolution of party alignments in the structured polities can be divided into three stages, corresponding very roughly to the decades between 1820 and 1850. The politics of the 1820s were characterized by extreme fragmentation, with political attachments formed on both personalist and regional bases. Alignments fluctuated rapidly, depending on the variable fortunes of certain leading figures. In many cases the alignments evident in this decade did not persist much beyond it.

During the 1830s, however, there occurred a coagulation of various conservative interests into identifiable establishment groups.

Finally, in the 1840s there occurred a kind of political crystallization in many countries, with emergent groups rebelling against the establishments of the 1830s. In the process there formed political groups with sharp ideological differences and strong party identities. Factionalism continued to flourish within parties, but in many places the politically active part of the population now thought of itself as belonging to either of two parties. Most commonly they came to be called "liberal" and "conservative". Such terms, particularly *liberal*, had been used during the 1820s and 1830s, but before the 1840s they were not the exclusive property of one party; until the 1840s, everyone considered himself "liberal". By the end of the 1840s, however, these terms had become firmly attached to particular parties and were the banners under which they went to war. In many countries the alignments formed in the 1840s tended to be more or less enduring.

This "radicalization" of politics at the end of the 1840s and in the early 1850s in turn divided some of the newly crystallized parties. The liberal parties in Mexico, Colombia, and Venezuela divided on slightly varying grounds between radical and moderate wings. Nevertheless, the mid-century alignments remained of enduring significance. For no matter how bitter the divisions between the wings of the post-1850 parties, their members in most cases continued to think of themselves as indelibly marked as either liberal or conservative.

Party affiliation must have been a question of great moment to members of the upper classes. Otherwise it is hard to explain the bitterly fought internecine conflicts of the nineteenth century. Much civil disruption amounted to little more than caudillistic coups d'état, in which broad interest often may not have been engaged; this was particularly true of those countries, like Peru and Bolivia, in which there was relatively little party development. But in Mexico, Colombia, and Venezuela, relatively greater party articulation meant that political conflict was more likely to occur on a broad scale.

What did party affiliation mean to the upper classes? For many it was largely a matter of government jobs. Lacking other economic opportunities in most places and lured on by the Spanish tradition of government service, those with secondary education often viewed political position as their principal economic resource. Even for those not directly involved as politicians, party affiliation meant access to or denial of favorable treatment in customs offices, in the settlement of government debts, in speculative purchases of public lands. In time of civil war, all substantial citizens knew that their party affiliations would determine whether or not forced loans would be exacted from them. For many members of the upper class, therefore, a political party was a brotherhood for their economic protection.

Halperín-Donghi (1973) and some others who view nineteenth-century politics in terms of contending economic groups see a dynamic that has its point of dramatic climax at mid-century. The better accounts agree that a kind of crystallization of politics occurred in such countries as Mexico, Venezuela, and New Granada in the years between 1845 and 1855. From several of the more interesting interpretations one can extract the following synthesis. In the political confusion and relative economic stagnation of the 1830s, the landowning–clerical–military coalition was able to dominate the urban sector rather easily. The development of export economies and commercial expansion in the 1840s in some countries, however, fostered the emergence of a new merchant class, which began seriously to challenge the dominance of the traditional power groups. At the same time, the expansion of foreign trade undermined native artisans, making them susceptible to the blandishments of the emergent bourgeois who would challenge the established power-holders. In the conflict between the old landed and the new commercial element, both sides made elaborate appeals to ideology in their efforts to curry popular support. The ruling coalition of landowners, aided by the clergy and military, responded to the middle-class challenge by making an intensified appeal to religion as a symbol that could hold the masses. The "new middle classes" (merchants, professionals), in many cases representing a new political generation, for their part held up the banners of a new secular religion – compounded of economic liberalism and the democratic republican spirit of the Revolution of 1848 – attracting the loyalty of artisans, small merchants, and other lower elements in the society. These ideological conflicts of mid-century were most clearly dramatized in the *Reforma* in Mexico and in Colombia's upheavals of the years 1849–54. In both cases, allegedly, the new bourgeoisie emerged politically triumphant but then, through purchases of land (often former church property), became incorporated in and assimilated to the traditional landowning aristocracy.

For all the authority behind it, the conception of nineteenth-century politics as a conflict between landowners and an urban bourgeoisie is not convincing. In the first place, the nature of most Latin American economies was such that there was not a clear opposition of interests between property-owners and merchants. In most places the overwhelming majority of the upper class had a stake in developing export economies – the landowners as producers for export and as consumers of imported luxury goods, the merchants as expediters of this exchange, and the lawyers as principal actors in the drama of land aggrandizement. The most common upper class vocations were complementary. Party affiliation therefore was unlikely to express a particular occupational interest within the upper class.

Even where one can perceive, in large, an opposition between urban and rural interest, as a practical matter it is hard to make a clear distinction between individuals or families belonging to a rural landed class and those belonging to an urban sector of merchants, professionals, and intellectuals. Most of Latin American society was not sufficiently developed for there to be a clear specialization of function. A member of the upper class active in politics was likely to be at once a landowner, lawyer, merchant, educator, littérateur, government employee, and, on occasion, military officer. Even in those cases where an individual can be assigned to a "major" function, the members of his immediate family, all with the same political affiliation, are likely to have encompassed most of the upper-class vocations. It is therefore very difficult to distinguish among individuals or families in the élite in terms of economic function.

If liberals and conservatives were similar in formal occupation, was there nevertheless a difference between them in economic style? A number of accounts view liberals as capitalist in spirit, conservatives as resistant to capitalist institutions and behavior.

The often-used distinction between commercially oriented or export agriculture and the static *hacienda* is an attractive and seemingly useful device for political analysis. In broad regional terms, one thinks of the notable division between the conservatism of the highland areas and the liberalism of the plantation lowlands in Ecuador. In Colombia the same pattern applies, in the same broad terms. Tunja and Popayán, neither involved in exporting, remained bastions of conservatism. The Caribbean coast and the Magdalena Valley tended to drift toward a liberal posture during the expansion of agricultural exports of the middle of the nineteenth century. But the Colombian case, as usual, presents anomalies. As one begins to look more closely at the picture, it tends to lose clarity. The Cauca Valley north of Cali fell under liberal dominion at least twenty years before it could effectively ship goods abroad or even to other parts of the country. And conservative Antioquia, while not in export *agriculture* until about 1880, was more heavily engaged in exporting, both as a gold producer and as the commercial organizer of other activities than any other region.

If one looks seriously at the economic behavior of individuals, the matter may become even more complex. Discriminating between "capitalist" landowners and "traditional" ones may present as many problems as distinguishing between merchants and landowners. There are notable cases of men who on different holdings were engaged both in export agriculture and in more traditional production for the domestic market. And one cannot assume, as Bazant does, that producers of "commercial" crops, such as sugar in Mexico or tobacco in Colombia, necessarily operated more "capitalistically" than producers of locally consumed staples.

Probably the most generally applicable statement to be made about economic categories and political affiliations in Mexico and Colombia is that capitalists could be found in either party but that they tended to hew to the center. And those who were most capitalistic, practically by definition, were those who attempted to shun any political identification and to find safety in the narrow interstices between the parties. One uncommon, but useful, way to look at the relationship of economic interests and politics is to view the truly bourgeois, the apolitical businessman, as opposed to the disruptive ideologies and ambitious politicians in both parties. For the true merchant-capitalist was disturbed less by the tenor of government policy, be it free-trade or protectionist, than by the violent upheavals, the changes in policy, the unpredictability with which politicians in both parties afflicted him. This resentment and distrust of politicians in both parties, documentable in the case of some merchants, may well have been characteristic of many landowners also.

What implications may this commentary have for the generally accepted picture of the dynamic of nineteenth-century politics?

What general statements may one make? In a number of cases, most clearly in Mexico and Colombia, there was a conflict between one element that identified with colonial institutions and another that sought a new order. It seems doubtful, however, that one can identify the defenders of the colonial heritage as a landed group ("feudal" or not), the new wave as an urban capitalist one.

Conservatives did tend to be anti-capitalist in some respects. Their belief in the necessity of a strong state and a strong Church (or Church-state) was such that they tended to resist, while liberals tended to promote, the alienation of the resources of either institution into private hands. Often conservatives found themselves defending mortmain, the tithe, and government monopolies, whereas liberals tended to attack these institutions as restraints on free exchange and efficient private capitalist exploitation of resources. On the other hand, it would be a mistake to characterize nineteenth-century conservatives in Mexico or Colombia as "feudal" or entirely backward-looking. Often they took the lead in creating modern capitalist institutions, particularly in the founding of banks and banking systems. Their differences with liberals tended to be not over the desirability of capitalism but over the role that state and Church might play in guiding capitalist development. Thus, while liberal movements of the era may be considered expressions of an upsurgent capitalism, they expressed only a particular version of capitalism. And they were opposed by conservatives less for their capitalist character than on other grounds (desire for order, religious piety, competition for public office).

One can say that the conservatives were an entrenched group, the liberals an emergent one. But conservative entrenchment was not localized entirely in the land; it was also represented importantly in government administration and in commerce. Nor did the liberals emerge entirely from urban areas and urban occupations; probably more of them came from landowning families in the provinces. In short, it seems much too simple to describe the conflict, at least in Mexico or Colombia, as one of *campo v. ciudad*.

For many countries regional differences seem to be more relevant to political alignments than divisions among occupational groups. The two approaches, of course, are not mutually exclusive. Even where class or occupational divisions may have utility, they are used most accurately with reference to specific regions.

Regional economic conflict may provide a key to political differences in many cases. But the approach requires some refinement. In the first place, there is a tendency to think of regions or localities as behaving in a solidary manner. This tendency to view regions as undivided units leads to unnecessary obfuscation. For within most regions and even within many if not most localities, there are marked divisions.

In the unintegrated countries perhaps the main object of regional economic interest would be the area's share of the national budget, in particular its share of funds for communications development. But in the first two-thirds of the nineteenth century a number of factors tended to reduce interest in the national budget. Ineffective revenue collection and the cost of supporting the military limited disposable government funds. Liberal ideology in the period further tended to limit the importance of the national budget. Internal improvements insofar as possible were handed to private enterprise. And in some cases, federalist influences also constricted the role of the central government.

The approach to the socio-economic analysis of political alignments that I most favor looks at the relationship of individuals or regions to certain structures of economic, social, and political power as they existed at the end of the colonial period and the beginning of the republican one. This approach does not dismiss questions of individual or regional economic interest, but it looks at these in a somewhat different way than economic interpretations often do. The important question in such an approach is not an individual's occupation or a region's economic activity, but rather the access of individual and region to structures of power. Regarding the behavior of individuals, it assumes that social origins are more predictive of political attachments than social arrivals. It is therefore not the adult occupation that counts but formative factors such as family position, family relations, and access to education. The approach differs from regional analyses as they are sometimes performed in suggesting that it is not so much where an individual is from, territorially, that matters, but what that fact may imply about his relationship to dominant institutions. One is concerned, then, less about his physical location than about his social location. It is a class analysis in the Weberian sense of class as a definition of life chances. Those in the élite whose close early relationships to the structures of power gave them strategic advantages at the beginning of the republican epoch were likely to end up being termed "conservative"; those who stood at a greater distance were likely to become "liberal".

Part III
Export-led Development

Introduction

As *O'Brien* points out above, the starting-point for an understanding of class formation and domination in Latin America must be "the specificity of the production process, and hence the immense complexity of relations of production". The selections grouped here focus on the crucially important period of export-led expansion between 1880 and 1930, and draw attention to the nature and the centrality of struggles between classes in the shaping of different outcomes from case to case. *Bauer*'s focus upon the specific forms taken by efforts by entrepreneurial land owners to secure a stable workforce, and the forms of resistance they encountered, reveals the role played by compulsion, but at the same time points to significant variations in the material basis for resistance and accomodation between contending classes, and to the implications for the extent of the transition from non-capitalist to capitalist forms of agriculture. The case study of Brazil provided by *Stolcke* and *Hall* reveals the nature of the problems facing the planter class in the coffee zones of São Paulo, outside the major areas of slave labour, in the years preceding and following abolition, and interprets changes in labour contracting in terms of both labour exploitation and labour resistance. The two remaining selections examine the formation of the urban working class and its political implications, and again suggest a degree of variety. *Knight*'s exploration of the role of the Mexican working class in the revolutionary period details the rift between urban workers and the peasantry, and ascribes the economism and reformism of workers in most modern industrial units to factors similar to those which operated in Europe at the same time. The closer to the peasantry (a peasantry, it should not be forgotten, shaped by the process of export-led development) the more likely the working class was to adopt a revolutionary stance. *DeShazo*, in some contrast, identifies the sources of the greater autonomy and ability to resist repression on the part of the Chilean working class in the same period. He pinpoints the inability of the state to win workers over to its side as an important explanatory factor with regard to the future

71

development of a labour movement unusually dominated by independent parties of the left. In different ways, the last two selections look forward to Part IV on "Latin American populism".

The readings here are best supplemented in the first instance by good case studies. On Mexico see Womack (1976) and Jacobs (1982) for contrasting studies of rural areas, and Anderson (1976) for the working class. On Peru see Albert (1984) and Blanchard (1982). On Chile see Bauer (1975), Kay (1975), Fernandez (1984) and DeShazo (1983). On Brazil see Dean (1976) and Holloway (1980). On Argentina see Brown (1982), Scobie (1964) and Munck (1984a). For some of the social consequences of the changes described, see *Journal of Family History* (1985). For a first class brief overview of the period as a whole see Albert (1983).

Export-led Production

Rural Workers in Spanish America: Problems of Peonage and Oppression

Arnold J. Bauer

[*It has been widely argued that the advancing of credit and the resulting indebtedness of rural labourers has historically been a key means of tying labour to the land. Bauer argues that this may sometimes have been the case, but that in general recent studies* (Bazant, 1973; 1974; 1975; Brading, 1975; Deas, 1977; Katz, 1974; Martinez-Alier, 1977; Tutino, 1975; Warman, 1980) *suggest that the bargaining power of workers may have been greater than has been appreciated.*]

What we have in all of these cases is an early stage of response to modern markets. The turn to sharecroppers and rental tenants makes sense when we recall that most of the rural people still lived in communities of smallholders, on the move seeking occasional daily work, or in loose squatter settlements in the interstices of various kinds of private property. Most of the rural people could not yet be brought easily into the orbit of the large estate. In the mid-nineteenth century less than one-third of all Bolivian peasants were attached to the *haciendas*; some seventy per cent in Chalco (Valley of Mexico) still lived in communities in the early nineteenth century; and for all of central Mexico the figure is probably roughly the same at this time. In Peru, coastal plantation owners must have believed it easier to reach 7 000 miles across the Pacific for laborers rather than attempt to pry them loose from their own sierra communities.

As demand for more labor began to grow, everyone complained of *escasez de brazos* (shortage of hands) and not without reason, for both the villagers and the marginal squatter were disinclined to work for the remuneration offered especially if, as in the case of villagers, access to their own land provided an acceptable way of life. If rental tenants and sharecroppers provided the *haciendas* with more income than before, it was not enough given the enormous possibilities now apparent as world demand grew, rail and steam lowered freight rates, and capital became more easily available. The next step taken by landowners was to apply pressure on the tenants by reducing their perquisites and pressing for greater labor service while at the

73

same time negotiating for a larger part of sharecropping arrangements. Following this, landowners attempted to gain more direct control over production by moving toward wage labor systems.

The problem now presented, from the landowner's point of view, was that the ordinary rural inhabitant was inclined to sloth, unreliable, lacked ambition, or at least was not yet adequately responsive to wage incentives. For their part, the tenants were reluctant to work more for less, the smallholder had his own and acceptable way of life, and the day laborer – who might himself be drawn from the families of either tenants or villagers – was unwilling to work at the pace and intensity now demanded. Under these circumstances the landowners, usually supported by the national government in which they had much influence, devised an entire range of strategies to bring people with precapitalist mentality into the labor market. These strategies were applied until mechanization and the massive demographic growth of recent decades shifted the labor-to-land ratio to the landowners' advantage and made possible the full development of capitalist agriculture.

Given the prevailing notion that men would work only out of necessity, it naturally followed that needs should be created; and this, in the later eighteenth and in the nineteenth century, takes two general forms. In the first place, the colonial devices of tax, clerical fees, and forced distribution of merchandise were increasingly employed in the later eighteenth century. The tribute was the most convenient form of creating obligations and the standard practice was for the entrepreneur, hacendado or *obrajero*, to pay the cash tribute for his workers while extracting labor service from those liable for the tax. All of these expedients – tribute, fees, forced purchase of merchandise – were designed to bring the ordinary person into the economy at a time when the subtle hard-sell consumerism of modern capitalism was unknown, the wares of city life had not yet penetrated into the hinterland, and the modern lust for possession had not yet become general. Everyone complained that workers had exceedingly minimal needs and consequently would not work beyond the point where their bare necessities were satisfied.

The other principal element in the pre-capitalist strategy was to deprive potential workers of alternatives to estate labor, or, to put it another way, to remove restraints in the formation of a free labor market. An early feature of the new strategy was the Bourbon assault on charity or on the kind of welfare which was believed to encourage idleness and sloth.

A much more effective measure was the nineteenth-century liberal challenge to the Church which inadvertently weakened charitable and welfare functions in addition to diminishing its economic and political role.

Much more important in the process of threatening the foundations of independent peasant existence was the absorption of village lands by private *haciendas*. In Mexico beginning in the 1870s, in Guatemala where the reduction of Indian lands was accompanied by anti-vagrancy laws, in Bolivia where two-thirds of the rural population became dependent upon *haciendas*, and in fact throughout the Andean spine, the resources and means of independent livelihood of a great many rural people were reduced. All of this is a familiar story. The process of separating peasants from their independent livelihood, which included access to *hacienda* land, village lands, or artisanal production, was rarely carried to the point of complete destitution. Peasant resistance was a factor in some cases and where the state was unable or unwilling to put itself squarely on the landowner's side, the costs of expulsion or appropriation were too high for individual landowners. There is also this question of social welfare. The pre-1870 *hacienda* had undoubtedly sheltered, fed, and underemployed far more people than required for production. The more cost-conscious landowners understood that village communities and their extended family networks provided important services for the wage-earning poor. Day laborers on the estates could return to the subsistence sector which fulfilled functions of social security which the *hacienda* was less and less willing to undertake.

In any case, the more common practice in Spanish America was not the complete destruction of communities — they still survive everywhere — but the reduction of them to the point where diminished resources forced villagers or their dependents into the labor market. And of course it was not just the reduction of village lands, but this combined with population growth which propelled rural people into the labor market. After the 1940s, the scramble for any kind of job by millions of landless rural people eliminated labor shortage and made the previous forms of compulsion unnecessary.

Let us now bring the various elements of our problem into sharper focus. The scheme below arranges the two principal features in the argument along vertical and horizontal continua. Along the left side is the range of workers' attitudes, the varying degree of their incentive toward gain. Implicit here is their changing perception of need and the acceptance and internalization of discipline. Along the top, ranging from Much to Little, is the degree of direct control over production on the part of the large landowners or rural entrepreneurs. Implicit here are change in capital investment with consequent division and specialization of labor, the landowners' power to

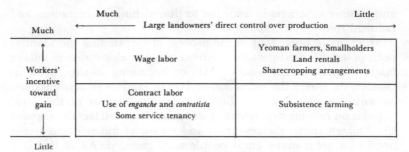

limit or block alternative ways of life for other rural inhabitants, and the landowners' increasingly rational or profit-maximizing attitude. At one extreme pole in this scheme, where there is little incentive for gain on the part of the workers and little control over production by a rural élite, the historical record generally shows a subsistence economy with little linkage to the market; the rhythm of work turns around seasonal demand. At the other pole where workers are keen to earn ever more and landowners have control (the case say, of California agribusiness, Tucumán sugar, and the Peruvian coast in the 1950s and 1960s), one finds a nearly pure wage labor system with overtime pay and bonus for extra output.

Between these poles are areas of ambiguity and conflict. Where workers emerge with strong incentive toward gain while landowners have but little control smallholders or villagers may hold on to their land and there are usually varieties of rentals for cash or crop or sharecropping on the estate. The system of *yanaconaje* which came into existence on the Peruvian coast in the late nineteenth century and endured until heavy capital investment in the late 1940s; the coffee workers described by Deas; Brading's late eighteenth-century Bajío; and Bazant's nineteenth century *acasillados* are all illustrative examples. As landowners increase their control through expropriation of village lands or when they benefit from a shift in the labor-to-land ratio, there is a tendency to reduce renters' perquisites, increase labor requirements, and eventually move to a wage labor system. Obviously, local or national political support is important in this process; without either, the transition to wage labor remains only a goal. Martínez-Alier's studies show how unsuccessful the attempt was in a number of highland Peruvian haciendas where neither the Cerro de Pasco corporation nor the Fernandini corporation had sufficient control to expel tenants.

The greatest conflict in our scheme comes when the market rather quickly opens enormous opportunities for landowners – through, for example, overseas demand, new domestic markets, the introduction of rail or new roads, or new sources of capital – while there is still a general resistance to wage labor and where pre-capitalist attitudes are still the rule. As landowners' control increases, they first, as we have seen, put the screws to the service tenantry and sharecroppers. Increasingly however, others, including villagers and the rootless or casual worker, must also be brought into the production process. How is the landowner to make the wage mechanism work? Advertisements are put in papers, but the word is slowly and imperfectly spread and only a few workers appear at the gates of the new sugar *central* or sisal plantation. Or, if they do appear, they work only to cover their own needs (defined by them very modestly) and then disappear, or they return for village fiestas or to work their own fields. One measure of how unresponsive or inconstant rural people were to wage offers can be seen in the price paid for Chinese laborers. In Cuba and Peru between 1847–74, over a quarter of a million Chinese were employed at a cost of $340 to $500 each. It is at this point – in the interstices between subsistence and rental arrangements at one pole and wage labor at the other – where other devices and mechanisms are employed by the landowners to obtain a work force. The power of landowners to block alternatives and their reluctant but eventual willingness to pay sufficiently high wages for higher quality labor (the United Fruit Company early initiated this practice) did bring workers into the wage labor market. But where the demand for labor was especially strong and potential workers dragged their heels, more direct measures were used. Landowners hired labor contractors or *enganchadores* whom they paid as much as 20 per cent of the wage bill for recruitment, transportation, and labor management. The contractors often found it necessary to give part of the total salary in advance to potential workers; in other cases landowners extended credit during slack times or charged corn rations, merchandise, or even clerical services against a tenant's or worker's account.

Until recent years, most students and observers have assumed that debt meant bondage. Because of this assumption and because the sources then available did not reveal the inner workings of rural estates, we have by and large an unreal and one-dimensional picture of rural society. New research based on sources closer to social reality now provides a basis for reevaluation. An explanatory context of course is still fundamental. To help with this, I have suggested the possibility of examining the change in values which occurred in the transition from non-capitalist to capitalist forms of agriculture.

From about 1870 onward, because of capital investment and technological change there was in many regions of Spanish America a fundamental change in the way men made their living. Alongside the quickening pace of economic life, the majority of rural people still lived a quiet existence, their attitudes toward work shaped by the rhythms of ordinary agriculture and the limited economic horizons of village life. The consequent disjunction between the demand and supply of labor brought about conflict and accommodation. A great many rural people were wrenched out of one social and mental world and ended up in another.

The years 1870–1930 represented a transition which in many ways is analogous to the period a century earlier in Great Britain and Western Europe. During these sixty years, landowners and rural entrepreneurs managed, gradually and incompletely, to tighten their control over production. This was done only rarely with the kind of Draconian measures described in *Barbarous Mexico*, or by the American envoy in Veracruz, or the novels of Ciro Alegría or Jorge Icaza. More commonly labor contractors, *enganchadores*, paternalistic measures, wage increases, wage advances, and in rare cases debt bondage were used to obtain the kind of labor needed by new types of plantations and *haciendas*. Reliable and productive workers were demanded at a time when rural people were not yet fully responsive to wage incentive; when, in other words, a free labor market did not yet exist. All of the landowners' devices were accompanied by only partially successful efforts to block alternatives to wage labor. Most of the new research is consistent in its rejection of debt as a controlling feature of labor. The closer we get to social reality, to the everyday workings of society, the better we understand that rural people are not merely passive victims; rather, they make choices, work out of self-interest. They and landowners alike make compromises and strike accommodations which are often mutually beneficial. To be sure, the world within which the relatively powerless make choices is narrowly limited and, in some cases, the indirect limitation of choice comes dangerously close to direct coercion.

By the 1940s, new labor habits were formed, men were alienated from their work, and the values appropriate to a smoothly working wage labor system became more common. This process is not yet complete. In those areas where labor was not needed, where markets were weak, where capital was not attracted, pockets of rural people were by-passed. But everywhere else we can see the breakdown of community, the creation of a rootless and alienated mass, and the triumph of the consumer society. For having accelerated this integration of rural people into modern economic life, we may thank the modernizing landowner, the effective *contratista*, and the rural workers' own capacity for spiritual self-destruction.

The Planter Class and Labour

The Introduction of Free Labour on São Paulo Coffee Plantations

Verena Stolcke and Michael M. Hall

Introduction

As a country with abundant land and a relatively scarce population, Brazil confronted special problems in the creation of a labour force. Until the 1850s, slaves made up the bulk of the workforce needed by large-scale export agriculture. By the mid-nineteenth century, however, as slavery came under increasing attack, at least some São Paulo coffee planters began experimenting with free labour. The abolition of the slave trade in 1850, moreover, coincided with the penetration and rapid expansion of coffee in western São Paulo, due to the decline of the other main coffee-growing region – the Paraíba Valley – and in response to the growing international demand for coffee. The introduction of free labour in São Paulo agriculture is, in effect, an instance of the creation of a free labour force in a situation of extensive agricultural development under conditions of potentially scarce labour supply. "Our soil offers unlimited wealth, but we lack labour", as one contemporary put the crucial obstacle to continued agricultural development which São Paulo planters faced in the second half of the nineteenth century. The most forward-looking coffee planters clearly saw after 1850 that a way of replacing slave labour, or at least supplementing it, would have to be found in the fairly near future in order to provide the sizeable number of workers required for this very labour-intensive crop. Slavery in fact continued until 1888, but it was precisely the increasing debate over the labour question, and the experimentation in the following decades by São Paulo planters, which eventually made possible a relatively non-violent transition to free labour.

The creation of a labour force is never an exclusively demographic question. In the absence of a readily available local reserve of labour, São Paulo planters resorted to the use of immigrant workers. However, their experience with slaves had made them acutely aware of the need for effective forms of labour control. Thus, the issue planters increasingly faced throughout the second half of the nineteenth century was not only that of finding a new source of labour to replace their slaves, but also of how to organize and control free labour efficiently. The development and organization of a free labour force for the São Paulo coffee plantations was both an economic and a political process. The dynamics of the situation derived from both the economic rationale of the planters and from the bargaining power available to labourers to resist the planters' impositions.

The objective of this article is to understand how São Paulo planters eventually solved their labour problems. The effective supply of labour at any particular moment is importantly affected by the sanctions and incentives available to employers to enforce their power over labour to extract profit. In the São Paulo case, the absence of an established labour market decisively determined the planters' choices of labour systems and their evolution. The early difficulties with free labour have repeatedly been attributed to the relative unprofitability of immigrant workers in comparison to slaves, yet what induced planters to introduce free labour in the first place was their increasing awareness that slavery was doomed. The more interesting initial question, then, is why planters first chose sharecropping as the labour system under which free labour was to be introduced, rather than a straight wage system or some other arrangement.

The absence of an established labour market not only decisively determined the planters' choice of labour systems but also their fortunes with them. The success of the labour systems introduced was not only determined by cost factors (in the narrow sense of the cost of obtaining immigrant labour), nor even by the planters' ideology (their supposed "backwardness" or, alternatively, their exemplary entrepreneurial spirit), but importantly by the struggle between planters' actions and workers' responses as shaped by the economic and political circumstances in which they found themselves. As we will attempt to show, it is this interrelationship between systems of labour exploitation and patterns of labour resistance which explains the successive transformations of the forms of labour contracting adopted.

The Sharecropping Contract

In 1847, Senator Vergueiro, the owner of a large estate near the town of Limeira, in the province of São Paulo, became the first planter to introduce immigrant labour for work in coffee production. Vergueiro, as his son later put it, had foreseen that the end of slavery was only a matter of time. Initially the immigrants seem to have been offered two kinds of contract: a sharecropping and a labour leasing (*locacão de servicos*) contract, but they opted for the former.

According to the sharecropping contract, the planter financed the immigrants' transportation from their country of origin to the port of Santos, advanced the cost of transport from Santos to the plantation, as well as the foodstuffs and tools the immigrants needed until they could pay for them with the proceeds from their first crops. The planter assigned the workers the number of coffee trees they could tend, harvest and process, and allotted them a piece of land on which to grow their own food crops. In addition, the immigrants were given a house, apparently free of charge. Their remuneration consisted of half the net profit from coffee and from the food crops. The labourers were obliged to repay the expenses incurred by the planter on their behalf with at least half of their yearly returns from coffee. The initial contract did not specify the length of its duration, but stated the amount of the debt owed by the immigrant on account of his transportation costs and other advances. For any amount outstanding after two years, the labourer was to be charged interest, which was to be the case with other advances after one year. Finally, the immigrants could not legally move off the plantation until they had repaid their debts. Should they do so, they incurred a substantial fine. Work was organized and supervised by the planter or his administrator. The labourers were explicitly required to conduct themselves in a peaceful manner.

The planters thus transferred all the expenses of obtaining immigrant labour to the labourers themselves. Consequently, such workers started out already burdened by a substantial debt. It was generally expected that a diligent labourer would take an average of four years to pay off his debt.

Since the recruitment of immigrant labour required an initial investment by the planters, one of their constant concerns was to guarantee this capital investment. However, for the immigrants, the initial debt weighed increasingly heavily on their income. In practice, their returns from coffee cultivation turned out to be markedly lower than the stipulated 50 per cent of net profit. The consequences were far-reaching.

The first serious sign of the mounting discontent among immigrant labourers came in mid-1856, when a group of Swiss workers revolted on the Nova Olinda plantation near Ubatuba. The trouble apparently started when cattle invaded their food plots, and disagreement over indemnity led to the intervention of the police. Eventually, when the Swiss consul visited the plantation, the central issue became the general conditions of the immigrants: quality of food plots, fulfillment of contracts, housing, etc. Planters typically attributed the events to instigation by subversive elements. The conflict was finally resolved when the consul promised the immigrants that they would be transferred to a government colony, that part of their debts would be forgiven, and that no interest would have to be paid. This conflict already reveals what were to become some of the crucial points of contention between planters and workers.

The most important revolt, however, began in December 1856, among Swiss and German labourers on Senator Vergueiro's model plantation Ibicaba. The presence of a Swiss school teacher, Thomas Davatz, contributed to converting the latent resentment of the immigrants into an organized movement of protest against what they felt were grave irregularities in the fulfillment of their contracts. They did not question the terms of the contract as such but protested against "the calculation of returns from coffee produced, the charging of the commission, the unfavourable exchange rate used to convert their debts into local currency, the charging of transport from Santos to the plantation, and the strange division of profits from the sale of coffee" (Davatz, 1941). What seems to have sparked the revolt was disillusionment with the results of the 1855 harvest which, contrary to their hopes, did not allow them to reduce their debts. As Davatz later wrote, what he and his compatriots demanded was no more than just treatment (Davatz, 1941, pp. 105–6). The revolt ended when Davatz was expelled and some of the other leaders left the plantation. One measure of the apprehension which the revolt produced among the planters was the accusation levelled against Davatz that not only was he in alliance with extraneous elements, but that he harboured communist and other terrible plots. Many planters appear to have been genuinely terrified that the revolt would not only spread to free labourers on other plantations (a link with the earlier Ubatuba conflict was repeatedly suggested), but worst of all might incite the slaves.

Much has been made of this revolt and of the frauds committed by planters which supposedly triggered it off. These are generally used to explain the failure of the sharecropping system under which the first immigrants were contracted, and the alleged decline of interest among planters in the use of free labour (see, for example, Dean, 1976). It seems, however, that these irregularities (fraudulent measures, dishonest calculation of profits, etc.) only added to the growing disillusionment of immigrants with their living and working conditions. The planters, for their part, acted under a serious misconception. They had not counted on the resources available to the immigrants in resisting what they considered unjust contractual conditions and impositions. The introduction of free labour required a capital outlay whose amortization demanded a level of exploitation which the planters were unable to enforce. The main obstacle was not the threat of possible reprisals from the immigrants' national governments, since protection was reluctant and limited at best, but rather, under the circumstances, the sharecropping contract did not adequately address the problem of creating a reliable labour force.

Why then did São Paulo planters adopt the sharecropping system?

Sharecropping in a situation of scarce labour is in fact more efficient than wage labour. It is a form of the use of labour similar to a carefully negotiated piecework system. Both are forms of incentive wage systems, a way of securing extra effort from labour, of making labourers work harder and better for only a small increase in total remuneration over that of wage labourers. Remuneration in the form of a proportion of the product constitutes an incentive for the labourer to intensify his effort since it is on the amount produced that his returns will depend. He will cultivate with greater care, again because part of the result will accrue to himself. In addition, the supervision required will be insignificant, since control of work is exercised by the labourer himself.

In the case of Sao Paulo, because of the absence of a local supply of workers, labour costs were at least initially high. Moreover, coffee is a very labour-intensive crop. Because of the incentive element characteristic of sharecropping it could be expected that sharecroppers would tend more coffee trees per worker than would wage labourers. Consequently, fewer workers would be required, and initial investment would be lower. Sharecroppers are usually contracted in family units. Thus, sharecropping also allows the landowner to benefit from the use of the sharecroppers' family labour. Planters had always opposed recruiting single men since it was argued that immigrant families were less prone to abandon the plantations. This may be so, but equally important was surely the fact that the immigrants' families constituted a cheap labour reserve. A sharecropper will usually accept a division of the product that will not fully cover the potential market price of family labour, which would otherwise remain under- or unemployed. Planters, in fact, sometimes prohibited immigrants and their families from working outside the plantation. The planter thus obtained this additional labour at a cost below that which he would have had to pay were he to contract it on the market as wage labour. Since labour needs during the harvest were about one-fifth greater than during cultivation, the workers' wives and children could satisfactorily cover this additional demand.

Labourers were also assigned a subsistence plot, which was a further way of reducing unit labour costs. These plots were usually granted on marginal lands not appropriate for coffee, or on virgin land later planted in coffee. Workers had no effective possession of the land. Ideally, they were expected to produce strictly what was needed for their own subsistence, in this way further reducing the cost of their own reproduction.

By reducing unit labour costs in comparison with wage labour, sharecropping must have initially appeared to the planters as the most appropriate substitute for slave labour. The incentive element must have seemed a satisfactory substitute for the coercion which made slaves work. The question was not merely to fill the potential gap in labour supply, but to do so in a profitable way.

Immigrants, however, were free workers. As sharecroppers, they were in principle free to decide on labour intensity and the allocation of labour. Their diligence and productivity in coffee thus depended on their own appraisal of returns.

Planters and immigration agents sought to create the illusion that immigrants would quickly be able to repay their debts and acquire their own land. In practice, however, immigrants usually had to wait for at least two years before receiving significant returns for their efforts. The share to which they were entitled from the first harvest took almost another year to be paid because of delays in the marketing of coffee; but, since the contracts stipulated that half of the workers' annual earnings from coffee were to be withheld to cover their debts, and in the meantime they had accumulated new debts from further advances, only in the third year could they expect to receive much cash. It is hardly surprising that the immigrants grew increasingly discontented.

The 1856 revolt remained an isolated event. The majority of the immigrants reacted in a less dramatic but at the same time more insidious manner by systematically restricting output in coffee cultivation. Planters soon grew concerned about the immigrants' low productivity in coffee. As late as 1870, an emissary of the Imperial government noted that "most plantations are not yet in a condition to receive free labour even under the sharecropping system, mainly when workers already start out burdened with a debt . . . The transportation costs are excessive and consequently the labourers' share is insignificant . . . The delay in the sale of coffee forces the workers to wait over eight months for payment . . . As a consequence, the workers generally tend a reduced number of coffee trees, preferring to plant food crops to supply their homes and cover their needs, in addition to obtaining immediate benefit. Yet it is evident that this system cannot be advantageous for the planter, whose main interest is coffee" (Machado Nunes, 1860, p. 15).

The initial debt, even without arbitrary additional difficulties created by the planters, discouraged any effort by the workers in coffee cultivation beyond what was strictly necessary. As another observer remarked: "They [the labourers] abandon the coffee trees, which as a result do not produce but deteriorate, and the planter is deprived not only of his share in the product but also of that of the immigrant which is the only source of amortization [of the debt] he has" (Valdetaro, 1858).

The contract left open the number of coffee trees to be tended by a family and the size of their subsistence plot. Both of these elements were initially left to the decision of the labourers themselves. This made it possible that, as immigrants became uninterested in repaying their debts within the expected time, they increasingly diverted their labour to food crops whose returns accrued to them directly and immediately. Although many observers remarked on the alleged laziness and lack of interest of the immigrants, in fact what happened was an alternative allocation of labour to food crops, rather than an absolute underuse of labour capacity.

Most of the immigrants in the early 1850s were members of the rural or urban poor who were driven by the severe economic crisis in Central Europe to abandon their home country, in many cases as a matter of sheer survival. What they probably initially hoped for was to make a secure living. Since the conditions they encountered in São Paulo made it almost impossible for them to obtain a profit from work in coffee, they preferred to dedicate a significant part of their efforts to food crops. As a result, productivity in coffee was low.

The planters' power to control labour and enforce a satisfactory level of productivity in coffee cultivation was limited by the circumstances under which free labor had been introduced, that is, in the absence of a local reserve of labour and under arrangements which required that immigrants repay their costs of passage and initial settlement to their employers. Planters presumably thought that the incentive element contained in sharecropping would effectively replace market forces in reducing wage costs. However, the initial debt cancelled out the incentive element, and the planters lacked any effective means of forcing their workers to produce coffee. The threat of dismissal, which is the usual form of persuasion used by employers to enforce labour contracts, was hardly practical since it would have meant the partial or total loss of the planters' investment. Although it was true that the immigrants could not legally abandon the plantation until they had paid off their debts, neither could the planters make them work beyond what the labourers themselves were willing to do. Even the use of state power, as in the case of the Ibicaba revolt, was of little avail. The leaders of the revolt were expelled, but those who remained did not work any harder.

The Labour-leasing Contract

By the late 1850s, planters faced a dilemma. Economic incentives had failed to produce the expected results: a reasonable level of productivity and amortization of debt within the expected time. After 1857 the sharecropping system was gradually abandoned in São Paulo. Free labour, however, by no means disappeared. While the number of immigrants engaged in coffee cultivation did not increase during the next two decades, it declined only slowly. Reports reaching Europe on the immigrants' hardships eventually persuaded both the Swiss and Prussian governments to take severe measures which practically halted emigration from the two countries to São Paulo. Nevertheless, in 1870 it was estimated that approximately 3 000 free labourers – some of them Brazilians – still worked on the plantations, a decline of about 500 since 1860, and the debate over possible solutions to the labour problem had not abated.

Many planters continued to explore alternative labour systems and to devise institutional safeguards which they hoped would allow a more effective enforcement of contracts. In order to deal with the related problems of control of productivity and amortization of debt, planters initially resorted to contract changes. Sharecropping was gradually replaced by a labour-leasing contract (*locação de serviços*). Instead of a share of the value of production, labourers were henceforth paid a pre-established piecerate for each measure of coffee produced. It was argued that by thus reducing uncertainty over income and eliminating long delays in payment, labourers would feel encouraged to apply themselves with greater diligence to coffee cultivation. In addition, the clause that surplus food production be shared with the planter was generally dropped, and increasingly the size of the food plot was fixed and/or let against a rent in an attempt to discourage immigrants from diverting labour to food crops. Moreover, free labourers no longer participated in coffee processing, either directly or through a fee. This task reverted to slaves until the

1880s, when it was then carried out by wage labour. Significantly, it was this part of coffee production, together with transportation, which were rapidly mechanized in the early 1870s as slave labour became increasingly problematic.

Labour-saving innovations, however, were not introduced in coffee cultivation. Mechanization of the harvest was not technically feasible, and the mechanization of weeding by the use of a cultivator would have severely upset labour demand throughout the agricultural year. Mechanized weeding would have either produced idle labour during the cultivation period, or a shortage for the harvest in a situation of general scarcity of free labour.

The labour-leasing contract continued the wage incentive system, but it still could not assure an adequate level of productivity because it did not resolve the basic problem of debt as a disincentive to increased productivity in coffee.

In addition, the quality of work appears to have deteriorated under the labour-leasing contract. Such a system of remuneration not only affects labour intensity, but may also have consequences for the care with which tasks are executed. In general, piecework is not used for many agricultural tasks because the quality of work suffers. There is evidence that under the labour-leasing contract, while the immigrants were keen on harvesting as much coffee as possible, they tended to be negligent in the weedings or abandoned outright part of the trees once they had been harvested.

In effect, neither contract changes nor the use of more severe labour laws succeeded in creating a satisfactory labour force because these measures failed to resolve the basic problem: the initial investment planters had to make to introduce free labour. Heavily burdened by their initial debts, immigrant labourers continued to work little in coffee and were troublesome.

The Colonato

Those planters who still worked their plantations with free labourers by the late 1860s gradually introduced further adjustments in the labour contract. While contracts initially had contained fines for abandoning the plantation before the worker's debt had been repaid, they now increasingly stipulated fines for the non-execution of weedings. As one planter noted, "for us the only advantage of slaves is in discipline, and once a planter wants to renounce a little control and patiently bears the faults of the *colonos*, he will gradually succeed, by means of the fines contained in the contracts, in making all *colonos* submit to regular work" (Jaguaribe

Filho, 1877, pp. 34–5). Food plots were now regularly assigned in proportion to the number of trees tended by the family. Finally, some planters began to introduce a new form of remuneration, a mixed task and piecerate system, the *colonato*, an arrangement which was to prevail on the coffee plantations from the 1880s until the 1950s. Under this system, coffee weedings were paid at a fixed annual rate per thousand trees tended and the harvest at a piecerate.

By paying a separate stipulated rate for weedings, a sort of fixed-minimum wage, which guaranteed the labourers a stable income independent of coffee yields, it could be expected that workers would not neglect the coffee groves outside of the harvest season. In addition, since part of the labourers' remuneration under the new contract depended directly on the number of trees tended and no longer on their yields, it could be assumed that they would feel encouraged to cultivate a larger number of trees. By maintaining the piecerate system for the harvest, however, labour costs could still be adapted to annual fluctuations in yields. Moreover, unit labour costs could be lowered through intensification of effort on the part of the immigrants' family at the time when labour demand was greatest.

By the late 1860s, however, there was a growing awareness among planters that contract adjustments and the existing labour laws were insufficient in themselves to assure a disciplined and profitable free labour force. The decade of the 1870s began amid predictions of an impending labour crisis, both in terms of future supply and of labour control.

Nevertheless, coffee production during the 1870s expanded to almost twice what it had been in the previous decade. In fact, planters were still able to postpone until 1888 the effective end of slavery. They temporarily solved the anticipated labour shortage by generally rationalizing coffee production. They managed to disarm the abolitionists with a very limited concession: the Rio Branco law of 1871 which declared that children born thereafter of slave mothers were to be free. Planters also continued to purchase substantial numbers of slaves from the Rio de Janeiro region and from northern Brazil. The great expansion of railroads, almost all located in the coffee-growing areas, which took place in the 1870s also helped postpone an acute labour shortage. The availability of railroad transport allowed planters to reassign to other tasks the slaves they have previously had to use in transporting their crop to market. Moreover, by lowering the cost of transportation and reducing the damage the crop suffered en route, the railroad helped compensate the planters to some extent for possible rises in the cost of slave labour.

The introduction of labour-saving machinery in the coffee industry was another important element in forestalling the crisis.

Although São Paulo planters managed to cope with their labour needs quite successfully during the period, they did not by any means abandon the question of how to organize the supply of free labour. The issue of negotiating the transition from slavery to free labour became increasingly urgent. It was the old problem: Brazil "possesses the best climate in the world, almost all the precious metals and a prodigiously fertile soil, but lacks population and for that reason is poor" ('*O. Lavrador*', in the *Gazeta de Campinas*, 20 February 1870).

At the 1878 Agricultural Congress, called by the government to evaluate the general state of agriculture, one group of planters opposed large-scale immigration as a solution to the labour problem because of its costs to themselves or to the country. They demanded, instead, laws to combat the alleged aversion of the local population to work.

In 1879, the 1837 labour-leasing law was replaced by a new regulation covering both labour-leasing and sharecropping contracts and providing prison sentences not only for abandoning the plantation without just cause but also for strikes and incitement of others to strike through threats or the use of violence.

Other São Paulo planters, in contrast, became increasingly emphatic about the need for the liberalization of labour contracts and legal reforms as indispensable prerequisites for a successful programme of government-sponsored immigration, which they regarded as the only solution to the labour problem. The relatively low coffee prices of the early 1880s, and the difficulties planters faced in securing credit, acted as further deterrents to privately sponsored immigration, since they left many planters unable or unwilling to advance passage money to immigrants. On the other hand, the 1879 law was largely ineffective and even counter-productive. As Antonio Prado, one of the most prominent São Paulo planters noted, immigrants in jail were neither repaying the planters' loans nor harvesting their coffee, and in addition the law only served to discredit Brazilian colonization in Europe. Prado further observed that the law would soon become unnecessary in any case, at least in São Paulo, since the Assembly of that province had approved a measure in 1884 providing free passage for immigrants who went into agriculture.

Planters by this point were generally aware that "it is impossible to have low salaries, without violence, if there are few workers and many people who wish to employ them" (Brazil, *Anais da Camara*,

1884, V, p. 50). The way out of this dilemma, and the essence of the São Paulo immigration system, was explained by another member of the Chamber of Deputies shortly after Abolition: "It is evident", he said, "that we need labourers . . . in order to increase the competition among them and in that way salaries will be lowered by means of the law of supply and demand" (*Anais da Camara*, 1888, IV, p. 23).

As long as coffee plantations could be run predominantly with slave labour, it was difficult to secure state-subsidized immigration on a large scale. However, by the early 1880s Abolition clearly had become unavoidable, and a comprehensive solution had to be found. The São Paulo planters, whose power in the government had been increasing steadily, then finally succeeded in imposing their solution to the labour problem. Although more than two years and several important modifications of the law providing for subsidized immigration were required before the system functioned satisfactorily, Prado was essentially correct in affirming that the problem had been solved by the mid-1880s. After 1884, the state, instead of coercing labourers directly, sought to achieve the same objective – cheap and obedient labour for the plantations – by flooding the labour market with subsidized immigrants.

By 1886 the provincial government had found an effective way to provide complete subsidies for immigrants, and the effect was almost immediate. By May of 1887, some 60 000 to 70 000 immigrants, by now predominantly Italian, had already been placed in the agricultural establishments of São Paulo. This figure exceeds the estimated 50 000 slaves who were being used on São Paulo coffee plantations in 1885.

Immigration policy remained essentially unchanged until the First World War. Between 1884 and 1914, some 900 000 immigrants arrived in São Paulo, mostly as cheap labour for the coffee plantations. The immigration programme allowed São Paulo planters not only to abolish slavery with only moderate inconvenience but the scheme – aided by at least initially high coffee prices – created the conditions for sustained expansion of coffee production. Between 1888 and 1902 the number of coffee trees planted in São Paulo increased from 221 million to 685 million.

Subsidized mass immigration and the creation of an effective capitalist labour market seemed to solve both of the difficulties planters had previously encountered with free labour – the debt and labour discipline. Since planters no longer had to advance passage money to immigrants and were assured of an abundance of fieldhands by the state, the 1879 law fell into disuse and was finally repealed in 1890 because "among the economic measures most strongly demanded by the present state of the country is the need to populate it, since public wealth develops in direct proportion to the increase in population". In order to attract sufficient numbers of immigrants the "shameful" law of 1879 needed to be abolished. Contracts henceforth should be "acts of pure convention based on mutual agreement which elevate the labourer to the category of partner in the contract" (Decree No. 213, 22 December 1890). The 1879 law, however, had not only served to enforce contract fulfillment, but also prohibited strike action. Among other liberal reforms of the period was one replacing the 1879 provisions with a decree on so-called "crimes against the freedom of work" which penalized the inciting of either labourers or employers to increase or reduce work or wages through the use of threats or violence.

Contract enforcement and labour discipline were henceforth to depend on the mechanism of the market. Planters did indeed employ coercion and violence under certain circumstances to keep labourers on the plantations and extract profit, but in general they preferred to deal with the problem of keeping down labour costs by increasing supply. Extra-economic coercion, which was at times substantial, served essentially to improve the planters' bargaining position in the labour market.

In effect, the massive influx of immigrants covered labour needs quite satisfactorily before 1914. Not only did subsidized mass immigration drastically reduce initial labour costs, but planters were now required to make only minor advances for food and agricultural tools. In addition, the disappearance of the burden of the initial heavy debt, coupled with stricter regulation of work and fines for non-execution of tasks, now possible to enforce because of the abundant labour supply, produced a marked increase in labour productivity in coffee. By the late 1880s the average number of coffee trees tended by an adult man ranged between 2 000 and 3 000, while women usually cultivated half that number.

Planters continued contracting immigrant labour under the mixed task and piecerate system coupled with subsistence production. The contract was now annual. Even with an abundant labour supply, the *colonato* system continued to be more profitable than straight wage labour for a number of reasons. Food prices were persistently high since foodstuffs were to a large extent imported as a consequence of the planters' almost exclusive interest in coffee. As the president of the province noted in 1887: "Coffee gives the best returns . . . it would be an error to disdain it in order to cultivate something else".

Food plots acted as an incentive for the labourers, at the same time reducing the cost of the reproduction of labour. Moreover, since food crops were grown during the coffee cultivation season when labour demands were comparatively lower, the planters could make full use of the immigrants' family labour throughout the whole year. As one observer noted in 1908, "what really enables the immigrants to make ends meet are the crops they have the right to raise on their own account" (Denis, 1911). Bonardelli (1916 p. 71ff) estimated that food crops grown by labourers made up one third of their income" (Denis, 1911). The right to grow food crops rather than constituting a payment in kind or a means of fixing labour, was primarily a way of extracting a labour rent in addition to the surplus produced in coffee cultivation. The combination of cash crops with subsistence cultivation was potentially problematic for economic development in general, and for the planters themselves – as late as 1922 planters stressed the need to restrict food crops since "the landowner cannot permit that labourers plant extensively in cereals when labour is lacking for coffee cultivation" (Maistrello, 1923). However, if effectively controlled, and as long as coffee was highly profitable, the arrangement was clearly advantageous for the planters.

A final way the planters devised to reduce unit labour costs was their growing preference, not only for families, but for large families, i.e. units containing at least three workers. A large number of workers in a family made it possible to depress wage costs further. The more workers per consumer in a family, the lower the cost of reproduction of each individual worker and consequently the lower the task-rate could be.

The planters' power increased in direct proportions to the growing powerlessness of the labourers. Almost all plantations had their band of *capangas*, armed guards in charge of carrying out the will of the planter and of controlling among other things the entrance and departure of labourers. Planters occasionally attempted to retain their labourers by such means as artificially delaying the end of the agricultural year when the final financial accounts were settled, thus making it unlikely that the labourer "could find work on another plantation where cultivation for the next crops had already begun" (Coletti, 1908). Nevertheless, the mobility of labour was generally considerable. Some 40 to 60 per cent of the labourers left their plantation each year. Planters exercised extensive control over their labourers, in itself an expression of their abiding fear of indiscipline or worse. Observers sometimes remarked on the *colonos'* "submissiveness, respectful and docile" behaviour, although this was often more apparent than real.

The obstacles to more than sporadic individual resistance were immense, and planters did what they could to suppress any expression of discontent. For example, all societies or associations of labourers were prohibited. Yet despite severe control, not only were individual labourers often turbulent and sometimes violent, but strikes occurred with some frequency.

Labourers acting individually or nearly so quite regularly carried out acts of violence against planters and overseers. One of the most famous instances, though by no means atypical, occurred in 1901 when Francisco Augusto Almeida Prado, a planter belonging to the prominent Prado family, was so careless as to stroll through his coffee fields one day without the protection of his bodyguards. Several of his labourers took advantage of the situation and murdered him, riddling his body with knife wounds, and chopping it into pieces with their hatchets and hoes. Diogo Salles, the brother of the President of the Republic, was murdered in 1900 by a labourer for attempting to rape the murderer's sister. This was an individual motive, but it is as much indicative of the extreme forms exploitation took, as of the underlying tensions. Other incidents arose from somewhat broader issues. In the Prado murder, the immediate cause was said to be the punishment he had imposed on his labourers for refusing to put out a fire on the estate of one of his relatives.

Collective action was also not infrequent. The first strikes after Abolition occurred in the early 1890s, and the Italian-language daily *Fanfulla* registers several dozen by 1913; from that year to 1930, the *Patronato Agrícola* (a state agency) and the labour press provide references to over a hundred strikes on the coffee plantations. Most such strikes were limited to the boundaries of one plantation, although in 1911 about 1 000 labourers struck on half a dozen plantations in the area of Bragança for twenty days and secured a slight increase in pay. The following year, labourers on more than a dozen plantations in the Ribeirão Preto area went on strike and also secured a small wage rise. The largest strike of the period took place in the same area in 1913. It mobilized between 10 000 and 15 000 labourers, but resulted in a total defeat. Strikes were generally carried out in an effort to secure an increase in wages, or in opposition to such measures as the non-payment of wages, attempts to reduce salaries, heavy and arbitrary discipline and fines, or restrictions on the planting of food crops.

From the beginning, the relations between planters and free labourers were fraught with severe and generally rather explicit tensions. Even had the planters desired to establish paternalistic relations of personal dependence – and the point remains unclear –

a number of elements limited the ready use of such arrangements to obscure exploitation and discourage resistance. Not only were São Paulo plantations large, but the work force was both new and foreign-born, thus depriving the planters of many of the traditional sanctions – religious and otherwise – which rural ruling classes have often enjoyed.

As long as sharecropping prevailed, struggle between labourers and planters centred around the share in net profit from coffee. Exceptionally, labourers revolted, but more generally they resisted by withdrawing labour from coffee cultivation. As long as food growing was not subject to systematic restraints, the labourers were able, without jeopardizing their own survival, to deprive the planters of part of their labour power. This does not mean, however, that labourers reduced their expectations. What they did was to divert a significant part of their productive capacity to food growing, beyond what they required for subsistence. Though essentially individual, these actions were decisive in determining the readjustment of the labour system.

The transition from sharecropping to the mixed task and piece-rate system, the *colonato*, was a process of increasingly systematic exploitation of labour, aided after the mid-1880s by the massive importation of immigrants. Once a capitalist labour market had been created, planting rights restricted to the basic minimum, and increasingly severe labour discipline instituted, conditions effectively disappeared for individual struggle at the level of work against what were considered unsatisfactory returns. By the turn of the century immigrant labourers constituted a homogeneous mass, subject to more or less uniformly harsh conditions. Under normal circumstances they had the possibility of exploiting regional differences to their advantage, or of abandoning São Paulo agriculture altogether either for work in Brazilian cities or in other countries. Labour mobility among plantations and outright departures were considerable. But for those who remained in agriculture, low wages or any additional exactions by planters, such as the non-payment of wages, the prohibition of food growing, or a reduction in wages, could trigger off collective action in the form of strikes. Contradictorily, by increasing labour discipline, planters created the very conditions for collective – and thus potentially much more damaging – action by the immigrants.

We have argued that São Paulo planters introduced free labour to replace or add to their slave force because the most forward-looking of them were aware by mid-century that some substitute for slave labour eventually had to be found. Under these circumstances, they were willing to experiment with new forms of labour, whose productivity they initially did not know. However, only a minority of São Paulo planters opted for free labour at the time, and the end of slavery was not immediate. Thus there was no acute shortage of slaves, and planters could continue to staff their plantations with slave labour, whose productivity was familiar to them, in case free labour did not respond to their expectations. Not only those who have studied the early experiments with free labour, but also the planters themselves repeatedly attributed the difficulties with free labour to its relatively low productivity in comparison to slavery. It may be true that slaves were more profitable than free labourers, but to go back to slavery was no permanent solution. Thus, to explain the failure of the sharecropping system by its comparatively lower productivity would be reasonable only if it were not for the impending abolition of slavery. The spectre of abolition left planters, in fact, with only two alternatives: either to find a satisfactory substitute form of free labour, or to abandon coffee cultivation altogether.

The planters who initially took it upon themselves to find some replacement for slave labour were the first of a remarkable group of agricultural and commercial entrepreneurs. Their decision to reorganize production using free labour is in itself symptomatic. They viewed labour as a cost and adopted a labour system, sharecropping, which they thought would assure them a cost per unit of output lower than that of straight wage labour, rather than comparing this with slave labour. That some of them became disenchanted with the experiment and temporarily returned to slave labour was due fundamentally to the absence of one essential prerequisite, a surplus population of free labour that would have kept their workers intimidated and subjected to exploitation. Under these circumstances, neither the economic incentives contained in the sharecropping contract, nor the resort to frauds and occasional coercion succeeded in assuring a profitable and reliable labour force. The immigrants systematically restricted output in coffee and/or rebelled. It is this which led some planters to conclude that "at the cost of any sacrifice the work of a slave is preferable to that of a free man" (Valdetaro, p. 93, quoting a planter whose labourers worked little and very badly). Others attempted to resolve their labour problems by introducing contract changes and more effective labour laws, yet with scarcely greater success. The permanent problem of labour productivity and discipline was only resolved in the 1880s when the state began to subsidize mass immigration and thus lay the foundations for an effective capitalist labour market.

The Working Class

The Working Class and the Mexican Revolution

Alan Knight

Like any major historical phenomenon, the Mexican Revolution can be viewed from a variety of angles. From one, arguably the most important, it was a rural phenomenon, rightly categorized by Eric Wolf (1969) as a "peasant war", hence comparable to the Russian or Chinese Revolutions. From another it can be seen as a generalized social and political (some might like to call it a "hegemonic") crisis, marking the end of the old oligarchic Porfirian order and characterized by mass political mobilization; as such, it bears comparison with the crises experienced in Italy and Germany after the First World War; in Spain in the early 1930s; in Brazil in the 1960s or Chile in the 1970s. But what it emphatically was *not* was a workers' revolution. No workers' party sought – let alone attained – political hegemony. No Soviets or workers' councils were established, as in Petrograd or Berlin. There were no attempts at workers' control of industry, as in Turin, Barcelona – or the *gran minería* of Bolivia. Though the Mexican working-class had to confront the realities of the revolution, and thus in turn contributed to its development, its contribution was limited and largely reflexive; it responded to events rather than initiating them.

The working-class (as defined here) was distinguished by two characteristics, and moulded by two formative influences: an urban environment and an immersion in the market, the two correlating closely. The significance of the urban environment has often been underestimated: perhaps out of exaggerated fear of theories postulating "urbanism as a way of life": perhaps out of a residual reluctance to admit the gulf (and a "cultural" gulf at that) which often separated working-class from peasantry, or the corresponding bonds which united working-class and "bourgeoisie". But Barry Carr (1979, p. 621) rightly stresses the "growing cultural gap which was separating the world of the urban artisan and workers from the world of the villagers of central and southern Mexico" at the time of the revolution. First, urban workers shared the higher literacy rates evident in the cities: in a country where average literacy was no more than 20 per cent, working-class literacy was nearer 30–35 per cent; the leadership of the railway union claimed 100 per cent literacy. This reflected not only the significant growth of secular education in Porfirian cities, but also the powerful educational drive mounted by the workers themselves, particularly the artisans, in response to what was evidently a strong demand. The plethora of working-class papers and pamphlets, the educational efforts of mutualist societies (libraries, discussion groups, *veladas*), were all indicative of this trend. In the industrial city of Orizaba on the eve of the revolution thousands of copies of the Constitution were sold at 10c apiece; the *Casa del Obrero Mundial*, famous for its political activism, began as an educational/cultural organization, which carried the stamp of its creators: the printers of Mexico City, who "saw themselves as catalysts for cultural revolution, duty bound to bring light to those still submerged in obscurantism" (Carr, 1979, p. 606).

Thus, the urban working class was open to a range of ideas, which could combine in bizarre but appealing constellations: liberal, socialist, anarchist, Catholic (the 1900s saw the efflorescence of Catholic social action in Mexico), and even Protestant. Foreign influences were important, but not all-important in this process: working-class politicization cannot be explained by some crude diffusionist theory. But certainly it was the capital, the major ports (Veracruz, Tampico, Acapulco), and communities in the border zone (Chihuahua, Juárez, Cananea), which were most affected. For these and other reasons, the cities became the focus for the oppositionist politics of the 1900s, in which the urban working class (in contradistinction to the peasantry) played an important, if dependent role. As elsewhere in Latin America, electoral politics flourished in the cities, while the countryside still languished under the control of cacique or coronel – or, in parts of Mexico after 1910, experienced violent rebellion and jacquerie.

The cities therefore contained *masas disponibles*, relatively unfettered by "traditional" authority. This had important political implications; but it did not therefore render the urban working class more "revolutionary", any more than the continued presence of "traditional" authority in the countryside necessarily rendered the peasantry more docile. On the contrary, forms of "traditional" authority (the village representatives of Morelos; the *serrano* caciques of Durango or Puebla) supplied a vital organizational pre-requisite for protest and rebellion; equally, it was the presence of "traditional" norms (and their apparently arbitrary violation) which in Mexico, as elsewhere, provided the stimulus to revolt (Moore Jr, 1978). Peasants rebelled in defence of a material and normative *status quo ante* (in a few instances they received the support of "worker-peasants"); and, among urban working-class groups, it was the declining artisanate (which had a retrospective point of reference, if not a contemporary capacity for organization, comparable to those of the insurgent peasantry) which showed by far the clearest commitment to violent protest. Elsewhere, the relative absence of both traditional authority and pre-existing traditional norms and expectations made working class rebellion more difficult and less likely; just as it made the working class itself more pliable, and politically *disponible*. The miners of Cananea, for example, came closest to the model of a classic, *déraciné* proletariat (Cananea had scarcely existed twenty years before the revolution); organization and protest, therefore, had to be built up from scratch – pragmatically, cautiously, by trial and error and imitation. The "moral outrage", the search for "justice untarnished by compromise", which characterized peasant rebellion, had no place in the cities (Moore, 1978, pp. 233–4, 241, 251, 257, 269–74; Smith and Cano, 1978, p. 188).

The ideas purveyed in the cities were heterodox, and working-class ideology was eclectic. For all its radicalism, it had a lot in common with progressive "bourgeois" thought. Traditional liberalism exercised a strong and not wholly irrational appeal to the urban workers: workers' demands were frequently couched in terms of constitutional right and the legacy of *Juarismo*; the workers of Orizaba, as already mentioned, snapped up copies of the Constitution at 10c apiece. The Constitution, after all, guaranteed freedoms of organization, expression and withdrawal of labour (all of which the Porifirian regime repeatedly infringed); it provided for democratic representation which (in theory) gave the working class a political voice. But there was also a strong working-class attachment to the values of what might be termed, at some risk of confusion, "social liberalism", or, at the expense of euphony, "developmentalism", or even the Mexican Protestant ethic. As early as the 1840s, artisan circles in Mexico City were preaching thrift, sobriety, education and hard work; the *Casa del Obrero Mundial* followed suit; and the ephemeral radical papers of the revolutionary decade also displayed a commitment to these values, which the working-class (or, at least, the working-class literati who publicized them) shared with "bourgeois" thinkers and polemicists of different political colours: Porfirian/positivist, social Catholic, *Maderista*/liberal. All agreed, for example, that drink was the curse of the working-class (though one suspects that many of the working class went along with Wilde's reformulation of the problem); and temperance was allied to anti-clericalism: pulque and priests were (for many – not, of course, for the social Catholics) the twin evils which had to be extirpated. Nowhere was the gulf between the enlightened urban worker and the obscurantist peasant clearer than in their respective attitudes towards – not necessarily the Church hierarchy but – the Catholic religion; nowhere else was the barrier between civilization and barbarism more imposing. Hence the *Zapatistas*, with their deferential references to God and their Virgin of Guadalupe banners and badges, appalled the anti-clerical progressives among the Mexico City working-class.

Finally, in addition to these ideological factors which sundered city and countryside, while creating a certain identity between working class and bourgeoisie, there was also a concrete material interest. Workers in the Federal District were offended as much by *Zapatista* depredations – which forced the outlying textile factories to close, curtailed the electricity supply, and halted construction work – as by *Zapatista* religiosity. Elsewhere, too, the logic of the workers' position gave them a vested interest in continued industrial or mining production (which they shared with other urban groups); and it made them critical of rural rebellion. They, after all, could not retreat into their *milpas* when times were hard. In the spring of 1912, for example, rural rebellion engulfed the Laguna; at Torreón – then witnessing strenuous working-class organization – production fell, businesses closed down, unemployment and prices rose, and mobs invaded the streets, demanding food. The workers' hitherto bold attitude towards employers and officials was converted into an enforced dependence; "consumptionist" demands now took precedence over the battle for wages; and, since the workers rightly blamed the revolution for this change in conditions, it was as much as the Army could do to prevent rebel prisoners from being lynched by the city mob.

The perceived identity of interest between urban bourgeoisie and working-class was reciprocated. Long before the revolution, Porfirian (even *Juarista* and *Lerdista*) leaders sought the political support of the urban working class; and began to concern themselves with the "labour question" (in contrast, *Porfiristas* saw the "agrarian question" in purely productive, rather than politico-social terms: it was a question of modernizing agricultural technology and boosting output, not benefiting the peasantry by way of reform). *Políticos* like Guillermo Landa y Escandón, Governor of the Federal District, took a lively, enlightened interest in industrial problems and sponsored mutualist societies; state governors like Reyes (Nuevo León), Dehesa (Veracruz), and Bandala (Tabasco) thought it worth cultivating the working class. This did not denote altruism. The regime had been shaken by the "year of strikes" (1906), and especially by events at Cananea and Río Blanco; in Mexico, as elsewhere in Latin America, the "social question" began to agitate men's minds; even the Mexico City theatre started to explore "social" themes. Landa y Escandón, like later revolutionary labour reformers, clearly attempted to curtail working-class protest, or divert it into acceptable channels. But the significant fact is that such an attempt was systematically made – in a way that was not when the regime confronted peasant protest. The peasant – especially the *indio* – represented barbarism; but the urban worker might be converted to civilization.

Both working-class protest and official thinking must be seen in the contemporary economic context; and here we come to the second distinguishing feature and formative influence, the market. The working class existed within a money economy, almost entirely governed by the laws of the market, free labour and the cash nexus. This carried two important implications, one secular, one "conjunctural". First, like many early twentieth-century working classes, that of Mexico was still in the making; the inculcation of the time and work discipline of industrial capitalism was still partial, in some cases incipient. Employers' complaints concerning the fecklessness, unreliability and absenteeism of workers were nothing new: they had been vocal enough in the 1840s and before; but now, with the rapid growth of industry, and the conversion of artisans and peasants into proletarians, the complaints came thick and fast. The separation of the worker (artisan or peasant) from the means of production guaranteed an abundant supply of labour, but not of suitably motivated labour. Employers lamented the chronic absenteeism of their workers; the old practice of San Lunes; the pernicious effects of drink; the lack of application and initiative. And they responded, roughly, in two contrasting ways. Some (in the troubled textile industry, for example) borrowed the "paternalistic" ways of the *hacienda*: instituting close supervision of the factory, compiling complex regulations, imposing fines, docking wages, keeping dossiers of supposed trouble-makers, hiring and firing at will. Though (as in some *haciendas*) a more benign, protective paternalism was also apparent, this was increasingly exceptional; under the pressure of the market, the inexorable trend was towards "stricter industrial regimes for the workers and harsher personnel practices" (Anderson, 1978, pp. 78; 95). As in the countryside, the growth of the market and of proletarianization did not necessarily dissolve old regulatory practices (which we are here calling "paternalistic") but often served to distort them, emphasising their coercive or oppressive aspects, while stripping away what reciprocity formerly existed. The hated *hacienda mayordomo* (often Spanish) had his counterpart in the hated factory foreman (also Spanish); *hacienda* and factory alike possessed their *tiendas de raya*; and harsh, arbitrary factory discipline (justified on the grounds of the workers' fecklessness) was a source of constant working-class complaint. Though more modern industrial enterprises faced similar problems (in the mines of Cananea it was difficult to ensure sustained work, over the week and the month) such companies – typified by the large, corporate, Anglo-American mining and oil interests – came to rely less on semi-coercive control than on calculated incentive: paying a premium, for example, at the end of a full week's work. They could count on their own favourable market position (vis-à-vis labour) and their financial resources (oil began to boom as textiles contracted); and employment in these sectors was better paid and sought after. Mexican industrialization during the Porfiriato can thus be seen (though it has been little researched) in terms of the secular struggle to implant the ethic of modern capitalism, to which there were divergent responses, hence divergent political and economic behaviour on the part of the workers.

While neither the strength of *hacienda* "paternalism", nor the prevalence of subsistence agriculture should be exaggerated, the fact is that both cushioned the rural population (peon and peasant) against the effects of the market; and these, in the 1900s, were largely detrimental. For, as population growth and agrarian expropriation swelled the supply of labour, as food production failed to keep pace, and as industry destroyed jobs faster than it created them, so real wages fell markedly. The years 1907–8 witnessed economic recession, 1908–9 consecutive bad harvests. Historians have readily inferred that these lean years provoked the revolution. We cannot enter that argument here, though it should be noted that recovery was well under way by 1910 and that – whether the focus is on regions, individuals or social groups – political dissidence and revolutionary proclivities usually antedated these years. More important here, it must be questioned whether economic indices and cycles (though superficially attractive as "hard" data) are necessarily so useful in explaining popular protest: not only are they often unreliable, and lacking any *causal* relationship with the phenomenon of protest (it is often just a question of *post hoc ergo propter hoc*); they are also suggestive of a rather crude, positivistic, correlative technique (recession in 1907, therefore revolution in 1910).

In fact, to the extent that tentative correlations can be established between wages and employment on the one hand, and the workers' *economic* struggle on the other (measured in terms of strike activity), the experience of Mexico in the years before the revolution is a familiar one: economic hardship and unemployment went with a fall in strike activity and decline in apparent militancy. The later years of the revolution produced a similar effect. But, as regards the much more complex question of popular, political protest (which underlay the 1910 revolution), such simple economic correlations may be misleading. Recent research, dealing with both peasant and working-class protest, has emphasized "non-economic" factors: the "moral economy", the violation of existing (tacitly) agreed norms of behaviour, the imposition of new, arbitrary authority, the capacity for "moral outrage" as a primary impulse and collective organization as a necessary basis of effective protest. Obviously, such arguments embrace the "economic", but they place it in context and do not exalt it (not even to the status of necessary "cause-in-the-last-analysis"). As regards the Mexican working class, therefore, a catalogue of bad times – unemployment, low pay, atrocious conditions of work – may have little explanatory power, as it stands. Aggregate economic data must be interpreted in the light of other more important (largely non-quantifiable) data relating to regions, industries, and social groups, to which data we now turn.

It must be noted first that the Mexican artisanate greatly outnumbered the classic proletariat. The 1910 census revealed between 90 000 and 100 000 factory workers (of whom about one-third worked in the textile industry), as compared with 67 000 carpenters, 44 000 shoemakers, 23 000 potters (and so on). But three subdivisions must be made. First, there were village artisans (potters, weavers, carpenters) who, protected by distance, local poverty, and ingrained custom, could survive in the face of industrialization. If their plight worsened, it was as a result of the general fall in rural living standards, particularly associated with the growth of large landholdings. Village artisans often played an important role in rural rebellion, figuring as leaders, or as "village intellectuals" – Felipe Neri in Morelos, Orestes Pereyra in the Laguna. But they were clearly marginal to the urban working-class, in terms of both location and organization. With regard to the towns, a second, crucial group was composed of declining artisans, engaged in a mortal struggle with factory production: of textiles, shoes, hats, candles, leather goods. Their sad lot was most apparent in the towns of the Bajío, where artisan crafts had long flourished in conjunction with the mines; but now the mines were past their peak, wages were depressed, and industrial competition (usually emanating from other parts of the country) was intense.

In Mexico as elsewhere handicraft workers of this kind found it notoriously hard to achieve any collective organization or mount collective resistance. They might share with the peasant a nostalgia for the world they had lost, or were fast losing, but they were less equipped to do anything about it. The artisans' characteristic response, during the revolution, was the urban riot: a form of popular protest particularly evident in the towns of the Bajío in 1911 (Ciudad Manuel Doblado, Pénjamo, San Miguel Allende experienced riots; at Celaya, León and San Francisco del Rincón they were narrowly averted). Rioters – identified at San Miguel as literate workers – ransacked tax offices and court-houses, opened gaols, and looted pawnshops. It is clear that longstanding grievances against industrialists (probably "putting-out" industrialists), officials and retailers were exacerbated by the economic effects of the revolution, which also afforded the political opportunity for grievances to be expressed. It is worth noting, too, that, after the artisans, it was the miners – but chiefly the miners in the older, declining centres, not the new, corporate mines of the north – who were most prone to riot: at Angangueo, Los Reyes, Hostotipaquillo, Pachuca and (a particularly grisly riot, reminiscent of *Germinal*) Concepción del Oro. But while these followed in the old tradition of the brawling miners of Bourbon Mexico, their colleagues in the collieries of Coahuila or the copper mines of Sonora eschewed riot in favour of unionization. Similarities between these riotous groups and events and their counterparts in pre-industrial Europe spring to mind. And, with the physical remoteness of their industrial competitors inhibiting outright Luddism, the Bajío artisans (and the "traditional" miners) shared with the pre-industrial mob a concern for issues of consumption (as against production): hence the repeated attacks on shops and pawnbrokers (many of them Spanish-owned).

The third category of artisans, the most diffuse, embraces those who survived, grew in numbers, and even prospered during the generation of the Porfiriato; it extends from those "artisans" who served the new, buoyant sectors of the urban economy (trams, public utilities, printshops, the construction and electricity industries), and who merge into the proletariat proper, to the aspiring, "petty-bourgeois" artisans, skilled, literate, and cast in the image of their Victorian counterparts. Despite the wide range which these groups spanned they shared important characteristics: they were skilled or semi-skilled, and were familiar with the urban environment, which they and their families had long inhabited; they were neither recent rural migrants, nor classic proletarians (in the sense of working in large industrial units), nor yet were they part of the large lumpenproletariat, the unemployed, underemployed, vagrants, beggars and criminals who constituted the *pelados*. And they displayed certain comparable political traits.

The aspiring artisan, the *artesano culto*, provided the backbone of the educational and cultural organizations already mentioned. Literate, aspiring and politically aware, he joined mutualist societies (where he might rub shoulders with the middle-class); he inhabited the new suburbs of the capital around Buenavista station; he may be seen graphically depicted in the woodcuts of Posada. Typical of this group were Aquiles Serdán, the Puebla shoemaker and first martyr of the revolution; Silvestre Dorador of Durango; the *Veracruzanos* Gabriel Gavira (a cabinet-maker) and Rafael Tapia (a saddler). Madero, in preaching to and mobilizing the disaffected middleclass, also singled out that "chosen element of the working-class which aspires to improvement" as an important source of support, which, indeed, it proved to be, as during 1909–10 mutualist societies metamorphosed into Maderista political clubs, often of hybrid middle-and working-class composition (Madero, 1908). But the political involvement of the artisanate was nothing new in Mexican history; nor was it confined to *Maderismo*. *Porfirista* officials also established relations with mutualist societies; and five years after the revolution began, it was the Mexico City artisans who pioneered the political alliance between the organized working class and the Constitutionalists.

With the obvious exception of the village artisans, the artisanate was typically, ineradicably urban. But, as already suggested, the making of the Mexican working class was very much in progress when the revolution occurred. As a result there were large semi proletarianized groups, who defy precise categorization (no doubt that reflects upon the categories in use; but for the moment we are stuck with them). From the perspective of revolutionary participation, furthermore, these groups were of much greater significance than the "pure" working-class. Roughly, we may discern two groups: the "worker-peasants" of central Mexico, who collaborated with the vigorous peasant movements of that region, Zapata's included; and the "semi-proletarian" or migrant workers of the north, who supported the Orozquists and *Villista* movements, and who may best be regarded as elements within the generic *serrano* rebellion (Knight, 1980, pp. 26–36). The worker-peasant, of course, was a central character in the revolution in Russia, where continued ties between village and factory served to fuse the discontents of both groups (elsewhere kept distinct), and where both the nature of the regime (highly autocratic and repressive) and the nature of factory production (large, self-contained, regimented units) inhibited the growth of organizations which might ameliorate the workers' conditions or socialize them into urban society. In Mexico this phenomenon was much less pronounced, hence much less productive of urban revolution. In Puebla and Tlaxcala, where "long-standing job mobility between rural villages and urban areas" was evident, relations between peasant rebels and urban workers were often close (displaying little of the cultural gulf apparent in the capital); thus, while the Tlaxcalan peasant movement obeyed familiar, agrarian motives – the recovery of land lost to expansionist haciendas – the shift of peasants into industry (textiles) encouraged a cross-fertilization of ideas, a degree of mutual trust and support, and an unusual capacity for collective worker/peasant action (Buve, 1975). Tlaxcala consequently witnessed the development of a radical worker/peasant movement, capable not only of rural insurrection but also of urban political mobilization, leading to the election as Governor of an ex-textile worker, who put out an allegedly "socialist" programme, gravely alarming property-owners in the state. In Puebla, too, factory workers of recent, rural origin, gave aid and comfort to *Zapatismo*. But this phenomenon – the collaborative protest of city and countryside, worker and peasant – was strictly limited, by both time and region. Generally, factory employment – while it lasted – acted as a disincentive to revolt; the revolutionary commitment of the Puebla workers was belated (it came in 1915, when production faltered), that of the Tlaxcala worker-peasants was exceptional. Elsewhere in Mexico, proletarianization was more gradual yet more complete than in Russia: it built upon a stronger artisanal base (which Russian industry lacked), and relied less upon mass, rural recruitment; hence ties between city and village, worker and peasant, were weaker. Furthermore, for all its black image, the Porfirian regime was less intransigent than its Tsarist equivalent: it not only allowed but sometimes positively encouraged the peaceful association of the workers, and their integration into urban society.

The semi-proletarian character of the northern revolution has been emphasized elsewhere; indeed, there is a risk of over-emphasizing it, for the northern rebels, too, were mostly rural folk, some of them classic peasants, some of them motivated by agrarian grievances analogous to those of the *Zapatistas*. True, the more mobile, market-oriented north witnessed the revolutionary recruitment of semi-proletarians, migrants and miners; hence it has been suggested that the northern revolution was, initially, a *révolution minière*, based on mining communities (Guerra, 1981). But such an occupational emphasis – derivative of industrial society – is misleading in societies where the division of labour was less advanced, and jobs were less functionally specific. Some rebels were ex-miners; but they were also ex-peasants, -outlaws, -cowboys (sometimes all four); and they were radicals or persons with a grudge against the authorities. In fact, mining communities almost never rebelled as collectivities, as some villages did (though they might engage in brief, violent *journées*); and throughout much of the revolution, the mines kept working, where they were permitted, to the evident satisfaction of their employees. *Serrano* rebellion obeyed motives which were largely divorced from mining, and the sporadic participation of miners or ex-miners in such rebellions scarcely imparted an "industrial" character to these revolts, or detracted from their rural, *serrano* origins.

Roughly, therefore, semi-proletarians participated actively in the armed revolution precisely because they were *semi-* and not *wholly* proletarianized (or urbanized). It was their contacts with or even membership of rural communities – the cells of revolution – which counted. Conversely, if the focus is switched to the classic, fully proletarianized groups, it is the *absence* of such revolutionary commitment which is conspicuous. Thus, where factory employment could soak up surplus labour – which, admittedly, it could not always do – the result was a diminution, not an accentuation of revolutionary potential. As Barrington Moore observes in the case of Germany, "industrialization solved the problem of the proletariat rather than created it" (Moore, p. 135). Once the process of proletarianization – the "making of the working class", be it English, German or Mexican – was well advanced, the dangers of violent revolution tended to recede, as the development of "modern" capitalism was matched by the development of "modern" working-class organizations, with a vested interest in continued industrial production; what has been called (by a Marxist, not a Panglossian modernization theorist) the "imbrication of working-class organization in the *status quo*" (Thompson, 1978). And this was particularly true during the revolution, when unemployment facilitated rebel recruitment (the Red Battalions were the classic but not the sole example), while stable employment often made recruitment impossible.

This is not to characterize the emergent proletariat – the railwaymen, dockers, textile operatives, and (proletarian) miners – as inert or politically indifferent. On the contrary, they displayed "a very marked tendency to associate" (Rafael Sierra y Domínguez to Trabajo, 13 March 1913), first and foremost in "economist" organizations (mutualist societies, *sindicatos*), secondarily in political formations. But the latter were strongly reformist and pragmatic in nature, and they were prepared to countenance alliances with parties and regimes of almost any type – left, right, and centre. Thus it was possible for groups like the miners of Sonora and Coahuila (a) to form combative unions; (b) to achieve tactical alliances with revolutionary politicians like Maytorena or Espinosa Mireles; while (c) avoiding active participation in the armed struggle (indeed, while demonstrating against revolutionary upheaval and in favour of peace, as the miners of Coahuila did in 1912). The dockers, who represented one of the most aggressive and developed sectors of the working class, behaved similarly, at Acapulco and Tampico; while a similar dual strategy – economic organization and wage bargaining, coupled with judicious political alignment – characterized the railwaymen. Even if anarcho-syndicalist ideology exercised an appeal (as it did in some quarters – perhaps not as many as often imagined) it was largely honoured in the breach. The most advanced sectors of the working class ("advanced" in terms of organizational strength; and incidentally, located in the more "advanced", high wage sector of the national economy) had no inhibition about mixing in bourgeois politics. And, as regards the central, "economist" struggle, the intransigence of most employers ensured that this was no soft option.

This was exemplified in the two famous, pre-revolutionary, labour disputes at Cananea (1906) and Río Blanco (1907), which should be seen less as political revolutions *manqués* than as bloody industrial conflicts, provoked by managerial intransigence. Come the Revolution, we should note, Cananea – though strongly oppositionist – did not rebel *en masse*, nor establish itself as an armed camp, like the Bolivian tin mines of the 1950s. Rather, production continued (under new, more enlightened, corporate management); the miners still pressed for "economist" gains; and they received a degree of satisfaction. Nor did Río Blanco live up to either revolutionary hopes or Porfirian fears in 1910. Not till five years later, as the economy crumbled, did rebel recruitment pick up; but, even then, the Orizaba factories (including Río Blanco) lagged behind those of Puebla, where links with the *campesinado* were stronger.

To summarize matters crudely: to the extent that enterprises conformed to the "modern" industrial norm (large units, an advanced division of labour, hence full proletarianization and a complete divorce from the countryside) so the workers' protest assumed "modern", associational forms – trade unions, involvement in reformist politics – and eschewed both armed revolutionary commitment and violent street confrontations. Violence was absent, the political order was (broadly speaking) accepted, and economic grievances focused on questions of production rather than consumption. The workers struck against their employers (angling for political support while they did) and did not lynch *jefes políticos* or ransack Spanish pawnbrokers. As the comparison with Russia has already suggested, this pattern of development depended on factors outside the control of the workers themselves: it required not only the growth of modern industrial units (many of them foreign-owned and managed) but also the increasing tendency of the government (Porfirian, *Maderista*, *Carrancista*) to seek a rapprochement with labour, if only the better thereby to control it. The workers' acceptance of the state, and preparedness to invoke the authority of the state, required that the state meet them at least part of the way. Parallels with Europe, and the growth of labour reformism there, are evident. Given half a chance, the organized working-class opted for unionism and reformism (sometimes camouflaged under revolutionary rhetoric); only when it was brusquely and brutally denied the chance did it entertain risky thoughts of revolution. Historically, the workers have not been born revolutionaries, but have had revolutions thrust upon them.

The Development of a Revolutionary Labour Movement in Chile

Peter DeShazo

The historical attachment of the organized labor movement of Chile to revolutionary ideologies has been unique in Latin America. Anarcho-syndicalists controlled most labor unions in Santiago and Valparaíso, and the Communists those of the nitrate and coal mining zones during the 1920s. From the late 1930s to the fall of Allende, a majority of Chilean labor unionists manifested their desire for socio-economic change by supporting the Communist and Socialist Parties at the polls and in the streets.

A leftist-oriented labor movement developed and survived in Chile because of the failure of élites either to eliminate independent working-class organizations by repression or to provide institutional means for incorporating workers into society. During the "Parliamentary Regime" (1891–1924), the fiscal dependence of the state on nitrate exports and the prevalent view among politicians and entrepreneurs that the government's role in the economy should be limited to guaranteeing a free flow of trade conditioned the relationship between the state and organized labor. Under normal circumstances, the national government did not intervene in the affairs of labor and capital. Legislation aimed at regulating industrial relations was introduced in Congress on several occasions during the early twentieth century, but no action was taken until the passage of seven labor laws in September 1924. Congress did produce a series of laws governing child and female labor, indemnity payments for work-related accidents, and Sunday rest, but employers generally ignored them.

In lieu of government regulation, workers and employers formed their own *de facto* system of industrial relations during the first decades of the twentieth century. Early efforts at unionization were met with dismissals and blacklisting. Strikes on many occasions more closely resembled industrial warfare than labor disputes. Employers considered any union demand not related to wages to be a frontal attack on their managerial prerogatives.

This unregulated relationship between labor and capital persisted until the repression of the unions by Colonel Carlos Ibáñez in February 1927. An industrial environment marked by a quarter of a century of malign neglect on the part of the state and constant resistance from employers helped create an independent, leftist-oriented labor movement in Chile. The tactics and outlook of anarcho-syndicalism guided many of the labor unions of Santiago and Valaparaíso through their first strikes between 1902 and 1908. Workers learned that direct action against employers, not political or mutual aid activities, won them material benefits. The presence of police spies in labor unions, the brutality of mounted troops during demonstrations, and unenforced "social legislation" convinced many that the State was their enemy. Either by choice or by circumstance, most workers did not vote and thus remained politically isolated from the parliamentary regime. Unemployment, rampant inflation, and increased poverty assaulted the working class whenever major fluctuations occurred in the nitrate economy. Under such conditions, revolutionary ideologies made headway on a step-by-step basis until nearly all the important labor unions came under anarcho-syndicalist or communist control by the early 1920s.

The Alessandri government (1921–4) at first gave half-hearted support to labor but, as soon as it became apparent that the unions could not break the lockouts, it shifted allegiance to the stronger side. Under attack from capital and retrenching everywhere, the major labor unions moved rapidly to the left by declaring their adhesion to communist and anarchist principles. A Communist Party of Chile (PCC) was formed in January 1922 and within two years dominated the FOCh through its control of unions in the nitrate and coal mining zones. Anarcho-syndicalists led the most important labor unions in Santiago and Valparaíso between 1917 and 1927, including those of printing, leather, baking, maritime, and construction workers. These organizations also became more ideologically committed as lockouts ensued.

Many factors stimulated the growth of an independent, leftist-oriented labor movement before 1927. The nature of Chile's political system and the composition of the working class greatly limited the capacity of the state to repress organized labor. As previously noted, executive officials from the President of the Republic to local police chiefs used force to break strikes and quell civil disturbances, always as a stop-gap solution. Despite the infiltration of police agents into most labor organizations, the arrest of union leaders, and other acts of harassment, the government did not attempt to dissolve unions permanently. The repression ordered by President Juan Luis Sanfuentes in July 1920 was the most determined effort of any regime before 1927 to eliminate major labor unions by force, but they regained their former effectiveness within six months.

Chilean Presidents during the parliamentary regime exercised limited powers and could not make far-reaching decisions without the co-operation of Congress. The host of political parties and their unstable congressional alliances paid little attention to the working class unless social upheaval threatened. In those instances, legislation calling for short-term repression such as the granting of state-of-siege powers to the President or increasing the size of the armed forces were the normal responses. Even when the major political parties clearly perceived the growing stability and leftist orientation of the labor movement, rivalry prevented them from enacting laws to prevent the continued independence of labor. Only under pressure from military *golpistas* in September 1924 did Congress finally pass legislation intended to subjugate organized labor to a government and employer-controlled system of industrial relations.

Other factors limited the government's repressive capabilities. Chile's independent judiciary system would not automatically convict and imprison arrested union leaders. Labor newspapers were protected by freedom of the press guarantees. An excessive use of force, especially in urban areas where violence was more visible, often embarrassed and politically weakened governing coalitions. Political parties both in and out of government could exploit public opinion regarding the "social question" to their own benefit. The overwhelming preponderance of Chilean citizens in the labor movement posed another barrier to potential repression by the state. In

Argentina and Brazil, where foreign anarchists established and led most labor unions during the first decades of the twentieth century, the government used "residence laws" and deportation to weaken seriously the power of the organized working-class. The Chilean Congress passed its own *Ley de Residencia* in November 1918, reflecting the misconception of élites that "foreign subversives" were responsible for the increased number of strikes and protest demonstrations. Only a handful of people were ever deported. Nor could the government pit native workers against foreigners by means of preferential treatment or appeals to xenophobia. Chilean workers did not consider revolutionary ideologies and labor unions to be useless baggage from the "old country" as in Argentina and Brazil.

Chilean workers remained isolated from the mainstream of national politics throughout the first quarter of the twentieth century. During that time, none of the major political parties enjoyed any sustained support from organized labor, due in some areas (Santiago, Valparaíso) to the anarcho-syndicalists' disdain for politics, and in others (Tarapacá, Antofagasta, Concepción) to the interest of labor unions in political alternatives. Legislation passed in the 1880s which extended the franchise to all literate adult males, and the high literacy rate (60–80 per cent in 1920) of city workers over twenty-one years of age should have guaranteed the urban working class a position of importance in Chilean politics during the parliamentary regime.

Few of those qualified to vote registered, however, and even fewer cast ballots. The presidential election of 1920, for example, captured greater working-class attention than any before 1925, and yet a mere 21,338 people, or approximately 23 per cent of those eligible, voted in the Department of Santiago. Considering that at least 20 per cent of adult male workers in Santiago were illiterate, it appears likely that only one in six cast a ballot in 1920. Traditional parties did woo the working-class elector, however, since a small number of votes often spelled the difference between defeat and victory in elections. The most common and effective means of obtaining working-class "support" was to buy votes. Elections during the parliamentary regime were won by the candidate or party which paid more per vote and exercised greater skill in stealing or stuffing ballot boxes. Genuine representatives of the mutual aid societies and labor unions, normally democrats before 1912 and socialists and communists afterwards, were occasionally elected to Congress, but vote-buying and fraud in registering voters deprived them of a firm base of support. No social democratic party such as the Socialist Party of

Argentina achieved the necessary legitimacy or power to provide Chilean workers with a means of formal political expression.

Arturo Alessandri was the first representative of a major political party to attract widespread support from the working class. While running for the presidency in 1920, his ceaseless demagogy promised working people nothing less than a new social order, and thousands believed what they heard.

Organized labor either supported Alessandri or, in the case of the anarcho-syndicalists, refrained from actively criticizing him during his first six months in office. Alessandri, in return, helped several unions to achieve favorable settlements in their wage disputes with private employers and the State railways. This brief "honeymoon" between the President and organized labor came to an abrupt end when Alessandri sided with employers during the nationwide maritime lockout and general strike of August–October, 1921. Thereafter, his relationship with the labor unions deteriorated to the point of open hostility.

Electoral politics up to the time of the Ibáñez coup of 1927 produced few, if any, concrete benefits for Chilean workers. Organized labor did, however, use other forms of political action in an attempt to influence the behavior of government in its favor. Massive rallies, general strikes, and one-day work-stoppages, all imbued with the threat of violence, were the principal weapons in labor's arsenal. On several occasions, such as the campaign of the "Workers' Assembly on National Nutrition" (*Asamblea Obrera de Alimentación Nacional*) to lower food costs in 1918–19, and the rent-strike movement of 1925, the government reacted to intense pressure by partially granting labor's demands and at the same time by taking steps to neutralize these popular movements. "Show of force" tactics rarely produced anything but short-term improvements in the economic lot of the working class. Attempts to by-pass employers and apply pressure for economic reform directly on the government further alienated workers from the state when no basic reforms came about. An increase in the number and intensity of rallies and protest strikes after 1917 eventually compelled élites to devise methods by which the organized labor movement could be controlled through incorporation in a legally-established system of industrial relations.

The organized labor movement in Chile developed and remained free of institutionalized control by either capital or the state before 1927. This was made possible by a system of industrial relations which pitted labor unions against employers in an unregulated struggle for more than twenty-five years. Neither side could vanquish the other. Employers failed to halt the spread of unions, although their tenacious opposition resulted in numerous setbacks for workers. Labor unions in most industries managed to preserve their organizational identity, but normally occupied the weaker position in collective bargaining. State intervention took place whenever the conflict between labor and capital seriously affected the economy or disturbed the *status quo*. The short-term, but often brutal, repression employed by the government on occasion deepened the already profound alienation of the working class from the state. Content to leave the "social question" in the hands of employers and the armed forces, political élites in Chile unwittingly fostered the spread of revolutionary ideology within the labor movement. Workers in many industries had cultivated the tactics of anarcho-syndicalism since the turn of the century and, by 1921, most of the principal labor unions of Santiago and Valparaíso openly declared their adoption of anarchist principles. The FOCh also turned leftward during the early 1920s by shedding its syndicalist identity and linking itself with the Communist Party. Even the normally complacent mutual aid societies took an active part in the rent strike and anti-labor law movements organized by the anarchists in 1925–7.

The independence and revolutionary outlook which most labor unions in Chile developed by 1927 had a major role in determining the course that Chilean politics would take in the following decades. Unlike their counterparts in Brazil and Cuba, Chilean anarcho-syndicalists did not become communists, nor were they displaced by communism during the 1920s. On the contrary, the communist-dominated FOCh appears to have been weaker numerically and in terms of economic effectiveness than the anarcho-syndicalist federations at the time of the Ibáñez coup. The existence of revolutionary, anti-communist forces within the Chilean working class of the 1920s facilitated the establishment of Latin America's only important Socialist Party in 1933. Evidence of the anarcho-syndicalist contribution to the Socialist Party is the sizeable number of anarchist union leaders and middle-class libertarians who held important positions in the Party during its first years of life. When organized workers in Chile became highly politicized in the 1930s as a result of their inability to bargain effectively with employers once the labor laws of 1924 were finally enforced, they did not abandon their former identification with the left, but turned to politics rather than job action as a means of achieving their goals.

Although Chilean labor unions were greatly weakened by the constricting terms of the labor laws of 1924 as codified in 1931, they did not fall under the political control of the state as in Peronist Argentina or the *Estado Nôvo* of Brazil. Instead, organized labor became an increasingly significant force on the left in Chilean politics.

Part IV

Latin American Populism

Introduction

As indicated in the Introduction, the range of movements and alliances which have come to be known collectively as "Latin American populism" are best understood in the context of the evolution and crisis of export-led economies in the region. To this extent they have a common source and origin, and may be differentiated from the forms of populism associated with the United States and Russia. Latin American populism has generally been urban in focus, opposed to the status quo where it has rested upon open export-oriented economies, generally oriented towards accelerated industrial development, and therefore likely to construct alliances linking an emerging working class to an industrial bourgeoisie. These groups are likely to be tied to and linked through the state, and attempts are likely to be made to minimize inter-class antagonisms through the propagation of a broadly nationalist ideology. However, forms of populism in Latin America have varied widely, in accordance with the nature of export-led development, the political alliances associated with it, the degree of urban and industrial development it promoted, and the forms of political opposition it produced. There is little to be gained by seeking inclusive definitions which encompass all those movements, regimes or alliances which have been termed "populist". It is more fruitful to explore the consequences of the loss of authority experienced by élites associated with export-led development as a result of the depression, the consequent vulnerability of their political arrangements, and the varied forms taken by attempts, promoted by urban counter-élites, to re-orient these economies and build new political and social bases of support.

In the selections presented here, *Roxborough* examines the three best known cases of "Latin American populism", those of Cárdenas in Mexico, Perón in Argentina, and Vargas in Brazil, and shows that in each case substantial class conflict was involved in the establishment of the alliances concerned; *Stein* discusses the element of social control inherent in such projects; *Laclau* proposes as a common element in all the diverse forms of populism an ideological nucleus which can be interpreted as arising directly from the manifold consequences of the crisis of export-led development, and provides a comparison of Brazil and Argentina which reveals the impact of specific national factors in shaping different types of regime, and *Cueva* provides a detailed analysis of the less well known case of *Velasquismo* in Ecuador.

Given the specificity of "Latin American populism", the readings here are best supplemented by case studies. Conniff (1982) is a useful comparative collection, though relatively weak on theoretical insight; Malloy (1977) is more ambitious, and has been influential. *Stein* (1980), from which the selection below is taken, is an excellent historical monograph. For Mexico, consult Ashby (1967) and Hamilton (1980). For Brazil, see Erickson (1977). For Argentina, see Baily (1967), and Rock (1975). Spalding (1977) offers a comparative discussion of organised labour which covers many of the issues discussed below.

Populism and Class Conflict

Latin American Populism

Ian Roxborough

The "classical" account of Latin American populism sees it as a phenomenon combining a particular form of ideology with certain organizational and social structural features. For "classical" theorists, populism in Latin America is a loosely organized multiclass movement united by a charismatic leader behind an ideology and programme of social justice and nationalism. In their view this linkage of ideology and organization is the *strength* of the definition; it links ideology with a definite mode of political participation. There is an implicit or explicit contrast with the supposedly class-orientated nature of politics in the advanced industrial societies of Western Europe. Popular participation in populist movements, it is asserted, does not take on a "class" character. Either the subordinate strata compose a "mass" or the working class does not yet have its own autonomous organizations. It tends, therefore, to be organized and led by other social classes or political forces in a heteronomous manner. The absence or weakness of an autonomous working class is central to the classical definition of populism.

The period of import substitution industrialization was accompanied by a displacement of the old agrarian oligarchies from state power and by the mobilization of perviously excluded classes and strata. A heterogeneous coalition of industrialists, the urban middle class, urban workers and migrants to the cities led this assault on the oligarchical state. Frequently with the aid of sections of the military, this coalition led to the installation of populist or Bonapartist regimes and to a new level of state autonomy from direct class pressures. Industrial expansion, growth in employment, and widespread rises in living standards were the material bases for the widespread support enjoyed by these populist governments.

Opposing this account, there is what might be called the "discourse analysis" school of thought. For these theorists, populism is first and foremost an *ideological* phenomenon: populism is an ideology, or strand of an ideology, which asserts that political conflict is between "the people" (who are seen as the "nation") and the

119

"oligarchy" or "imperialism" (Ionescu and Gellner, 1969; Mouzelis, 1978; also *Laclau*, below). Hence, whenever a political leader makes an appeal to "the people" he or she is a populist, and his or her movement or government may by extension be described as "populist". In this definition, nothing is said about the causes of populism, about its social base, about its policies, or about its organizational style. Having defined the phenomenon with reference to a particular form of ideological appeal, it remains a matter of empirical enquiry as to whether this appeal to the people is associated with particular features in the genesis, structure, social base, and outcome of the movement. The "discourse analysis" definition is, therefore, a minimal definition; while some theorists would argue that populism is more than this, none would argue that it is *less* than this. Moreover, if populism is an "appeal to the people", it does not follow that those to whom this appeal is addressed actually heed it. Whether the subordinate classes and strata of Latin America support populist leaders because they accept the validity of this appeal to the people, or whether they support such leaders because this is a rational choice among alternatives, given their interests, remains an open matter.

A corollary of this minimal definition of the term is that one must expect to find "populism" in a wide variety of contexts, and this is, indeed, the case in Latin America. Populist appeals to the people were made by the Christian Democrat Eduardo Frei in Chile in the 1960s, by Mexican presidents throughout the twentieth century, by the Peruvian military government of the late 1960s and early 1970s, and by a motley host of civilians and military men in a wide variety of contexts. The proponents of the "classical" account of populism see in the paradigmatic cases of Perón, Vargas and Cárdenas attempts to mobilize subordinate strata from above into multi-class coalitions behind an industrial-developmentalist project of the state and/or the national bourgeoisie.

The available evidence, however, suggests that the fit between the classical definition of populism and these three cases is open to question. Indeed, of the three paradigmatic examples of "populism" (according to the classical account), one of them – the 1930–45 Vargas government – fails even to fit the minimal definition. During the period from his seizure of power up to the calling of elections after the Second World War, Getúlio Vargas' discourse was *not* noted for the frequency of its appeals to the "people". His was a conservative, authoritarian and demobilizing regime that is hard to describe as "populist" under any definition. It was only with the advent of competitive politics in the period *after* 1945 that

Vargas made any sustained appeal to the people. In this second period, indeed, Vargas may justly be described as a populist, and the heyday of Brazilian populism may perhaps be dated as 1945–64. But Brazilian ISI was well under way in the 1930s and had begun considerably earlier. The "fit" between economics and politics in this paradigmatic case is rather loose.

In the cases of Cárdenas and Perón there is little doubt that they meet the minimal definition of populism. But the classical account of populism goes beyond this minimal definition to include the notion that mass support for populist movements was not organized primarily along class lines. That is, the support for populist leaders was not a multi-class alliance, with independent trade unions lending the support of an autonomously organized working-class to a Bonapartist figure, but rather an amorphous mass movement or coalition with direct ties between individuals and the charismatic leader. This analysis springs basically from Weber (charisma) and Durkheim via mass society theory.

For the classic definition of populism to have any utility, it must be demonstrated that we are dealing with a situation in which subordinate classes or strata are organized into the populist coalition in a *heteronomous* manner. If this is not the case, then we are dealing with an alliance of classes, rather than with populism. The available evidence suggests that, at least in the early phases, both Perón and Cárdenas were supported by autonomously organized working-class institutions, i.e. relatively independent trade unions. These movements may, therefore, be analyzed in terms of more or less explicit and deliberate alliances of the working-class with individuals holding state power. No reference to the concept of populism is necessary to explain this, nor does the notion of populism add anything to the analysis. It is only at a later stage that the unions lose their autonomy and the working-class becomes subordinate to the state. Empirically, neither early Peronism nor the Cárdenas government fit into a classical account of populism.

In the case of the early Peronist movement, Juan Carlos Torre (1976) has shown how the supposedly "spontaneous" demonstration of the poor people of Buenos Aires on 17 October 1945 to demand the release of Perón had been called for and organized by the principal trade-union confederation, the CGT. Moreover, at the meeting of the CGT's executive committee where that decision was taken, the union leaders were deeply divided over their attitudes to Perón. On the one hand were those who wished to have nothing to do with Perón; in a slight majority were those who, despite considerable distrust and misgivings, decided to support Perón as a lesser evil. Moreover, the notion that it was recent migrants to Buenos Aires from the interior –a "new" working class – which provided Perón with his principal base of support has come under sustained attack. Little (1975), and Murmis and Portantiero (1971) have argued that Perón's support was drawn from all sectors of the working class; repressed by conservative governments since 1930, Argentina's urban workers and trade union leaders saw in Perón a potential, if ambiguous, ally. There was, therefore, considerable continuity in working class political behaviour, at least during the early phase of the regime. Of course, this was all to change. Union leaders erred in supposing that they could retain control over relatively independent unions in the face of a deliberate strategy by Perón to establish complete state control over labour. It is at this point, as di Tella (1981; also see Horowitz, 1983) has suggested, that the mobilization of previously non-participating sections of the working class may have some role in explaining the nature of Peronist control over the trade unions. In any case, the evidence suggests that with Peronism we are dealing with an attempt at an alliance between the working class and the state, an alliance in which the state gradually gained the upper hand and increasingly subordinated the working class to its control. By conflating the later subordination of the unions to the state (1947–55) with the period of genesis of the Perón–union alliance (1943–7), the classical account seriously understates the autonomy of working class action and, by describing this phenomenon as "populism" implicitly ascribes motives and orientations to the working class which were less than rational. There is no doubt that Perón's discourse, at least until 1952, was populist. However, to infer from Perón's massive support that this appeal was successful is to make a series of possibly unwarranted assumptions about working class motives.

Similar considerations apply to the Cárdenas period. Most analysts have argued that the Mexican unions were in a state of disarray when Cárdenas came to power in 1934 and that, in any case, the Mexican working class had a long tradition of state tutelage. In a bid to break away from the power behind the throne exercised by Plutarco Elías Calles, the new President actively mobilized working-class and peasant support on his behalf. The outcome of this was the reorganization of the dominant party along corporatist lines and the formation of the *Confederación de Trabajadores de México* (CTM) in 1936. Such an account is not, however, entirely accurate. Although the earlier union movement had been subordinated to the state through Luís Morones' CROM, there had always existed independent dissident unions. By 1933, together with breakaway elements from the CROM, the CGT and the Communist Party unions (the CSUM) were experiencing a period of growth and revived militancy. When Cárdenas was elected President, the union movement – after considerable initial hesitation – rallied to his support in the struggle against Calles. This switch in the position of organized labour was in part due to the change in Comintern tactics in 1935 towards a policy of popular fronts. Even when the CTM was formed, the Communists and independent leftists retained considerable support within the union movement as a whole, and it was only with the purges of 1948 that the union movement was definitively brought under state control. As in the case of Peronism, we have here an independent labour movement entering into alliance with the state and subsequently being subordinated to that state. The notions of a "mobilizable mass" or of a coalition involving a heteronomous working-class – crucial to the classical definition of populism – are inapplicable.

The empirical evidence, then, does not lend strong support to the notion that the governments of Cárdenas, Perón and Vargas can reasonably be described as "populist". In all cases the organizational features held to be defining characteristics of populism (in the classical version of the definition) are absent. In terms of the minimal definition of populism (i.e. a particular type of ideological appeal), both the Cárdenas and the Peronist governments may be labelled as "populist". The result, however, of using such a minimal definition, as Laclau has argued, is that a great many otherwise diverse movements, including Nazi Germany, must also be labelled "populist". The utility of the notion of "populism" as a description for a particular stage in the development of Latin American societies is, therefore, open to serious question.

Social Control

Populism and Social Control

Steve Stein

The fundamental distinction between the twentieth century and preceding ones in the history of Latin America has been the growth of the popular masses in size, in importance, and as a potential threat to the status quo. National populations have expanded spectacularly, communications networks from roads to radio waves have begun to crisscross nations, bringing new awareness to formerly isolated peoples. Huge numbers of men, women, and children have streamed into Latin American cities, which in turn have become ringed with squatter settlements that have arisen to house the new arrivals.

With conditions of unremitting poverty for most of the new masses and in the face of social and economic inequalities seemingly as eternal as they are profound, many observers have reasoned that established structures and institutions would be subjected to intolerable pressures; some predicted that violent revolutions must soon engulf the whole of Latin America. When Fidel Castro took power in Cuba in 1959 and less than three years later defiantly identified his nation with Marxism–Leninism, his movement seemed only the first manifestation of a larger revolutionary process. Latin America's move to the left appeared inevitable; the outstanding issues were how far, how fast, and by what means?

Yet events subsequent to the initiation of the Cuban Revolution have negated these predictions. The "enforced stability" of countries like Chile, Argentina, Uruguay, Bolivia, and even Mexico has confirmed a rightward trend in Latin America, with nations ruled by socially conservative and politically authoritarian regimes. And, upon re-examination, even when authoritarianism has not come to the fore the expected buildup of popular pressures for revolutionary change has not occurred.

Major questions remain as to how societies essentially oppressive of large portions of their populations have survived intact in most countries, or why, in other words, Latin America's ferment has not boiled over into more far-reaching transformations. Why have genuine popular revolutions been the exception rather than the rule in contemporary Latin America? This extremely complex question has no easy answers. For most Latin American nations any approximation about the absence of expected popular disruptive activity would have to stress the various mechanisms of social control that have long helped maintain the status quo throughout the continent.

With the upsurge of repressive governments in contemporary Latin America, physical repression clearly emerges as a major form of social control. At various times in Latin American history when groups and individuals have attempted to change existing structures or conditions they have been met with force. Repression has been exercised in many ways in modern Latin America, from the primitive *hacendado* who personally chastises "misbehaving" peons to the sophisticated military units trained in counter-insurgency and mob control who root out guerrilla bands or torture political prisoners. Despite the effectiveness of repression, to view Latin American countries historically as a series of armed camps is highly misleading. For mass social control, the general climate of fear created in all societies where extensive repression has taken place has proven more important than isolated repressive acts. When the powerful, whether individuals or governments, can and have shown that they will summarily punish signs of dissent from below, those with less power must think twice about manifesting or acting upon their dissatisfaction with the existing system.

By focusing on Latin America's present wave of political authoritarianism one might tend to exaggerate the long-term importance of physical coercion as a form of social control. At the same time that the high concentration of power in the hands of narrow élite groups has for centuries made varied forms of repression possible in Latin America, it has also helped spawn a system of patrimonial values and institutions that have strongly supported basic inequalities and worked to defuse mass protest. As an ideology originally produced by the semi-feudal colonial systems of Spain and Portugal in America and continually buttressed by official and folk Catholicism, patrimonialism has stressed hierarchy and organicism. To the powerful it has taught charity; to the powerless, dependence on the charitable. As an extensive network of reciprocal patron–client relationships between actors of highly disparate power and status, patrimonialism has provided a framework for vertical personal dependence by offering concrete channels, commonly in the form of ceremonial kinship, through which working-class men and women have "private" access to those above them. As an institutional framework for politics, patrimonialism has appeared in the form of party machines and corporatist governments in which elaborate patronage organs have exercised a seminal role in linking together the rulers and the ruled. In all its forms, patrimonialism has encouraged the popular masses to look upwards, to reject individual, group, or class protests of adverse conditions in favor of dependence on forces more powerful and influential than themselves for the amelioration of immediate or prolonged suffering.

In twentieth-century Latin America the single institution that best demonstrates the interaction of the various elements for social control is populism. Urban-based populist movements were a conspicuous feature of Latin American political life between the 1930s and the 1960s to the point that this whole era of the Continent's development has been called "populist". As James Malloy (1977, p. 7) has written, "in one manner or another all political forces from left to right have been forced to structure their behavior in response to the populist challenge. For good or ill, populism has, since its inception, been the major political force in Latin America". To appreciate the impact of populism as a political force one need only enumerate some of the most prominent movements commonly labeled as populist: Peronismo in Argentina; the administrations of Getúlio Vargas and João Goulart in Brazil; the Cárdenas government in Mexico; Peru's Apra party, the regime of Manuel Odría and the Acción Popular party of Fernando Belaunde Terry; the presidencies of Arturo Alessandri, Jorge Ibañez, and Eduardo Frei in Chile; the Acción Democrática and COPEI parties of Venezuela; the followers of Jorge Eliezer Gaitán and Gustavo Rojas Pinilla in Colombia; and the brief regime of Juan Bosch in the Dominican Republic. The term continues to be applied to certain contemporary institutions, notably the Peruvian military government in the 1968–75 years.

One immediately distinguishing feature of populist movements is that they have arisen at times of profound discontinuities in the political and social systems of their respective countries. Populism constituted a political response to the severe structural crisis that accompanied Latin America's transition from a series of agriculturally centered export societies in the nineteenth century to the rapidly urbanizing, massifying societies of the twentieth century. That crisis contributed to the political bankruptcy of a traditional élite political system which seemed incapable of neutralizing large concentrations of working-class people that had emerged in modernizing and increasingly complex nations.

In bridging the gap between orderly oligarchy and mass society, populist movements have constituted the principal political form of social control in modern Latin America. With their strikingly patrimonial style they have provided an effective political blend of the hierarchical, elitist modes of the past and the new currents of mass society. Easily outpacing and directly helping to undermine autonomous worker parties which sought to oppose lower-class interests to those of other social classes, populists built vertical coalitions whose very *raison d'être* was the integration of the masses into national politics without greatly disrupting the existing system. Through the distribution of material and symbolic concessions by a group of highly charismatic, personalist leaders, these movements succeeded, for a time at least, in bringing ever larger numbers of lower-class elements into politics while preventing them from "subverting" the process of national decision making. In the very act of providing a form of structured participation to working-class people, populist movements have functioned as an institutional restraint to those sectors of society with the greatest potential for social explosion, converting them instead into a new base of support for an established system in crisis.

Despite the continuous presence of populism in recent Latin American history, few movements have been the subject of extended analysis, and considerable confusion has arisen over an accepted definition of the phenomenon. Existing literature on populism often contains contrasting, even contradictory arguments regarding the nature of populist movements. Some observers stress the extreme dependence of lower-class groups on the higher-class leaders of populist coalitions and the ad hoc, transitory nature of populist organization. Others affirm that populism has involved genuine political mobilization, pointing to the establishment of mass-based parties and unions and to a new sensitivity of populist decision makers to the needs of those below them. Still others combine both views in the same analysis. Given such a diversity of approaches, should the term *populism* be retained in the Latin American political vocabulary?

Even within Latin America literal comparisons are difficult to draw between movements which have appeared in different contexts yet which are equally classified as populist. The prospects for mass recruitment by populists in post-World War II Peronist Argentina, for example, with its relatively high level of urban industrial employment were quite different from those that Apristas faced when they began seeking a following in post-World War I Peru, where only a minimal development of an industrial labor force had occurred. Mexico's or Bolivia's revolutions, which acted as preludes to populism, had no parallels in either Argentina or Peru. And the case of Brazil, where the foundation of populist institutions if not an actual movement under Getúlio Vargas in the 1930s seemed to predate rather than react to a social crisis, does not fit any of the above instances.

Given such diversity of circumstances, should the term *populism* be thrown out entirely as a proper classification for these movements? I think not, for at least three reasons. First, it has been commonly utilized both in and outside of Latin America to refer to movements like Peronism, Apra, the MNR, etc. Second, many of the disparities between populist experiences are attributable to the different historical contexts in which they emerge, that is, to the varying levels of national development or specific international economic and political conditions affecting single countries or Latin America as a whole. Third and most important, though these groupings are hardly identical, a number of basic commonalities exist among them. While a strict definition of populism in Latin America is risky as it surely would fail to contend with innumerable exceptions, a discussion of commonalities is a useful tool for understanding the movements' internal dynamics and their place in history as well as providing a start down the rocky road of conceptualization.

Most Latin American populist movements have exhibited several common traits: (1) the formation of electoral coalitions of upper, middle, and lower social sectors with potentially conflicting interests; (2) the appearance of a popularly exalted leader figure capable of appealing to the emotions of large portions of the citizenry; (3) an overriding concern for gaining control of the existing state for power and patronage without envisioning a major reordering of society; and (4) the explicit rejection of the notion of class conflict with the advocacy instead of the creation of a corporate-style state to rule the national family hierarchically. Each of these populist parallels is worth discussing at greater length.

Latin American populist parties have developed mainly in large cities, with their members drawn from all levels of the urban social pyramid. In terms of their composition, two sectors have habitually predominated: middle and upper middle-class groups that have assumed leadership positions and working-class groups that have formed a mass electoral base. In nearly all cases members of the middle sectors initiated the movements and then attracted the lower-class contingent into them. From the standpoint of middle sector populists, the impetus to form such coalitions stemmed from a complex set of factors. As a general rule, they were individuals discontented with their circumstances. Perhaps they were *nouveaux riches* still to be accepted by the reigning social élite. Or they may have been the offspring of the wealthy families of old who had been unable to keep up with the changing conditions of dependent development and had consequently fallen into relative poverty. Then again, they may have been counted among the increasing numbers of highly educated individuals for whom the existing system had not expanded fast enough to offer an occupational status to fit their aspirations. For all of these men, politics offered a way of improving their circumstances. Perceiving that the working classes were increasing in size and importance, it became obvious to prospective middle sector leaders that the masses were the indispensable basis for political legitimacy, especially on the backdrop of the decline of traditional élite rule. Furthermore, there was a pervasive feeling on the part of both working- and middle-class groups that acting independently would be less effective than working in alliance. Finally, it was to the decided advantage of many of the more privileged strata to direct the masses' integration into politics rather than risk a buildup of popular political frustration that could lead to a "revolutionary" situation.

One of the most striking facets of populist movements is that they derived their real cement from the presence of a strong leader with whom people could identify above all in emotional terms. These leaders have generally built their appeal by effectively translating a series of positive individual traits into a personal political style. Many have been ideal *"macho"* types; strong, authoritative, *simpático*. Their special leadership qualities have often seemed to make them particularly effective guides in times of distress, men with an unusual practical talent to achieve concrete ends. Successful populist leaders have not spontaneously arisen by virtue of their "exceptional qualities". Nor has their ascendance rested on traditionalist legitimacy or hereditary claim. Rather they have been men who, more than others, have consciously exploited their personalities and their surroundings to build a special rapport with large segments of the population.

The relationship between the leader and his mass followers has been the key to understanding populist political dynamics in Latin America. The most striking feature of that relationship has been its personalism. The working-class participant identified with his leader not in class or interest terms but as one individual to another, without institutional mediation. Most often assuming the role of protector along traditional patron–client lines, the leader was seen as a particularly benevolent man who *donated* his help, often before it was asked, because he intimately understood the needs of the masses. He was perceived as a generous father figure who could capably direct the political affairs of his less sophisticated children.

In large part, the success of the populist leader depended on his ability to extend this paternalistic relationship into the formation of a political movement. Or in other words, he used loyalty to and identification with his person for the creation of a vertical political coalition able to incorporate individuals from diverse sectors and levels of society.

The tutelary nature of populist politics has severely limited the possibilities of autonomous mass participation.

The subordinate position of the working-class populist suggests that at the same time these movements have contributed to the integration of specific sectors of the popular masses into the political system through their utilization of mass followings in the pursuit of power, they have also limited the impact of that integration by severely constricting the political activities of their followers to the realm of leadership support.

The goals of populist movements have been generally amorphous with the exception of the immediate and concrete enterprise of getting their leader into office. Once this goal was attained it was expected that the leader would employ his power, in a usually undefined way, to better the existence of his supporters. The role of the leader figure as the central uniting force of the populist movement implies that his political style may indeed have been more important than issue-oriented political platforms in the workings of populist politics. It follows that to understand populist dynamics one must concentrate more on the political symbols generated by the movement than on the stance a populist party might have taken on specific issues.

Where populist parties have elaborated explicit programs of action, they have seldom proposed a major transformation of economic and social structures. On the contrary, they have generally made little pretense of radically changing the shape or mixture of the existing social and economic pie, being content to seek a larger piece of that pie in order to provide top-down payoffs to their followings. Commonly in these movements the populist leader's appeal has revolved in part around his perceived ability to ameliorate the real discontents and grievances of his political clientele by distributing jobs, material rewards, and other payoffs. Whether this political clientelism resulted in any concrete redistribution of income by populist government towards the popular sectors depended in large part on prevailing economic conditions. Juan Perón, for instance, was able to raise workers' real wages perceptibly during the first years of his presidency (1946–50) by dipping into the large surpluses generated by Argentina's wartime trade. When those surpluses ran out and the economy began to decline, the workers' real wages followed suit. In Mexico under Lázaro Cárdenas the picture was even more spotty, with rises and falls in real wages occurring throughout his administration. More evident than any identifiable redistributive trend is that those changes in the status quo produced by populists in power have focused on the expansion of the administrative state, particularly its patronage mechanisms. In this respect populist governments have closely resembled the old political machines of large cities in the United States, stressing short-term, particularistic handouts and functioning as informal welfare agencies for their loyal supporters.

The content of populist ideology distinctly reflects these movements' reluctance to come to grips with the kinds of social costs required in a program of substantial national restructuring. The supreme importance of the personalist leader has militated against the generation of ideology, "in the sense of codified, rationally elaborated systems of thought which illuminate the causes of man's problems and describe paths of action for remedying them" (Evinson, 1977, p. 204). Nevertheless, these movements have made more or less coherent statements of their beliefs about the nature of society and the basis of political action. The recurring theme of those statements has been the simultaneous rejection of class antagonisms and fostering of social collaboration, not surprising in the light of the multi-class composition of populist coalitions. Equating the concepts of people, family, and nation, populists have denied the existence of irremediable conflicts between the social classes that make up the citizenry. Since all "the people" belonged to the same family, differences, inequalities, and competition between groups were said to be outweighed by their common interests. All potential discord was to be eliminated, or at least smoothed over, by the emphasis on the fraternal and filial over the more conflictive prospects implied by workers *v.* owners, peasants *v.* landlords, or consumers *v.* producers. The unity of the family was provided by the Nation, a construct within which all groups could find mutual identification. In the context of Latin America's long-standing condition of dependency, the populists' insistence on national solidarity also accentuated the idea of class harmony as imperative for the defense of the fatherland against threats of domination by the world's more developed countries.

Thus far my analysis of the creation and political course of populism in Latin America has emphasized the seminal role of the leader figure in everything from recruitment to ideology. But the leader's pre-eminence cannot take away from the fact that without the existence of certain objective conditions populist movements would never have evolved so extensively. The presence of an organizable mass as a source of populist support and legitimacy was a first necessity for the emergence of populism. Historically in Latin America this populist following has appeared in major cities as a result of substantial discontinuities in social structure touched off by rapid urbanization. Some agrarian forms of populism have developed, as in the cases of Mexico and Bolivia, where national revolutions forced the incorporation of large population sectors from the interior. But it was mainly in the major cities that the process of intense rural–urban migration led to the compact massification necessary for populist mobilization. That same massification brought to bear growing pressures on traditional institutions whose resilience determined to a great extent the point at which populist movements eventually arose. When the closed élite political systems born in the nineteenth century found themselves in crisis, whether the result of a loss of internal cohesion or of their inability to handle the expanding masses – in most instances a combination of both – a power vacuum originated at the national level. The decline of traditional politics provided a point of entry for populist movements.

Social scientists have for years tended to downplay the role of political parties in Latin American development. And they appear correct in asserting that for many countries parties have had only a minimal impact on the basic facts of social and economic life. But it would seem that in their oft-stated disappointment with and consequent belittling of these institutions for failing to either advance the growth of democracy or affect significant change, many have ignored the enormous importance of some parties – perhaps more movements than parties – as effective elements of co-optation. In the region's expanding mass societies, where the process of co-optation can no longer proceed on an individual level, populist organizations have repeatedly taken the place of person-to-person clientage by creating clientelist systems, and in some cases clientelist states, to act as decisive conservatizing agencies.

To summarize briefly, Latin American populist movements have been socially multi-class, structurally hierarchical and authoritarian, and ideologically nationalistic and semi-corporatist. Their central dynamic has been the personalistic particularistic ties between powerful leaders and dependent followers. They have appeared in conjunction with large-scale social massification generally brought on by rapid urbanization. They replaced traditional political élites whose ability and legitimacy to rule had been seriously eroded by the social discontinuities attendant on the massification process. The primary impact of most populist movements in terms of political development has been to increase popular participation while at the same time directing it into paternalistic forms that have served to bolster an exploitative status quo. Hence, populism has been a major force throughout modern Latin America for the reduction of pressures on established social structures, for the management of potential and real conflict, and for the maintenance of passive, non-revolutionary popular masses.

Many of the specific characteristics of individual populist movements have been influenced by the international context in which those movements arose, their political antedecents, and their social composition. In post-World War II Argentina, for instance, a rapid rate of industrialization and the existence of a large industrial working-class encouraged Peronismo to favor import substitution industrialization as an economic and political response to the growth of the masses. Fifteen years earlier, in a largely pre-industrial Peru with only a small industrial proletariat, industrialization was given relatively minor emphasis in the political programs of the two populist movements that vied for power. And in the Mexico of the 1930s, populist politicians faced the aftermath of what was in some areas of the country a peasant revolution by making agrarian reform a mainstay of their rule. Also, the final outcome of populism has depended on certain special conditions. When accepted by the powerful, populist movements have commonly promoted the political pacification outlined above. If, however, they have been repressed by inflexible ruling sectors, these movements have sometimes given rise to a greater radicalization of the working classes. This latter situation has been a particularly strong possibility in those countries where populist parties were dismantled after exercising some measure of political power. After Perón's ouster in 1955, the Peronista worker groups in Argentina moved increasingly leftward as their high expectations formed during the Perón presidency were ruthlessly quashed by successive military and civilian regimes. And in the Dominican Republic in 1965 the aroused followers of former populist President Juan Bosch battled US Marines in the streets of Santo Domingo in the name of their exiled leader. But even in those cases where "radical populists" have gained office and wielded their power to alter positively the lot of the popular masses, those advances have often been short-lived. Achieved through the beneficence of paternalistic leaders as opposed to autonomous effort or within an institutional framework, working-class populists generally have lacked the united resolve to preserve their attainments when the leader-figures departed the scene. A case in point is post-Cárdenas Mexico where government-sponsored unions for years have presided over a steady decline in the real wages of organized labor without significant protest. As Paul Drake (1978) has observed, populism "is likely to be more effective at mobilizing protests by the underprivileged than at securing their organized participation in national decision making or at delivering substantial benefits to them".

Ideology

Peronism in Historical and Comparative Perspective

Ernesto Laclau

To understand the specificity of the populist rupture, from which Peronism emerged, it is necessary to understand the nature of the previous dominant ideological system in Argentina, and its characteristic articulating principles.

In Argentina before the crisis of 1930 the hegemonic class in the power bloc was the landowning oligarchy, and the basic articulating principle of its ideological discourse was liberalism. The reasons for this are to be found in a double circumstance common to all Latin America from the mid-19th century to 1930: if on the one hand the full incorporation of the Latin American economies into the world market necessitated the constitution of nation-states, which created the conditions of political stability and institutional continuity necessary for economic activity to develop, on the other hand, political power remained in the hands of local landowning oligarchies. Now if in Europe these two constellations were contradictory – since the liberal state arose largely in the struggle against feudal particularism – in Latin America they were complementary, since it was the landowning oligarchies who were seeking to maximize their production for the world market and who, therefore, sought to organize a central state. The emergent Latin American political systems sought to give expression to this dual situation: centralized states were formed in which the representation of local oligarchical interests pre-dominated. The formula most adapted to this situation was a parliamentary liberal state with a strong predominance of the legislative over the executive. The degree of decentralization of power varied greatly in the different Latin American countries. In some cases the executive was reduced to a mere arbitrator – think of the old Republic in Brazil or of the constitutional reorganization of Chile after the revolution of 1891. In other cases, like Argentina, where the ensemble of power and wealth was concentrated in a relatively limited area of territory, the decentralization was less and the executive enjoyed greater autonomy. But in all cases, whatever the form, the central state was conceived as a federation of local oligarchies. Parliamentary power and landowning hegemony became synonymous in Latin America.

The very historical process of the implantation and consolidation of the oligarchic state in Argentina explains the specific connotative domain with which liberal ideology was articulated. *In the first place*, liberalism initially had little ability to absorb the democratic ideology of the masses and integrate it into its discourse. Democracy and liberalism were opposed to each other. Imperialist penetration and the incorporation of the country into the world market in the second half of the 19th century necessitated the dissolution of previous forms of social organization and pre-capitalist relations of production. This involved a violent and repressive policy towards the dominated classes. The struggles between the interior of the country and Buenos Aires, the Montonero Rebellion of the 1860s, the uprising of Lopez Jordan in the early 1870s, were episodes in this struggle through which the liberal state was imposed. *In the second place*, liberalism was throughout this period connotatively articulated to economic development and material progress as positive ideological values. (Note that this is not a necessary articulation: after 1930 liberalism and developmental ideology were definitively to lose any capacity for mutual implication.) *In the third place*, liberal ideology was articulated to "Europeanism", that is to say, to a defence of the European way of life and ideological values as representing "civilization". There was a radical rejection of popular national traditions, considered to be synonymous with backwardness, obscurantism and stagnation. *In the fourth place*, Argentinian liberalism was consequently anti-personalist. The emergence of national political leaders with direct contact to the masses, which could take precedence over the local political machines with their clientelistic base, was always viewed with mistrust by oligarchic power.

These four ideological elements, of which liberalism was the articulating principle, constituted the system of coordinates defining the ideological domain of oligarchic hegemony. Positivism was the philosophical influence which systematized these distinct elements into a homogeneous whole. Popular ideologies – that is to say, that complex of interpellations constituting popular subjects in their opposition to the power bloc – exhibited the opposite features. It was therefore natural for popular resistance to be expressed in anti-liberal ideologies; for it to be nationalist and anti-European; for it to defend popular traditions against the corrosive effects of capitalist expansion; for it to be, therefore, *personalist* and to lend support to popular leaders who represented a politics hostile to the *status quo*.

The problem is then: to what extent did the dominant oligarchic bloc during this period succeed in neutralizing its contradictions with "the people" and in articulating popular-democratic interpellations into liberal discourse? This is exactly the problem discussed by Macpherson (1975 pp. 10–11): to what extent was democracy liberalized and liberalism democratized? To what extent was the ideological discourse of the dominated classes neutralized and its protest maintained at the stage of *popular parties*, and to what extent did it become jacobinized and lead to populism?

The answer to this question leaves no room for doubt: the land-owning oligarchy was completely successful in neutralizing democratic interpellations, and in no case did popular resistance reach the point of populist radicalization. The reason lies in the success of the incorporation of Argentina into the world market and the great redistributive capacity of the land owning oligarchy during the expansive cycle of differential rent. I have discussed economic aspects of this process elsewhere. What is important for the present purpose is that two basic consequences followed from this process: (1) the power bloc was highly cohesive, since no sector of it either opposed the agricultural and livestock orientation of the country or was in a position to dispute oligarchic hegemony; (2) the redistributive capacity of the oligarchy enabled it to include nascent middle and working classes within its expansive cycle and to co-opt their respective leaderships into the power bloc. That is to say, there took place neither a crisis at the level of the power bloc nor a collapse of transformism – both of which are, as we have seen, pre-conditions for the emergence of populism.

What existed in this period in the way of a systematic attempt to create a coherent anti-liberal ideology was the very opposite of populism: it was a right-wing nationalism, emphasizing whatever was authoritarian, elitist, clerical and anti-popular in the anti-liberal tradition. This ideological trend reflected, from an opposite perspective, the very high degree of fusion between democracy and liberalism in Argentina: because its exponents despised democracy and the "radical scum", *and saw them as an inevitable result of liberalism*, they defended an authoritarian state which found its source of inspiration in Maurras. Later, on the eve of the 1930 revolution, a new element was incorporated into this tradition: *militarism* – for the role of the army was now to transform itself, in the theories of right-wing nationalism, into the historical agent of an anti-liberal revolution.

The most notable feature of the ideological structure of the working class of the epoch was that it made not the slightest effort to articulate popular-democratic interpellations into its political discourse. Three reasons combine to explain this phenomenon: (1) Due to the principally agrarian character of Argentina, the working class was confined to small enclaves in the big coastal cities. During this period workers were therefore marginal to the broader confrontations in which "the people" as such was constituted. (2) The working-class of this period was recruited overwhelmingly from European immigrants. This had two consequences: firstly, the fusion between their class ideology and the popular–democratic ideology of the country to which they had come, could not but be a slow process; secondly, those aspects of their new country which seemed most comprehensible in terms of their European experience were precisely the liberal state and its institutions. Hence their tendency to interpret any incomprehensible element in terms of European paradigms as the residue of a more primitive cultural stage which material progress, the expansion of the liberal state and the progressive Europeanization of the country, would finally eliminate. The condensation of these three elements – Europeanism, liberalism and material progress – into a unified ideological discourse reproduced the kind of articulation which, as we have seen, characterized oligarchic liberalism. (3) To this it is necessary to add the specific way in which the strictly populist element was integrated into this ideology. As we know, the most characteristic structural feature of socialist ideology at the end of the 19th century and the beginning of the 20th was class reductionism, which confined the proletariat to a pure-class ideology that viewed any popular interpellation as the ideology of a class enemy. Naturally this obstructed any form of socialist populism. *What is important is that this class reductionism, applied by the immigrant working class in Argentinian society, came to identify the diffuse democratic ideology of the masses as pre-capitalist residues which the progressive Europeanization of Latin American societies would finally eliminate.* Hence the close and increasing unity between hegemonic liberal ideology and socialist ideology.

An analysis of these ideological ensembles – which of course were not the only ones present – enables us to understand the system of ideological alternatives in pre-Peronist Argentina: an increasing unity between liberalism and democracy in the dominant discourse, a marginal authoritarian ideology, *both* anti-democratic *and* anti-liberal; class reductionism in working-class ideologies. These three aspects, *taken as a whole* expressed oligarchic hegemony.

The decade of the 1930s saw important changes in this ideological crystallization, presaging the decline of oligarchic hegemony and the emergence of new contradictions in the power bloc. In the first place, the power bloc experienced a deep crisis: the world depression led to a process of import-substituting industrialization that created new antagonisms between nascent industrial sectors and the land-owning oligarchy. Secondly, there was a crisis of transformism. As a result of the economic depression, the oligarchy could no longer tolerate the generous redistributive policies characteristic of the Radical governments, and had to ban the middle classes from access to political power. In order to do this, it established a parliamentary system based on electoral fraud. The democratic demands of the masses and the ideological symbols which represented them were less and less absorbed by the liberal regime, to a point where the scission between liberalism and democracy became complete.

The decade of the 1940s thus challenged Radicalism with the disarticulation of its tradition political discourse: it now had to opt for liberalism *or* democracy. The perfect synthesis between the two which had characterized Irigoyenism was dissolved.

Right-wing nationalism also underwent important changes. The implantation of an oligarchic liberal regime, which had buried their corporativist hopes, made right-wing nationalists think increasingly of an alternative military solution; the corrupt character of the conservative regime and its servile subjection to Great Britain led them to denounce imperialism; while the need to break imperialist links and to transform Argentina into an independent power led some nationalist sectors to demand an industrialist reorientation of the economy. These two new components of authoritarian national-ism – anti-imperialism and industrialism – implied a growing confrontation with oligarchic liberalism. It also presented right-wing nationalism in the 1940s with a clear alternative: either to accentuate the anti-imperialist and industrialist character of its programme which – given the increasing opposition to the latter on the part of the oligarchy   could only lead to a quest for support from a mass movement, and a consequent renunciation of the élitist and anti-popular elements in its ideology; or to retain those elements but at the cost of diluting the radicalism of the anti-oligarchic programme.

Finally, working-class ideologies also underwent a process of crisis in this period. Internal migrations had incorporated into industrial activity a new proletariat from the interior of the country, whose ideology was not based on the class reductionism of the old prole-tariat of European origin, but on a particular type of discourse in which popular–democratic interpellations were central. Mean-while industrialization was now transforming the role of the prolet-ariat in the political process; from being a relatively marginal sector –

as it had been in the Argentina of agriculture and livestock – it came to be the most concentrated social sector, and the backbone of all those forces interested in the expansion of the internal market and opposed to the continuation of oligarchic rule.

We can see, then, the extent to which the decline of oligarchic hegemony was reflected in a crisis of the dominant political discourse. This – as in any ideological crisis – consisted of a progressive disarticulation of the constitutive elements of that discourse. Liberalism and democracy ceased to be articulated; democratic interpellations could less and less be integrated into liberal ideology. For authoritarian nationalism, the possibility of a simultaneous anti-democratic and anti-liberal posture became increasingly problematic; there arose, particularly after anti-imperialist and industrial components had been incorporated into its discourse, a possibility previously non-existent: democratic authoritarianism. Finally, class reductionism and proletarian ideology ceased to be necessarily correlated and the possibility arose of a working-class populism. This disarticulation meant, among other things, that the power bloc's ability to neutralize its contradictions with the people had diminished; in the mirror of liberal ideological forms, now broken and murky, new and unforeseen combinations were possible. This was a breach opened at the ideological level, and with it the possibility of populism. For populism in Argentina was to consist precisely in a reunification of the ensemble of interpellations that expressed opposition to the oligarchic power bloc – democracy, industrialism, nationalism, anti-imperialism; their condensation into a new historical subject; and a development of their potential antagonism towards a confrontation with the principle of oligarchic discourse itself – liberalism. The whole effort of Peronist ideology at this stage was bent towards the aim of detracting liberalism from its last links with a democratic connotative domain and presenting it as a straightforward cover for oligarchic class interests. Peron declared, in a revealing speech [12 February 1946] during the electoral campaign: "I am, then, much more democratic than my adversaries, because I seek a real democracy whilst they defend an appearance of democracy, the external form of democracy. I seek a higher standard of living to protect the workers, even the poorest, from capitalist coercion; while the capitalists want the misery of the proletariat and its abandonment by the state to enable them to carry on their old tricks of buying and usurping ballot-papers . . . In conclusion: Argentina cannot stagnate in the somnolent rhythm of activity to which so many who have come and lived at her expense have condemned her; Argentina must recover the firm pulse of a healthy and clean-living youth. Argentina needs the young blood of the working-class."(see Peña, 1972, p. 10)

This attempt to distinguish between liberal ideological forms and real democracy dominated the whole of Peronist discourse. Look at this claim: "For the truth is this: in our country the real problem is not a conflict of 'liberty' against 'tyranny', Rosas against Urquiza, 'democracy' against 'totalitarianism'. What lies at the root of the Argentinian drama is a contest between 'social justice' and 'social injustice'. The fraud and corruption to which we have come is simply repugnant: it represents the greatest possible treachery against the working masses. The Communist and Socialist parties, which hypocritically present themselves as workers' parties whilst serving capitalist interests, have no qualms about carrying out electoral propaganda with the aid of cash handed over by the bosses . . . To use a word of which they are very fond, we could say that they are the true representatives of continuism: but a continuism in the policy of workers' slavery and misery"(Peña, p. 9).

It is not our intention to study the evolution of Peronism as a movement, since we wish only to point out how the strictly populist moment in its ideology was constituted. But in any case we should note certain significant facts. Firstly, if the strictly populist element in Peronist ideology was the radicalization of anti-liberal popular interpellations, Peronist discourse consisted not only of these interpellations but also of their articulation within a discourse which sought to confine any confrontation with the liberal oligarchy within limits imposed by the class project that defined the regime: the development of a national capitalism. Hence the antagonism of popular interpellations was permitted to develop only up to a certain point. Peronism sought to limit their explosive potential by presenting them always in articulation with other ideological elements which were anti-liberal, but were not popular – military or clerical ideology, for example. Secondly, if Peronism was undeniably successful in constituting a unified popular–democratic language at the national level, this was due to the social homogeneity of Argentina, exceptional in the Latin American context: lack of a peasantry, overwhelming predominance of the urban population, substantial development of the middle classes, development of trade-unionism throughout the country. Thirdly, the massive presence of the working class in Peronism gave it an exceptional ability to persist as a movement after the fall of the regime in 1955. Whilst other Latin American populist movements did not survive the fall of their regimes, the fact that Peronism was rooted in the working class enabled it to continue as a political force and even to extend its influence into the middle classes, radicalized in the last two decades as a result of the contradictions created by the expansion of monopoly capital. Fourthly, if the antagonism of popular interpellations developed only within the limits tolerated by the Peronist regime while it existed, it was impossible to impose these limits once Peronism was proscribed and started to reorganize its cadres from below. To the extent that Argentinian liberalism, restored in 1955, demonstrated its complete inability to absorb the democratic demands of the masses and resorted more and more to repression, the potential antagonism of popular interpellations could develop to the full. Popular ideology became increasingly anti-liberal, and in the most radicalized sectors increasingly fused with socialism. "National socialism" was the formula coined in the course of this process. The return to power of Peronism in 1973 proved that the change was irreversible: successive attempts to turn the clock back and to articulate popular–democratic ideology in a form assimilable by the bourgeoisie all failed. The regime of Isabel Peron collapsed into repressive chaos without having achieved any stable form of articulation between popular interpellations and bourgeois ideology.

The singularities of Peronism can be more clearly seen if we compare it with the other major populist experience in Latin America of this period, to which it is often likened: Varguism. Let us recall its origins. The Brazilian revolution of 1930 was the product of an accumulation of contradictions which, in the Argentinian experience, had been successively resolved. Inter-regional conflicts had ceased to be of decisive political importance in Argentina after the federalization of Buenos Aires in 1880. The accession to power of the middle classes with their redistributive projects within the agro-exporting system had occurred with the electoral victory of Radicalism in 1916. The new contradictions between the agrarian and industrial sectors only became important after 1930. We find in Brazil, on the contrary, that these contradictions had not been resolved and that they accumulated in the revolutionary process of 1930. Inter-regional conflicts, in which less influential states opposed the increasing predominance of São Paolo, played a decisive role in the alliance which carried Vargas to power. The Brazilian middle classes, due to the extreme regionalization of the country, had not been able to create a political party with national dimensions as Irigoyen had done in Argentina. The result was that they could not prevail against the political machines of the local oligarchies – witness the fruitless attempt of Ruy Barbosa in the presidential elections of 1910 – and no internal democratization of the liberal regime took place, as had occurred in Argentina or Uruguay. These frustrated liberal–democratic tendencies – perfectly represented by the Democratic Party in São Paulo – also played an important part in the revolution. Finally, the *tenentes* were of prime importance in the seizure of power – radicalized sectors of the army which sought to carry out a programme of democratization and modernization of the country, via a complete break from the oligarchical political system and the liberal state. It was in these sectors that we can find the first traces of a populist ideology.

Vargas had to manoeuvre amidst a highly complex coalition of contradictory forces, and only in 1937 was he able to establish full political control through the Estado Novo. But even then, and throughout his entire political career, Vargas was never able to become the leader of a unified and homogeneous movement like that of Perón: on the contrary, he was always to be an articulator of heterogeneous forces over which he established his personal control through a complicated system of alliances. If in the more industrialized areas of the country he was able to establish firm bases of independent support in the working class and vast sectors of the middle classes, in the interior of the country he had to seek his support from traditional political machines. This fragmentation of his political support was reflected in his inability to form a unified political party: the forces which rallied to him were organized in two parties. The Social Democratic Party (PSD) grouped the conservative forces in his coalition; the Brazilian Labour Party (PTB) was based on urban sectors, especially the working class, and attempted to develop a populist jacobinism. The dual face of Varguism – accentuated by the fact that the importance of the working class in Brazil was incomparably less than in Argentina – was reflected in an inadequate and fragmented populism, which did not succeed in constituting a political language of national dimensions. Varguism was never, therefore, genuinely populist. On the contrary, it oscillated in a pendular movement: at moments of stability its political language tended to be paternalistic and conservative; at moments of crisis on the other hand, when the conservative elements abandoned the coalition, it swung in a "populist" direction – that is to say, one that developed the antagonism latent in democratic interpellations. But precisely in these crises an elementary political logic imposed itself: the social bases for a populist discourse have always so far been insufficient in Brazil to guarantee political power. This was to be demonstrated by the fate of Vargas in 1945, 1954 and finally by the fall of Goulart in 1964.

We may conclude this section by indicating why populist experiences have been less frequent in Latin America in the last two decades. I think the reasons lie in the following factors:

(a) Transformism has entered into a definitive crisis. The capacity of Latin American power blocs restructured under the hegemony of monopoly capital to absorb the democratic demands of the masses is extremely limited. Its consequence is that today the dominant blocs do not even attempt to take popular initiatives – that is to say, to articulate popular – democratic ideology into the discourse of power. On the contrary, the new type of military regime in contemporary Latin America tends to rest more and more exclusively upon its repressive apparatuses. The result has been to throw into crisis not only the various populist experiences, but also the limited transformism needed for the minimal subsistence of a liberal regime. This also explains why despite the increasing authoritarianism of Latin American military regimes, they have not been able to assume in a fascist orientation for, as we have seen, the ideological base of fascism was a peculiar articulation of popular ideologies, whilst the orientation of current military dictatorships in Latin America seems to preclude *any* such articulation in its discourse.

(b) In the past a crisis of transformism led, as we have seen, to the creation of various forms of populism by dissident fractions of the dominant power bloc. Any development in this direction now, however, seems improbable for the following reasons. In the 1930s and 1940s, the power blocs were deeply divided due to the crisis of oligarchic hegemony, and at least a fraction of them was ready to move in the direction of a national independent capitalism and to seek mass support to this end.

Today, on the contrary, the nationalist experiences have collapsed and the power blocs have been reunited under the control of monopoly capital. In these conditions, there are no antagonisms sufficiently deep for a fraction of the power bloc to reorient in a populist direction. The second reason for thinking that a new populism of the dominant classes is unlikely is that, in the course of the experiences of the last twenty-five years, the Latin American masses have developed the antagonism inherent in democratic interpellations to a point where it is very difficult for any fraction of the bourgeoisie to absorb and neutralize them. This has led, in turn, to a consolidation of the power blocs and an accentuation of their repressive policies towards the dominated classes. For the latter, however, a new, long-term ideological perspective is opening up: to develop the radicalization of popular–democratic ideology and increasingly fuse it with socialist ideology, at a stage when the bourgeoisie as a whole is more and more engulfed in repression and barbarism.

Velasquismo: An Interpretation

Agustín Cueva

In the period immediately preceding the emergence of *velasquismo*, a lapse of barely ten years witnessed the failure of three formulas of domination in the country. Between 1922 and 1925 the mechanism assembled by the Guayaquil bourgeoisie crumbled (liberal formula). In 1931 the petit bourgeois Julian government collapsed, overtaken by the economic crisis and its own weakness (military–reformist formula). In 1932 the Sierra landholders' "solution" failed in the battlefield (conservative formula).

This led to a power vacuum, which was to last long and constitute fertile soil for *velasquismo* to flourish in. The agricultural exporting bourgeoisie could not reclaim political power by electoral means, given its unpopularity and the weakening undergone as a result of the economic crises of the 1920s and 1930s. Nor could it gain power by military means, since the army was openly opposed to so-called plutocratic domination. Even fraud, a caricaturesque substitute of "representative" democracy, which was itself a symptom of the bourgeoisie's political weakness, was no longer viable.

The Sierra landholders, who were in a position to win elections by mobilizing those sectors ideologically controlled by the clergy, could not assume power without the acquiescence of a hostile military, in addition to strong opposition from the Littoral bourgeoisie. At the time of the emergence of *velasquismo* the middle class was also unable to regain military control; its failure in 1931 had shown the impossibility of carrying forth a reformist policy in times of crisis. The paradox of a situation, which had not allowed for the concentration of all the elements of social power into one single class, became an impasse: economic dominance was in the hands of the agromercantile bourgeoisie; ideological hegemony belonged to the Sierra landholders; and the capability to "arbitrate" by force of arms was the privilege of an officialdom closely linked to the middle class.

This power crisis is the first element to be taken into account for an accurate analysis of the Velasco phenomenon, without overlooking the wider framework of the economic crisis of the 1930s. This is an important fact if one remembers that Velasco's most impressive victories coincided with similar situations: the apotheosis of 1944 occurred at a time of inflation, and the caudillo's devastating victory of 1960 came about at a critical point in the "banana economy".

Neither an economic nor an hegemonic crisis are enough to explain the birth and development of a "populist" solution such as *velasquismo*. The latter owed its success to the structure of a new socio-political context in Ecuadorian cities since the 1930s (a process related to the crisis of the system as a whole).

During his short tenure in office (1932–3), President Martínez Mera suffered constant harassment by the "populace, groups of youths, and the underworld", according to bourgeois historians. In the words of its leader, *velasquismo* began "in the Guayaquil marketplace and the modest numbers who deigned to listen to me in the Chamber of Representatives". Velasco won in 1933 owing to a dynamic campaign, streetwise and exalted, filled with promises to end privilege, factionalism, monopoly, and all the ills of the republic.

The question is why the reaction found it necessary to appear as a democratic and mass movement; that a president was forced to abandon his post due to popular harassment; and a political movement born in the marketplace was successful owing to the type of campaign described above. The answer is clear: the urban social composition underwent such change that traditional élite politics, with the old parties of notables, became obsolete. It became necessary to accept a new political form which, without threatening the interests of the dominant classes as a whole, would be appropriate to the new context. It was indispensable to take into account eventual reactions by the masses, which thereafter would no longer intervene, as before, only in extreme cases of insurrection or riot, but also in conventional "civil struggles". Fraud became risky, no less than decisions made at the level of the "small electoral club". A certain degree of popular participation in national politics had to be tolerated.

What masses were these and how had they developed in recent years? To answer this question we must touch upon the effects of the capitalist crisis of the 1930s in some sectors of Ecuadorian society. Let us begin with the peasants. Those of the Sierra the least affected, not only inasmuch as agriculture for domestic consumption suffered less than that for export, but also because the remuneration system predominant in the Andean area, in terms of natural resources or in kind, was less sensitive to market fluctuations. Yet some of those peasants, especially in Pichincha province which was more developed because it included the nation's capital, became unemployed and had to emigrate to Quito. This was also the fate of temporary workers, who according to a 1933 estimate numbered 300 thousand for the country as a whole. The Littoral peasant suffered immediate effects from the depression. "In times of normal and satisfactory business activity, cocoa producers usually paid a daily wage of 1.20 to 1.40 sucres, whereas at present not only has there been a decrease in the number of laborers employed in those cocoa *haciendas*, but their wages have also dropped to 1 sucre per day" (Carbo, 1953, p. 526).

Neither unemployment nor the drop in the standard of living caused serious conflicts in Littoral agriculture, but rather induced an exodus of the peasantry to Guayaquil, resulting in this city's growth, between 1929 and 1934, at an unprecedented annual rate of 5.33 per cent. During 1909–29 its population had grown at an annual rate of 1.45 per cent; and even later, in 1934–46, it grew at a rate of 2.5 per cent. Immigration to Quito and Guayaquil (the latter in particular) at a time when neither city was able to employ those groups amounted to a rural–urban shift in unemployment. This relieved "congestion" in the countryside, avoiding the crisis there, but the price was the emergence of new areas of tension in the cities due to the creation of a marginal urban sector. This sector was not exclusively formed by those immigrants, but also by the impact of depression upon popular urban sectors with no stable employment, regular wages, or basic legal guarantees such as the proletariat. Hawkers, unskilled construction workers, loaders, longshoremen, and small salesmen of occasional goods generally, which in Ecuador constitute the majority of the urban poor, either became unemployed or saw their income and range of activities considerably reduced.

The capitalist crisis of the 1930s and not a crisis of the traditional sector, as is commonly stated, created a lumpenproletariat with a specific political behavior. Initially the latter was politically controlled in Quito by those who had dominated the Andean population. The landholders and clergy had organized the *Compactación Obrera Nacional*. But this control slipped quickly away, the moment the lumpenproletariat adopted behaviors more in accordance with their socio-economic situation. If there were reasons why this marginal sector escaped the conservative control of the clergy, there were also reasons why they should not fall under the ideological rule of the liberal bourgeoisie. None of the dominant groups was able to impose its norms of political behavior upon the lumpenproletariat because the latter's marginality, which involved a displacement with regard to basic socio-economic roles foreseen by the system, also placed the lumpenproletariat outside of the mechanisms of social control previously used. The ex-*hacienda* laborer, for example, turned "free" salesman of occasional urban services, could no longer be ideologically dominated with the same ease as in his previous situation.

This social sector remained politically available and awaiting a "redeemer". Unsatisfied with their new fate, impoverished and psychologically forsaken, more unruly inasmuch as traditional social controls had little impact upon them, yet incapable of finding a revolutionary outlet – those lumpenproletarians could only impel a populism such as that inaugurated by Velasco.

In 1952, 1960, and 1968 Velasco rose to power owing to the overwhelming majority of votes obtained in three provinces: Guayas, Los Ríos, and El Oro, which have taken in the largest number of immigrants in the past few decades (e.g. during the intercensus period of 1950–62, they absorbed 80 per cent of the nation's total internal migrations). Velasco's stronghold in Guayaquil has been the suburbs, as election results show. In the other cities the caudillo has also been successful in areas whose residents' socio-economic status was comparable to that of the population in the port suburbs. Even in non-urban areas of the Sierra, Velasco votes derived from locations where structures had come into crisis, allowing the formation of social groups which escaped traditional controls, in small towns and villages.

The grass roots of *velasquismo* are in all those groups made marginal with the development of dependent capitalism, either by uprooting them from previously stable positions in the traditional sector, or by periodically displacing them from precarious "modern" positions.

The question remains as to why, the economic crisis of the 1930s having occurred, the traditional mechanisms of political domination broken, and urban mass conditions created, this was not put to use by the Marxist parties.

An objective hypothesis might be that Marxism in Ecuador never bloomed because the urban popular sectors had, during the period being analyzed, a distinctly lumpenproletarian composition. The latter group, given its socio-economic status, does not lend itself to revolutionary politicization – except in situations in which the proletariat had already created an appropriate context.

Let us examine some figures regarding the quantitative pre-dominance of the lumpenproletariat among the urban population. In Guayaquil, Ecuador's most industrialized city, the occupational breakdown for 1962 was as follows: professionals and technicians, 7.79 per cent of the economically active population; managers and administrators, 1 per cent; clerks, 13.06 per cent; salespeople, 20.57 per cent; fishermen, 8 per cent; farmers and woodcutters, 1.97 per cent; wood dealers and quarrymen, 0.16 per cent; truckers, drivers, railwaymen, 6.22 per cent; craftsmen, 3.79 per cent; workers and laborers, 9.67 per cent; domestics, 18.09 per cent; others, 9.68 per cent. The sum total of salespeople and domestics, mostly lumpenproletarians, amounts to almost 40 per cent of the economically active population; while workers and laborers do not even represent 10 per cent (aside from the fact that many laborers are in effect lumpenproletarians in terms of their work and living conditions).

If we accept the Marxist criterion that for revolutionary consciousness to prosper poverty is not enough, that the concurrence of other social conditions is indispensable, we must reach the conclusion that it would have been extremely difficult for Ecuador's lumpenproletariat to develop such a consciousness without the encouragement of another social class. But during the period under study the social agents of revolution were too weak to get it off the ground. The main one, the proletariat, has been incipient in nature from every point of view; and the peasantry, for reasons we shall examine further on, has been unable to move beyond a historical performance laced with heroic *journées* but lacking true revolutionary perspective. Under such unfavorable circumstances the lumpenproletariat became the grass roots for a caudillo-style, messianic, and paternalistic populism, perceived as a symbol of the "popular will" and of open challenge to more orthodox schemes of domination.

From an overall historical perspective *velasquismo* can only be seen for what it is: an element for the maintenance of bourgeois order, highly functional in terms of having allowed the system to absorb its more visible contradictions and overcome at the lowest cost its worst political crises, maintaining a "democratic" or at least "civil" façade with apparent popular consensus. From this point of view *velasquismo* has been the most viable solution for the dominant classes. Who, for example, would have been able to capitalize on and mystify the 1944 popular movement which reached insurrectional proportions, better than Velasco? Which of the men or parties would have been better able to first seize and then dissolve the anti-imperialist and anti-oligarchic sentiment of 1960?

Yet *velasquismo* has developed amidst a constant tension vis-á-vis the dominant groups and their corresponding political parties (conservative and liberal). This seems to be a contradiction. Yet one must consider that the actual historical answer tending to maintain the system is never in strict agreement with the particular scheme of domination of one single hegemonic group (a class or fraction thereof). That is why *velasquismo* acquires a complexity and appears as a non-orthodox, almost illegitimate formula of domination, insofar as it represents, on the one hand, a compromise among competing dominant groups, and on the other, the latter's adjustment to actual conditions for the exercise of power.

It is obvious, for example, that the dominant classes would have preferred not to have urban mass conditions such as those described, so as to continue exercising more comfortable formulas of political domination through the "classic" parties and the mechanism of fraud. Once urbanization accelerated – a process beyond these classes' control – they had no recourse but to adapt to the new situation, within which populist *caudillismo* was the lesser evil. These classes have witnessed with alarm the periodic rise in the nation's political temperature, including the psychological unleashing that Velasco gave vent to within the masses carrying the social malaise. Since such malaise existed independently of Velasco, the latter's symbolic banishment of the oligarchy was preferable to an actual one.

Both the liberal bourgeoisie and the conservative landholders would have preferred to govern directly without the mediation of a fickle caudillo. Yet lacking a party consensus and faced with difficulty of overcoming their own contradictions, they opted for allowing government by a third party – who offered advantages such as guarantees against the "hungry jaws of demagogy which claim to suppress private property, the only real belief of Ecuador's bourgeoisie", and such as having proclaimed himself both liberal and Christian, no less than being popular among the poorest and less submissive sectors of urban population. Originating from the Sierra and beloved by the Littoral lumpenproletariat, Velasco even turned out to be an ideal formula to overcome regional opposition. This is why Velasco, despite having intuitively and ably represented the interests of domination as a whole, maintained tense relations with each hegemonic group in particular. *Velasquismo* has only satisfied the aspirations of the speculative sector of the bourgeoisie, those who deal in foreign currency, goods of prime necessity, or benefit from shady business under the protection of the Velasco chaos. This sector has "financed" Velasco Ibarra's electoral campaigns.

Velasco's relations with the middle classes were complex. He had the support of some sectors, such as drivers, whose loyalty to the caudillo has been one of the remarkable phenomena of the last few decades. To a lesser degree, he had the support of small and medium-size business and craftsmen, when they escaped the traditional control of landholders and the clergy. Hardly interested in structural changes, although unsatisfied with oligarchic domination, these self-employed workers (petite bourgeoisie *per se*) have benefited from populist policies such as building of schools, medical facilities, roads, etc. Given their generally mestizo origins, they saw in *velasquismo* a way to symbolically challenge an aristocratizing society which had openly scorned them. The caudillo had restored, as he might have said, their sense of human dignity.

One need only peruse Velasco Ibarra's speeches to ascertain the extent to which demagogy has accomplished this spiritual healing: "Your profession is so sublime! How often have I thought if only I could be a driver! That is why, because your profession is so sublime, has so much of the sublime, that is why your soul is so independent and so free", he would tell drivers. He even instilled into them an ideological sense of greatness, encouraging their individualist tendencies derived from the experience of a non-team job ("that is the driver's psychology: the individual man, man alone, man technically alone, friend of the wind", etc.). Insidiously suggesting that by this very fact they were vastly superior to the working class, to "those poor men [who] are not persons, those poor men [who] are barely one-fourth individual being, one-tenth individual being". Velasco has psychologically redeemed these sectors from the double original sin of being manual workers and mestizos, which has complemented their technical and economic integration into "modern" society, in some cases (e.g. drivers), or its functional substitute on others (e.g. craftsmen).

Velasco's relations with the middle class *per se* (intellectuals and technobureaucracy) have been extremely tense. The same conditions that gave rise to *velasquismo* partly explain this phenomenon; the caudillo rose over the debris of Julian reformism inspired by the middle class. The latter therefore believed that Velasco had seized their rightful political leadership at the very time when they were beginning to acquire political personality and weight. Velasco had always openly expressed his contempt for Ecuador's intellectuals. He told educators, for example, that they were "slaves of the latest European book, the latest magazine, the latest bad translation; our ambition is to parade erudition, facts, and figures. Incapable of creating anything, we have been inept at teaching children to think and do so eventually on their own". Likewise, he told a journalist and writer that "it is unnecessary for an Ecuadorian mestizo to write long essays on Cervantes, Lope de Vega, or Hurtado de Mendoza, since truly erudite Spanish thinkers have already covered these subjects in depth".

Ecuador's middle-class intelligentsia, alluded to with the term *mestizo*, was all the more sensitive to this kind of attack because they lacked self-assurance, given their recent formation (mostly intellectuals of popular extraction, promoted as a result of the liberal revolution). Since they had already "redeemed" themselves from their condition as mestizos, owing to intellectual pursuits and the ideology of "mesticization" as the "essence" of national culture, Velasco was not even useful to them in the sense that he was for the petite bourgeoisie. On the contrary, he became a drawback to the extent that his populism broadened the gap between elitist ideologies and popular idiosyncracies.

It is also easy to infer from the above the contempt of a traditionally educated man such as Velasco for the upwardly mobile mestizo intellectual. Velasco has said that "the rural Indian does no wrong. He feeds the nation with his work. But the urban Indian is highly dangerous. He has read books". This does not express contempt for the people, as his adversaries have stated, but his aversion toward the country's new intellectual class. A strong aversion, to the extent that flaws and all, this group has at least attempted to think for itself and establish its independence, something unacceptable for a caudillo who had never admired in others any virtue but loyalty toward himself.

For technobureaucracy, the Velasco chaos was a constant nightmare. Periodic and indiscriminate dismissal of civil servants, the unforseeable whims that determine sanctions and raises, the caudillo's lack of confidence in bureaucracy and technical advice, have all kept this sector in a state of permanent anxiety. As the technobureaucracy improved its situation (mainly as a result of the banana boom), its anti-Velasco feelings grew. Anxious to achieve security, in 1960 it preferred the developmental alternative of Galo Plaza; in 1963 it felt a military technocratic government to be more "reasonable" than Velasco's ambiguous populism. And in 1968, when federated civil servants were determined to move from the traditional individualist–clientelist attitude to a clear organized-group behavior, there was an open clash with Velasco.

Nevertheless, *velasquismo* was useful for the middle-class unemployed, aspiring to latch on to bureaucracy via opportunism. Owing to his famous "sweepings" of employees, Velasco allowed these clients to come into public administration, thus creating a curious mechanism of bureaucratic alternation which may well have been another – albeit precarious – element of equilibrium for the system. Thus *velasquismo* functioned as the political movement of the marginal sectors.

The fact that Velasco the candidate moved in a different orbit than Velasco the ruler explains the unusual phenomenon that an idol of the multitudes should have been overthrown so many times, with relative ease and with his partisans doing nothing to defend him. His theoretical and programmatic ambiguity, so useful during campaigns when it allowed him to agglutinate the most heterogeneous elements around an abstract ideal upon which everyone projected hopes and interests, turned against him in the course of government.

First, the predominantly popular base disintegrated after "victory" due to the lumpenproletariat's lack of organization and goals. Velasco himself wrote, after his first downfall: "No president can remain in power if, aside from bureaucratic elements, he does not have the support of some coherent social group, aware of the goal and the road". Second, opportunism soon appeared, especially among those middle sectors which had supported him: "To a great extent, by seeking support among these kinds of sectors (which have an obviously opportunistic and ambiguous attitude and an immediate perspective) he frustrated the possibility of remaining in power". Ultimately Velasco was no longer faced with "his" people but with society's organized groups.

The initial part of his administrations have always been a colorless moment of great anticipation. All groups requested definitions and exerted pressure to get a piece of the pie. At first the caudillo resisted, trying to remain above particular interests. He sought to unite all Ecuadorians and maintain a sufficiently equivocal verbal policy so as not to alarm the oligarchies nor disillusion the people. But this satisfied no one. Pressures increased and the situation began to deteriorate at all levels when, tired of words, a few organized groups such as labor unions adopted concrete postures while hegemonic sectors, exasperated by what they considered Velasco's indecisions and fickleness, presented him with an ultimatum. Velasco then had to descend from Olympus and decide on one of the contenders. He ended up with an open pact, be it with the conservatives or liberals (in any case with some hegemonic group, since Velasco was no revolutionary), or by seeking the support of the army and even attempting a coup. In so doing, he sent the opposition not only to the organized sectors among the people, but also to those factions of the dominant class which had remained outside of the "pact".

Leftist opposition manifested itself through student demonstrations and workers' strikes. Tension mounted. The class or fraction thereof with which the caudillo had struck a deal then evaluated the situation: If Velasco, who had been accepted as an instrument for the people's manipulation, lost that role and became instead a "disturbing" element, he would then be overthrown from power and the dominant class as a whole would seek the most "reasonable" solution. The lumpenproletariat, with which the caudillo had in the meantime lost contact, abandoned him with all the more ease inasmuch as the messianic echoes of his campaign speeches had long been silenced. Alone and forlorn, the "apostle" of the multitudes had to resign himself to step down.

Ecuador's intellectuals and politicians have repeatedly expressed their surprise at Velasco's ideological chaos. As early as 1929 the latter wrote that "the entrails of society harbor the most diverse tendencies" and "between those tendencies there is no real contradiction". A few months before assuming the presidency for the first time he stated that his "ideology is definite: liberal-individualist", but "if socialism has acceptable, beneficial issues, they should be utilized. If conservatism has something that might be convenient, it should not be rejected. Nor should acceptable statements of communism be excluded".

Faithful to these precepts, Velasco has had no compunction in proclaiming himself both liberal and Catholic, even emphasizing his admiration for socialism. "This is *velasquismo*: a liberal doctrine, a Christian doctrine, a socialist doctrine", he said in a speech on 23 November 1960. The surprising and troubling fact is not that Velasco's mind should have concocted this amalgam, but rather the social phenomenon that such an ideological admixture should have been so successful.

To understand this phenomenon it is necessary to go back to a fundamental point: Latin America, and in this particular case Ecuador, is a dependent society, whose ideological superstructure is characterized, on the one hand, by its "exotic" origins (in the sense that it has not emerged from the Latin American socio-historical formation), and on the other, by the permanent tension involved in the need to adapt those ideological elements to the particular Latin American context. This determines a relaxation of the internal cohesion of theoretical ideologies (or a sometimes total redefinition of the elements of pragmatic ideologies) as well as the loss of many implications or connotations originally present in the social context which produced them.

Velasco seemed to have understood or at least felt this and wisely combined (as a function of domination) the ideological elements accumulated in society. From Catholicism he took the perceptive models and symbols, which respectively became the ideological matrix and semantic repertory of his political message. From liberalism he retained an abstract aspiration for liberty, and from socialism a no less abstract yearning for social justice. By reducing them to equivocal principles, to merely formal sentiments, he had no difficulty in making them compatible. After all, there need not be a necessary exclusion among a Catholicism defined as "balsam for pain and inextinguishable light in the darkness of human destiny", a liberalism "reduced" (sic) to "respecting man's conscience and personality", and a socialism which would be nothing but "a feeling of love, of generosity, of magnanimity", according to Velasco Ibarra.

Aware of the fact that the institutional power of the church was waning, Velasco did not attempt, like the conservative politicians, to seek support within the clergy. On the contrary, from the beginning of his career he declared himself to be against church intervention in the affairs of the state. But he was also astute enough to understand that the secular process of Catholic colonization had left indelible ideological marks in the population. His cleverness consisted in not resorting to the visible clergy, exerting little authority on the marginal population – especially along the Littoral – but rather to the invisible clergy which remained within the consciousness of this social sector.

An examination of Velasco's speeches shows that he never focused on problems in socio-political terms, but rather from a strictly religious and moral perspective. Aside from his multiple statements to the effect that Ecuador's problem was moral (which he kept repeating during forty years of political activity), his "doctrine" consisted in presenting the nation's dilemma as resulting from the confrontation between "good" and "evil". As early as 1929 he invited Ecuadorians to "consecrate themselves to the struggle against evil". In 1969 he had not modified his views by one iota: "Persian philosophers explained the tragic human agitation between murky depths and luminous heights as the struggle between Good and Evil, both substantively personified. The battle was to be decided in favor of Good owing to cooperation among men. Maybe this metaphysical-poetic version, as all poetry, contains much truth".

That such a clearly religious vision should have been transposed

to the political arena and been accepted and wildly applauded by
large sectors of the population, can only be explained by the fact that
the latter were strongly influenced by Catholic models of perception,
which have even served to redefine those "liberal and socialist
principles" incorporated into Velasco's amalgam.

Here, then, are the most relevant aspects of *velasquismo*, a phenomenon which has imposed its original mark upon Ecuadorian
politics during four decades. As we have tried to show throughout
this study, it is not a simple phenomenon of caudillismo reducible to
the leader's personality, but a complex process deeply rooted in the
historical singularity of Ecuador's social development. This particularism must be defined mainly by the condition of dependency,
without which it is impossible to explain a political phenomenon
which, like *velasquismo*, emerged at the time when the crisis of the
world capitalist system shook the fragile structure of a society
articulated to that system through its agroexporting sector, predominant in the formation of Ecuador. That crisis, which implied a
temporary slackening of ties with the metropolis, did not provide
Ecuador with the opportunity for industrial take-off, but rather
emphasized certain specific internal contradictions originated in the
profound structural heterogeneity of Ecuadorian society.

Given the importance of servile modes of production at the
national level, the social forces rooted in that re-emerged to the
forefront of the political stage under the protection of the crisis of
1929. *Velasquismo* was not born as a formula of arbitration between
the industrial bourgeoisie and the agroexporting oligarchy, nor as an
instrument of manipulation of the emerging proletariat – as was the
case for Argentine and Brazilian populism – but as a formula of
transaction between an agromercantile bourgeoisie in crisis and a
still powerful landholding aristocracy, and, on another level, as a
means of manipulation of predominantly lumpenproletarian masses.
Later, *velasquismo* further developed as a factor of precarious equilibrium of the interests of a weak and splintered dominant class, as
well as a complex expression of the phenomenon of marginality.
This was an inevitable consequence of the nature and crisis of the
predominant capitalist mode of production, and of its conflictive
articulation with world economy and national precapitalist sectors.
Even at an ideological level, *velasquismo* represented a combination of
heterogeneous structural elements amalgamated under the fires of a
mystifying demagogy. Bound to a precise moment in Ecuador's
history, it is therefore natural that *velasquismo* should have ended for
reasons beyond its leader's personal exhaustion. This subtle form of

perpetuation of political–ideological conditions of domination at the lowest social cost, ended not only as a function of a growing awareness by the masses, but also due to the extinction of the historical phase that originated it.

Part V

Agrarian Structure and Change

Introduction

In the last decade the focus of the analysis of the Latin American agrarian structure has changed. Part V shows clearly this new tendency. All the authors take as a point of departure the expansion of capitalism in the countryside based on the introduction of new technology, the transformation of the demand for agrarian products, the impact of modernizing policies of the state and the rapid growth of wage labour. *Goodman* and *Redclift* point out that it is necessary to examine carefully different cases in order to depict dissimilar paths. The Brazilian case presented by *Brandão Lopes* illustrates a "traditional" capitalist development with the constitution of proletarianized labour, the mechanization of the labour process and the increase in the organic composition of capital. In the Northeast of Brazil the exploitation of a fully proletarian labour force was accompanied by an expansion of peasant production due to an increase of regional urban food demand that the capitalist sector cannot satisfy. The same can be said in relation to Mexico, Ecuador and Peru. Nevertheless in all these countries and in different epochs agrarian reforms program were launched. These reforms aimed to solve the acute problems created by an uneven land tenancy system but in reality functioned as an incentive to capitalist development. In the case of Mexico and Ecuador the consolidation of efficient private capitalist enterprises is mentioned in the articles by *Warman* and *Archetti* and *Stölen*. This last article shows concomitantly that the analysis of new social factors is of special importance in order to characterize the emergent social structure. In Latin America the expansion of capitalism is related to the transformation of traditional landlords and the impact of agribusiness but, in parallel, a new rural bourgeoisie has emerged. The mobility of land, labour and capital has produced in different countries and regions a complexity of social actors and strategies that the different articles try to grasp. *Kay's* article on Peru argues that in the case of the most radical agrarian reform the main consequence has been the consolidation of a state capitalist sector. The landlords were eliminated, but not capitalism.

Capitalism in the agrarian sector co-exists with different peasantries. The peasants have resisted, adapted and accommodated to this new pattern of agrarian change. In this process different strategies were followed. *Warman* argues that in the case of Mexico the response to capitalism has been a rapid demographic expansion. For the Mexican peasants the most rational behaviour against capitalism is to intensify the work in the small plots and in order to decrease the impact of the drudgery of labour force the rapid growth of their families is the best solution. However, the communities have resisted through different adaptive strategies. *Archetti* and *Stölen's* study in Ecuador can be easily generalized at the level of the main findings: peasants units of production are viable only if their members can sell their labour force in the capitalist sector. Finally, *Deere* presents the impact of capitalism on woman.

As a general comment we can say that the existing agrarian structure is a combination of efficient large and middle size capitalist enterprises, viable family farms and a vast amount of peasant–proletarian units of production that feed the different capitalist rural and urban labour markets. The empirical combination and the weight of each group varies greatly. The main aim of Part V is precisely to indicate the variation, and to point at the crucial variables that must be taken into account.

Perhaps the most comprehensive recent account of trends in Latin America's agrarian structure, focussing on the role of the state and the increasing marginalization of peasant farming is de Janvry (1981). Goodman and Redclift (1981) provides essential complementary reading with a summary of the debates on the theories of capitalist transition in agriculture and case studies taken from Brazil and Mexico of the impact of government planning on agriculture and of the strategies adopted by both peasant and capitalist farmers in the context of urbanization and economic centralization. The collection of essays edited Duncan and Rutledge (1977) is a very useful overview, containing rich historical material, of the changing relationships between estate owners and peasantry throughout Latin America. A collection that provides a sense of the complexity of the peasant's situation in the contemporary period is that edited by Lehmann (1982). Some of the articles in this collection also provide detailed anthropological accounts of the nature of Latin American Indian society and the varying impact of capitalist penetration on that society. The reader should also consult Grindle (1986) for an overview, and case studies of rural communities or of regional agrarian structures. One recent example is Mallon (1983). Another is Zamosc (1986).

Peasant–Proletarian Transition

Paths of Transition

David Goodman and Michael Redclift

Before considering in detail the way that estates and peasant communities change under the impact of capitalist economic relations, we need to consider the factors which give rise to these relations. Among the most important are changes in demand for food, in part prompted by urbanization in the peripheral country and also, in some cases, by the necessity to produce foodstuffs at a price which will make them competitive with imported produce. These changes in demand reinforce, in turn, technological developments in agriculture – both biological technologies which are "land saving" and mechanical technologies which make savings in labour. In addition, according to the "unequal exchange" theorists, it is in the interest of the industrial bourgeoisie that wage costs are low, in order that they should derive advantage from their insertion within the international market, where (in more developed countries) they are higher.

Evaluating the Empirical Evidence of Transition

We argue that different forms of capitalist penetration – direct or real subsumption through the process of production, and indirect control of production relations through markets – have different implications for agrarian structure. In practice, whether transition is effected through "internal proletarianization" or "external proletarianization", both forms of penetration can prove to be important. Thus changes in the market can herald a process of conversion to wage labour within the estate system; they can prompt changes in the internal organization of the agricultural enterprise. By the same token the creation of "new" enterprises from within the estate can lead to an increase in the direct employment of wage labourers. The empirical complexities of each case are such that a discussion of individual cases is left for a later section of this discussion, where material is presented from Peru, Ecuador and Chile. For the moment we are principally concerned with the evaluation of empirical evidence for more general processes, and the need for caution in interpreting it.

Our first hypothesis is that introduction of wage labour marks a process of specialization, through which the "polyvalency" or multiple role playing which characterizes the peasantry is replaced by fewer roles that are more clearly class-based. This hypothesis encounters two principal difficulties – first, the survival of wage labour needs to be related to different forms of surplus appropriation in specific cases, and second, wage labour is frequently an additional role which complements the traditional activities of self-provisioning carried out by the peasantry.

The second hypothesis is that the penetration of capital leads to a convergence between the former estate and peasant smallholder systems of production. Following the Leninist models it is suggested that the outcome of increasing peasant differentiation is similar to that of internal proletarianization. Such a hypothesis encounters difficulties in many parts of Latin America where peasant smallholders living in communities possess corporately owned resources. It is difficult to generalize concerning the likelihood that the penetration of capital will be associated with a convergence between estate and smallholder systems. The peasant economy is sometimes looked upon as "structurally dependent" on the estate because of the latter's superior economic power.

However, in different circumstances, new forms of entrepreneurship, which require a reorganization of the estate enterprise, more specialization of production and a closer relationship with the market, might force apart the peasant and estate economies, making them more complementary but less dependent. In a reference to his own anthropological fieldwork in the Ecuadorian Sierra, Archetti shows how the development of a dairy economy, by requiring permanent access to fodder crops, as well as more capital investment, has forced apart the "parallel economies" of the *huasipunguero* (service tenant) and the landlord (see *Archetti and Stölen*, below). Changes within the landlord's enterprise precipitated changes in the size of landholdings, which in turn put pressure on the economic viability of the peasant holdings. After 1970 the Ecuadorian state helped reinforce these changes by making credit much more easily available to commercial milk producers. A similar process, in another part of the Ecuadorian Sierra, is mentioned by Preston and Redclift (1979), in which the developing milk-economy forced landowners to reduce the number of men who worked for them, and introduce women into the labour force as milkmaids.

The third hypothesis which can be advanced in explanation of empirical changes in agrarian structure concerns the proliferation of *minifundia* in many parts of highland Latin America. It is sometimes suggested that an increase in the number of smallholders in existing areas of *minifundia* is a prelude to eventual landlessness. The lack of access to additional land forces peasant families to subdivide exist- ing holdings in an effort to provide for new family members. This process of "agricultural involution" is similar to that which Geertz (1971) described for rural Java. There can be little doubt that the peasantry accommodates to resource ratio decline by subdividing holdings. However, it is less clear that this inevitably leads to landlessness.

The view that increased use of wage labour is an outcome of resource-ratio decline in areas of *minifundia* is well established. This was one of the principal arguments of the Inter-American Com- mittee for Agricultural Development (CIDA) studies undertaken in the 1960s (Barraclough, 1973). However, few empirical studies of resource depletion in Latin American agriculture have adequately considered the role of capital. It is difficult, therefore, to establish which is the independent and which the dependent variable.

The Development of "Peasant" Capitalism

Recent research undertaken in the Central Sierra of Peru, and in other parts of the Andes, suggests that we should also consider another aspect of capitalist market relations. This is the emergence of small-scale entrepreneurs in areas of smallholder agriculture (*minifundia*), where proximity to urban markets and freedom from the coercion of large landlords, has enabled families of middle peasants to accumulate capital. In areas such as the Mantaro valley we can identify families of peasant origin who both accumulate capital and employ wage labour on a small scale. This interest in the reinvest- ment of surpluses, in buying land and acquiring more capital goods, does not make these entrepreneurs into fully-fledged capitalist farmers. According to some interpretations, such enterprises are neither properly "peasant" nor properly "capitalist". The small- scale entrepreneurs of the Mantaro valley are able to develop their enterprises through the use they make of family labour and regional networks. In doing so they come to occupy an important structural position within the regional economy.

The peculiar characteristics of "peasant" capitalism in *minifundia* communities deserve close attention. Roberts states that this "local- level activity":

is itself part of, and a dynamic part of, the contemporary capitalist transformation of Latin American countries. I do not view this transformation as mechanically dependent upon external capitalist stimuli; it is basically an internal process of transformation that, while often initiated by foreign capital, has its own logic and power of transformation (Roberts, 1974, p. 6).

The development of family enterprises, many of which do not confine themselves to agriculture, is possible because of their flexibility and resourcefulness. Such enterprises are able to use very small surpluses to create new opportunities, and sell their products to even the poorest peasant. By diversifying into a number of activities, and operating in a number of different ecological zones, the disadvantages of their small scale and inadequate capital can be turned into advantages: "survival depends upon combining and co-ordinating existing and new resources; this permitted a sufficient specialization to rise productivity, but not enough specialization to encourage centralization" (Roberts, 1974, p. 22). Such enterprises may not develop into large-scale concerns, but it would be wrong to assume that they play no part in determining the form that economic and social development take in a region. Indeed, it would be more accurate to say that social differentiation, and the class structure, are the outcome of both the structural limitations placed on such enterprises and the development imperatives created by the enterprises themselves. A dialectical process, in fact, which serves to transform the structures which provide the original momentum.

State-induced Transitions: Technological Projects

The antecedents of the "technological" approach to rural development in Latin America are to be found in the "modernization" theory propounded in the early 1960s. Before considering the contemporary contribution of new agricultural technologies to the agrarian transition, it is important to review the modernization thesis briefly.

The modernization thesis was that the agricultural economy of Latin America would experience development if private land ownership increased, and this were combined with improved access to modern inputs and technologies. Land reform was conceived in terms of juridical changes in the status of small producers, offering titles to tenant farmers, and thus enabling them to obtain agricultural credit. The traditional highland *hacienda* was expected to be transformed into a modern capitalist enterprise once incentives existed for landowners. These incentives were to be provided by opening up their land to the market. Once this was effected they would cease to be *rentiers* and would be transformed into modern entrepreneurs.

Modernization through land distribution was nowhere attempted on a large scale. Landlords, powerful at both regional and national levels, opposed any tampering with existing tenurial relationships. Instead of a radical redistribution of landholdings, successive governments fell back on colonization schemes and the adoption of technologies which would raise aggregate production. The significance of traditional forms of labour exaction was never fully grasped by those who wished to reform them. Nor was it recognized that the land distribution was likely to perpetuate existing divisions and open the way for greater differentiation, as those who were better able to take advantage of market conditions exerted economic pressure on those who were not. In retrospect it is easy to see that rural underdevelopment would not have been attributed to the absence of capitalism if the liberal reformers had been able to recognize the diversity of forms which the penetration of capital had taken.

The arrival of agricultural technologies which could produce dramatic increases in production without recourse to policies of land distribution effectively shifted the balance of advantages even further towards the large landowning groups. In the view of most "modernization" theorists, structural changes in land ownership, and capital investment in agriculture, were a pre-requisite for agricultural growth and increase in production. To some extent the high-yielding varieties of rice and wheat offered a way around the political difficulties which agrarian reform presented. Structural changes were certainly an outcome of the introduction of new technologies in agriculture, but they no longer needed to be legislated for in advance. According to the United Nations, since the 1960s large-scale agricultural enterprises:

> have assumed more importance for the balance of payments and foreign exchange position (of Less Developed Countries). These circumstances have contributed in putting a brake on plans to reform land tenure structures. It is argued that any modification in land tenure would put in jeopardy a country's capacity to honour its international commercial responsibilities (CEPAL–FAO, 1978, p. 1396).

State-induced Transitions: Agrarian Reforms

The circumstances of state involvement differ markedly, and we shall confine ourselves to situations in which the state has attempted to reverse existing trends in the agrarian sector, or where it has established institutions which enable it to accelerate some processes and retard others through the direct management of land and agricultural enterprises.

It would be a mistake to assume that the changes introduced through agrarian reforms are necessarily the outcome of purposeful and preconceived policy. Caballero has argued that the Peruvian military had few clear ideas as to the form that agrarian reform would take – what ideas they had were elaborated in the course of the reform (Caballero, 1976, p. 85). Similarly, Harding (1975) has suggested that popular reaction to the military's policies, at least on the north coast of Peru, was instrumental in changing some of these policies. Elsewhere it has been argued (Redclift, 1978) that pro-duction shortages and peasant unrest provided an opportunity for the Ecuadorian state to introduce an agrarian reform, in the rice zone, which took much of its inspiration from local-level changes effected by the Agency of International Development (AID).

In conclusion, we can make a number of observations about "state-induced" transitions, drawing on the evidence we have pre-sented from Chile, Peru and Ecuador. First, it is clear that the state has sought to establish new structures of production and distri-bution which allow it to increase agricultural production and control the marketing and distribution of this production much more closely. In Chile under Popular Unity this process might have benefited poorer groups, including much of the urban population. The areas of *minifundia*, which feed most of the rural population (and much of the urban population) have been ignored altogether or, as in the case of highland Ecuador, they have been opened up to market forces by the government's changes in land tenure (Preston and Redclift, 1979).

Second, local-level cooperatives introduced or developed by the state – *asentamientos* and CERAS in Chile, CAPs and SAIS in Peru, *empresas agrícolas* in Ecuador – have revealed the diversity of existing exchange relations between different segments of the rural class structure. Each of these experiences of agrarian reform has broken the power of traditional landowning classes, only to replace the power that they derived from land-tenure institutions and market linkages with a new political bargaining process from which the poorest are unlikely to benefit. A "tug-of-war" develops between the privileged members of the reformed sector and the state bureaucracy over the use that is made of the surplus appropriated from the non-members. Advanced agricultural technologies, and the avail-ability of foreign exchange, assist technical personnel to maintain political control. In the guise of "statist" innovations, market forces are strengthened rather than weakened, a small number of peasant families consolidate their position under government patronage and the remainder become transformed into a rural proletariat permanently alienated from the land.

Brazil and Mexico: Case Studies in Transition

Mexico and Brazil can be usefully compared from several standpoints. In both countries the agricultural sector has contributed significantly to the post-war import-substituting industrialization process but without completing the "classic" trajectory of agrarian transition. Small commodity production remains an important component of these rural social structures and is characterized by a variety of production relations. Agricultural development strategies also reveal important similarities, notably the use of strongly discriminatory policies to promote the technological modernization of large-scale production units. The following discussion examines the structural effects of state intervention in some detail, emphasizing how the design of post-war rural development strategies has been dictated largely by the imperatives of urban–industrial capital accumulation. In both Brazil and Mexico, the state has played an active role in recent agrarian change by promoting and directing the penetration of agricultural production and distribution by different branches of capital.

In post-war Brazil, the dynamic of output expansion has shifted from the "extensive frontier" and the incorporation of new land towards exploitation of the intensive margin and the acceleration of productivity growth through utilizing modern inputs and capitalization of the production process. The Brazilian "path", vigorously promoted by the state since the 1964 military coup, has been described as one of "conservative modernization". The benefits of subsidized technological innovation and capital investment are heavily concentrated in large-scale enterprises, reinforcing the inequitable distribution of rural income and wealth. The agricultural production process is being "industrialized", creating new opportunities for accumulation and realization for various forms of capital and strengthening the agroindustrial complex. The strong bias of modernization policies towards export crops and large enterprises was modified slightly in the 1970s with the re-emergence of severe urban food supply problems. Special credit and investment programmes have been introduced to capitalize production and intensify commodity relations in small-scale family agriculture, traditionally a major source of domestic food staples.

As a case-study, Brazil illustrates the structural re-articulation between urban and rural sectors in the process of accumulation and growth. This articulation, based earlier upon the extension of peasant agriculture, now increasingly involves an intensive pattern of output growth incorporating industrialized inputs. This shift is effected by the penetration of different forms of capital and closer input-output linkages with agroindustry and accompanying changes in the institutional apparatus of state intervention. Its real significance arises, however, from the fundamental redefinition of agriculture's integration in the circuit of capital. There is considerable evidence of overt proletarianization in the recent period, both in peasant agriculture and areas of large landed property, due to the transformation of previous labour control systems and the expulsion of resident workers. Some writers regard this as the dominant tendency in agricultural relations of production. Equally, other processes can be identified which appear to reinforce the diversity of production relations in Brazilian agriculture.

Mexican agricultural development has paralleled that of Brazil in many respects. The Mexican state provided the expensive irrigation infrastructure that has largely benefited commercial farming interests, including the rich irrigated *ejidos*. Rainfed agriculture was virtually ignored after 1940. However the existence of the *ejido* has provided an opportunity for political rhetoric that did not exist in Brazil. Most peasant producers, many of them *ejidatarios*, and thus effectively tied to the Mexican government through constitutional guarantees, have had to search for employment outside the rainfed regions. As in Brazil agroindustry has been promoted, most of it providing exports which remain competitive partly because of cheap labour costs. The Mexican model has been highly "dualistic", but it is a structural dualism that has enabled only one sector, the capitalist one, to prosper.

Since the early 1970s it has become increasingly clear that this model cannot provide the food crops which are desperately needed by Mexico's burgeoning urban population. Consequently, under Lopez Portillo, a battery of policies was introduced in March 1980. The Mexican Food System (Sistema Alimentario Mexicano SAM) ostensibly provides the means for a new alliance between state and small-scale agriculture. In fact, by providing production incentives for the marketed surplus, the SAM programme will probably increase commoditization and contribute to the further demise of much of the Mexican peasantry. The Mexican state is effectively renegotiating the subsumption of labour to capital and, in doing so, is stimulating increased social differentiation within the peasant sector.

Capitalist Development and Agrarian Structure in Brazil

Juarez Rubens Brandão Lopes

Brazil's agrarian structure has, throughout its history, been dominated by the large agromercantile enterprise, whose *raison d'être* was the production of tropical food crops for the world market. Such a predominance by large mercantile landholdings has outlived slavery. The *latifundia* system, control of access to land ownership by a minority and, consequently, cheap labour and, itinerant primitive agriculture, with very low levels of capitalization, are the main characteristics of a picture that, for most rural areas, is still valid.

More recently, however, two developments began to be noticed by analysts. First, with industrialization and growing urban markets, food supply, even while maintaining its primitive nature, has grown rapidly and has kept up with demand. This has been true, for instance, in the northeast, one of the most backward parts of the country. Second, the socio-economic organization of agriculture in the centre-south has been changing. It is being rapidly capitalized and commercialized and these trends have been accompanied by a drastic proletarization of the labour force, i.e. the substitution of former *moradores* and *colonos* by pure wage earners.

It is first necessary to examine the general nature of the industrialization process that (beginning in the 1930s) has taken place in Brazil and then examine the role of the various agricultural sectors in that process.

In the 1920s the agrarian situation in the two regions was already becoming differentiated. In the centre-south region, the *colonos* on the coffee plantations were tending to become pure wage labourers. Thus the food crops obtained from the plots they received from the landowners were less significant to them than was the case for the *moradores* in the sugar plantations of the coastal humid zone of the northeast. Also, obligations to work for the landowner, in exchange for the plots of land – common in the northeast and even in the sugar zone – did not exist in the coffee region. With the depression of coffee prices in the 1930s, coffee plantations in the older areas, where yields were diminishing, were split up, either being sold or rented in smaller parcels. As a result, small and medium-sized family farmers multiplied, and, with the growing industrialization and urbanization of the State of São Paulo, such farmers were soon quite market-oriented. It was at this time that family operated *sitios* planting cotton began to emerge alongside the large coffee plantations. In fact in this region the peasant economy was rapidly disappearing and giving way to petty commodity production. However in the northeast, apart from the large-scale estates which preserved their *latifundium* characteristics (i.e. the extra-economic forms of control of their labour), the peasantry expanded.

The state played a large role in industrialization from the start. Looking back at the 1930s and 1940s it is clear that the state changed the institutional rules of the game in order to displace the large landed estates which were producing for exports from the centre of the economic system, increasingly turning industry into the main axis of capital accumulation even though this process proceeded in a contradictory fashion with many temporary setbacks. It was a composite state, reflecting the interests of many classes and social groups, especially the agrarian bourgeoisie, the *latifundistas*, and the industrialists. It also had to take into account the urban masses. However, the rural working classes, including the peasantry, were excluded. In this situation, it was broadly true that the interest of industry became dominant, without achieving hegemony.

During this process, industry and agriculture were in a very ambiguous relationship. Let us look at the two principal agricultural sectors. First, the sector of export agriculture (coffee, cocoa, sugar, etc.). This sector was being transformed from its central position in the economic system into a kind of a substitute for department I of the economy. Thus it became the "supplier", through export revenues generating import capacity, of the capital goods (raw materials, intermediate goods and equipment) required by industry. The ambivalent and conflicting relationship to industry is, therefore, easy to see. Since Brazil had meagre capital funds, if industrialization was to proceed income had to be transferred from the export sector where it had accumulated. This was done through a series of mechanisms, especially those which determined the price of foreign exchange. However, this could not be pushed too far for fear of killing the goose that laid the golden eggs. Continued export revenues were essential for the establishment and growth of the industrial economy.

The sector of agriculture directly oriented towards the internal market was still extremely small. With relatively few exceptions it was the *latifundia*-peasantry system that supplied the urban centres with food as it still does to a great degree today. So, on the one hand the agrarian export sector acted as the supplier of capital goods, and on the other the peasant-labourers on the *latifundia* and peasants on their own land provided their food surpluses in order to supply a major part of the "wage goods" of the urban working class. This type of food production only involved the very low level of the "cost of reproduction" of the peasantry, therefore cheapening in its turn the cost of reproduction of the urban labour force. It was then the provision of food by the *latifundia*-peasantry system, instead of by commercial agriculture, that – among other things – made it possible to fix a low level of minimum urban wage and this is still so today. Primitive agriculture – as well as primitive urban services – are fundamental aspects of capital accumulation in the urban–industrial sectors.

One of the internal aspects of the current "model" of development, that had begun in the 1950s, was the advancement of industrialization from non-durable to durable consumer goods, with production of the latter by the local branches of multinational corporations in association with other local companies. The car industry – consisting of a few foreign-owned assembly companies, linked to numerous small nationally-owned parts suppliers – can be taken as the prototype. Eventually the heart of the economy consisted of a monopolized durable goods sector under the dominance of foreign capital. But before this new model of development could flourish, an authoritarian and repressive political regime had to be instituted and, during the stagnant years from 1962 to 1967, a profound restructuring of the economy and of its relation to the state was also effected. By then, a new power bloc had been formed. The central fact of interest here was that the dominant agrarian classes were excluded from this bloc, as, of course, was populism, and hence also the formerly powerful union leaders and any influence the urban masses had previously had. As a result wages, already low, were deliberately further depressed, and a productive structure, oriented in its central and most important part to the supply of expensive durable goods obtained its necessary counterpart, namely a still greater concentration of income. Further, market outlets were provided by the subsidization of the exports of the simpler manufactured goods. This provided a temporary source of growth for industry whose home market was restricted due to the general lack of purchasing power.

We can now consider agrarian changes in the more advanced centre-south rural region (located near the major area of urban–industrial capital accumulation) and in the more backward northeastern areas. The agriculture of the São Paulo region will first be discussed. Drastic transformations have occurred here during the last decade. From 1966 to 68 mass dismissals of the permanent workers of the *fazendas* took place all over the region. These displaced ex-*colonos* formed new rural *bairros* or settled on the periphery of towns where they could easily be recruited in gangs for temporary work in the plantations of the region, being moved by trucks from one place to another as and when their labour was needed. This was a purer rural proletariat than the *colono*. An industrial reserve army, in the strict sense of the term, had been formed. But this time, mechanization and other modern agricultural methods (chemical fertilizers, herbicides, etc.) were clearly visible in many areas of the region. Here at least if not elsewhere, the classic arrangement whereby a primitive agriculture facilitated accumulation in the economy as a whole was disappearing. The usual explanation for the substitution of capital for labour was that the new legislation by making obligatory a minimum wage, paid vacations and holidays, etc. made labour too expensive. This will be discussed further below.

In fact the constitution of proletarianized labour, the mechanization and the increase in the organic composition of capital by a fundamental reorganization of the productive unit had all been occurring gradually over a long period.

The precondition for all these processes was the intense capital accumulation in the region which occurred as coffee production was succeeded by industrial development as the main focus for accumulation, bringing as a result a vigorous development of urban markets. São Paulo, and a whole network of other cities and towns grew rapidly. By 1950 over 50 per cent of the population of the region was urban; in 1970, it was close to 80 per cent urban. Urban demand rose for *new* food products (*new* in the sense that they were not part of the diet of peasants or agricultural workers and, therefore, were not produced in the subsistence plots). This demand was met by the commercial production of *sitiantes*. This urban market for foodstuffs (already increasingly met by the production of a growing stratum of small family producers) was already part of the process by which, at one and the same time, a market for food and a labour market appeared in the "mature" rural areas.

The stage was set for the recent and more dramatic tendencies in the *paulista* agrarian situation. These were triggered off by the effects of the new model of development (that corresponded to the phase of "internationalization of the internal market") and the socio-political characteristics it assumed in Brazil. The extension of the labour law to the rural areas was a result of the intensification of the class struggle in the early 1960s; its implementation and maintenance was due to the new constellation of the power of the regime post-1964, although a few years elapsed between its enactment and its definitive implementation in the areas of more commercialized agriculture (mass dismissals only began occurring in 1966 to 68). The character of the new economic model also explains the recent emphasis on capitalization of agriculture which has included subsidization of capital inputs and other incentives. This development follows from the character of the new policy alliance. Capitalization of agriculture is occurring as a part of the strategy of capitalist development *per se*, because its former distinctive features (those related to its different kind of labour with its specific circumstances) are rapidly disappearing. Agriculture is becoming just one sector among others suitable for the investment of capital. It is subjected, as the others are to the conditions and planning strategy laid down by government, in response to the social forces impinging on it. Subsidies for the acquisition of tractors and other agricultural inputs, by cheapening these products, at one and the same time, led to agricultural technical development, stimulated the corresponding industrial branches, and – together with other measures – expanded agricultural exports. These state actions completed the capitalization of agriculture in many areas in the region. Labour laws, especially the minimum urban wage, were extended to the rural areas, at a time when the real value of this minimum wage was being depressed. In such a conjuncture, labour power became "expensive", relative to constant capital (because of governmental policies). These changes completed the transition to a purer proletariat, the labour market was unified in many areas; and, through the suppression of the hitherto general non-monetary components of the "remuneration" of rural labour, an approximate equality between the cost of reproduction of rural and urban labour was achieved. Finally, a single industrial reserve army (in the strict sense of the expression) was created.

The economic and socio-political effects of the new style of development on the agrarian structure varied. An examination of the trends in the northeastern rural areas helps one to understand the peculiarities of the case of São Paulo, and its preconditions.

In the greater part of the *Sertão* and the *Agreste* the last decades have seen a growing specialization of the peasantry in pure cultivation. Other adjuncts of the old peasant economy (e.g. craft production and trading) were slowly eroded. The purely agrarian character of the peasant economy of the hinterland has been accentuated, as has its dependency on the sale of food surpluses which provide the major part of the urban food supply in the region. The intense urban growth in the northeast, and hence the growth in demand, has been met by this food supply which has resulted from the horizontal expansion of the peasantry. The form, rhythm and direction of this expansion has been greatly affected by the new economic model and state action to implement it. An important role in the economic system was played by a dynamic car industry and this required as a counterpart massive public investment in roads. This began in the late 1950s and was intensified in the 1960s and 1970s. Road building increased the supply of "free" land. This was a factor facilitating the expansion of the peasantry and the redirection of migration flow towards the west.

On the other hand, with increased land supply, the extension of the peasantry and hence of subsistence agriculture inhibited the emergence of commercial agriculture supplying food to the urban centres in the region. Besides expansion towards frontier areas, an increase in the peasant tenantry has occurred. As commercial agriculture in the region (sugar, cotton) stagnates, suffering from the competition of agricultural products from the centre-south, landowners instead of selling out, rent their land in very small parcels. Increase in tenants is, in fact, greater than the growth of squatters on the frontier lands. It is from this growing tenantry that most of the region's urban food supply comes. Landowners transform themselves into rentiers and oligopsonist buyers of the numerous small food surpluses which derive from the subsistence activities of their tenants. As tenants are not commercial producers, rising food prices in the cities do not benefit them, but are pocketed by the intermediaries, especially the landowner-rentier, and from them funnelled into urban capital accumulation. In these circumstances with such low prices for the producer, large commercial growing of food is impossible, despite rising prices in the cities. Anyhow, even if commercial undertakings were set up, e.g. in the form of a transformation of the peasants into petty commodity producers, they would have to compete with the more productive agriculture in the centre-south which is highly capitalized. So the character of the new model of development – by making possible the modernization of the centre-south (and even the small family farmers there), and in drastically unifying markets – inhibits a similar transformation in the more backward regions and results in the continued reproduction of primitive agriculture.

Lastly I want to consider briefly that part of the northeast, the humid sugar-cane coastal region especially, where there have been some changes in the direction of capitalist development. Here non-monetary forms of labour and extra-economic methods of control have only slowly given way to wage-labour, and only in a vacillating and incomplete fashion. The process of proletarization, to the extent to which it has occurred, has been parallel to that in the centre-south region. However, once again there have been inhibiting factors. One may point to the fact that the competition of the far more productive sugar agroindustry of the centre-south has been, for a long period of time, somewhat mitigated by the quota protection established by the Federal government. A more important inhibition, however, is the presence nearby – in the *Agreste* – of a large peasantry, which was used in the sugar region as seasonal labour. As wage-labour and peasant at the same time (with the families working a plot in the *Agreste*), the cost of reproduction of this labour power was low. This, perhaps, more than the quota system permitted a less productive sugar-cane sector to withstand competition from the *paulista* sector, and to retain its somewhat primitive character.

In conclusion, capitalist development in Brazil is, in certain areas of the country, transforming the agrarian structure and conditions rapidly in the direction of purer capitalist forms. Elsewhere, however, it not only is failing to do this, but it is actually preserving and reproducing the primitive forms. So, in specific ways, combined and unequal development is occurring in the country.

Rural Bourgeoisie and Peasantry in the Highlands of Ecuador

Eduardo Archetti and Kristi Anne Stölen

One part of the debate over agrarian capitalism in the highlands has been concerned with the classical problem of feudalism/capitalism and the more general problematic of the articulation of modes of production and forms of reproduction in relation to the more concrete level of socio-economic systems. It appears clear, in the case of Ecuador, that by 1954 the percentage of *huasipungos*, or plots which the peasants obtained by means of payment of a rent in labour, was extremely low: only 7.6 per cent of all plots in the highlands according to census data. We might suppose that by this time, especially on account of the extensive and cyclical character of the process of production, there existed different forms of utilisation of labour power, ranging from the *huasipungo* plot to wage forms proper, and that this varied from zone to zone and, undoubtedly, from *hacienda* to *hacienda*. One should not be surprised, therefore, by Baraona's findings in the first sociological study of the Ecuadorian *sierra*, carried out in 1963.

Baraona combined two variables, the type of management and the social relations of production, and found distinct types of *hacienda*: *modern*, with centralised managerial control and exclusive use of wage labour; *common traditional*, in which management is indifferent, and both wage labour and *huasipungos* are used; *traditional in disintegration*, in which managerial control is ineffective due to internal pressure from the *huasipungeros*; and *infra-traditional*, in which in effect the workers control the running of the units of production. On the basis of this typology Guerrero (1977) indicates that in the wake of the transformations which took place in the 1960s the last two types have disappeared, and the first two have been transformed. The modern holdings have been transformed into capitalist farms with the forces of production developed to a high level, production highly specialised, and, in some cases, processes of industrialization introduced (the production of milk, cheeses, and yoghurt). The common traditional *haciendas* have abandoned the system of relations of production based upon *huasipungo*, but have not specialised, and exhibit a low level of development of the forces of production (Guerrero, 1977).

Barsky (1978) also takes Baraona's typology as a point of departure, but introduces a modification in the case of modern holdings. He distinguishes two types of modern *hacienda* in this period – extensive and intensive. As a result there are three types in the process of transformation rather than two: those above, and the common traditional form. From these three, two types emerge at the end of the process of modernisation: the *intensive modern* form with a high level of capital accumulation and investment, and the *extensive modern* form with a low level of capital accumulation and, as a consequence, a much lower level of incorporation of modern technology.

In these accounts, the discussion centres on the role of traditional *haciendas* which undergo a process of "bourgeoisification" and modernization, while the emergence of a new class of "rural bourgeois" is never raised explicitly as an issue. Modernization, technological transformation and the history of highland agrarian capitalism are linked to the capacity for political manoeuvering which sectors of the landowning class may have at different times, to impose their own project and give meaning and content to processes of social change.

In an article by Murmis (1978) the problem of relations between this landowning fraction and what he calls the "middle bourgeoisie" makes an explicit appearance. Murmis states that the landowners initiate the transformation, which pulls along in its wake a "middle bourgeoisie" capable of reorganising a unit of production from 100 to 600 hectares in size. He detects a confluence of interests between this landowning class and the control of the state, from 1964, by the military and a new technobureaucracy. This makes possible an agrarian reform, in the sense of the elimination of the *huasipungo*, and modernization, with special emphasis upon production for the internal market and the substitution of wage goods. In this particular, the capitalist process in the highlands of Ecuador is "original" in that there is no direct investment from multinational corporations, either in the production of inputs for agriculture or in the industrial transformation of what is produced. There is therefore an economic and political space for the vanguard role of the *hacendados*, and the conversion of some of them into hacendado-industrialists, almost in the Junker style. In this context mention must be made of the importance of the oil boom and the availability of enormous financial resources, which could be used generously in the following ways: credits for modernization (credits to the agriculture and livestock sectors rose from 4 000 million sucres in 1962 to 11 300 million in 1971), credits for the purchase of land, subsidies for milk (20 per cent of the final price paid by the consumer), the importing of inputs (pedigree cattle, seeds, fertilizers, machinery), which rose from US$50 million in 1962 to US$72 million in 1970, and the creation of special agencies for research and extension work. Was this process accompanied by the rise and/or strengthening of this "middle bourgeoisie" of which Murmis speaks? If the answer is positive, the puzzle returns with the question: Who are they? What did they do before the oil and milk boom? What are they doing after it? In other words, how is it possible for them to respond in such a rapid and "modern" manner to these incentives? What is the relationship between commerce, intermediation, and this class of "modern producers"? In our view this is one of the principal enigmas in this process of capitalist development in highland Ecuadorian agriculture, and we shall attempt to present some leads which will take us beyond Murmis's correct intuitions.

At the same time, we should ask what is happening to the peasantry. If capitalism is growing, does this imply complete proletarianization, real subsumption to capital, and, in consequence, the crystallization of a true class of rural proletarians, deprived of all control over the means of production? If at the same time that capitalism is growing, the peasantry is too, does this not indicate a merely formal subsumption in which different labour markets and different forms of utilization of labour power co-exist? What is the relationship between these two parallel and convergent movements, how do capitalism and the peasantry, real and formal subsumption, co-exist side by side?

Our fieldwork was carried out in the south of the province of Pichincha, within the canton of Mejia. The zone selected lies 8 km from the town of Machachi, and at an altitude which ranges between 3 150 and 5 200 metres above sea level. The limit at which natural pasture can be exploited is found at around 4200 metres. The whole zone, therefore, lies within what is called the intermediate level, between the lower part of the valleys and the plateau. The climate is characterized by a low annual average temperature, from 10° to 12° up to 3 600 metres, and from 3° to 6° above that level, and by abundant rainfall. This area has traditionally been described as being particularly suitable for extensive livestock farming, and, consequently, as suffering severe limitations where intensive agriculture is concerned.

Types of Production on Units of 50–500 hectares

It would not be possible to give a detailed description of each unit and each family, so we shall present some general information. If we are seeking to characterize this new bourgeoisie, we should look for the origins of initial capital, within or outside the agrarian sector. First of all, we should discard the notion of industrial origin. In every case the previous activities of the present owners and those of their parents were in the agrarian sector. Of the fourteen, only two could be classified as belonging to aristocratic "lineages", and in one of the two cases the family was not Quito-based, but a traditional provincial one. The origin of initial capital in each case was the sale of properties received as legacies in other areas, and the purchase at a later date of land in this locality. The two had university education, one in agronomy in the United States, and a modern, entrepreneurial attitude. These producers represent a new "layer" of the traditional landowning class, with technical education and a "bourgeois" attitude: the land is not a source of prestige, it is not used to maintain the prestige of the "lineage", it is not converted into a source of local or regional power. In their view, what is important is to invest, modernize, and thus obtain the highest possible return.

Of the rest, 50 per cent (six producers) have commercial origins. It is impossible to comment extensively upon the importance of commercial capital; we may simply observe that highland agriculture functions and reproduces itself on the basis of a complex system of mercantile transactions. As is the norm, these transactions are more complex, the less the agrarian sector is integrated with the industrial sector. This means, in other words, that industrial capital does not penetrate the commercial sphere, or that the nexus between it and the producers is made by specific and specialized agents in a hierarchical and interlinked system of fairs and markets. As a consequence, commercial capital permits commodities to circulate, and knits together relations between producers and consumers, and between producers and the agroindustrial sector. An example may be drawn from milk production. There is a modern processing plant, but this does not itself collect the milk; the process of collection is controlled by a multitude of truckdrivers with one, two or three trucks, who guarantee that every day the milk produced will reach the factories. The litre of milk which is sold for 3.60 to 4 sucres is thus purchased by the industrialist for 5.20.

With the turnover of capital being extremely rapid, as in the case of every product, and the chains of transactions different, there are different niches which traders can occupy, and which guarantee, in one way or another, a substantial return. In no case are we dealing with small traders who deal directly with consumers in local fairs or markets of minor significance. In more than half the cases, these are wholesale traders of agricultural produce, potatoes and broad beans particularly, who operate or did operate in Quito or Ambato, whose regional market is one of the most important in the Ecuadorian highlands. There are two cases of retail traders, one in Quito and one in Machachi, but with daily stalls on a fixed site, and a very wide range of produce for sale. In one of the cases we find a typical social type of the zone: the truckdriver who is sometimes a truckdriver and sometimes, or at the same time, a trader. The owner of two trucks, he buys and sells at one fair or another or at urban markets, or simply carries goods on behalf of other individuals from the highlands to the coast.

For the majority, the preferred strategy is as follows: commercial activity for a number of years, and the subsequent purchase of land. When exploitation of the land begins to get under way, and income stabilizes, commercial activity is generally abandoned. As is easily imagined, commercial activity requires considerable assiduity, it involves risk, a great proportion of circulating capital is tied up in credit to small traders and small producers, and the life it permits is far from sedentary, even in the case of wholesale traders in the larger towns. In comparison, farming appears the very opposite. Frequent (we might say permanent, but to do so would be speculative until we have a better knowledge of case studies and life histories) exits from the market and from trading to farming and livestock gives the commercial system a degree of flexibility and perhaps avoids the consolidation of the process of concentration which can be observed as a trend in recent years. There is as a result great pressure upon the market and price for land, and this stems, in large part, from the conversion of this commercial bourgeoisie into a rural bourgeoisie.

The remaining producers (six in number) come from a background of agriculture itself, making the origins and formation of this social class even more complex. In the case of the present owners and of their parents these are producers who began with less than 50 hectares, in this zone or in other neighbouring areas, especially in the province of Cotopaxi which borders on the canton of Mejia. Two types of strategy are pursued. The first is less mobile: once settled in this zone they take advantage of the highly favourable cycles of certain products, particularly potatoes and some other vegetables, and they purchase little by little until the opportunity to buy a whole unit appears. This allows them to sell their scattered plots and consolidate a much more viable unit of production in which it is possible to centralize the process of production and control over it. The second strategy implies geographic mobility: the sale of a unit in another region, and a move to this new locality. In all the cases mentioned, prior ownership of property allowed the securing of mortgage credits, which were generous after 1966, and this made possible the expansion of the units controlled.

A move into milk is the general tendency, but even in our locality there are in this group three who are primarily livestock farmers, and one who was in the process of becoming one while we were in the zone. Only in ten of the fourteen cases is the production of milk central. Even when milk herds occupy 80–85 per cent of the surface area, agricultural activity has not been abandoned. The co-existence of milk and agriculture has important implications for the analysis of labour markets and the articulation of the peasantry.

As we have said, agricultural production revolves almost entirely around potatoes and broad beans. This type of production determines the other labour market, and one with very different characteristics to that in milk. The year-round work of raising crops is in the hands of permanent peons and tractor hands, and additional labour is hired only for the harvest and for other tasks such as weeding potatoes. In these seasons there is work for some 150 rural wage-earners, who are either day labourers or well paid on a piecerate basis. This obviously generates a transitory labour market, subject to different laws. The co-existence of these two labour markets is central to an understanding of the type of relations which are established between these operations and the seventy small production units.

The Peasantry

The strategy of production is typical of the highland peasantry: beans, potatoes, and some vegetables (particularly onions). Only the surplus is sold in the Machachi market. The money thus earned is used, among other things, to buy fertilizer and hire tractors from the local branch of the Agriculture ministry. Given the lack of land, the producers cannot keep draught animals, and therefore need to use the tractor to plough and tend the crops. Guinea pigs and some pigs and hens contribute to the diversifications of the diet. Only if the holding is in excess of 5 hectares do cows appear, and in some cases the milk is used to produce cheese for sale in the locality or in Machachi.

Let us now explore the manner of insertion of this group into the labour market. Of those who were wage-earners before becoming proprietors, 72 per cent were so on a permanent basis. This percentage indicates a type of sequence in the process of restructuring: proletarianization first, and then "peasantization". But this peasantization is not permanent and definitive; it does not generate a "classic peasant" group capable of constituting units of production and consumption independent of the capitalist labour market. The holder of less than 2 hectares is condemned to a difficult life, a continuous struggle for survival. Our data show that of seventy heads of family and owners, there are forty-two who work as day labourers or pieceworkers, particularly in the weeding and harvesting of potatoes and beans. In the multiplication of strategies in order to obtain the hundreds of extra sucres which are needed every year we thus find wives and daughters working as milkers, and sons working on a temporary or permanent basis within the rural proletariat. The strategy of reproduction combines production on the small plot with continuous contact with the capitalist labour market. As we might expect, this process of proletarianization–peasantization–proletarianization is highly correlated with the size of plots. Within those of less than 2 hectares (thirty-one of seventy), 57.6 per cent of adults (above the age of sixteen) are proletarianized. This percentage falls to 44.5 per cent for the plots of 2.1–5.9 hectares, and to 21.2 per cent for those of 6–10 hectares.

We do not imagine that this phenomenon is confined to our locality, or to Pichincha, or to Ecuador. What is original about it, however, in our view, is the sequence of proletarianization-peasantization–proletarianization, and not the end result, semi-peasants or semi-proletarians. This, it should be stressed, is a product of the very process of capitalist development in agriculture. The impact is not simply external to family or quasi-family units of production, but also affects them directly at the most intense moments of the labour process – the harvest, or the weeding period. We found that 23 per cent of small units made systematic use of outside labour, and paid for it in cash. The exchange of labour (*"prestarse mano"*) is still important, but its importance is declining. Paradoxically or not, the units which have to sell the labour of their members to survive have to compete, at the same time, as if they were capitalist units, at times when competition for the labour force is revealed in all its intensity. Production units of this type are not only integrated through commercial exchange and the labour market; it even appears that relationships of kin and neighbourhood are stripped of their previous meaning, and mediated through these processes.

In order to gain a more complete picture of the process of social differentiation in the locality, let us examine the situation of producers with between 10.1 and 50 hectares. Although we have only five such cases, we can find less distressing life histories, and more fortunate individuals. First of all we should say that they all come from families of old settlers, and their fathers were either *mayordomos* (four cases) or, in the last case, a farmer with more than 10 hectares. The role of *mayordomo* is important in the hierarchical system of the *hacienda*, as he is the owner's right-hand man, enjoys his confidence, and as a result may obtain favours which are denied to others. The direct intervention of these individuals in the sale of larger plots, of 6–10 hectares, to their children, appears uncontestable. This has been accompanied by a parallel process of proletarianization of the present owners, and, therefore, by the accumulation of an initial sum of money. When the land market loosens up these producers already have a plot which allows them to accumulate surpluses and thus to compete on favourable terms in the purchase of new land.

We also find among these producers the polyvalent production strategy of the smaller producers: potatoes, beans, and vegetables of other kinds. But we notice a very important change which could already be glimpsed among the owners of 6–10 hectares: the production of milk. The size of the plots allows them to maintain herds with five–ten cows producing milk. The preferred strategy is to convert this milk into cheese, rather than to sell it to the industrial plant. This undoubtedly allows them a higher return, while retaining an artesanal family type of production which allows them to maximize the use of domestically available labour. As a result of this, only 11 per cent of the adults in this group experience proletarianization, and all the units employ wage labour at peak times.

The development of milk production is based upon two pillars: on the one hand the agrofood industry capitalism present locally in the processing business, and on the other agrarian capitalism, the specialized milk producers or those on the way to specialization who use paid labour. Nevertheless, and this is an important characteristic, the division is not clear-cut, as agrofood industry capitalism functions at the same time as agrarian capitalism: in other words, the owners of the plants are owners of important milk-producing *haciendas*. Another original characteristic is the presence of commercial capital as an independent sector outside the control of agrofood industry capital. Commercial capital and the different types of trader as concrete agents of exchange continue to play a central role insofar as the relations of exchange between the first two sectors are exercised through means of transport and collection which the former effectively control. At the same time, this commercial capital guarantees the sale of calves and of reject cattle for the agrarian capitalists in the traditional highland fairs and markets. These three classes, the landowning–industrial bourgeoisie, the agrarian bourgeoisie and the commercial bourgeoisie, seem "articulated" and at the same time opposed. We cannot elaborate at length here upon these contradictions, but for the case with which we are concerned, that of the "rural bourgeoisie", they are important, and they limit their room for manoeuvre. We may briefly consider why this is so.

In the context described, the *rich peasants*, those with 10.1–50 hectares, are at the margin of agrofood industry capital, occupying a niche which the latter has not yet fully occupied: the production of fresh cheese which circulates at local and regional level. The milk produced by this sector appears as a finished product, and this is possible because of the size of the units of production. Specialization – or in other words the abandonment of agriculture – signifies increased production of a product which does not keep. This undoubtedly obliges many of these producers either to increase the production of cheese or to deliver the milk to the plants. The first strategy appears to offer few prospects, as agrofood industry capital is tending to move into this niche, and therefore the second appears more realistic.

Beneath this privileged group of peasants we find the majority of peasant producers and rural wage-earners. Owners of small plots, with insufficient livestock, without draught animals, subjected to capitalist laws and transformations in agriculture, they survive only through a multiplicity of strategies. But these strategies depend upon the constraints of the local and regional labour markets and the mobility of the factor land. The expansion of the internal frontier, or access to small properties, was a consequence of the crisis of the *hacienda* and the agrarian reform. But this is as true for the agrarian capitalists as it is for them. Therefore, the expansion of the one takes place at the expense of the other, and it is at this level that this social structure appears in all its brutality. Proletarianization is as necessary after becoming proprietor as it was before. At one and the same time proletarians with land and peasants without enough, they experience both real and formal subsumption to agrarian capital at different times of their lives and of the lives of their families. In Ecuador today the changes which are taking place in the most capitalist areas are affecting not only the way of life and of consumption, but also the technical process of production, as the majority of the means of production (machinery, seeds, fertilizers, insecticide and pesticide) have to be bought in the market, and this means a considerable reduction in the quantity of means of production produced internally. Although the objective is mere subsistence, this passes through an increasing commercialization of exchange. If the central purpose is to obtain a monetary income, the net income of which Chayanov speaks, production has in some way lost its original purpose and is subject to turbulence of all kinds. The destiny of production does not depend upon the turbulence of the domestic cycle, but on the turbulence generated by capital. As a result the peasants compete among themselves to sell their produce, to buy the land, to sell their labour power, and, paradoxically as we said before, to buy labour power as well. Social, ethnic, kin and neighbourhood relations appear mediated by the rigour of the capitalist market, by the instability to which production is linked, by specialization and by the greed of the merchants.

Achievements and Contradictions of the Peruvian Land Reform

Cristobal Kay

Between 1969 and 1980 the Peruvian military government undertook one of the major recent agrarian reforms. The agrarian reform has a parodoxical character – a military government implemented a collectivist reform to develop and strengthen the capitalist system. The economic and socio-political map of the countryside before the reform is extremely complex. A series of factors – marked regional variations, differing technological levels, access to markets, demography, politics – have contributed to the shaping of a wide variety of closely articulated production and social relationships both between and within regions. As will be seen, the agrarian reform, which set out to restructure and resolve some of the key contradictions arising out of this socio-economic formation, itself created a number of contradictions, some of which can be related to the pre-existing pattern of economic and social relations of production. Finally some general reflections are offered on the way in which the Peruvian agrarian reform relates to wider theoretical discussions, particularly those concerning the various roads of transition to capitalist agriculture.

Three main agrarian systems can be identified in Peru – plantations on the coast and *haciendas* (large landed estates) and peasant communities in the Highlands. *Haciendas* and peasant communities have a long history of conflictual relationships. The Highlands, particularly the peasant communities, also supplied labour to the coastal plantations. A series of articulations developed between non-capitalist and capitalist forms of production.

The uniformity of the terrain, the absence of marked seasonal fluctuations and the necessity of major irrigation works have all favoured large-scale agriculture on the coast. Production was largely for the export market and, as this expanded during the second half of the nineteenth century, a major process of land concentration took place. This process was most extreme in the case of the sugar plantations and foreign capital played an important role. It was far less extreme on the rice and cotton plantations, as these were much smaller in size.

The sugar plantations developed many features of a dual labour market structure. Most Highland labour was contracted on a temporary basis as *eventuales* who had to perform the more menial tasks, such as cane cutting and loading. The permanent workers undertook the more specialized jobs. On average the permanent worker's wage was significantly higher than that of the temporary worker. On many plantations permanent workers were also often given a small garden plot in usufruct to grow foodstuffs.

Unlike sugar, the rice and cotton plantations relied to a large extent on tenants and sharecroppers for their labour. On some estates tenants and sharecroppers cultivated over half the land. The labour tenancy system on the rice estates was the *colonato* whereby the tenant or *colono* was given a small parcel of land to grow rice and some other subsistence crops. Share-cropping, or *yanaconaje*, was more common on the cotton plantations. The main difference between *colonato* and *yanaconaje* was that while the *colono* had to work a substantial number of days on the demesne ("central enterprise"), the *yanacona* rarely had to. While both paid rents in kind and/or money, the *colono* also had to pay a labour rent, as he had to work on the demesne for less than the going wage. A *colono* was, therefore, a more direct part of the estate's labour force, while a *yanacona* was more of a small-scale producer. Landlords began expelling or proletarianizing *yanaconas* from the 1940s onwards as wage labour became more profitable. This process proceeded at different paces and continued right up until the agrarian reform. Expulsion or proletarianization was most intense on the more capitalized estates and was generally strongly resisted. *Yanaconas* on traditional estates could purchase their tenancy, a practice which later spread to modernizing estates as owners feared expropriation through agrarian reform.

In the Highlands two types of *hacienda* can be distinguished: the vast livestock estates and the not-so-large livestock-crop estates. On the livestock *haciendas* shepherds called *huacchilleras* (sheep-tenants, a type of *colono*) looked after the landlord's flock in return for the right to graze their own animals. As landlords and *huacchilleros* competed for the same pastureland, landlords attempted to dispossess the *huacchilleros* totally and transform them into shepherds paid only with a wage. The main factor behind the proletarianization of shepherds was the increasing productivity of the landlords' sheep as a result of investments to improve the quality of their stock. *Huacchilleros* resisted their further proletarianization as it meant losing what little entrepreneurial independence they had and because they believed that the wage payment would not compensate for the income lost if they gave up their herds. In the 1950s an average of half the *hacienda*'s pastureland in the Central Highlands was still used by *huacchilleros*. Only on the better administered estates, often belonging to corporate enterprises, did the proportion fall to about a fifth. As the enclosure process did not proceed so far in the South, landlords there did not exert such direct control over sheep rearing as in the central region and peasants often retained over half of the total livestock population.

On the livestock-crop or solely crop *haciendas* the process of proletarianization was not very advanced, as landlords relied mainly on *colonos*, or *feudatarios* as they were often called, for labour. These tenants were largely in charge of production as they cultivated most of the *hacienda*'s cropland and owned most of the livestock. On the more traditional *haciendas*, landlords were often absentee owners and retained only a fraction of the estate's land under direct cultivation. This meant that surplus was extracted in the form of product rent or more exceptionally money rent, rather than in the form of labour rent. The technology used on the small demesne did not differ substantially from that of the peasants. Productivity was low and little capital accumulation took place. On some *haciendas* a process of proletarianization of the *colonos* was, however, beginning to take place. Landlords on these *haciendas* took a greater interest in the running of the estate and the demesne was larger than on traditional *haciendas*. In recent decades the *colonos'* labour services were partly remunerated with a small kind and/or monetary payment which gradually took the form of a "reduced wage".

The other major agrarian system in the Highlands is the peasant community. A community is distinguished by economic links between members as well as by shared social, political, cultural and religious bonds. The peasant community is an association, membership of which conferred certain rights and obligations. In the past community authorities determined the proportion of land to be worked collectively and distributed individual plots in usufruct to members. Pastureland was always used communally. Members (*comuneros*) worked collectively that part of the land whose proceeds went to finance communal activity and were also called upon to undertake collective tasks such as construction and maintenance work. The reciprocal exchange of labour between members for the cultivation of individual plots was common practice.

This picture began to change with the intrusion of the *hacienda* into community land and with the penetration of capitalist market relations. The conflict between *hacienda* and community was permanent and often erupted in land invasions by *comuneros* demanding the restitution of their lands. The invaders were usually forcefully evicted and *comuneros* were often casualties in the ensuing clashes. The loss of community land to the *hacienda* forced some members to become labour-service tenants on the estates or to rent pastureland from the *hacienda*. Some members later sought seasonal wage employment on the Highland estates and, above all, on the coastal plantations. Others migrated for good. The penetration of capitalist market relations began a process of privatization of communal cropland. Legislation also speeded up the establishment of private property relations over cropland which *comuneros* had previously only held in usufruct. Natural pastureland was generally exempt from this privatization process, being too costly to fence and of poor quality. In any case, communal ownership did not prevent richer *comuneros* from grazing a larger number of privately owned animals than poorer members. Consequently collective work arrangements had over time dwindled to essential construction and maintenance work.

Comuneros also became differentiated in the wake of the capitalist development of labour and product markets. Richer *comuneros* contracted some wage labour but they were mainly differentiated from poorer members by their incursion into other economic activities – commerce, transport and small-scale crafts. Poorer *comuneros* had increasingly to sell part of their labour for a wage, eventually forming a semi-proletariat. The traditional free exchange of labour between *comuneros* was gradually replaced by monetary payments, although some forms of reciprocity survived. At first only the richer *comuneros* sold a significant part of their agricultural production on the capitalist market and bought commodities in return. Later the majority of *comuneros* were incorporated into the product market and monetary exchange supplanted barter.

All these processes meant that peasant communities had largely evolved into associations of private peasant producers before the agrarian reform. Privatization and differentiation notwithstanding, however, *comuneros* retained their organization and many non-*comunero* peasants attempted to form legally constituted peasant communities as a way of pursuing land claims more effectively and of obtaining credits and other services from the state.

The structure of land ownership before the agrarian reform was very unequal. In 1961 the estates (1.2 per cent of farms) held 52.3 per cent of the land while the *minifundios* (smallholdings) and peasant communities (84.6 per cent of farms) owned 40.8 per cent of the land. The land concentration was far higher on the Coast where the plantations (5.4 per cent of farms) had 86 per cent of the land, while in the Highlands the *haciendas* (3.7 per cent of farms) only controlled 52 per cent of the land.

The *latifundia-minifundia* land tenure structure generated both inequality and inefficiency. Landlords owned too much land and employed too little labour while peasants had too little land and used too much labour. Large estates left a high proportion of their land idle and cultivated the rest less intensively than the peasants. Peasant farms were small and fragmented into numerous plots which were located at different altitudes and ecological levels. This allowed spreading of risks and formed part of a rational production and life cycle.

During the 1960s the agricultural sector stagnated. The inability of production to keep pace with population growth reflected a generalized crisis of the rural sector. The agricultural sector grew at an average yearly rate of 3.7 per cent between 1945 and 1961. The population growth rate for the same period was 2.2 per cent per annum. This positive *per capita* rate of growth turned negative from 1962 to 1969 when agricultural production grew by only 1.1 per cent yearly and population at three per cent per annum. Agriculture was certainly the least dynamic economic sector, its contribution to the gross national product falling from 23 per cent in 1950 to 15 per cent in 1968. Agricultural production was particularly stagnant in the Highlands.

The military seized power in late 1968 with the intention of carrying out major changes in economy, society and polity. A new concept of "national security" came to form part of military thinking, whereby the solution of internal conflicts was seen as a prerequisite for the defence of national sovereignty. By mid-1969 a new agrarian reform decree-law (No. 17716) came into effect. The underlying objectives of the agrarian reform were not always explicitly stated in legislation and sometimes only came to light with the unfolding of the process. The agrarian reform law and related legislation also underwent changes over time as a result of group pressures. At the economic level, the main aim was to increase the agricultural marketable surplus for the rapidly growing urban centres as well as expanding the internal market for the incipient local industry. The military government not only continued the import-substituting-industrialization strategy but assigned a new urgency and a greater directing role to the state in pursuing this development strategy. At the political level, perhaps the more important for the military, the agrarian reform attempted to incorporate the peasantry into the political system under the tutelage of the State, widening the social base and thereby legitimizing its rule. This aim formed part of the military government's wider objectives to create a strong, autonomous national state, free from oligarchic control as in the past.

The military government first expropriated the twelve enormous sugar estates on the coast, striking at the heart of the oligarchy's economic power. Within 24 hours of the issuing of decree No. 17716 the sugar estates were militarily occupied and taken over. Unlike Belaunde, the military government thus started by expropriating the most profitable and capital-intensive agricultural enterprises, showing their determination and ability to liquidate the rural oligarchy. Expropriations in the Highlands came later but followed the same pattern of starting with the most economically significant *haciendas*.

Expropriated landowners were entitled to compensation. The amount of this was calculated by basing land values on self-assessed values as registered in the 1968 returns of the newly established land tax. Other fixed assets were paid at book value and livestock at market value. Forms of compensation differed according to how efficiently the farms had been managed. Compensation was partly paid in cash, the remainder taking the form of non-inflation-proof bonds. However, the amount of compensation landowners actually received was undercut by the fact that book values were well below real market values, and by the high levels of inflation in the Peruvian economy.

As for the military's plans for the organization and functioning of the reformed sector, these were aimed at developing co-operative forms of organization at enterprise and regional levels. Expropriated land could be adjudicated to groups of peasants or to individuals. The land allocated to groups of peasants could be organized into *Cooperativas Agrarias de Producción* – CAPs – (Agrarian Production Cooperatives), *Sociedades Agrícolas de Interés Social* – SAISs – (Agricultural Societies of Social Interest), *Cooperativas Comunales* (Communal Cooperatives) or *Grupos Campesinos* (Peasant Groups).

The military government planned a massive land redistribution, expropriating most of the estates. This programme, which it hoped to complete by 1975–76 fell somewhat behind schedule, especially with regard to adjudications. By mid-1979, ten years after the promulgation of the law, the reform had largely been completed: 15 826 farms (10.5 million hectares) had been expropriated, though only 7.8 million hectares had been adjudicated, favouring 337 662 families. Thus about 40 per cent of the nation's land had been adjudicated to 35 per cent of agrarian families.

The co-operativist character of the agrarian reform clearly predominated and little land had been adjudicated in private property. Most of the land (62.3 per cent) was distributed to fully or partly collectivized, large-scale farm units – 604 CAPs and 60 SAISs. Land concentration increased, as most expropriated estates were consolidated into even larger units, particularly in the Highlands, with the aim of obtaining economies of scale.

The overwhelming predominance of collective, community and group farming is only apparent, since about half of total adjudicated land (in standardized units) is actually farmed on an individual basis despite strong government pressure to the contrary. The high incidence of individual farming reveals the enduring influence of the pre-reform agrarian structure. Firstly, most of the land distributed to peasant groups and peasant communities was farmed privately as, prior to the reform, the beneficiaries had been tenants, small owners and *comuneros* accustomed to private farming. Second, given the former dominance of tenant-labour relations in the Highland *haciendas* it is not surprising to find that 52 per cent of the Highland collectives' land (in standardized units) is farmed individually. By contrast in the coastal plantations where centralized management and a proletarian work-force had largely predominated only 18 per cent of the land is cultivated individually.

The enduring influence of the pre-reform situation on the functioning of the reformed enterprises manifests itself in production patterns, technology, labour structure and the articulation of conflicts. The performance of a particular SAIS or CAP is conditioned by the pre-existing degree of capitalization and of centralization of its production process, which had implications for the degree of proletarianization of labour and the level of technological development. In general, estates which had more developed capitalist relations of production tend to perform better as co-operative enterprises after expropriation than those which were relying largely on pre-capitalist relations of production.

In order to understand the dynamics of the co-operatives it is crucial to analyze their contradictions. Two tendencies have been at work within the co-operatives, leading to an erosion of their co-operative character. The first conflict and principal contradiction is between *socios* and the state. On the sugar co-operatives, the *socios'* main aim is to maximize personal disposable income in the form of wages and other benefits. The state, however, has a clear interest in increasing the share of the surplus vis-à-vis wages to ensure that taxes and debts get paid and investment takes place. Furthermore, the state has an interest in increasing the size of the surplus itself by raising work intensity, a process which *socios* naturally resist. On the rice and cotton co-operatives the tug-of-war between *socios* and the state centres around the question of land allocation. Former tenants exert constant pressure to appropriate more co-operative land and water for private benefit and thereby to reduce the size of the collective favoured by the state. If this process of *asedio interno* or internal encroachment goes unchecked the collective will eventually subdivide completely into various individual farms operated by former tenants who privately appropriate the surplus generated by employing cheap, *eventual* labour. Some members could develop into prosperous capitalist farmers. In a bid to save the co-operative model, the state sought to limit the autonomy of the co-operatives from early on.

The second conflict is connected with the existence of divisions within the work-force between members and non-members. In general, the *eventuales* who form a quarter of the coastal co-operative's labour force work more hours per day, do the most irksome tasks and receive considerably lower wages than the *socios*.

Their generally higher productivity and lower wages create a surplus which is appropriated by the co-operative, over which they
have no control. As non-members, *eventuales* have no say in the
running of the co-operative and they do not receive a share of profits
or other benefits which *socios* receive. In the sugar co-operatives *socios*
tend to shift to administrative, technical and supervisory positions,
substituting *eventual* labour for their own.

The increased level of state intervention in the CAPs raises the
question of whether the CAPs are best characterized as state capitalist or self-managed enterprises. Since their establishment the
CAPs have formed a type of hybrid enterprise, characterized by a
changing emphasis on state control and workers' self-management.

Turning now to the historical conflict between peasant communities and the *hacienda* system, a large part of the Peruvian agrarian
reform's originality lies in the SAIS model, which was set up to solve
just this conflict over external proletarianization. The SAIS model
favoured large-scale agriculture by maintaining the original estate
or merging several estates into an even larger unit. At the same time,
local peasant communities were incorporated into the SAIS as
associate members, which gave them a majority presence in the top
decision-making body and a major share of the distributable surplus
generated by the SAIS's production units. However, profits were
generally meagre or nil and *comuneros* revealed their discontent by
staging several invasions of "their" enterprises, taking over collective lands. As has been seen, profits of the SAISs' central enterprises
were kept down by the ex-tenants' gradual and persistent appropriation of central resources. Thus, in some cases, external encroachment was precipitated by internal encroachment, bringing *comuneros*
into indirect conflict with ex-tenants and wage workers. Where
profits were reasonable, little remained for re-distribution to peasant
communities after deducting agrarian debt payments and investments in the central enterprise. In any case this was not distributed
individually but consumed in public works which the state should
have paid for anyway, so *comuneros* perceived little economic advantage. As a result the SAISs were unable to prevent the further
external proletarianization of *comuneros*, thereby prompting the invasions.

Peru's agrarian reform remains to date one of the boldest experiments of its kind undertaken in Latin America. It effectively destroyed the hitherto existing oligarchical order and created a new
institutional framework. This having been said, the question must
be asked: to what extent have the reforms actually succeeded in

bringing about desirable changes in the basic problem areas of Peru's rural economy and society?

The agrarian reform did have some positive effect on employment, although far less than anticipated. The 0.9 per cent yearly rate of employment growth achieved between 1969 and 1978 is almost three times the annual rate of male agricultural employment growth from 1961 to 1972. Owing to agriculture's still low rate of absorption of labour, the high rate of rural out-migration continued.

General economic policies of the state must bear a major responsibility for the poor performance of the post-reform agrarian economy. As already noted, the military government continued the "import-substituting-industrialization strategy" which discriminated against the agricultural sector. The foreign exchange policy favoured agricultural imports and penalized agricultural exports even more than before. Price controls on agricultural products were further extended and more strictly enforced. Furthermore food subsidies were introduced in 1973 to prevent food prices from rising. Over 80 per cent of these agricultural subsidies went to imported food products, creating unfair competition for local producers.

The co-operative model had the best chance of success on the sugar plantations, as large-scale agriculture and wage labour predated the reform. Upon expropriation the state took over large, centrally-managed and capital-intensive enterprises. The sugar workers saw little advantage in dismantling the estates. Economies of scale had benefited them in the form of higher wages, so there was little pressure for privatization.

In the Highlands (and non-sugar coastal co-operatives) the greater presence of tenant labour and the existence of peasant communities meant that the model met with strong opposition from its inception. The peasants' opposition to the co-operativist scheme, expressed in both internal and external encroachment on the central enterprise, struck at the very heart of the model, making for a much more conflictive situation in the Highlands.

Although peasant resistance was strong, the government chose not to wage an all-out battle to secure its model in the Highlands. The terrain is difficult, the number of units involved overwhelming, and their economic importance not so great as in the case of the coastal sugar plantations.

Rather the government has responded to peasant pressure with a number of concessions such as restructuring boundaries (*redimensionamiento*) to deal with external encroachment and permitting the development of individual peasant enterprises in response to internal encroachment. Unlike the coastal sugar workers, the Highland peasantry do enjoy a greater degree of self-management but of an individual nature.

The ability of the peasantry to resist the agrarian reform model in the Highlands and to organize and stage strikes on the coastal sugar estates points to the government's failure to fulfil its political objective of co-opting the peasantry via the agrarian reform.

Finally, where does the Peruvian case stand in relation to types of agrarian reform and debates about modes of transition to capitalist agriculture? According to Lipton's (1974) distinction between a distributivist and a collectivist reform, the Peruvian reform can be characterized as a collectivist one. However the Peruvian case has some features which – with the single exception of Israel – are unique. This is a collectivist reform taking place within the context of a capitalist system. It may be more appropriate to refer to the Peruvian reform as state capitalist, particularly as the most significant economic enterprises are controlled by the state.

In short, the Peruvian agrarian reform spawned a new form of transition to agrarian capitalism: the state capitalist road. At the same time, and unwittingly, it also gave a new impetus to the peasant road. The contradictions generated by the state capitalist road may restrict it to being a transient form. It is likely that both the coastal sugar collectives and the Highland livestock collectives will remain as state farms for some time. The remainder, however, may be subdivided and, in particular, the central enterprise (former demesne) may be separated from the internal peasant enterprises (the former tenancies) and appropriated by capitalist farmers. In some cases a part of the collective's land might be transferred to peasant communities. It is almost certain that in Peru, as in other underdeveloped countries, smallholders with their corresponding petty commodity mode of production will be able to resist full proletarianization yet fail to become capitalist farmers for many decades to come. Thus the structural conditions of underdevelopment determine that the peasant mode of production will survive both in spite and because of the development of world capitalism.

The Division of Labor by Sex in Agriculture: a Peruvian Case Study

Carmen Diana Deere

Until the publication in 1970 of Ester Boserup's *Women's Role in*

Economic Development, little attention had been given within the development profession to the economic participation of women in the Third World. In particular, little was known about women's agricultural participation, and even less was understood about the factors which influence the sexual division of labor in agriculture. Boserup's seminal work did much to correct this lacuna by demonstrating the important role of women in subsistence production as well as in the rural labor force of many Third World economies. This discussion seeks to extend Boserup's analysis to the Andean region of Latin America through a case study of the sexual division of labor in agriculture among direct producers in Cajamarca, Peru.

Boserup's most important contribution was to draw attention to the cross-cultural diversity in the division of labor by sex in agricultural production. The heterogeneity that she found in men's and women's agricultural work demonstrated that the sexual division of labor cannot be just biologically or physiologically determined. Moreover, her analysis suggested that the sexual division of labor in agriculture was not based only on particular cultural perceptions of what tasks and activities are considered correct and proper for each sex to engage in. Rather, she illustrated that the division of labor by sex in agriculture varies over time in accordance with changes in socio-economic variables. Her analysis paid careful attention to such factors as changes in land tenure, type of cultivation, technology, employment, and outside intervention in local productive processes in bringing about changes in men's and women's participation in agricultural production.

Boserup began her analysis by distinguishing between male and female farming systems in subsistence agriculture. In the former, food production is carried out by men, with little help from women; in the latter, food production is the domain of women, with little help from men. She suggested that two factors were of particular importance in establishing the prevailing sex differentiation of work: differences in the type of agricultural system, and differences in the patterns of social hierarchy.

Female farming systems are generally based on extensive shifting cultivation, whereas male farming systems are usually characterized by intensive plow agriculture. Boserup demonstrated the importance of type of cultivation in influencing the sexual division of labor by comparing community survey data from Africa and Asia. Women constituted a much greater proportion of the total family labor force in Africa (extensive shifting cultivation) than in Asia (intensive irrigated agriculture).

Boserup also argued that social stratification, as reflected in land-tenure systems and in the composition of the labor force, was of great importance in explaining different patterns in the sexual division of labor. A major difference between shifting and plow agricultural systems is whether land is privately owned. The use of the plow is associated with private appropriation of land as well as the existence of a large class of landless rural families. She argued that, in such a situation, the greater proportion of farm workers may not come from the family but from the rural proletariat. Drawing on population census data for four major regions of the world, Boserup then illustrated that where there are few agricultural proletarians, as in Africa and in some parts of Southeast Asia, women make up a high proportion of family workers in agriculture. In contrast, in areas where agricultural wage laborers form a large part of the agricultural labor force, as in the Arab nations and in Latin America, women form a low percentage of the familial labor force.

The objective of this discussion is to explore precisely this relationship between women's participation within the familial agricultural labor force and the process of agrarian-class formation in a case study of the Andean peasantry. It is shown that census data are inadequate for the task. In at least the Peruvian case, census data underestimate peasant women's participation in agricultural production. Consequently, Boserup's proposition concerning the association between low female participation in the familial agricultural labor force and the presence of a substantial agricultural wage labor force in the Latin American case requires reexamination. Drawing on peasant household survey data, I demonstrate that Boserup's insight of the role of social hierarchies in varying the sexual division of labor in agriculture is of considerable import if social hierarchies are defined in terms of the process of social differentiation among direct producers. However, in this Peruvian case study, it is found that Boserup's conclusions hold for only the middle and rich strata of the peasantry: women's participation in the familial agricultural labor force is indeed less among peasant households with sufficient access to land to employ wage labor. But the majority of peasant households are either near-landless or smallholders with insufficient land to produce all of their subsistence requirements – they are increasingly integrated into the labor market as semi-proletarians. Among these groups, women's contribution to agricultural field work and decision making within the familial labor force is most significant.

The focus of this study is the province of Cajamarca which is the economic, geographic, and political heart of the department of Cajamarca, the most populous Sierra department of Peru. It stands in contrast to the rest of the Sierra for its predominantly mestizo,

Spanish-speaking peasantry. The bulk of the population of the province is rural, located in the inter-Andean valleys that range from 8 000 to 11 000 feet in elevation. The area is characterized by rain-fed agriculture, principally the cultivation of corn, grains, and potatoes; livestock and sheep-raising activities are also important.

Haciendas (large agricultural estates characterized by a dependent labor force) represented the dominant economic institution of the Cajamarcan region until the 1950s. The establishment of a milk-processing plant in the area in 1947 had significant repercussions for the land-tenure system and the development of a local wage labor market. The majority of the *haciendas* were transformed into modern dairy farms by the landed elite. The peasantry that once obtained access to *hacienda* lands through the payment of rent in labor services, in kind or in cash, were largely displaced. Some found employment as wage laborers on the dairy farms, but the majority were simply expelled from the *haciendas* as their former usufruct plots were turned into improved pastures. In many cases, however, the concomitant parcelization of the *haciendas* provided the opportunity for peasants to purchase land as private property. Today, the area is characterized by a numerically large independent sector of peasants, the vast majority of whom have insufficient land to produce their subsistence requirements. Since the early 1940s, this area has provided increasing numbers of seasonal and permanent migrants to the northern Peruvian coast, and today the majority of the peasantry participate in local as well as regional labor markets.

The Magnitude of Peasant Women's Agricultural Participation

Census estimates of women's agricultural participation in Latin America uniformly indicate that women's participation in agriculture is insignificant compared with men's. Moreover, the census often suggests that women's participation among the agricultural economically active population (EAP) has declined steadily in Latin America from the late 1930s to the 1960s and 1970s. Both of these trends are apparent in the Peruvian data. In 1940, women made up 19 per cent of the agricultural EAP over 6 years of age; in the 1972 census, women accounted for only 9.6 per cent of the corresponding EAP.

I propose that rather than a marked shift of women out of agricultural activities, the variation in female agricultural participation rates over time reflects different census definitions of the economically active rural population. Further, I contend that the low female agricultural participation rates are due to faulty conceptual categories for measuring women's agricultural participation. The objective of this section is to illustrate the sources of error in measuring rural women's agricultural participation and to propose an alternative measure of the extent to which women participate in agricultural work.

The female agricultural participation rate is particularly sensitive to the definitions of economic activity utilized in the census as well as to the operationalization of these definitions in the actual census questionnaire. For rural women usually hold dual occupations: that of housewife and mother as well as that of remunerated or unremunerated worker in an income-generating activity. In international practice, persons who dedicate themselves to housework are automatically included among the economically inactive. If the first question asked in a census questionnaire is the person's principal occupation, Latin American peasant women uniformly reply that they are housewives. In a patriarchal society, women's first responsibility *is* toward home and children. Cultural norms require women to project what is thought "right and proper." In contrast, if a questionnaire begins with a description of the activities in which the person engages for remuneration or which contribute to family income, the response is quite different. This differing methodological approach appears to provide a major explanation for the differences in female participation rates in agriculture in the 1940 and later Peruvian census.

The census data for the department of Cajamarca are illustrative. Women constituted 38 per cent of the total EAP over 6 years of age in the 1940 census and represented 19 per cent of the agricultural EAP. In this census, the persons interviewed were first asked to describe the income-generating activities in which he or she engaged; this description then served for the later categorization of a person's principal occupation. The 1961 as well as the 1972 census first asked the person's occupation. The majority of rural women now appear as housewives. Women make up only 7.3 per cent and 3.8 per cent of the agricultural sector EAP, respectively.

The decreasing percentage of women among the agricultural sector EAP over time is also explained by considering the changing census requirements for inclusion among the economically active for those who do consider their occupation to be one other than housework. In the 1940 Peruvian census, no time limitation was placed on a person's exercising his or her occupation. People were simply asked in which activities they participated, for whom they worked, and if they worked that week. The majority of women agriculturalists were classified as unremunerated family workers but included among the economically active rural participants. In the 1961 and 1972 censuses, a specific time requirement was placed on unremunerated family workers to be considered economically active. In the 1961 census, a family worker must have worked in the family enterprise at least one-third of a normal working day during the week prior to the census. In the 1972 census, the family worker must have worked 15 hours in the family enterprise during the week of the census to be included among the economically active. However, these requirements of actual time on the job were *not* applied to other occupational categories such as independent or self-employed workers. The differential treatment of self-employed and unpaid family workers is itself questionable, but cultural norms make this measurement problem sex specific. In most Latin American peasant households, men are considered the principal agriculturalists if they reside in the household; thus it is men who are classified as the independent workers in agriculture and women as their "helpers," the unremunerated family workers, irrespective of the relative amount of time that each sex may spend in agricultural activities.

It should also be taken into account that the seasonality of agricultural work makes census classifications of economic participation based on arbitrary time requirements particularly inappropriate. A census taken during a harvest period would yield significantly different results than a survey taken during the months of relative agricultural inactivity. In the Peruvian case, since the time limitation for inclusion among the economically active applies only to unremunerated family workers, it is only women's agricultural work that is obscured.

A rigorous measure of agricultural participation and, specifically, of the division of labor by sex, must be based on an accounting of the actual number of days of agricultural work performed by different household members over the agricultural cycle. But this raises the problem of what tasks actually constitute agricultural work. A broad definition of participation in farm activities would include not only the tasks associated with crop production (such as field work) and animal care but also the related activities, such as the collection of inputs, crop and animal processing, and marketing. If some of these activities are sex specific, their exclusion may bias the measure of the sexual division of labor in agriculture.

Even if one's concern is only the sexual division of labor in field tasks associated with crop production, attention must be given to the myriad of tasks which are necessary to the productive process. Take the case of meal preparation for field hands. Frequently, within peasant economies, the number and quality of meals to be served during the agricultural workday constitute an important component of the remuneration to non-family labor. And it is usually peasant women who must combine their participation in field work with meal preparation in addition to child and animal care. While women often alternate work in the fields with meal preparation, if a large noonday meal is required a woman may dedicate more of her time to cooking than to field work. If meal preparation for field hands is excluded in the tasks considered to be part of agricultural field work, then women's contribution to agricultural production would be underestimated. This will be illustrated in the subsequent section.

In the Cajamarcan case, survey data show that women are active agricultural participants even if only a restricted definition of what constitutes agricultural field work is taken into account. Women contributed 21 per cent of the total number of agricultural labor days employed on peasant agricultural units. Although the data are only roughly comparable with census estimates (since the survey results apply only to peasant agriculture), the underestimation of women's agricultural participation is apparent. Whereas women constituted only 3.8 per cent of the 1972 agricultural sector EAP, they contributed slightly over a fifth of the total estimated labor time employed in field work in peasant agriculture, substantiating the proposition that women's agricultural participation has been greatly underrated.

Table 1 (Deere, 1978) illustrates the division of labor by sex by form of labor procurement. Family labor includes the labor of household members as well as that of children in separate households who perform unremunerated labor for their parents. Reciprocal exchange labor represents unremunerated labor which follows a day for day accounting in the exchange of labor services (known as *ayni, desquite, un tal por otro tal*, etc.); wage labor includes labor remunerated in kind or in cash. Whereas women contribute over 25 per cent of the total number of family labor days employed in agricultural production, their participation accounted for slightly less than 12 per cent of the exchange or wage labor days employed on peasant farms. The data suggest the importance of women's participation among unremunerated family members and that it is particularly this form of participation that has been subject to undernumeration in the census estimates.

Table 1 *Division of labor by sex by form of labor procurement – family labor, reciprocal exchange labor, and wage labor – based on actual days spent in agricultural work on peasant farms during 1975–6 agricultural season (93 households)*

	Family Labor (%)	Reciprocal Exchange Labor (%)	Wage Labor (%)	Total (%)
Women	25	13	10	21
Men	75	87	90	79
Total	100	100	100	100
Labor Days	(3 336)	(724)	(666)	(4 726)

The Agricultural Division of Labor by Sex and the Differentiation of the Peasantry

In this section I analyze women's agricultural participation in terms of the process of social differentiation among the peasantry. I demonstrate that peasant women's agricultural participation is by no means uniform; there is a marked difference not only in the relative importance of women's participation within the familial agricultural labor force but also in the nature of the agricultural tasks in which women participate among the different strata of the peasantry. Women's greatest agricultural participation, relative to men's, is found among the poorest strata of the peasantry, those without sufficient access to land to produce their full subsistence requirements.

The land-tenure data for the province of Cajamarca are indicative of the extreme inequality of landholdings among the peasantry. The vast majority of peasants have insufficient land to support a family: 71.3 per cent of the total number of land units in the province consist of parcels of less than 3.50 ha. Some 18.5 per cent of the land units can be considered middle peasant holdings, ranging from 3.50 to 11.0 ha in size. Only 7.6 per cent of the land units are in the 11.00–30.00 ha range, while 2.6 per cent of the landholdings consist of units of over 30.00 ha. Unequal access to the means of production – principally land – determines the range of activities in which peasant households participate and whether peasants become integrated into the labor market, as wage laborers, or into the product market, particularly as commodity producers that hire wage labor (Deere and de Janvry, 1979).

Once a proxy for class is taken into account, there is considerable variation among the peasantry in the predominant form of labor procurement for agricultural work as well as in the familial division of labor by sex. As would be expected, the use of non-family labor in the production process increases relative to the total labor employed as the size of farm increases. Whereas among the near-landless and smallholders family labor constitutes over three-quarters of the total labor input in agricultural production, family labor makes up barely half of the total labor input on medium and rich peasant farms. In terms of non-family labor, it is the use of wage labor, rather than reciprocal exchange labor, which strongly differentiates among strata of the peasantry. Whereas only 5 per cent of the labor requirements of the near-landless and 10 per cent of those of smallholders are met by wage labor, 21 per cent of the labor requirements of middle and rich peasant farms are met through wage labor. But, while there is no significant difference among strata in the sexual composition of the non-family labor employed on the farm, there is a striking difference in the sexual composition of the familial labor force by strata.

Table 2 (Deere, 1978) illustrates the relationship between female participation in the familial labor force and land-size strata. Whereas women in near-landless households provide one-third of the familial labor requirements, women from the fully constituted peasant farming sector, the middle and rich peasant farms, provide only 21 per cent of the familial labor employed in agriculture. These results suggest that, indeed, the sexual division of labor is responsive to material conditions of production, and that women's greater relative participation in agriculture is related to the family's dependence on familial labor power and, concomitantly, to decreasing farm size.

Thus far, only the division of labor by sex for agricultural field tasks has been taken into account. As noted in the previous section, one of the principal problems in measuring women's agricultural participation is that women must often combine participation in field activities with responsibilities for meal preparation as well as child and animal care. If we include the labor time dedicated to cooking for agricultural field hands, women's total contribution to the productive process increases accordingly: women contribute 39 per cent of the total number of family labor days worked in agricultural production. Once cooking is taken into account, there is no significant difference in the total number of days spent in agricultural activities by women of the different land-size strata relative to the total number of familial agricultural labor days. But the qualitative difference of the work

Table 2 *Participation in the familial labor force by sex and land-size strata – female and male agricultural labor days relative to the total familial labor days in agricultural field work*

Land-size strata	Female (%)	Male (%)	Total (%)
Near-landless peasants (≤ 0.25 ha; N = 12)	35	65	100
	(65)	(121)	(186)
Smallholders (0.26–3.50 ha; N = 58)	27	73	100
	(563)	(1 530)	(2 093)
Middle and rich peasants (3.51–30.00 ha; N = 23)	21	79	100
	(220)	(837)	(1 057)
Total	25	75	100
N = 93	(848)	(2 488)	(3 336)

The sample size, *N*, refers to the number of households. The number of labor days corresponding to each category is in parentheses ($\chi^2 = 23.1$, $P < 0.001$).

process is apparent: whereas the majority of women from near-landless and smallholder households are involved in field work, the majority of middle and rich peasant women spend their time cooking for field hands. To what extent, then, is the contrasting division of labor by sex among the strata a function of the increased requirements of cooking as the amount of land under cultivation, and the corresponding demand for non-family labor, increase? Here it is relevant to consider the actual agricultural tasks in which women participate in order to discern whether there are important variations in what is considered socially appropriate work for women of different socio-economic class positions.

In order to isolate the relationship between class position and agricultural work, female respondents were asked if they would usually engage in a series of agricultural tasks. Over 90 per cent of the women indicated that they normally participate in planting activities, placing seed in its furrow, or shaking soil free from the roots of weeds. Over 90 per cent of the women also indicated that they usually weed by hand, a task characterizing the cultivation of the grains, and that they participate in each of the following harvest activities: harvesting by hand (collecting corn ears, beans, or peas), husking corn, or sweeping up the grain during the threshing operation. In these tasks where the overwhelming majority of peasant women participate, over 75 per cent of the respondents considered men and women to work in the activity with equal productivity.

In another three agricultural tasks, all involving the use of agricultural implements, some 70 per cent of the women participate: breaking ground with picks (*piqueando*), hoeing (*deshierbe* or *aporque*), and reaping grain with a sickle. Only half of the respondents felt that women worked with the hoe or sickle as well as men, while only one-third felt that women were as productive as men in the use of the pick. Women's lowest participation is in those tasks that involve the greatest physical exertion: plowing, threshing grain, and carrying in the crop from the fields for storage. Nevertheless, 15 per cent of the respondents felt that women threshed as well as men, while one-quarter responded that women could carry a heavy burden with the same ease as men.

Aggregating over all tasks, there is marked variation in the tasks in which women will participate by land-size strata. Whereas women from near-landless households participate in 74 per cent of the 15 agricultural tasks, women from middle and rich peasant households participate in only 62 per cent. The most notable difference in women's participation across the strata is in the activities in which agricultural implements are utilized. For example, whereas only half of the women from middle and rich peasant households hoe with a pick, whether breaking up clumps of dirt or harvesting potatoes, 77 per cent of women from near-landless and smallholder households do so. While 63 per cent of the women from the poorer households cultivate potatoes or corn, only 39 per cent of the women from the upper strata occasionally participate in these tasks. And the only women who admitted to plowing on occasion were women from smallholder households suffering from the lack of family labor as well as a lack of funds to hire wage labor.

The data support the proposition that there is a significant difference in the agricultural division of labor by sex by strata of the peasantry. Not only do women from near-landless and smallholder households participate more in agriculture relative to total familial labor employed on the farm plot, but women from these strata participate in a wider variety of agricultural tasks. Women from the middle and rich peasantry dedicate more time to cooking because more non-family labor is utilized in the production process, and these women do not consider it proper for women to participate in a good number of agricultural tasks. The use of agricultural implements provides the clearest boundary of the type of agricultural work which is considered right and proper for women to do. Whereas poor peasant women are much more likely to participate in what generally are regarded as male tasks, women from the middle and rich peasant strata most strictly conform to behavioral norms. The data suggest that, among the Andean peasantry, the participation of women in agricultural production is related to rural poverty. Economic necessity requires full familial participation in agricultural activities and a flexible division of labor by sex.

The Effect of Proletarianization

The salient characteristic of Cajamarcan agriculture is that the vast majority of the peasantry have insufficient land from which to produce even a portion of their subsistence requirements. Less than one-quarter of the mean annual net income of near-landless and smallholder peasant households is derived from farm production. In contrast, middle and rich peasant households derive 55 per cent and 82 per cent, respectively, of their mean annual net income from farm production; the median income of this latter group is some three times higher than that of near-landless and smallholder peasants.

Without sufficient access to the means of production from which to produce familial subsistence, increasing numbers of peasants have been forced to engage in wage labor. In 1973 some 72 per cent of near-landless households and 55 per cent of smallholder households had at least one labor market participant residing in the Sierra household whereas only 39 per cent and 35 per cent of middle and rich peasant households did so, respectively. What has been the effect of the integration of the peasantry to the labor market on the agricultural division of labor by sex? If a trade-off exists between agricultural work and wage work, and the wage earned by men is higher than women's, we might expect women's participation in agricultural production activities to increase significantly with the men's absence from the farm. But if there is insufficient land to absorb a significant portion of the available familial labor power, as well as surplus labor with respect to employment opportunities, there is no reason a trade-off between agricultural work and wage work should motivate the sexual division of labor.

The data on the actual number of days dedicated to agricultural production are indicative of the extent to which agricultural production cannot employ the familial labor force. On farms of less than ¼ ha in size, only 20 labor days a year are dedicated to agricultural production; on farms of up to 3.50 ha, the total labor requirements do not exceed 2 months a year. These days of full-time agricultural work are, of course, spread out during the year, but since they are calculated in total labor time, they indicate the extent to which agriculture can be only a complementary activity, not fully occupying even the male head of household.

Nonetheless, the data indicate that women's agricultural participation is related to male proletarianization. For example, the participation of mothers relative to fathers in agricultural field work only approaches parity in households where the father is a full-time wage worker. This ratio is slightly higher than the sample mean in households where the father works only part-time, but the difference in ratios is not significant. The average length of employment of the part-time wageworkers in the sample was 66 days in 1976. Given the minimal labor requirements in agricultural production on small plots, as well as the prevailing labor market conditions, it is not surprising that women work only as much as men do in peasant agriculture if the man is employed full-time in non-farm activities. Although peasant women in Cajamarca are not the principal agriculturalists of the family unit in terms of the relative amount of time dedicated to agricultural production activities, it is apparent that the division of labor by sex is much more flexible among the smallholders and near-landless peasants who constitute the majority of labor market participants than among the middle and rich strata of the peasantry.

Agricultural Decision Making and the Differentiation of the Peasantry

The relation between the division of labor by sex in agriculture and material conditions of production is also apparent in terms of the process of agricultural decision making among different strata of the peasantry. In this section I examine agricultural decision making in terms of the control over inputs, the organization of the productive process, and product disposition by sex and strata. The Cajamarca data suggest the proposition that, as agriculture becomes less important as the family's principal income source – principally among the near-landless and smallholder households – women's participation in agricultural decision-making activities relative to men's increases concomitantly with their increased participation in field work.

Consider, first, control over inputs. In the majority of households women are charged with seed preparation, selecting and storing the seed after the harvest, and cleaning it again before the planting. Men, aided by their children, generally take responsibility for fertilizing, collecting manure from the animal corrals and spreading it over the fields. Whenever seed or fertilizer is purchased, however, it tends to fall within the men's domain. Aggregating over all input-related activities, women's greatest responsibility is found among near-landless households; men and women tend to share input-related responsibilities principally among the smallholder households. Male dominance in these activities is a characteristic of middle and rich peasant households.

This trend is accentuated in terms of the indicators of control over the organization of the productive process. The key decisions of agricultural production concern what crop is to be planted, in what field, and when. When the decision is one of timing only, principally among the near-landless and smallholder farmers (since there is often only one plot of land to plant and the crop is pre-determined by the elevation of the area or lack of irrigation), in the majority of households the decision is characterized by family consultation. The principal factors to be taken into account are the amount of rainfall and the availability of oxen for plowing as well as of family labor. Among middle and rich peasants, the decision-making process includes the crop mix; in 79 per cent of the households in this stratum the organization of the productive process is carried out by men alone. In contrast, in fewer than one-third of the landless and smallholder households do men alone organize the productive process.

Contracting or arranging for non-family labor to participate in the agricultural task, as well as contracting for oxen, tends to be a male responsibility among all the strata, characterizing 79 per cent of the households. These tasks tend to be taken up by women only when they are single heads of household. In contrast to the generally male responsibility for arranging the agricultural work party, the actual co-ordination of the work process in the fields tends to be a shared task between men and women of all strata. This largely reflects the women's role as "hostess" in deciding when the breaks in agricultural work are to be taken for refreshments or meals. But if both husband and wife are working in the field, either may assign people to specific tasks or actually commence the work, although wives will defer to their husbands, if such are present. Women alone co-ordinate the field work only if they are heads of households.

Once the crop is harvested, the family must decide how much is to be stored for the family's use over the year ahead and how much is to be sold or bartered. Cajamarcan women in general play a greater role in decisions over product disposition than they do in the other facets of agricultural decision making. In the majority of households of all strata, women also take responsibility for storing the crop and for allocating the harvest to consumption, animal feed, and seed for the next planting. In only 7.5 per cent of the households, concentrated among the middle and rich strata of the peasantry, do men enter into what is generally regarded as the female domain. It is only in these strata, as well, that consumption decisions are shared between men and women – this being an exclusively female domain among poorer peasants.

Marketing is an exclusively female task and arena of decision making among 60 per cent of near-landless households and 45 per cent of smallholder households; in the remaining households, marketing decisions are shared between husband and wife, although the woman generally carries out the sale. In contrast, in only 9.5 per cent of middle and rich peasant households is marketing an arena of female decision making alone. The degree of female participation and control of product disposition is closely related to the integration of the farm unit to the commodity market. Small farmers market a minimum of agricultural produce, selling small quantities of their principal crop on a weekly basis in the retail markets. The marketing activities of these women are a direct extension of their management of the family's consumption; they sell what they have in order to purchase their necessities rather than engaging in marketing as an occupation. In contrast, middle peasants are much more likely to market their crops wholesale to middlemen right after the harvest. Here the decision as to how much is to be sold, to whom, and at what price tends to be made in consultation between husband and wife, although men tend to carry out the transaction in the majority of households. Barter follows a similar pattern in that it is sensitive to scale.

A striking feature of the cross-strata comparison of control and participation in decision making is that men and women among the poorer strata tend to share those decisions made only by men of the upper strata. Women from near-landless households as well as from the smallholder sector tend to control those activities which are shared by men and women on medium-size farms. Figure 1 illustrates the relationship between the relative number of households where women alone control the decision-making process, aggregated by types of decision over inputs, process, and outcomes, by land-size strata.

Women from near-landless households play a much greater role in all forms of agricultural decision making than women from other strata. And women from the smallholder sector certainly play a greater role in agricultural production and decision making than do women from middle and rich peasant farms. Taken together with the data on households where both men and women share responsibility, the proposition that women's greater participation in agricultural field work relative to men's is related to women's greater participation in agricultural decision making is supported. But it should be recalled that women's relatively greater participation in agriculture is strongly tied to material conditions, agricultural production being a declining activity both in terms of income-generating importance and in terms of the time absorbed by the activity.

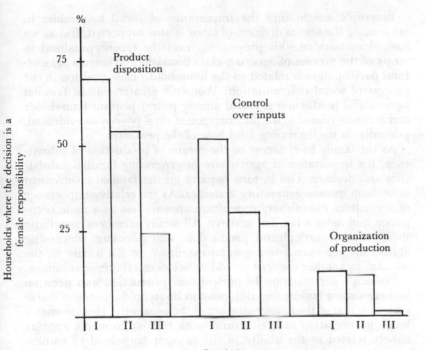

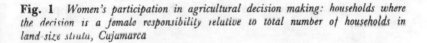

Fig. 1 *Women's participation in agricultural decision making: households where the decision is a female responsibility relative to total number of households in land-size strata, Cajamarca*

Conclusions

This Latin American case study conforms to Boserup's general proposition concerning the relationship between the sexual division of labor and type of cultivation. In the Cajamarca area, where the farming system is based on plow agriculture, men are considered to be the primary agriculturalists and do contribute the greater proportion of familial labor to peasant agricultural production. Nonetheless, female agricultural participation is most important, suggesting that rather than a *male* farming system, this Andean region should be characterized as being family based. The survey data confirm that it is principally women's participation among the familial labor force in agricultural production that has been underenumerated in census estimates.

Boserup's insight into the importance of social hierarchies in influencing the sexual division of labor is also supported. But as we have demonstrated, this proposition must be reconceptualized in terms of the process of agrarian-class formation. Women's agricultural participation is related to the household's class position in the process of social differentiation. Women's greater role in familial agricultural production is found among poorer peasant households and is closely related to the phenomenon of rural poverty as evidenced, primarily, in the decreasing land base of the peasantry.

As the family loses access to the means of production of subsistence, the importance of agriculture in generating familial subsistence also declines. This in turn requires greater familial involvement in off-farm income-generating activities. As the relative importance of agriculture diminishes, agriculture appears less as a male occupation and more a familial activity. All family members contribute their labor to agricultural production, and decisions concerning agriculture are shared to a greater extent by, or fall totally to, the woman, as another concern to add to her domestic responsibilities.

Women's participation in agricultural production and decision making among middle and rich peasant households contrasts markedly with that of the poorer stratum of the peasantry. Here women's lesser participation in agricultural work relative to men's appears closely related to the ability of the peasant household to employ wage labor. It is the upper strata of the peasantry that conform to Boserup's observation concerning the lower participation of women in the familial agricultural labor force where a sizable rural proletariat exists.

Peasant Production and Population in Mexico

Arturo Warman

In my work on the peasants of Morelos, Mexico (Warman, 1980), I have tried to analyze the interaction between two different ways of organizing life, of more correctly two modes of production: the peasants, on the one hand, and the conveyors of industrial capitalism: ranchers, farmers, businessmen or government officers, the promoters of modernism and development, on the other. Both modes co-exist and depend upon each other; neither can explain or conceive alone; they are like Siamese twins joined by the same spinal cord. However, these twins not only do not look alike, but also hold very different positions: one dominates, while the other, the peasant, defends himself in a thousand ways in order to subsist, in order to remain a peasant. Sometimes he defends himself by dying, paradoxical as it may sound. This happened during colonial times, in the sixteenth century, when the conquerors had to grant and recognize ancient rights to the natives, running the risk of killing the hen that laid the golden eggs, the only source of wealth. At other times, as in the agrarian movement led by Emiliano Zapata, in the beginning of the twentieth century, the peasants defended themselves by fighting, by making a revolution. At still other times, their defence consisted in multiplying themselves, in increasing the number of peasants needed to survive.

On this occasion, I shall try to explain this last strategy: peasant population growth as one of the ways of adapting to a deeper exploitation. I shall present the analysis in general, abstract terms, and the concrete peasants will scarcely appear. However, they will be always present, especially those from the eastern part of Morelos, the real teachers of this lesson.

The limited flexibility of basic resources for cultivation is employed in different ways according to the nearness of physical and technological limits that mark the point of diminishing returns for human labour. The handling of plants, with greater flexibility, is the most desired and less onerous alternative. It takes place through agricultural system of long fallow, especially the so-called slash-and-burn or swidden. The use of fire helps prepare the biotic community, and allows the planting of selected species with only very limited tools and without touching soil water. To operate the system, it is necessary to have abundant land, which has to be fallow to replace the natural vegetation that makes possible the sporadic growth of cultivated plants. Under long fallowing, the yield per cultivated unit of land is very high, but it is low if it is calculated in terms of the total area needed for operating the system. Short fallowing, in which the soil "rests" at least one cycle for each one that is cultivated, is almost always associated with the use of work animals, since the yield per cultivated unit of land is lower, and thus greater surfaces must be covered. On the other hand, the yield of the total area is higher than under the slash-and-burn system. In short fallowing the soil is handled, plants are not too varied and highly specialized, mostly cereals or grains. Partial restoration of the destroyed biotic balance is one of the crucial (but not always achieved) requirements. The introduction of irrigation increases the yield per hectare, and the yield of the total land area, since the soil is used more frequently, in some cases continuously. With irrigation, not only the water but also the soil must be levelled, or terraces must be built to permit regular water-flow, whether animals or only tools are used. Irrigated agriculture uses all resources with more intensity, human work included. The different systems are not mutually exclusive, and can be combined in many ways depending on the last resource, human labour. People, then, obviously hold a peculiar position: they are at the same time an element of energy for production, and the only existing reason for the complicated and arduous process of cultivation. This, too, because it is so obvious, is often forgotten. People are not the human resource of production as a supreme aim, but rather people produce in order to live.

From the combination of resources with very little or no elasticity at all, and human work, autonomous and flexible, a relation appears that seems constant in agriculture that only uses biological energy (also called traditional agriculture). This law, the formulation of which does not originate with me, can be stated thus: the more intense use of agricultural land results in an increase in total production and a decrease in labour productivity. In other words, if production is duplicated in a given surface, the amount of labour necessary to obtain it will grow in a larger proportion, since there is the need for more quantity and more complexity in the tasks of pushing other resources near their limits. And still another way of saying it: if more labour units are invested in a limited amount of land, the average productivity per unit will decrease. Well, and with this I stop insisting: the peasant works more and harder but obtains smaller increases in his production, as long as the territorial area remains constant.

Evidently, the hypothesis contradicts the generalized dogma that the greatest production – the "scale" that constitutes the efficiency model of capitalism – is a condition to raise labour productivity. It also contradicts the productivity measures that are made through capitalism's optics. In capitalism, work productivity is almost always measured per capita and in long periods of time, while in this essay productivity is measured per work unit in fact invested, per hour of effort. In the first sense, in the capitalist sense, peasant productivity increases with intensification; but in the second one it decreases, because labour demand grows more than production. Sometimes we are shown that modern technology, measured in a lot or a hectare during an agricultural cycle, makes work more productive, more profitable, and better paid: yet at other times, not even this can be shown. In calculating these figures, using business micro-economy, facts are in many senses obscured. The result may be totally contradicted by hidden facts, such as work-day length and its drudgery; what people do when the agricultural cycle – which only covers part of the year – is over; what is happening in non-cultivated or fallow land; or what is the meaning of the monetary units in which productivity is measured in terms of subsistence and satisfaction of needs.

The recent history of rural Mexico shows a constant tendency towards the intensification of soil utilization to increase total territorial production. If we apply the above-mentioned law, we find that the work needed to raise production increases in greater proportion. Data from many different sources fully confirm this fact. The central question is now pertinent: What motivated the growth of production and the more than proportionate increase in the efforts dedicated to achieve it?

Several obvious answers come to mind. The defendants of liberal capitalism cite their reasoning: peasants produce and work more because they wish to live better, as if the protestant ethic had suddenly fallen on them. The facts contradict this optimistic and naive vision. Contemporary peasants still do not exceed the strictest level of subsistence. All their effort, larger all the time, scarcely gives them enough to stay alive; without speaking of saving, much less of investing, or even counting on reserves for a bad year, for illness, for marriage or death. If anything like this happens, and it always does, one has to borrow and work harder yet in the future. There exists an almost unanimous consensus among peasants that the quality of their daily life has deteriorated: one works harder but enjoys less and even eats worse; everything becomes more difficult; "it's tough going", as they say.

Another obvious reply, that I shall attribute to ecological pessimists, is that peasants produce and work more because they have reproduced themselves irresponsibly, like rabbits. The answer sounds logical because evidently peasants are more numerous, double the number they were twenty years before, but it is completely false. The facts show without doubt that production growth came first and was higher, at least until 1970, than rural population growth. In other words, peasants worked harder before they had more mouths to feed, and no hope of saving or investing, or even the illusion of living with less debts; on the contrary, to pay overdue debts. Peasants are forced to produce more by external pressures. The real price of their products has been falling in relation to the price of the articles they have to buy. They have to buy more things that they do not produce, because their resources have been alienated. They have to pay 100 per cent interest to money-lenders, and each year they have to borrow more money for the benefit of middlemen and merchants. As free labourers, peasants earn the lowest wages in Mexico and only for short periods of time. Salaries are established in terms of complementing peasant autonomous production, and they are below the cost of subsistence and reproduction of other groups in the society. To say it pompously, peasants must pay a fee of increasing exploitation to the benefit of the capitalistic industrial sector, because they are dominated through the market, by the forms of land ownership, by institutions and by the legal or armed violence that shields them. The mechanisms of domination are another story that I shall not go into now, but evidently, they are a central part of this essay.

The facts firmly suggest that it is domination, the growing exploitation that benefits other groups, that is the principal motivation for the increase in rural population. Thus, rural population growth is not a cause but a consequence, a defensive reaction. Let us go back to the above-mentioned law: to each increase in production corresponds a more than proportionate increase in work expended. Now we can also state it in this way: for each value unit that the peasant transfers to the capitalistic industrial sector, his work effort grows in greater proportion. Every time the price of maize falls relatively, and it has not stopped doing so for the past thirty years, the work needed to compensate the fall is greater than the ratio of price deterioration. Faced with a demand for greater production and a diminishing productivity of labour, the peasant has to increase the size of his labour force. He is forced to reproduce himself in order to increase the availability of labour, so that he can keep intensifying agricultural crops even at the risk of cutting down his level of consumption, his standard of living. The peasant adapts and defends himself from an increasing exploitation through reproduction.

With this a vicious cycle develops and a Pandora's box opens. The rural population must reach the necessary size to saturate the maximum labour demand for crops in a constant process on intensification. The maximum demand is, generally, of very short duration, given the seasonal and variable nature of agricultural production. Water, land, and other resources are not available to give constant employment. The saturation of maximum demand implies "unemployment" for the rest of the agricultural cycle, a remnant labour force temporarily idle, which is characteristic of today's peasant populations. From the standpoint of the dominator, the remnant labour force has a potential for exploitation. "Under-employment" becomes determining under the increased level of exploitation, which again regenerates intensification and, obviously, unemployment that must be eliminated.

Part VI

Urban Poverty and Survival

Introduction

One of the phenomena that most clearly differentiates Latin America from other areas of the underdeveloped world is the scale and pace of urban development. Latin America is the most urbanized of the less developed areas and in 1984, over 50 per cent of its population was living in towns and cities of over 20 000 people. This urbanization has long roots and, at the beginning of the twentieth century, Latin America was already the most urbanized parts of the underdeveloped world (Roberts, 1978, p. 6). One reason for this rapid and early urban development is the continent's close integration into the world economy, reviewed in previous sections. The character of this integration changes in the twentieth century as Latin America industrializes in response to a growing internal market for manufactures and construction. Those countries which industrialize and urbanize first are those which first develop an extensive internal market, such as Argentina on the basis of European immigration and the agricultural prosperity of the Pampas or South Central Brazil, again through extensive European immigration and the wealth created by the coffee boom.

However, almost all Latin American countries were showing industrial growth by the 1940s and the proportions of their populations living in urban centres were rising fast. This rapid urban growth was not simply a response to employment opportunities in industry and in associated services, but was also fuelled by a population exodus from the rural areas due to population increase and the forces for agrarian rationalization discussed in Part V. In the decades following the 1940s, urban growth rates of 5 per cent and more per annum were common throughout Latin America. Moreover, this urban growth concentrated in the largest urban centers of the country, emphasizing urban primacy throughout Latin America, in which the major city – or, in the case of Brazil, the two major cities – were several times larger than other urban places. By 1984, for example, Mexico City had some 18 million people and was expected to reach 30 million before the turn of the century. Commentators were, at first, most struck by the scale of urban growth and by the apparent mass of unemployed and under-employed people that resided in the cities. Terms such as "overur-banization" and "marginal mass" were used to denote the social and political consequences of the lack of fit between the rapid rise in urban populations and the slower rise of secure and adequately paid employment opportunities. Many of the new industries were based on high technology and used little labour relative to their produc-tion. Indeed, there was an evident contrast between these modern industries and associated modern urban infrastructure, such as high rise office blocks, brilliantly illuminated supermarkets and super-highways, and the street peddlars, small workshops and the un-paved, badly lit squatter settlements or the crowded tenements which housed the majority of the urban population.

In this section, we look at the two sides of this urban process. First, we consider the economic and political forces that structure the city in Latin America and, second, we examine how people, particularly the urban poor, respond to and make use of the oppor-tunities created by the urban economic and political structure. We start with *Kowarick's* characterization of urban development in Brazil as responding to the "logic of disorder". The forces he discusses are present in most Latin American cities: speculative use of land; an economic growth – based, in part, on paying low wages, avoid-ing regulation and not contributing taxes to urban infrastructure; and the inability of the poor to pay for anything but the most rudimentary and interstitial housing. The Latin American city and its chaotic form is, from this perspective, a product *not* of economic stagnation, but of economic growth. The excerpt from *Portes and Walton* places this economic growth within an international perspec-tive, stressing the extent to which the Latin American economies have grown industrially on the basis of the "cheapness" of their labour, thus creating an urban situation in which the poor "subsi-dize" economic growth by themselves providing much of their subsist-ence through caring networks, petty commodity production, self-construction of housing and even the self-installation of urban infrastructure. Consequently, employers are able to pay low wages and avoid the high taxes necessary if the full costs of providing an adequate urban infrastructure were to be met.

The extent to which the urban poor must take care of their own welfare raises the issue of collective consumption and whether it represents a force for political mobilization (Castells, 1983, pp. 175–212). The account of *Moises and Stolcke* explores one dimension of this: the train riots that occurred in São Paulo in the late 1970s.

They link these riots to the type of urban development described by Kowarick and also to the authoritarian regime that had foreclosed other avenues for the expression of political discontent. The mobilization of the urban poor is, however, double-edged. Their desire to obtain cheap and secure accommodation serves also as an opportunity for politicians, political parties and authoritarian regimes to obtain their support in return for small favours (Cornelius, 1975).

How the poor "make–out" in the Latin American city is the subject of the last three excerpts. *Lomnitz* and *Roberts* provide contrasting descriptions of these strategies of survival. Roberts, using data from Guatemala City, one of the poorest and least industrialized of Latin America's major cities, emphasizes the job and residential mobility of the urban working-class – a mobility that is experienced by all the urban working class and which undermines collective action and limits the development of cohesive communities. Social relationships are vital resources for survival in this situation, but they do not create solidarity amongsts groups of the poor or among sections of the working class. Lomnitz, in contrast, differentiates the working class into an "élite", and more marginalized mass and puts greater emphasis on exchange relationships as bases for solidarity among these different groupings. The debate over the potential bases for solidarity and organization among the working class must, however, be placed in the context of the structural contrasts highlighted in the first articles of this part: the survival strategies of the poor are inevitably shaped by the framework of political and economic opportunities with which they are confronted.

Gavin Smith demonstrates the rationality that underlies what to the casual observer are haphazard and reactive survival strategies of the poor. He points to the importance of the household, singly and in combination with others, and of the domestic cycle, as determining the ways in which people get by in the city. He shows that city dwellers in Latin America should not be viewed or researched as individuals, atomistically struggling for survival but as members of social units that can straddle not only urban neighbourhoods, but city and village. Indeed, an important point arising from his account is the weakness of rural–urban boundaries in Peru, as in many another Latin American country.

These last three articles are based on neighbourhoods which are squatter settlements. This should not be allowed to obscure the fact that most of the urban poor live in different types of neighbourhood: in legal, though usually poorly serviced, neighbourhoods at the fringes of the city or in inner city tenements. Also, rental, often from other poor people, is as common a tenure as is the ownership that comes through squatting and self-construction. Analysis of these distinctions and of their significance for the coping strategies of the poor is, however, well covered elsewhere (Gilbert, 1983; Gilbert *et al.*, 1982).

There is now a wealth of reading on Latin American urban development. The reader who wishes to obtain an overview of the issues can consult such accounts as Portes and Walton (1976); Roberts (1978); Butterworth and Chance (1981); Gilbert *et al.* (1982). A very useful account of the urban land question and of state intervention in the provision of urban services is Gilbert and Ward (1985). For further reading on the related issue of urban social movements, Castells (1983) provides both a clear theoretical argument and interesting case material from Chile, Peru and Mexico. A detailed overview of urban politics and the question of access is provided by Nelson (1979). The reader should also consult the six available volumes of *Latin American Urban Research* of which the most recent is volume Six edited by Wayne Cornelius and R. Kemper (1978). Some of the most interesting reading on urban issues is to be found in the case studies of particular aspects of urban development, such as urban poverty or urban politics. Lewis (1961) remains fascinating reading, but should be read in conjunction with other ethnographies, such as Lomnitz (1977), Peattie (1968), Perlman (1976) or Cornelius (1975).

The Logic of Disorder

The Logic of Disorder

Lucio Kowarick

Greater São Paulo is the dynamic centre of Brazil. Here, industrial production, the financial system, *per capita* income, in fact all indicators of vigorous economic growth, denote an area of great economic potential, especially in comparison with other areas of the country.

While such evidence indicates the degree of economic development, it does not necessarily reflect changes in the "quality of life" of the population. It fails to link up two processes which would in Brazil appear frequently to be interconnected: economic growth and the deterioration in living conditions of large sections of the working-class. Living conditions are dependent on a series of factors, of which working conditions are possibly the most important. Nevertheless, some insight into these conditions can be gained from an examination of the conditions of urban expansion, including its services, infrastructure, space ratios, social relationships, and consumption levels – all closely related to economic growth.

In the early phase of industrial growth, before 1930, the problem of housing was partly solved for skilled and some unskilled workers by the employer. Firms built "workers' towns", which were usually constructed alongside the factories, and the houses either let or sold to the employees. This kind of solution was viable as long as the number of workers to be housed was relatively small – it was especially designed for labour in short supply – and worked as long as the low cost of land and building was compensated for by securing the services of workers for the firm. In this case, the cost of reproducing the labour force, at least as far as housing was concerned, was borne directly by the employers. This was the origin in the 1920s and 1930s of industrial districts in São Paulo, like Bras, Mooca and Belem, where life centres round the "hooters of the textile factories".

As the process of "import substitution" accelerated, the numbers of workers increased and so did the pressure on available low-cost housing. The cost of both industrial and residential land rose, and this meant that firms no longer found it economical to build houses for "their" workers, especially as an increased influx of migrant labour had created a surplus of workers. Firms therefore transferred the cost of housing – the purchase, rental and maintenance of property – as well as the cost of transport, to the worker himself, and transferred the cost of basic urban services (where they existed) to the state. From this point onwards the "workers' towns" tended to disappear, and the problem of housing was resolved henceforth by the "economic laws" which govern the real estate market. There appeared on the urban scene what has come to be known as the "periphery": housing agglomerates, illegal or not, which had no infrastructure, but which housed the workers on whose efforts the economic machinery depended.

In this explosive context of metropolitan growth, the public authorities armed themselves with legal instruments which appeared to try to impose some order on the use of land, but which came into use only after the layout of the city had been established. In any case, official action continued in the main, to restrict itself to servicing the settlements created by the private sector, thus helping indirectly, by means of its own urban development schemes, to justify the speculation of the real-estate and building sectors.

Some figures illustrate the results. In the capital there are 4.5 square meters of green land per inhabitant, whereas the desired minimum is 8 square meters. In the metropolitan area, out of 8 000 km of roads used by traffic, only 40 per cent are paved; 870 000 inhabitants live in houses with no electric light; only about 30 per cent of homes are connected to the drainage system, and 53 per cent to the water supply system.

In the "periphery" of the capital the situation is even worse: only 20 per cent of the houses are connected to the drainage system, and 46 per cent to the water supply. To have some idea of the high rate of environmental pollution, it is sufficient to say that at least three-quarters of the dwellings in the "peripheries" empty their drains into simple blind sewers. Even in the capital itself there are large areas, mainly in the Southeast, Northeast and East, where more than two-thirds of the roads are unpaved and 70–80 per cent of extensive areas have no electric light.

Here it would be useful to trace the dynamics of the process which produced this situation. In the disorderly process of urban expansion the property sector forged ahead, controlled the use of land, and kept vast spaces empty near the central areas to await the rise in prices. In the meantime, it opened up outlying areas, with no infrastructure, for sale to the poorer classes. Thus the settlement of new areas, far from following a planned programme, was based on the withholding of more central land for speculative reasons. Hence, in the city of São Paulo, vacant lots abound, principally in the peripheral zones to the East, West, Northwest and Southwest, and it is becoming increasingly common in Greater São Paulo.

The staggering demographic growth of the region – 6.8 per cent per annum between 1960 and 1970 – combined with the process of land speculation, greatly increased the urban area's spread. There is thus an increase in the number of people settling far from their place of work, typified by the "dormitory towns", which in fact are encampments lacking infrastructure. In this context, apart from work and housing, an analysis of which will follow, transport becomes one of the crucial problems.

Queues, over-crowding, delays, loss of a day's work cannot be called simple "transport problems". Those who depend on buses and trains to get to work waste an enormous amount of time waiting for transport and actually travelling. In other words, subjected to the pressures of the economic machinery from which he is unable to escape, the worker, in order to reproduce his condition as a wage-earner and urban householder, has to submit to a period of fatigue which constitutes an additional drain on what he has to offer: his labour power and energy. And, as the labour power of at least the unskilled and semi-skilled workers is in excess supply, the economic machinery can afford to waste it without doing itself much harm.

It should be emphasized again that the transport situation illustrates the effects of the close connection between the siting of workers' housing and the interests of development speculators.

Hence the "peripheries" have become such a common feature in all the urban areas of Greater São Paulo that today nearly 96 per cent of the inhabitants of the region live in them. Obviously land speculation does not occur only because of land retention between a central area and its peripheral zones. It is vigorous in those very central areas where stagnant or run-down zones receive investment in the form of services or basic infrastructure. The appearance of a highway, the piping of a small stream, in fact urban improvements of any kind have an immediate effect on the price of land. In this context, perhaps the most recent and flagrant example is found in the areas surrounding the present, and planned, underground railway routes. The fact that certain zones of the city will be serviced will change the use and type of existing properties, causing a staggering rise in the price of any plots of land available. Thus – and the public sector frequently has a direct role in the process – a new urban configuration emerges with its target usually being the wealthy buyer, while the lower income groups tend to be "expelled" to more remote districts.

The siting of shanty-towns tends to follow the location of industries. They spring up overnight in areas where there is a market for unskilled labour. When the pressure from speculators increases or the freezing of certain areas intensifies, the shanty-towns disappear, or are simply moved on to neighbouring municipalities where land-development deals are not yet so lucrative. A typical example of this is the case of the removal of the São Caetano shanty-towns to the near-by municipality of Maua, a flagrant example of a "slum clearance" operation in an area marked out for intensive property development.

There are 130 000 people living in shanty-towns in the city of São Paulo. There are also 615 000 people living in slum tenements, and 280 000 people who are forced to share a dwelling unit. There are, furthermore, and this is an important point, 1.8 million people who live in the "precarious housing" of the periphery. These figures refer only to the city of São Paulo itself, and in spite of the lack of data, the precarious housing situation can be clearly seen in the other municipalities of the metropolitan area, to which the working population has been channelled in recent times.

It is important to note that more than half the private homes in Greater São Paulo are owner-occupied, or in the process of being bought. The middle class, through the National Housing Bank (NHB) are becoming house-owners settled in well-serviced more central areas, while the working class are being settled in the peripheral areas, building their own houses in their spare time, with the unpaid help of family, relations and neighbours.

Building one's own home is a practice which fits in admirably with the logic of the exploitation of labour, for it reduces the cost to the worker of his own reproduction, of which housing is an important element. In the final analysis this allows wages to be fixed at low levels.

The periphery, as a formula for reproducing the labour force, has emerged out of the process of economic development experienced by Brazilian society in the last few decades. On the one hand it has allowed for a high rate of exploitation of workers, and on the other, it has allowed destructive patterns of urban living to be imposed on the working class. There are, in addition, 615 000 inhabitants of slum dwellings which are concentrated in decaying parts of the more central districts of São Paulo: Bom Retiro, Bras, Bela Vista. As a result of the housing shortage as well as the "slum clearance" operations in other areas, these slum tenements tend to spread, following especially the run-down areas adjacent to the railway lines: Perus, Pirituba, etc. Faced with the choice of worse housing or worse location, people in these areas live at a rate of 3.6 persons to a room – of which a quarter have no outside windows – but 67 per cent spend less than half an hour in getting to work.

Like the shanty-towns and the jerry-built houses on the periphery, these tenements house the working-class, who live in enormous numbers in the old mansion houses, in sheds or in cellars, basically because their family earnings are, on average, only two-and-a-half or three minimum wages a month. The background to this process of exclusion has been the development of workers' incomes. Not only has the real value of the minimum wage fallen considerably in recent years, but at the same time, the proportion of families whose income is not more than a few minimum wages has remained very high.

One cannot repeat too often that the recent process of the accumulation of wealth has brought absolute impoverishment to a considerable proportion of the working-class, certainly to the greater number of those workers who are unskilled or semi-skilled and whose wages have declined in real terms. In order to meet basic expenses – food, housing, transport – those workers earning one minimum wage must work for 466 hours and 36 minutes a month, that is so say 16 hours a day for 30 days a month.

These figures take on their true significance when one adds that in Greater São Paulo even in 1975 18 per cent of workers earned no more than one, 56 per cent no more than two, and 75 per cent no more than three minimum wages a month.

It is in this sense that one can talk about an increasing exclusion from wealth: low incomes are linked to sub-normal housing conditions, to long travelling times to work, to unsatisfactory nutritional conditions and to the greater risk of premature death. Furthermore, as a result of accidents at work, or premature ageing through the enormous physical and mental strain of a workers' urban life, the worker is not able to remain long in the labour market and soon becomes, at best, underemployed.

This process does not arise by chance. On the contrary, it is linked directly to the logic of the accumulation process pertaining in Brazilian society, which is able to count on a vast industrial reserve army and on a working class bereft of trade union and political organization, resulting in their being exploited at a rate which brings a great many workers to a state of absolute impoverishment, while at the same time, imposing upon them urban living conditions which waste away their working energy. But at least at the level of unskilled workers, they can easily be replaced by the employers.

The heavy increase in the number of accidents at work which occur in Brazil is symptomatic. The state of São Paulo, far from being an exception to the rule recorded 712 000 accidents at work in 1973, and 780 000 in the following year. This represents nearly a quarter of the registered work force, and takes on its real significance only when compared with the rate of such accidents per man year in, for example, France, where it is one-third as much.

These are the principal characteristics of the work situation and urban living conditions of vast numbers of the working class.

Clearly such processes do not affect everyone in the same way. On the contrary, in recent years a considerable amount of wealth has been created which has benefitted a section of the working class, particularly the skilled workers who, with the development and diversification of the manufacturing sector of industry, have been able to increase their wage levels, and who share to a modest degree in the benefits of industrial society. Even for them, however, the future is clouded by the rapidity of technical change and the deskilling that this often involves.

It is possible that, in spite of absolute impoverishment and the deterioration of urban living conditions, for many of those who come to São Paulo from other parts of Brazil, settling down in the capital has provided social and economic improvements. But this improvement should not be exaggerated, because it is the same process, after all, which is responsible for the total destitution experienced by increased numbers in the rural area. Furthermore, the fact that the migrant has a marginally higher income in town says little about the quality of life. The universally expressed feeling of migrants that they would like at some point to return home is an indication that the case is not cut and dried. Furthermore, in view of the deprivation of the urban work-force, expressed in low salary levels, and, consequently, in basic consumption levels, it is reasonable to suppose that even where the illusion remains that "life has improved" such an evaluation often results from an impression of participation and the hope of improvement which may be quite unrealistic, but which arises from a mass society which manufactures through the media what could be called "a market of illusions". It is the world seen in the shop window, on the television screen, the world of the "outdoors", where those who have risen in society serve as an example and a symbol of hope to those who can only share in their imagination the life-style of their fellows who have achieved success. The final turn of the screw comes because lack of success is branded as personal failure, hence providing a very powerful inducement to refuse to confront it as fact.

Limits are set only by the damage that depredation might do to the process of the accumulation of wealth, and not by "social" imperatives which transcend the logic of the economic machinery. On the contrary, where it has been profitable for private enterprise it has used easily replaceable labour with the utmost callousness and without the slightest concern to integrate it, even partially, in the benefits accruing from development. Obviously in the longer run this has its price, which could be reflected in the process of capital expansion itself, for physical wastage, ecological or urban depredation, imply, at least in the future, the destruction of resources which could be channelled into productive investment. But the dynamics of capitalism is not concerned with this; it is centred around profit-making, in the short run disregarding the depredation that is taking place in society.

Finally, it must be recognized that the state is not the patron saint of society as a whole. It considers the demands of the working class only when they can exert pressure on the decision-making centres. When that pressure is dulled and controlled, it represents unabashedly the interests of private appropriation. It deals with the negative effects of this only insofar as these threaten to affect the logic of capitalist expansion. The working-class, weakened in its social and political dimensions, becomes merely a factor of production. The loss of its capacity to defend itself allows the economic system to exploit and savage the work force and to substitute wasted workers with new blood, using the plentiful industrial reserve army, and creating wealth at the expense of the absolute impoverishment of the great majority of the working class. Furthermore, the loss of working-class organization results in a process of growth which raises the possibility that urban living conditions may deteriorate even more, if capital deems this to be in its interest.

The simple facts must be stated: it is capital – and not the labour force – which causes urban life to deteriorate. For the capitalist, the metropolis and the worker is of interest as a source of profit. For the worker, the metropolis in which he lives is the world in which he must seek to develop his human potential. Between the two there is a world of difference.

Collective Consumption

Urban Transport and Popular Violence in Brazil

José Alvaro Moises and Verena Stolkce

I

Beginning in 1974 Brazil's largest industrial cities, Rio de Janeiro and São Paulo, were swept by a series of riots directed at the suburban railways. The riots were not only a sign of the growing discontent of the urban poor with their living conditions, but also a consequence of their loss since the military coup of 1964 of any adequate means of political expression. The purpose of this paper is to attempt to trace the immediate causes of the riots, and to indicate their political significance both for the government in power and for the participants themselves.

The first of the trains was set on fire and partially destroyed in July 1974. There had been earlier outbreaks of popular violence against public transport, but these had been localized and quickly suppressed. The July 1974 riot, however, was not to be simply one more isolated instance of popular unrest. It was merely the first of a wave of popular protests against transport conditions in the rapidly expanding industrial centres of Brazil.

The following analysis of events is based on newspaper reports. Both the wealth of information available and the candour of the reporting are striking if one considers Brazil's present political situation. That such a conservative newspaper as *O Estado de São Paulo* should have so widely publicized the lamentable state of public transport must, however, be attributed in part to its own running campaign against the government's interference with the principles of free enterprise. The disastrous performance record of the state-owned Federal Railway Company provided the newspaper with a welcome pretext to express its dissatisfaction with the government's economic policy.

As the riots recurred, a new term was coined: *quebra-quebra* ("break-break"). The riots were not the result of fare increases. The cause was always linked to the frequent delays of the suburban trains, the incessant breakdowns, and the occasional fatal accident which turned every trip into a nightmare. All of the riots occurred early in the morning, when any disruption to the service might, by delaying arrival at work, threaten these predominantly working-class passengers with loss of job, and thus of livelihood.

In some European countries action groups have emerged in recent years in response to the deterioration in the quality of urban living or as a reaction to increases in the cost of basic services. These new forms of political participation have as a rule been, if not actually founded, certainly quickly taken over and controlled by parties of the left, but only very exceptionally have they assumed a violent character. Usually those involved have been driven to protest by what they felt was a threat of some kind or other to their way of life.

In Brazil the living conditions of the suburban population have been consistently poor since the beginnings of industrial expansion. The geographical concentration of production in a few cities, and the consequent development of sprawling suburbs from the 1930s onwards to accommodate the rapidly expanding labour force, created a growing need for public services, but this need was only partially and inadequately met by the city authorities and the government. In 1975 no less than 80 per cent of the houses on the outskirts of São Paulo still lacked proper drainage, and 54 per cent had no reliable water-supply. In addition more than two-thirds of the streets were not surfaced; between 70 and 80 per cent lacked public lighting; and houses built on about five thousand illegal developments were located on twenty-six thousand "officially non-existent" streets. The situation in Rio de Janeiro was basically no different. Rapid urban growth not only created an urgent demand for such basic services as water, drainage, public and domestic lighting, but in particular, because of the considerable distances between home and work, for a system of public transport that was fast, efficient and reliable.

The total lack of some public services and the unreliable state of others goes a long way towards explaining the growing discontent of the suburban population. But these conditions alone do not tell us why the protests erupted in 1974 rather than at any other time, nor why they were focused specifically on the problem of public transport. Nor are they in themselves any sufficient reason for the spontaneous, unorganized, sustained and violent nature of the riots. There had, as we have said, been earlier transport riots – for instance, in São Paulo in 1947 and in Rio de Janeiro in 1959 – but there had been nothing to compare with the wave of riots that began in 1974.

It could be argued, following the classic examples of "spontaneous eruptions" of the urban crowd, that there comes a point when the labouring poor feel that the only way to improve their lot is by means of open rebellion. In 1974 real wages in Brazil reached their lowest point since 1964. The decline in purchasing power must certainly have contributed to the creation of a favourable climate for revolt, though it still does not explain why public transport should have become the specific target of the riots. For such an explanation we must look at the actual conditions of urban transport and the ways in which these affected the suburban population's living conditions.

Expenditure on transport on average took up less than 10 per cent of the budget of a working-class family, with 39 per cent being spent on food and 23.5 per cent on housing. Money was not the main problem, and the principal grievances were not associated with fare increases. The central issue was the fact that the increasingly unreliable state of public transport threatened the working population with loss of wages, unemployment, even death – that is, it might actually deprive the passengers who depended upon it (predominantly wage- or salary-earners) of the very basis of their survival.

The suburban railways of Rio de Janeiro and São Paulo are owned by the state and run by the federal government, not by regional or city authorities. The Federal Railway Company, formerly the Central do Brasil, serves over ninety stations in the suburbs of Rio de Janeiro, and in 1973 carried about 700 000 passengers a day in 715 trains; in 1975 the suburban trains of São Paulo carried about 900 000 passengers a day.

In spite of their importance to the functioning and development of these two cities, the state of the suburban railways has continuously deteriorated over the years. Despite a growing demand for transport the total number of trains has actually declined. And there are continual breakdowns. In 1974 there were 1 720 train stoppages on the Central do Brasil because of some failure or other, and a breakdown at any point on the line often meant the disruption of the entire network.

What were the reasons for this deplorable situation? As *O Estado de São Paulo* stated in June 1975 after one of the riots: "In Brazil the railways . . . are the responsibility of the ministry of transport, and during the last administration 87 per cent of the ministry's budget went on roads, while railways were forced to share with port authorities the remaining 13 per cent". Significantly, while public transport stagnated, the number of cars in São Paulo rose from 120 000 in 1960 to almost a million in 1974.

What was the effect on production and productivity of the loss of working hours caused by the lamentable state of public transport? General attrition of the working population would only be recognized as a problem by management if the satisfactory operation of industry was seen to be affected. But the nature of the labour-market and the fact that the majority of the workers were unskilled allowed for easy replacement within the labour force. Individual hardship was ignored. The overall situation thus allowed employers to remain largely insensitive to the transport problem. Instead of exerting pressure on government to effect an improvement in public transport, they simply penalized those of their workers who had to depend on the railways, either by deducting money for time lost or by outright dismissal. In the words of one passenger: "what makes us wreck the trains and stations are the constant delays, because most of us know that if we are not at work on time we lose our pay for the day and for Sunday".

Some employers no longer accepted the "delay certificates" issued by the railway company, while others practised a policy of selective employment. As one employer warned: "if things continue in this way it will no longer be possible to employ people from Mauá, Riberão Pires and the other suburbs which rely on the trains" – a somewhat impractical attitude, one might think, as the bulk of the labour force lived in precisely suburbs such as these, and as private transport by car was not at the time economically viable for the majority of Brazilian urban workers. Moreover stoppage of pay or outright dismissal were also counter-productive, since it was in part exactly this sort of reprisal which fuelled the anger of the workers. As one passenger complained:

> things are allowed to go so far, and then the people explode. They give vent to their fury. When you get to work in the morning you have to tell your boss: "I am late because the train broke down". The next day you get there and you say: "I am late because the train was delayed". The next day . . . and so on. Do you think the boss will go on believing you, or that he can be bothered with your train?

A significant percentage of the passengers travelled as *clandestinos*, that is, without paying their fares. In 1975 the proportion of *clandestinos* was estimated at around 27.5 per cent, and this, of course, further aggravated the railway company's difficulties in improving the service. Also the low wages of the vast majority of the passengers made it practically impossible for the company to set realistic rail fares. For many of the passengers even the single fare of 60 centavos was too high: "Nobody risks his life for fun . . . Many times I have run along the track to reach the platform [bypassing the ticket barrier] because I did not have 60 centavos for the fare", said one of the passengers who invariably travelled on the outside of the train.

The situation of one particular worker, reported in *O Estado de São Paulo* after two riots had occurred on the same day in July 1975, was probably representative of a significant number of passengers. His income was 900 cruzeiros a month:

> each day he leaves home at 5:30 a.m., taking the train at 6:15 a.m. to be at work by 8:00 a.m. He takes 5.00 cruzeiros with him, 1.20 cruzeiros for his train fare and the rest for cigarettes. For his main meal of the day he has a handful of rice and beans and once a week some meat. In his pocket he carefully keeps his working register, for without it he could be picked up by the police. If he were to take the bus he would have to pay 4.70 cruzeiros for the return trip. And if he spent more than 5.00 cruzeiros in a day "the children wouldn't eat".

In the 6 years from 1970 to 1976 the average amount of time spent on travel to and from work increased by about 30 per cent. Passengers living on the periphery of the towns spent as much as three to four hours every day travelling. Moreover a large part of the labour force attempted to make up for the decline in real wages by regularly working overtime. The passengers that crammed the station every morning thus faced each new day exhausted. The struggle for a place on the train, and the journey itself, often standing the whole way, only served to exasperate them even further.

Another reason why popular unrest should have been directed specifically against their means of transport may be the "collective" nature of travel. This not only offered favourable conditions for joint action without the need for any prior organization, but by contrast with, for instance, collective action in the factories (which was banned) the daily crowding of the station platforms and the trains gave a measure of anonymity and therefore a degree of impunity.

II

The continuous erosion of purchasing power and the steady deterioration of public transport were reason enough in themselves for the people to riot. Indeed in view of the general conditions in which they lived and worked it is perhaps surprising that they did not riot more often. The systematic nature of political repression since 1964 and the power and ubiquity of the police forces – even the Federal Railway Company had its own police force – made any sort of organized movement almost impossible.

While the permanent display and use of force may have deterred many from openly manifesting their discontent, repression may itself have generated direct popular action. The riots were not simply a response to economic hardship. They were also the product of a political system which blocked all legitimate outlets for dissent.

Since 1964 the Brazilian working class has lacked independent organizations for social and political representation through which it can express its grievances in an organized manner. The labour unions are firmly under state control. Moreover São Paulo, Rio de Janeiro and the other state capitals have been deprived of their political autonomy, with their mayors (and also, more recently, state governors) thereafter being nominated by the president. In 1965 all political parties were banned, being replaced by a two-party system: the Alianza Renovadora Nacional (ARENA), the official government party, and the Movimento Democrático Brasileiro (MDB), an official opposition. Popular participation in the electoral process was restricted to the election of municipal councillors and state and federal deputies and senators, but even these elections were strictly controlled.

The federal elections of November 1974 were preceded by a period of relative political freedom. It can thus be plausibly argued that this provided the opportunity for some degree of mobilization by the working classes, however basic the actual level of organization. In this sort of political climate people might have managed to shed some of their fears and ventured to express their discontent openly. However, the wave of riots which began in São Paulo in January 1974 took place at a time of renewed repression, when several federal deputies had been dismissed from Parliament on the grounds of being affiliated to parties which had been banned, and even the political activities of the official opposition party were openly suppressed.

In short, while the material conditions of wage-earners steadily deteriorated during these years, periods of relative political toleration alternated with periods of harsh repression. The lack of organization and the spontaneous and violent character of the various transport riots must be viewed within their particular political contexts. However, this still does not explain the actual timing of the riots, which took place in *both* political contexts.

E. J. Hobsbawm (1959) has suggested that in any industrial society urban crowd activity and movements such as these riots tend to be superseded by the more typical modern labour movements, because of the emergence of an industrial working class and the increasingly efficient nature of the apparatus of public order. "Only outside Western Europe can the ordinary citizen of large towns still be expected to have experience of the pre-industrial riot and the pre-industrial mob". However, though we are concerned here with a non-European country, the settings for the riots are, of course, the largest industrial centres in South America. Moreover it is well known that the "apparatus of public order" is particularly well developed in Brazil. It is also clear that a large proportion of those involved in the transport riots belonged to the industrial proletariat. Yet still the riots occurred. This hardly bears out Hobsbawm's point. We would, therefore, like to put forward the hypothesis that in those industrial societies where autocratic political regimes have assumed power and suppress popular discontent, spontaneous riots may tend to occur once again. In a context where political rights have been reduced to a minimum, riots are after all one of the few possible forms of popular political expression. Viewed from this perspective they are not pre-political but eminently political. Only on the surface do the riots appear "irrational", "anarchic" though inevitable reactions to hardship. Their spontaneity and violence are the consequence of the working class's *formal* exclusion from politics. The people reacted in the way that they did, not out of any historically determined political backwardness, but because, in the circumstances in which they found themselves, this was the only means available to them to make themselves heard. After all, the almost total exclusion of the masses from the political process is precisely the consequence of their latent political potential.

Repression succeeded in temporarily stifling the riots, but it did not put an end to them. It may be that it was precisely the absence of leaders and the lack of organization that made the suppression of the riots so difficult.

If we compare these transport riots with the food riots of eighteenth-century England analyzed by E. P. Thompson (1971)a further aspect stands out. As one of the passengers warned after the devastation of Engenheiro Trinidade station in São Paulo in 1976: "now everything is calm. It is in the mornings that this becomes a madhouse. Tomorrow the people will take the train again and then we will see whether or not *they* now understand what *we* want; if *they* do not take any action *we* will start another fire". Who are *they*? By contrast with eighteenth-century food riots the suburban populations of Rio de Janeiro and São Paulo did not riot in order to defend traditional prerogatives – after all, public transport had been in a shocking state for a very long time – but rather against one of the several manifestations of a growing exploitation. The suburban railways were owned and run by the federal government. The legitimacy of the passengers' protests derived from the feeling that the state should, but did not, provide the basic services essential to their livelihood. Their hostility was directed not at subordinate or intermediate agencies, but in the final analysis at the state itself. In so far as the idea of a paternalistic state lingered on (a remnant of the pre-1964 populist mass politics), such recourse to rioting pointed to the crumbling of this idea. Being under direct attack, the state had to react. Faith in a paternalistic state was further eroded by the repressive action taken by the police and military to suppress the riots. The riots constituted a "delegitimization" of established authority and had distinct political implications and consequences. The choice of target was not random. The riots were caused by a collective feeling of distress, the result of the participants' identical situation as members of the labour force, and finally the people demanded recognition of their grievances by the state.

III

The most difficult problem is to reconstruct the crowd's own attitudes and expectations. It is possible to obtain some idea of these by analyzing the actual course of events.

In October 1974 one of the early-morning rush-hour trains broke down and stopped between the stations of Augustó Vasconcelos and Santíssimo (in the Baixada Fluminense, Rio de Janeiro). A crowd of about three thousand passengers, "exasperated by the interminable delays", set three carriages on fire and stoned another twelve. This was only the beginning. Passengers on a second train, "forced to stop at a barricade thrown up on another line by the passengers on the first train" (presumably to obtain alternative transport), joined the riot. Armed with "tufts of dried grass, wooden benches and some railway sleepers they joined in the burning of the three carriages". According to some of the onlookers it was like "a real war". The riot only ended after the arrival of a squad of railway police. The driver of the first train was also attacked. Something of the spirit of the crowd is revealed by the solidarity of the passengers of the second train with those of the first. Although the former were in effect prevented by the latter from continuing their journey, they nevertheless immediately joined the riot.

In the following year, 1975, transport riots became both more frequent and more extensive. Around the middle of the year, within the space of a single month, there were no fewer than six *quebra-quebras*, five in Rio de Janeiro and one in São Paulo. All of them were triggered by breakdowns and delays or were the direct result of accidents.

Although, according to the press, the crowd was "panic-stricken" it did not in fact simply destroy everything blindly, but acted as though it had a specific target. The resources of the state in the form of its forces of repression, the army and the military police, were mobilized.

The choice of targets, therefore, was not random. Action was not blind. But were the actions of the rioters perhaps in the final analysis simply an end in themselves, a kind of ritual of redress lacking any clear notion of the social forces behind the conditions against which they were rebelling? Perhaps the riots were basically symbolic, even though their consequences might go much further. Lacking the means and the power to reach directly those ultimately responsible for public transport, the state itself, the crowd manifested its rage by destroying such things as were immediately to hand: the trains and the stations. In one of the riots in 1976 the rioters at the station of Engenheiro Trinidade, outraged by the death of some *pingentes*, not only set fire to the station, but also tore down the station clock which was running six hours late at the time, stamped on it and broke it in pieces.

Over and above such symbolic destruction the passengers themselves defined the target of their action quite explicitly: "I only hope that God will bless the men of government and enlighten them so that they will understand the situation of the poor", sighed a woman passenger, infuriated by the state of public transport. In political circles it was fully appreciated that the riots had an ulterior motive and meaning. As a candidate of ARENA for the municipal elections of 1976 remarked: "the people vote for the opposition because they think that the government is to blame for the delays". One of the passengers recalled the time of Getúlio Vargas when, he asserted, the president would have dismissed those responsible for the accident within twenty-four hours. Even though immediate blame might lie with the railway company, it was thus assumed to be the function of the state to ensure that the company satisfied the public's needs. This explains one aspect of the rioting that seemed incomprehensible to the head of the regional department of the Federal Railway Company when he exclaimed: "they destroy their own means of transport. I cannot understand it!". The logic of events seemed to be that only such radical action as the destruction of public property as a demonstration of the latent or potential power of the crowd would move the authorities to take any action.

How then did the state react to these incidents, either indirectly, through its intermediate agencies, or directly? The Federal Railway Company often attempted to explain away the various accidents as the result of "possible human error" and, whenever anyone was injured, as a consequence of the irresponsible stoning of the trains. The *pingentes* were said to be typical of "the youth of today, constantly seeking some form of self-affirmation and obsessed with the prospect of excitement and adventure"; they thus had only themselves to blame if they were killed. In this way the railway company tried to divert attention from its own responsibility for the delays and the accidents. Besides, by explaining away the accidents in the way they did, the authorities could deny that the riots constituted any sort of legitimate collective response.

The crowds thus rioted against the conditions of public transport in the hope of persuading the state to take the necessary measures. In a sense, therefore, their actions were aimed at reform. But one should also look at the way that actual participation in the riots might have affected the perception that the masses had of themselves. Collective action of this type clearly goes a long way towards shaping the masses' awareness of their potential strength. The numbers involved in each of the incidents ranged from between three and five thousand. Only a small fraction of these actually took part in the work of destruction, but these few were supported by the wider consensus of the crowd as to the legitimacy of their actions. Moreover there was a clear "demonstration effect" at work. As one passenger in São Paulo put it: "The rule now is to set fire to things, because the present situation is simply unbearable". He was referring to the events in Rio the previous year.

Unable to offer any quick and effective solution to the transport problem, the only alternative left to the authorities was repression. The passenger just quoted was arrested shortly afterwards with seven of his "comrades" because, as a station employee later explained, "the situation was becoming more and more tense and a riot liable to start from one hour to the next, just as it had in all the other places". Each new incident reinforced the future potential for revolt. The actions of a single passenger, perhaps one who happened to be more daring or exasperated than the rest, might be enough to spark off the riot. As one participant in the Mauá riot explained after his arrest: "I got to the station when the riot was already well under way. Sympathetic to what was going on I joined the crowd, shouting *quebra-quebra* . . . people outside the station also joined in". Another, arrested under similar circumstances, described his own experience as follows:

At 5:00 a.m. I went to the station to catch the train to Pirituba where I worked . . . while waiting for the train I went to the bar for a drink . . . when I came back the riot was already under way . . . I saw a mulatto of medium height tearing down a telephone and kicking it, and *decided to imitate him* . . . then I was arrested.

There seemed to be no pre-arranged plan, but similarity of living and working conditions generated a common purpose: "let us see whether or not *they* have understood what *we* want". Despite the daily struggle for a place on the trains, "when it actually comes to getting on the train . . . the passengers help each other. They all know one another, at least by sight", declared another passenger, "we at least know who belongs to us".

In 1976 São Paulo became the principal scene of the riots. The various security measures implemented in Rio de Janeiro, together with government promises to improve the suburban transport system, appear to have discouraged passengers from taking any further action there. But in the first six months of 1976 São Paulo was the setting for no fewer than ten riots. The first of these occurred at Engenheiro Trinidade:

the train was overcrowded. As it neared the station the *pingentes* holding on to the carriage doors began to be knocked off. It was just after 6:00 a.m. . . . . There were about two thousand passengers on the platform and these immediately began to riot; they threw the railmen out of the station, broke up the benches and station fittings, and set fire to the ticket-office. When it was all over the number of injured was thirty-four.

Postscript

The first draft of this article was completed in June 1976. Since that time the state of suburban transport in Rio de Janeiro and São Paulo has changed very little. Delays, breakdowns and accidents continue as before. The elaborate measures for ensuring public order have not succeeded in preventing renewed outbreaks of violence, and transport riots have become practically endemic in the two cities since 1974. For this reason the analysis presented in this paper has to be open-ended. Riots are an important aspect of the growing political tensions in Brazil. Any effective improvement not only in public transport but to public services generally would require nothing less than the reformulation of the government's economic priorities and this seems unlikely for the time being. Some modification of the present political system to allow greater popular participation in the processes of government, which would contribute to the easing of these tensions, seems equally unlikely, though political reform along these lines is being urged with growing insistence by different sectors of society. It is doubtful whether political liberalism on its own, without any corresponding improvement in living standards, would have the desired effect of neutralizing popular discontent. As regards the transport problem, the only possible solutions for the time being appear to be stopgap measures and the tightening of "security". The following statement is perhaps revealing. *O Estado de São Paulo* reported in June 1977 that the design of a new subway line to serve the low-income suburbs of São Paulo "has been especially adapted to meet the particular characteristics of the passengers who will use it ... The carriages have been reinforced against the inevitable vandalism that will occur, since these passengers have a lower standard of living and less education than those who travel on the other lines".

Economic Growth

Unequal Exchange in the Urban Informal System

Alejandro Portes

The presence of the urban informal sector makes possible a condition of high surplus labor extraction by compensating for concessions made to the organized segment of the working class with the continuing exploitation of unorganized informal workers. Stated formally: The amount of surplus value, V, is the difference between total wages paid, W, and the total exchange value produced by employed labor, T. The difference between W and the cost of subsistence, S_1, defined in biological and social normative terms, can be generally attributed to past working-class organization and the resulting labor contracts and protective legislation.

These protective covenants and the strengthening of working-class organizations tend to increase the difference, D, further, between subsistence and average wage levels. For capitalist firms, the means to maintain and even expand V while yielding to increases in D is to push S to a minimum. This is not done directly by the firm, but by the organization of the entire economy.

Two values of S might be distinguished. S_1 represents the theoretical cost of subsistence, if the full value of necessities had to be purchased as commodities in the market. S_2 represents the actual costs of subsistence, including household-produced goods and services and those acquired through informal channels. The size of the gap between S_2 and S_1 is fundamentally different between core and peripheral economies. Whereas even in advanced countries S_2 and S_1 do not coincide, the distance is much larger in the periphery.

Stated differently, the portion of D represented by the distance between S_1 and S_2 is the quantity of surplus labor extracted from informal sector workers. Although such labor may not directly produce surplus value, it affects the relative level of W and hence the rate of surplus value in the formal sector. It permits an average level of wages in formal firms that is above subsistence while being, at the same time, a fraction of those predominant in the centers. In this manner, the labor of unpaid family and informal workers eventually

241

finds its way into the coffers of large industrial corporations and finance houses.

The next sections illustrate this argument by examining the actual modes of articulation of the informal and formal economies as documented by recent research. Examples are divided according to what appear to be the three major "in-come" producing strategies of urban working-class households outside the formal economy: (a) subsistence and networking activities; (b) petty commodity production and trade; and (c) informal land occupation.

Subsistence Networks

Household subsistence activities include the production of goods, such as foodstuffs and services. Though more limited than in the countryside, food production in the city is not insignificant. It includes animal products such as eggs, milk, and meat and vegetable crops. In his study of Guatemala City shanty-towns, Roberts noted the quantity of animals kept even in the most densely populated areas. Some residents not only raised poultry and pigs for their own consumption, but had enough to sell in the market (Roberts, 1978, p. 112).

An identical story is told by Birkbeck (1978) in his study of garbage-dump pickers in Cali. Birkbeck found garbage picking to be a highly organized informal enterprise and one where workers would use the refuse to feed animals at home, both for consumption and sale.

A consistent finding of studies dealing with urban squatter settlements is the opposition of inhabitants to be relocated into government projects where animal raising and gardening are impossible. Ray (1969) reported this trend among Caracas squatters relocated into multistory "superblocks". Identical opposition to resettlement plans was found by Mangin (1967) in Lima, Portes (1972) in Santiago de Chile, and Leeds (1972) and Potengy Grabois (1973) in the favelas of Rio de Janeiro. In each case, what appeared to outside officials as a marginal economic activity was regarded by the settlers as a primary source of livelihood.

Urban subsistence activities are not limited to direct production of food, but to its procurement through channels that bypass costs in the formal marketing system. The unpaid labor of unemployed family members is frequently used for that purpose. A study by Luz Joly in Panama outlines the existence of informal networks through which village products, such as pork meat (*puercos brujos*) and vegetables, are channeled directly into the squatter settlements of Panama City. By avoiding costly government inspection procedures, urban families involved in the networks can acquire these products at considerable savings relative to formal market prices.

Similar mechanisms for informal transportation and distribution of village products into urban working-class areas are reported in studies of Lima's squatter settlements by Mangin (1967), and Roberts (1976, pp. 99–132) and of Santo Domingo by Cortén (1965). The unpaid labor input of kin and friends appears to be a prerequisite for efficient access to village production and the consequent lowering of prices.

A third important subsistence activity is housing construction. Unlike their counterparts in core economies, a significant proportion of workers in the periphery build their own houses. In most instances, this is housing erected after the spontaneous or organized occupation of vacant land or after purchase of a small lot in one of the "pirate" subdivisions encircling peripheral cities (Portes and Walton (1976, ch. 2).

More recently, governments and international agencies, such as the World Bank, have sponsored "sites-and-services" programs in which squatters are given access to an urbanized lot and credit for the purchase of construction materials. Evaluations of some extensive sites-and-services programs, such as those conducted by the Salvadoran Housing Foundation and the "Operación Sitio" program in Chile, indicate that urban squatters generally prefer this type of program to those involving the purchase of a government house or apartment.

Reasons for this preference involve the lower costs of purchasing a lot and the opportunity to tailor home construction to family needs, including the conduct of other subsistence activities. At the start, a temporary shack may be built in the back of the lot, while construction materials are bought and accumulated. Construction proceeds as resources and time permit and involves the labor of family members, other kin, and neighbors.

The theoretical importance of self-built housing in peripheral cities is not limited to the fact that it solves the housing problem for the poor. Rather, its significance is that it solves a crucial problem for capital insofar as the latter requires the *in situ* reproduction of a low-wage urban labor force. Wages paid to workers in the formal sector are generally insufficient to permit access to the "regulated" land and housing markets characterized, in most large cities, by unbridled speculation.

Stated differently, the cost of providing shelter to all members of the urban working class through conventional market channels would require a quantum increase in wages or, alternatively, massive state subsidies. Self-built housing is cheaper than any comparable form, including low-cost government projects, because there is a large input of labor by the worker himself, his kin, and his friends.

By permitting workers to engage in a traditional form of subsistence activity – house building – in squatter settlements or encouraging them to do so in new sites-and-services projects, the formal sector capitalizes on vast amounts of unpaid labor. Such labor allows the continuation of wage scales bearing no relation to the level of rents in the regulated housing market. To a greater extent than food production, part of the cost of a crucial element of reproduction – place to live – is thus shifted into the informal economy.

Subsistence activities are not, however, conducted in isolation. In the preceding chapter, the concept of social networks was introduced as a key mechanism for the survival of workers in peripheral economies. The work of Lomnitz (1977, pp. 133–50) in Mexico City remains the most exhaustive account of this survival strategy involving the pooling of resources and information and a constant exchange of credit and other favors. Food production and procurement, housing construction, as well as information on job openings and small loans, are among the items exchanged within such networks.

Informal Land Occupation

A substantial proportion of the urban working class in peripheral countries lives in officially non-existent neighborhoods. Hundreds of such "pirate" or "parachute" settlements surround the perimeter of large cities. The population living in such areas ranges from an estimated 25 per cent in cities like Rio, Lima, and Santiago to 40 per cent in Caracas and Cali and over 50 per cent in Recife and provincial Peruvian cities.

The subsistence production of housing by the urban working class can obviously not occur without access to land. The urban land market in capitalist peripheral countries is governed less by need than by use of land prices as a safeguard against inflation and as a profitable and secure investment. Speculative prices brought about by rapid urban growth are seldom regulated, much less seriously taxed by governments. The landowning class can thus appropriate values produced by an expanding urban economy without any significant investments or improvements of the land.

Studies of the urban land market in Latin America register increases of 400 per cent in central city prices in Caracas over a 10-year period; 800 per cent in Cali, Colombia in 3 years; and 6 000 per cent in residential areas of Mexico City over two decades. Unbridled speculation and the absence or inadequacy of government subsidies bars the urban working class from access to normal market channels for land acquisition.

This situation has resulted in the emergence of informal means for land acquisition in every major peripheral city. Whereas the specific strategies vary, the final result is the constitution of working-class communities, often numbering in the tens of thousands, which stand in violation of private property laws and are, in turn, officially unrecognized by the state. There are three major informal strategies for land acquisition:

1. *"Spontaneous" settlements* are formed gradually in illegally occupied land. The emergence of these settlements is not dependent on deliberate collective decisions. Instead, settlements grow by accretion, with a few families setting up residence at the start. If not expelled, they are soon joined by others until the entire area is occupied. The absence of any prior planning results in a haphazard layout of alleys and houses. The pressing need for housing leads to high densities and to the construction of precarious two- and three-story structures. This pattern is common in the *favelas* of Rio de Janeiro and is also found in the *villas miseria* of Buenos Aires and *barriadas* of Lima.

2. *Land invasions* are the result of prior deliberate organization by a group of homeless families, sometimes with outside political or economic support. Lots are allocated to each family in advance, the entire site being surveyed prior to the invasion. The actual land occupation is planned to maximize external support and to contain repression by the police.

   Invasions usually involve large number of participants, a pattern designed to call attention to the plight of the invaders. Land invasions are the most drastic and frequently the most dangerous strategy for urban land acquisitions. They represent the dominant form in Lima's *barriadas* and were common among Santiago's *poblaciones* before the 1973 military coup. In Colombia, they are dominant in Cali, Medellin, and Barranquilla. They have also been reported in Asian cities.

3. *Clandestine subdivisions* are established by landowners who sell cheap lots to poor families. The buying and selling of clandestine lots constitutes an informal extension of the formal pattern of land speculation for profit. Owners are able to offer comparatively low prices by failing to meet minimal public regulations on the size of lots and the provision of services. Buyers receive bare land and a dubious title without access to water, electricity, transportation, or social services.

Clandestine or "pirate" subdivisions are the dominant form in Bogota. They are frequent in the southern periphery and are found in the hillsides surrounding the city and beyond the river Bogota, subject to periodic flooding. "Pirate" urbanizers are not usually landowners, but middlemen who acquire land from old proprietors of the *sabana* and sell it through informal contracts. Lot sizes of 72 m² sell at present for between US$10–30 per square meter, without water, sewage, or electricity. Clandestine settlements also exist in Chile under the name *loteos brujos* and appear to be the dominant form in Mexico City and San Salvador.

Illegal land occupation results from wage scales bearing no relationship to the market price of land. Squatter and other illegal settlements represent a subsidy to the reproduction of the urban working class outside formal capitalist relations. Access to land enables the worker and his family to engage in the direct subsistence activities of home building and food production. More generally, the constitution of the settlement brings together workers employed in the formal economy and those employed in informal petty production and trade.

The settlement, as a social community, is the context wherein networks of exchange and mutual support are created. It is also in this context where the articulation of money wages with informal sources of supply permit the simultaneous reproducton of the different segments of the working class. Subsidized illegal settlements and the gamut of informal economic activities based on them are ultimately appropriated by capital in the form of lower wages. Squatter settlements and land invasions do not represent an abnormality or a contradiction in peripheral economies, but are, instead, an intrinsic component of the process of capitalist accumulation, as it occurs in them.

Constraints on the Expansion of the Working Class

The reduction in costs of subsistence for the segment of the working class employed in formal capitalist enterprises is not the only means of ensuring high surplus value extraction. As mentioned previously, the wage scales and social security benefits of this segment represent, under conditions of social disarticulation in the periphery, a political constraint on capital. Firms seek to further reduce labor costs by avoiding expansion of their organized work force and reaching down directly into the pool of informal sector workers. Through this strategy, minimum wage, health, social security, protection against arbitrary dismissal, and other clauses of labor legislation can be avoided.

Economists have frequently noted the slow absorption of labor by the manufacturing sector of peripheral countries. In Mexico, one of the most heavily industrialized peripheral nations, the manufacturing sector absorbs roughly one-fifth of the economically active population, having increased its share by only 5 per cent since the early days of the Revolution. The general explanation given is that peripheral industrialization is based on imported capital-intensive technology, which demands little labor.

A neglected factor in this explanation is the increasingly apparent use of informal sector workers by formal enterprises to perform labor intensive or seasonal work. Manufacturers limit expansion of their organized labor force by the use of intermediaries that carry out the stipulated tasks with unorganized informal workers. Widespread use of this strategy, a fact not registered by official statistics, can have a significant impact on the rate of labor absorption by the "modern" sector.

Conclusion

The class structure of peripheral urban economies can be described in terms of four broad categories:

1. Domestic and foreign capital owners, senior executives, and state managers
2. Salaried professionals and technicians in public and private employment
3. Clerical and manual wage labor in public enterprises and private industry and services
4. Casual wage labor, disguised wage labor, and self-employment in petty production and trade

The first three classes comprise the formal sector. The interests of the first class are, however, structurally opposite to those of the other two. Class 1 members are dependent – directly or indirectly – on the rate of surplus value. Although for some this may be tied to expansion of the internal market, the structure of sectorally disarticulated peripheral economies leads to the dominance of the export sector. This translates in turn into a consistent drive against the portion of the product going as salaries and wages to Classes 2 and 3.

The organization and political mobilization of these classes counteract the interests of capital and prevent their monetary returns from reaching the minimum possible under a "free" labor market. In this situation, the preservation of the share of the product going as profits to Class 1 requires a reduction of the costs of consumption for the other two classes, a reduction of their size relative to the available unorganized labor, or both.

Depending on the specific situation, the relationship between the urban classes is one in which Class 1 – the owners – uses Class 4 against the intermediate classes, or one in which Class 1 allows Classes 2 and 3 to exploit Class 4, thereby cheapening their costs of reproduction and reducing upward pressures on wages. In whatever version, the fundamental point is that the informal sector subsidizes part of the costs of formal capitalist enterprises, enabling them to enforce comparatively low wages on their own labor.

The reliance on family subsistence activities for the reproduction of the work force is not a new phenomenon in the history of capitalism. Nor is it the employment of unorganized and vulnerable labor in "putting-out" and similar arrangements. Those familiar with the early history of capitalism in Europe and the not-so-old rise of industrialism in the United States could point out to a wealth of similar examples. The fundamental difference and the reason why our analysis of the informal economy has not been assimilated into the abundant literature on similar European experiences is that the two phenomena took place at separate moments in the development of the world economy.

Putting-out and informal labor exploitation, the existence of vast layers of semi-proletarianized labor, accompanied the autonomous expansion of industrialism in the centers. They gradually gave way to full proletarianization as the system was transformed by the rise of finance capital and imperialism. Indeed, the capacity of the central economies to bring their working classes into fully commodified relations was, in part, dependent on their reach abroad and the exploitation of peripheral labor.

It is impossible to assimilate the informal economy as it exists today in peripheral countries to the earlier "transitional" stage of advanced capitalism, for the present situation is the deliberate and continuously reproduced consequence of a new worldwide structure of accumulation. Thus, informal enterprise is not a vestigial presence, a lag from pre-capitalist times, but rather a very modern and expanding creation. It is an integral component of peripheral capitalist economies and its development is mandated by the conditions in which these economies are incorporated into the contemporary world-system.

Because the context is different from that of the "transitional" stage in Europe and the United States, there is no reason to expect that the informal sector will disappear through gradual "involution" and every reason to anticipate that it will continue to exist and expand. The continuously increasing relative gap in wage levels between core and peripheral workers at comparable levels of productivity requires it. The constantly expanding gap between formal sector (Classes 2 and 3) and informal sector living conditions within the periphery and the increasing number of informal enterprises and of the urban "self-employed" provide evidence of it. Such has been the experience of the last decades despite orthodox economic theory and its adherents. Conditions can change, but they will not do so to reproduce, mirrorlike, the particular evolution of nineteenth-century European capitalism. The system itself has changed.

Two final clarifications of our argument must be made: First, the distinction between manual workers in the formal and informal sectors refers to the separation between types of labor and not between physical individuals. Workers frequently alternate between periods of formal and informal employment and the same individual may simultaneously hold jobs in both sectors. The attributes of formal and informal employment and the interrelationships between them must, therefore, be understood as characteristics of the economic structure and not of physically separate groups. Second, the preceding analysis of peripheral classes indicates that the informal sector's subsidy to consumption is not limited to Class 3 workers. The same applies, though less directly, to salaried technicians and professionals.

Direct subsidies to reproduction by informal to formal-sector labor are also indirect subsidies to core-nation capital and, hence, means to defend the rate of profit on a world scale. The concrete forms that this transfer takes range from low-price raw materials and foodstuffs to an increasing flow of cheap manufactures. Paralleling the mechanisms of rural subsistence enclaves, but in a far more diversified and complex manner, firms are thus able to exploit not only the work energy of their own workers in the periphery, but those of their kin, neighbors, and friends as well.

The Poor in the City

Urban Careers and the Strategies of the Poor

Bryan R. Roberts

The declining significance of locality for job recruitment means an increase in job mobility and a greater discontinuity in the occupational careers of these workers. This occurs partly because age and literacy are not qualifications that commit an individual to any particular type of job. Consequently, a worker can seek out better job opportunities, but lack of personal commitments also means that he is more easily replaceable. Also, with the proliferation of small enterprises the work situation itself becomes more unstable and sensitive to changes in the economic climate of Guatemala. Newly established enterprises do not have stable relationships with a clientele in city or countryside. In time of prosperity, the number of enterprises increases and established ones take on additional workers to meet the demand, but during economic depressions or those fluctuations occasioned by political events, enterprises fail and lay off workers.

Under these conditions, a successful occupational career is one in which a worker seeks out stable and well-paid employment moving from one job to another as circumstances change. Those who are old and illiterate and cannot easily compete are thus likely to remain in, or soon enter, a marginal occupation where the income fluctuates with economic change or is so low as to make no difference. In contrast to those situations where the change occurs because large enterprises demand higher qualifications of their workers, individual characteristics become important to job recruitment in Guatemala City as a worker shifts from one small, ill-equipped workshop to another, as he sets up his own workshop with no more equipment than a sewing machine or a few rudimentary tools or helps others to peddle merchandise around the city. In the contrasting case of Monterrey, Mexico, the increasing importance of qualifications appears to occur through large-scale industrial enterprises raising their recruiting standards – see Balán (1969). This movement does include larger and more formally organized enterprises where literacy is more closely tied to job position; but, in general, the emerging significance of literacy and age occurs as workers move from job to job, seeking better employment or trying to avoid entering low-paid marginal employment.

To convey a sense of the type of mobility that is being discussed, two cases of job mobility are presented; one of these is city born and the other is a migrant. Both cases emphasize the diversity of the mobility and its sensitivity to economic and political events.

Luis: A Migrant, Literate, in his Late Thirties

Luis came to the city at age fourteen from a departmental capital located some 150 miles from the city. His elder brothers had preceded him and were working as tailors in the city. He came to live with them, and they got him an apprenticeship in the small clothes factory where they were working. There were about forty-eight workers in the factory supervised by three specialist tailors. The factory was local. Luis describes his 10 working years in the factory, emphasizing the prosperous economic conditions of the early revolutionary years: "Peasants would come to the city to buy shoes, clothes, food, and would not even bargain". Working conditions were being improved by industrial legislation that protected the worker, guaranteeing a 6-day week, overtime, and a minimum wage. A union was formed in Luis's factory, and, in the last years of his stay that coincided with the regime of left-wing President Jacobo Arbenz, Luis was active in labor disputes. He had married and describes this 1952–54 period as one when he was working hard to maintain his wife and yet active against exploitation by the factory owner. Luis was still living close to his brothers. With the fall of Arbenz, Luis describes the worsening conditions in the factory due partly to the owner's taking advantage of the conservative regime to reduce workers' benefits and partly to an economic recession. Luis quotes the figures for the reduced output of the factory in this time. In 1956 he lost his job shortly before the factory closed due to the bankruptcy of the owner. He set up independently as a tailor in the zone. At first, he claimed to do reasonably well and soon bought sewing machines and hired assistants to help with the work. Then, his business failed and Luis began to work in small tailor shops. He describes his work in this period from 1956 onward as moving from shop to shop in search of adequate work. He claims that, due to competition from Salvadoran products, it was becoming increasingly difficult to get enough work to make ends meet. Where before he was given five pairs of trousers to work on in a day, he was now given five pairs to work on in a week. Finding his rented accommodations too expensive and having married again and had children, he invaded the shanty-town. In subsequent years, while still seeking work from tailor shops, he sought other forms of remuneration, often, as we shall see, political. He also occasionally travels to the provinces, especially the remoter parts, taking his sewing machine with him and hiring a mule to carry his equipment. He sets up in village fairs and does on-the-spot tailoring. He claims that his income in 1968 from tailoring was about a third of what it was in 1954.

José: City-born, Literate, in his Early Forties

José's father apprenticed him in his early teens to a local butcher's trade, but he did not like the conditions of work and a few years later he joined his uncle in his small business of making such leather goods as saddles, bags, and the like. He served out his apprenticeship and began to work, but, after getting into trouble in the city, he took to the provinces and moved around small towns working for months at a time as a leather worker. He returned to the city just before the revolution of 1944 and became an active participant. For his efforts, he became a member of a city police force set up to keep order in the period following the revolution. He returned to work with his uncle and continued working there until 1954, in the meantime moving his zone of residence several times. In the disturbances following the counterrevolution of Castillo Armas, he left the city and took a job as a docker in the port of San José. This job he got through a contact there. In the same period he applied for and got a small parcel of land where he located his family and started a small farm. He got into trouble on the docks, being prominent in labor disputes, and lost his job, then dedicated himself full-time to the farm. This work went well, but again personal and political disputes surrounded his rights to the piece of land, and influential people desiring his land had him removed from it. He tried again with a poorer piece, but eventually in 1962 he returned to the city, went straight to the shanty-town to get a lot, and started to work in his old trades of leather work and pork butchery. He finds that leather working is no longer remunerative because of the decline in demand for saddles and competition from imported material. Increasingly he set himself up in independent work, buying pigs and cattle, slaughtering them, and selling the meat to wholesalers and retailers. He continued in this work full-time until 1968, when his work in political organization got him an office job with one of the political parties.

These examples merely dramatize something that results from the structure of job recruitment under the conditions of the rapid growth of Guatemala City. These discontinuities are also true for those who remain within their occupation. Thus, the rapid increase in the labor force also means that within an occupation there is increasing competition for the good jobs and the good profits or wages. Workers, as in the case of Luis described earlier, who began their careers in the city in the years up to the late 1940s speak with nostalgia of the stable working conditions of jobs in these years. Traders, for example, emphasize that they could sell for higher profits and turn over more merchandise than they can now. Craftsmen such as tailors and shoemakers, who face increasing competition from factory-made products often originating outside Guatemala, cite the much higher incomes they earned in the early years of the revolution. However accurate these complaints, the important thing is that workers in most occupations believe that their material condition has not substantially improved, and the reference points they use in interpreting present possibilities often are their early career experiences.

Apart from these general discontinuities, there are those discontinuities that arise because the careers of the workers straddle the changes that have taken place. Basically, we have been describing a change in the way different generations of workers enter the labor market. During a worker's occupational prime, what matters for his subsequent mobility is the job category in which he starts, and there is little evidence that, during their prime, workers move between jobs in established enterprises and those in trade, services, or construction, or between being employed and being self-employed. Looking again at the data on the three cohorts born in 1911–21, 1922–32, and 1943–53 there is little difference between the first and subsequent jobs of each cohort as to whether they are in established enterprises or not. Indeed, comparing the very first urban jobs of the whole sample with their occupations in 1968 also indicates considerable continuity as far as these broad distinctions are concerned. Of those who started in self-employment, 78 per cent continued in it in 1968, and, of those who began in trade, construction, or the services, 70 per cent were still in those categories in 1968.

One major way in which the change in the basis of job recruitment has affected workers in the neighborhoods is to differentiate the job careers of the different generations. Younger workers, for example, are less likely to have experience in workshops or factories than older workers who, in turn, may be less familiar with the emerging trading or service activities. This means that fathers and sons are less likely to have jobs in common and to be of use to each other on the job. Less than half the eldest sons of workers in the sample have followed in the same general job category as their fathers, let alone in the same job or enterprise; it was noticeable during field work that many parents made a point of advising sons not to follow in their occupations. Thus, craftsmen such as tailors, shoemakers, or carpenters, when commenting to me on the difficulties they encountered in making their living, would often turn and point to a son and say that he was in, or was going to enter, a different type of occupation.

We can now construct a general description of the types of occupational career experienced by low-income workers. At the beginning of a worker's urban occupational career, he has neither the experience nor the contacts to find good employment and, especially, good employment in established enterprises. Also, the decline in the proportion of apprenticeships means that both migrants and city born are likely to take whatever job is available. As they accumulate experience and contacts, they move relatively frequently before stabilizing their occupations around age twenty if they are city reared and later if migrants. If they are literate they are usually successful in finding some relatively well-paid job in established enterprises; but if they are illiterate they are more likely to begin in low-paid employment and to remain in such employment despite changes of jobs.

As they grow older, workers shift to self-employment or low-paid marginal occupations; illiterate workers are especially likely to do so. Yet for all these workers, it seems that sooner or later age makes them marginal to being employed in established enterprises and one of the most frequent topics of conversation with workers in such enterprises is the prospect of their becoming self-employed or taking on some service or trading job. This means that workers, as they grow older, must take into account not only the social relationships relevant to their present occupation but also those that will aid them in a future and often quite distinct type of occupation. In this way, the life cycle has a dynamic of its own with respect of the job behavior and social relationships that an individual considers relevant to his interests. Much of the movement described is not forced through losing a job, but brought about by an individual's assessment of his present position and prospects. This is even true, as we saw in Pepe's case, of many moves to self-employment and to other unstable occupations. As workers grow older they may prefer less arduous work and a more flexible timetable.

Separation of Work and Residence

The proliferation of small enterprises and the occupational mobility that has been described are associated with an increasing separation of the place of work and the place of residence of these workers.

The process that is being described is a consequence of the rapid growth of the city unaccompanied by substantial and evenly distributed economic development. The purchasing power of the mass of the urban population has remained low and thus there is not the extensive market available for the stable growth of a large number of urban industries catering to the population. Instead, there are a number of establishments catering to an international, national, and local middle and upper class clientele that accumulate sufficient funds to enable them to directly or indirectly finance a chain of smaller enterprises. A shoe factory, for example, may have a retail outlet in the center of the city and also "put out" work to a large number of small craftsmen.

The significance of increasing centralization is that it is a career experience of many workers in the two neighborhoods that they must take into account as they consider their next occupational move. For some workers, it means the increasing relevance of social relationships with social and economic superiors who have the social and geographical span needed to influence the allocation of jobs or credit. Many workers have experienced a shift from a work situation where they depend on local businesses or a local clientele – where they reside close to those with whom they did business or by whom they were employed – to a situation where their working relationships are divorced from their residence and often depend on socially and spatially remote people. Workers in the two neighborhoods have neither come to work in large-scale enterprises nor have they remained working locally and for a local clientele. These workers have neither social relationships binding their work and their residence, nor do they have the opportunity to form relationships with workers in the same category through common employment in large-scale enterprises.

The change in the basis of occupational recruitment is thus part of a transition in which individual workers must construct their own occupational careers with the aid of whatever contacts and qualifications they have at hand. A person's job is thus increasingly divorced from a stable context of family and friendship relationships, and movement along an occupational career does not reinforce existing relationships by adding common work interests to kinship and common residence. Though kin and friends may provide the information or contacts needed to obtain a job, they rarely are acting to include the worker in their sphere nor are they determining his career. Instead, a worker's job mobility is influenced by economic fluctuations beyond his control, and the successful worker is one who uses whatever resources are at his disposal to manipulate the range of opportunities. In terms of his work, a worker thus develops an extensive rather than an intensive set of relationships and this has important consequences for his orientations to acting with others.

Under the conditions we have described, the working world of low-income workers is characterized by the emergence of distinct occupational paths. Thus, for workers in marginal occupations whose mobility is over, social contacts have a less immediate significance than for literate migrants expecting to be highly mobile. These latter maintain and develop contacts with those who can help them to better employment. Conversely, those facing the prospect of becoming self-employed must think in terms of a different set of relationships to assist them in the transition. The nature of the path that the low income worker is describing and his stage along it becomes an important determinant of his readiness to enter into social activity and gives him differing perspectives on how to order his environment. In this sense, neither neighborhood represents a community of workers who can be bound to an activity by some overriding common interest; for each location contains people describing different paths and differently interpreting the social meaning of interaction.

Under these conditions, neighborhoods are made up of people at different stages of their jobs and residential mobility who are not bound by long established ties of interest and interaction. Their mobility, and especially the type of occupational mobility they experience, makes it difficult for them to reinforce existing relationships by adding new strands of shared interests. Yet, neither the occupational nor the residential paths that people describe are formalized by the existence of set skills or qualifications prescribing when and where a move must be made. Instead, personal relationships remain important as a means of seeking out opportunities and countering difficult situations.

This indeed is one of the central dilemmas facing these families in their urban careers; for they must have a wide span of relationships to effectively cope with their environment, but their mobility makes it difficult to establish strong and stable relationships. Also, since the paths people follow are distinct, they have different demands to make on their relationships. It is the various attempts of differently placed people to cope with these dilemmas that give its peculiar character to the organization of low-income families; looking at these families at one moment of their lives should not obscure the fact that the dynamic of their activity comes from the convergence of many different and ongoing careers.

Confederations of Households: Extended Domestic Enterprises in City and Country

Gavin A. Smith

Multi-occupational Households in Lima

Migrants from Huasicancha, a village in the central highlands of Peru, arriving in Lima during the 1950s, sought out relatives or friends living in one of a number of inner city locations called *corralones*. These are makeshift huts put up on vacant lots in the central area of Lima. During the 1950s and 1960s ex-residents moved out to a number of locations on the fringes of the city. As the city expanded, the earlier settlements were embraced while, over time, houses were built out of more permanent materials. Such areas are neither inner city slums, like the *corralones* and *callejones* of the city core, nor are they shanty-towns, like the *barriadas* (shanty-towns) constructed on the city's periphery throughout the 1960s.

Huasicanchino ex-residents, then, can be found in one of three different kinds of settlement. Today there exist two *corralones* entirely inhabited by ex-residents of the community. One was started in 1948 and is now in the heart of Lima's upper-class residential area, Miraflores. The other was started in the early 1960s and is on the other side of the city's motorway, near the bus depots and market. Other ex-residents are found in concrete buildings, settled in the late 1950s and located beside the road to Lima's airport. The land was "invaded", but all Huasicanchinos now have legal title to their houses. Finally ex-residents can be found in one of two *barriadas* on the edge of Lima, where land "invasions" occurred in the late 1960s and early 1970s. Structures here are less permanent and titles to land are non-existent. The distance of these *barriadas* from the city centre is substantial, the journey taking anything from one hour to one and a half hours by bus.

Those who arrived in the city during the 1950s usually began earning their livelihoods in economic activities characterized by considerable uncertainty, such as selling cold drinks near to the markets, or assisting others on a day-to-day basis. In many cases, ex-residents continue to depend on such hazardous forms of livelihood. But, during the 1950s, it was found that the hazards of ambulant fruit selling could be alleviated somewhat if others from the community were similarly involved. Increasingly, ex-residents were introduced to fruit selling and especially, between November and January, strawberry selling. While many Huasicanchinos in Lima, especially those recent arrivals of between sixteen and twenty-six years of age, continue to depend on fruit selling for a large proportion of their income, others have used fruit selling as a base to branch off into other activities which they undertake while continuing to sell fruit. Still others have gradually moved away from their initial commitment to fruit selling and are now committed to the operation of a truck, the manufacture and repair of vending tricycles, the operation of small buses in the city and so on. I am not interested here in those who are almost entirely dependent upon fruit selling, nor in those who have committed themselves through investment to one enterprise, such as the *transportistas* or the *taller* owner (making tricycles). Together these two groups may constitute 50 per cent of the Huasicanchino ex-residents in Lima.

The fruit seller is, in most cases, attempting to build up an extensive set of sources of income which will have the effect of tying his or her household into a network of other households. Many continually fail in this attempt. At the other extreme, there are people attempting to sever their ties and to concentrate their capital into one operation. They may succeed; they may not. Indeed they may appear to have succeeded for one or two years and then find they are driven back into dependency on previously neglected ties. This makes it difficult to make any clear distinctions or to assess the numbers of Huasicanchinos involved in multi-occupational enterprises. Nevertheless, I believe that this kind of operation provides the core for the economic rationale of the Huasicanchino enterprises in Lima. What follows is a case study of a representative multi-occupational household in Lima.

Vicente Hinojosa is thirty-eight years old and he came to Lima over 20 years ago. He was the third child among seven. On arrival in the city he moved to what was then the only concentration of Huasicanchinos – an inner city *corralon* (squatting on a vacant lot in the central area). He alternated between the quarters of his elder sister's husband and his father's brother, both of whom were early Lima migrants. Vicente no longer lives in the *corralon*. His sister is now dead and his uncle has moved elsewhere, but Vicente keeps up ties with the *corralon* and has another younger unmarried sister living in a shack there. His eldest brother, Victor, still lives in Huasicancha. Each year, Victor comes down to Lima after he has planted his crops in the village and sells strawberries. He stays with Vicente or with one of the other two brothers living in Lima. If he finishes work late and does not want to travel out to his brothers, he stays the night with the unmarried sister.

The *corralon* has seventeen shacks in it, all inhabited by Huasicanchinos. Vicente is one of seven men who use the facilities of the inner city location, but do not actually live there. Since 1959, he has lived with his wife and four children in a *barriada* outside Lima. When he originally arrived in Lima he sold soft drinks in a poor market area. He then turned to fruit selling, progressing from ambulant basket seller to the more mobile tricycle seller as the years went by. Today Vicente pursues a multitude of activities. He has a contract to provide a certain number of strawberry-pickers to a *hacienda* near Lima each season. Throughout the year, he uses his old pre-war Ford pickup to transport fruit from the central wholesale market to the *corralon* where he and other Huasicanchinos keep their tricycles for easy access to fruit retailing in the central area. (Most of the *corralon* residents themselves are ambulant sellers or are involved in some occupation which – usually due to irregular night hours – makes it difficult for them to move to a *barriada*, even if they wanted to). Vicente therefore spends very important parts of the day at the *corralon* and most of his interaction with other Huasicanchinos centres around there, rather than the *barriada* where the nearest other Huasicanchinos live two or three streets away. He is at the *corralon* from 8:00 a.m. to 9:30 a.m. and often again at about 6:00 p.m. or 7:00 p.m. During this time, inevitably, village and migrant news is discussed and information exchanged.

Although Vicente spends from about 9:30 a.m. to 3:00 p.m. or 4:00 p.m. touring the streets with his tricycle, he is also involved in a number of other activities in the city. On the opposite side of Lima from the Hinojosa's *barriada* there is another, somewhat older, shanty-town where a number of Huasicanchinos live. Beyond there can be found an area of small irrigated plots of land. With five other Huasicanchinos – four of whom live in the older shanty-town – the Hinojosa family own and farm a plot of land. Although their ambition is to grow entirely cash crops, each year family demands make it necessary for them to grow a combination of subsistence and cash crops, with an emphasis on the former. Still further removed from the city, a truck journey of at least one and a half hours from the centre, Vicente has a small piggery. It comprises what at first appears to be a random pile of old bedsteads and bits of chicken wire, within which are found eight to ten surprisingly healthy-looking pigs which are largely fed on the spoilage from the fruit selling. What with his other commitments, Vicente cannot get to the piggery each day. But he is in partnership with seven other Huasi-canchinos who also have makeshift sties and they take it in turn to make the daily visits.

During the strawberry season, which runs from November to the end of January and thus coincides with post-sowing slack periods in the village, Vicente spends the early morning supervising strawberry-picking on a *hacienda* near Lima. He pays the owner a set price and then sub-contracts to others who pick a controlled amount which they then sell on the streets of Lima during the remainder of the day. The business is fraught with conflicts since the *hacendado* has to unload large amounts of fruit when prices are low and often wishes to preserve his plants from overpicking when a sudden drought has driven prices up. He relies, therefore, on somebody who can control his workforce and who can expand or contract this force quite easily. Vicente uses both seasonal migrants from the village and residents of the inner city slum in order to carry out this task.

In the cases which I have presented here, it is clear that the common feature of the domestic enterprise throughout history — be it in the city or in the village — has been the extreme instability of any single source of support. In the village, livestock rearing became increasingly threatened by the expanding *hacienda* and arable crop-ping at such high altitudes was subject to great variations. In the city, the unpredictable nature of fruit selling was reduced as more Huasicanchinos became involved in the activity; it nevertheless remained a risky occupation.

Confederations — of which migration became but one dimension — were a means of minimizing risk and uncertainty by embracing different forms of productive enterprise over a wide area, such as occurred in the past when interhousehold relationships attempted to take advantage of the Andean vertical ecology. However, over time, these confederations have generated their own rationality and I have attempted to show this in the case study of the Hinojosa family which was, as it were, that part of the iceberg most visible in the city. Indeed, in studying the workings of any one confederation, so interrelated are the various households which make it up, that it becomes difficult to isolate the household unit as the most suitable unit for study. While production and consumption decisions do take place within these units, the factors taken into account have much to do with the situation of other members of the confederation. Hence the degree of risk to be undertaken in a particular operation depends on the comparable risks faced by others of the confederation (not simply the degree of risk, but whether or not it is a risk of the same kind e.g. being laid off versus over-extending capital invested in stock). Similarly, investment in capital equipment will depend upon the cash needs of other confederation members, since such needs would prevent the tying up of cash in equipment.

The same is also true with respect to the way in which the domestic enterprise makes use of labour. Were this simply a function of the enterprise's commitment to the domestic unit as a pool of labour, a kind of Chayanovian rationality might prevail. But, as the cases clearly illustrate, each domestic enterprise adjusts the strategy of its labour use to conditions arising in the other units of the confederation. Factors affecting the use of labour, therefore, are neither perfectly Chayanovian, nor perfectly capitalist.

What this means is that the internal rationality of any one domestic enterprise is crucially a function of its relationship to others. The specific features of each of these others feed back on the original unit, making it very hard – for both operators and ethnographer alike – to envisage the domestic unit apart from these linkages.

Nevertheless, this interdependence should not be overstated. The kin ties and strong sentiments of community membership of Huasicanchinos provide institutional channels through which production relations are expressed. One such institution is the confederation. This is a dynamic relationship experiencing fragmentation and reformulation resulting from the changing economic requirements of each household unit (for labour, for capital, for access to differing sectors of the economy, etc.). One enterprise might release itself from the confederation or there may be an overall slackening of obligations among members. Some families may then seek new sets of alliances or, for one reason or another, remain isolated from such intricate ties.

To get at the causes of this dynamic process, it is important to recognize the connection between the imperatives of household production and the social institutions which are used to meet those imperatives. Such imperatives are essentially of two kinds. Firstly, a division of labour on the basis of family roles within the domestic unit affects the interhousehold relationships as the family progresses through its generational cycle. This puts the confederations in a perpetual state of schism and reformulation. One household hitherto able to provide extra labour to other members, for example, may find one son marrying and setting up on his own, while another (perhaps precisely through the connections offered by the confederation) goes off to the mines. This changes the relationships both to confederates needing labour and to this household's previous ties to wage labour and the mining sector which can now be replaced by the unmarried son.

Secondly, there are imperatives which derive from beyond the household and refer to the other set of linkages (besides the confederations) enmeshing the household unit, namely those tying it to specific sectors of the Peruvian economy. As changes occur in the composition of the Peruvian economy, so households linked to differing sectors of the economy are affected differentially, and this affects the schisms which occur in confederations.

The emergence of a contradiction between the imperatives of the household enterprise and the institution of the particular confederation into which that household is tied usually expresses itself in the form of a succession of failures to meet obligations to other confederate members. This often begins as a reflection of changes in household composition as described above, but may then be exacerbated as the household begins to initiate new alliances, thus introducing itself into a new, and more appropriate, confederation. In other cases, the enterprise cannot, or will not, activate new alliances but gradually releases itself from any confederation. Needless to say, other households are unable so easily to discard the obligations accrued through the confederation and hence remain involved, as one informant put it, "like a fly in a web, struggling to be free and each time getting more caught".

This last statement suggests that confederations of households are not always equally advantageous to all members. This, together with the fact that developments in particular sectors of the economy affect enterprises differentially, suggests that the institution of confederations of households may give rise to exploitation between households. The idiom of reciprocity appropriate to the confederations acts to disguise this process and, in some cases, explains the continued participation of the more prosperous members.

Once a particular enterprise becomes more productive than its associates, it faces two conflicting tendencies. On the one hand, not only does the confederation continue to offer labour, for example, at a cheaper rate than the open market, but also other households may attempt to keep the enterprise within the net of obligations as a means, however ineffectual, of in some way benefiting from the more productive enterprise. Such a situation constrains the enterprise from leaving the confederation. On the other hand, the greater productivity of the unit encourages its members to adopt a more strictly capitalist rationale, trying to lock up cash and labour within the enterprise, where returns are greater, rather than in the confederation as a whole. Such incipient capitalists can be seen to be beginning to isolate themselves from other households, often through a series of events whose logical outcome is not entirely clear to them.

In any discussion of domestic production, it is useful to distinguish between the production of use values, the production of commodities and the sale of labour for a wage. Like most peasant households, many Huasicanchino households engaged in all three forms of livelihood, in varying degrees. With the penetration of capitalism the peasant jack-of-all-trades has not been replaced by a more specialized peasant, but by a more diversified one. Nevertheless, the social cost of the skills and equipment necessary for this diversification has increased relative to any one household's buying power. Confederations tie households into these three forms of livelihood, while allowing each household to take best advantage of local conditions for one or other of them. In a sense, households participating in confederations have diversified while at the same time specializing.

This makes for some difficulty in assessing the various characteristics of the household as an economic unit. Where the entire source of livelihood for a household is derived from wage labour, it may be possible to draw some conclusions about the economic rationality of that unit. Where a male labourer in a household migrates to the mines, while women maintain the farm production for that household, the situation is rendered more complicated. But, in the cases discussed here, there are household units all of whose members are engaged entirely in wage labour or commodity production, but which are nevertheless subsidized by the production of use values through linkages with the confederation. Thus, many household enterprises ostensibly engaged in one main livelihood – such as petty commodity production in the city – are, in fact, closely tied to the logic of another – such as subsistence production of use values in Huasicancha. The variety of "mixes" possible for each household makes the assessment of its logic as an economic enterprise a complicated task.

Nevertheless, the confederations provide linkages between different sectors of the economy and, in each sector, surplus is extracted more or less efficiently and in a variety of ways. This means that household enterprises strongly committed to one sector of the economy may be able to take advantage of other sectors, both because of the greater productivity of their sector and, also, because of the fact that they make use of use values produced within the confederation itself. Thus, despite demands to spread investments, there are always some households attempting to withhold resources from circulation throughout the confederation. The need to invest capital within the enterprise acts to push such an enterprise away from confederations. But its frequent need for cheap labour, often for once-off jobs and often where remuneration for work done may be delayed and, even then, take a variety of forms – all these are factors pulling such an enterprise back into the household confederation.

At the other extreme are those households who find it increasingly difficult to maintain the obligations of the confederation. As one operator in Lima began to lose contract business for his small workshop, he was unable to continue to offer seasonal jobs to family members of two confederate households in Huasicancha. They, in turn, began to lose interest in caring for his land or livestock. He therefore had to send his son back to the village. The loss of the skilled labour of the son led to a further reduction in business, eventually resulting in the collapse of the workshop and in the household's inability to participate in any confederation.

Between these two extremes, the confederations maintain their resilience; the economic rationality of each unit depending upon the "mix" of its operations, its linkages to other units and the constraints of the economy at large. It would be misleading to discern an historical trend towards the polarization of enterprises or the increasing separation of manufacturing and commercial from agricultural ventures. And this may often be so despite the intentions of participants. It was precisely those informants most firmly embedded in confederations who most strongly voiced the economic rationale of individual (household) accumulation with no obligations to those beyond the household. In contrast, it was those whose past five years' history revealed a trend towards increasing accumulation within the enterprise, towards the use of wage labour and a growing trend towards avoiding the reciprocal ties of the confederation of which they were members who most vigorously contrasted the immorality of capitalism with the need for Huasicanchinos to stick together and share their personal strength resourcefully.

Networks and Social Marginality

Larissa Lomnitz

Some of the major concepts in this book have evolved over a period of time, as undercurrents of thought rather than as isolated factual findings. In this section I shall make an attempt to summarize the basic concepts used in describing the reality of Cerrada del Cóndor. None of them were present in my mind at the time of the fieldwork; therefore, they may truthfully be said to represent central research findings of this investigation.

A cleavage is developing in the Latin American working class. A new social stratum, the urban industrial proletariat, is rising to prominence. This emerging labor élite is becoming increasingly differentiated from the peasantry, on the one hand, and from the migrants of rural origin on the other. To the extent that they have not become integrated into a modern industrial system, the traditional masses have remained largely segregated from the urban economy. Marginality was once regarded as a transient phase of the industrialization process in Latin America; however, in shantytowns such as Cerrada del Cóndor it appears that the second generation of shanty-town-born settlers has, on the whole, even less opportunity of access to industrial jobs than their parents had.

Yet the rural migrants keep streaming into the cities from the countryside. By their own standards, migration to the shanty-towns is a successful process. How do they survive? In order to do justice to this question it becomes necessary to view the marginal reality in all its complexity. I have attempted to develop a global ecological framework that integrates the closely interwoven problems of marginality, shanty-towns, migration, and urban poverty. Cerrada del Cóndor is not treated as a "community" in the traditional anthropological sense, but rather as a part of the national ecosystem. The field data are interpreted in terms of nationwide statistics. I have tried not to lose sight of the causal thread running through the history of urbanization and industrialization in Latin America, leading up to the modern plight of the settlers of Cerrada del Cóndor.

What is marginality? Physical segregation in shanty-towns is one part of the story. As one examines marginality as a way of life, one finds that the major economical barrier is the *security* question. The industrial proletariat is protected by legal safeguards (unions, social security), but the marginals have access only to jobs that are temporary, intermittent, menial, devalued, and generally unprotected. Underemployment is the rule.

The marginal dilemma, then, is not so much a problem of how to live on an inadequate income as of how to survive during the recurrent periods of zero income. There is one way out of this dilemma: using the social resources of the individual. Kinship, *compadrazgo, cuatismo,* and friendship are the resources used by the marginal for this purpose. This is also true for the relatively more skilled segment of the marginal population (artisans, skilled foremen) who work on a contract basis and therefore lack the job security of an industrial worker.

How are the social resources of the marginals converted into economic security? The process is not a new one. Kinship and other forms of social solidarity have provided the mechanisms of survival during much of the history of mankind. The settlers of Cerrada del Cóndor may be compared to the primitive hunters and gatherers of pre-agricultural societies. They go out every day to hunt for jobs and gather the uncertain elements for survival. The city is their jungle; it is just as alien and challenging. But their livelihood is based on leftovers: leftover jobs, leftover trades, leftover living space, homes built of leftovers. Even their poultry and livestock are raised on leftovers. To borrow an example from ecology, the marginals live like crabs, they inhabit the interstices of the urban industrial system and feed on its waste.

From the point of view of the urban industrial economy, although marginality may be said to represent a "surplus population" in some respects, in other respects it performs important though perhaps as yet unrecognized social functions. In particular, the rise of an urban middle class in Latin America is greatly indebted to cheap labor and services provided by marginals: domestic servants, gardeners, delivery boys, drivers, and a host of menial helpers of every description. If there is a symbiotic relationship between urban society and marginality, its major beneficiary is undoubtedly the middle class.

Networks

Since marginals are barred from full membership in the urban

industrial economy they have had to build their own economic
system. The basic social economic structure of the shanty-town is
the reciprocity network. This is not a social group or institution;
rather, it is a social field defined by an intense flow of reciprocal
exchange between neighbors. The main purpose of a reciprocity
network is to provide a minimum level of economic security to its
members.

The principal findings about shanty-town networks may be summarized as follows:

1. Reciprocity networks are groups of neighbors who cooperate
in the daily task of mutual economic survival.

2. Membership in networks is based on family units, not
individuals.

3. The networks are constituted and disbanded according to a
dynamic process ruled by economic and social factors, such as the
historical evolution and property structure in the shanty-town, the
geographical origins and family structure of the settlers, the major
incidents in the life cycle, and the daily ups and downs of shanty-
town life.

4. The size, stability, and intensity of exchange in a reciprocity
network depend on the social closeness between member families.
All-kin networks tend to be more stable, more self-sufficient, and
larger in size than networks of non-kin neighbors.

5. Association in networks is based on a fundamental equality
of wants among member families.

The reciprocal exchange of goods and services among shanty-
town settlers was found to be a central fact of their economic
existence, so much so that many other features of the social and
economic life of the marginals were organized around or in terms of
networks of reciprocal exchange. Family structures, residential patterns, occupational structures, household organization, leisure time
activities, alcohol consumption, and the use of traditional institutions such as *compadrazgo* and *cuatismo* were all modified and directed
toward protecting and furthering reciprocity relations among kin
and neighbors. Some examples of adaptive changes in traditional
structures and institutions found in Cerrada del Cóndor are the
extensive use of *compadrazgo* among members of reciprocity networks, whether kin or non-kin; the widespread use of the jointed
household as a means of preserving the extended-family structure in
the fragmented property and land ownership conditions of the
shanty-town; the prevalent recruitment of *cuate* groups and drinking

circles among the male segments of reciprocity networks, and the egalitarian ideology that stresses and idealizes reciprocal assistance and solidarity under conditions of mutual equality of wants.

It is hardly possible to overlook the large extent to which prevalent rural patterns of individualism and mistrust have become superseded by powerful tendencies toward integration, mutual assistance, and cooperation. Rural migrants are housed, sheltered, and fed by their city relatives in the shanty-towns; the men are taught a trade and oriented toward available urban jobs, in direct competition with their city kin. The reason for such "altruistic" behavior must be sought in the fact that migrants become integrated in local kinship reciprocity networks, which represent an overriding survival value to all their members. Contacts between the migrants and their communities of origin in the countryside become oriented in terms of the new reciprocity structures in the shanty-town. Kinship is the major factor promoting migration. The extended family in the shanty-town has become a unit of production and consumption. Important economic collaboration is provided by women, old people, and children. The result is a complex economic system largely based on the sale of unskilled manual labor by the men, service occupations by old men and women, and the active gathering of surplus and waste materials by all members of the household. A new typology of households for Latin American marginality is a result of this study.

Living in Cerrada del Cóndor

Nearly 70 per cent of the heads of families and their spouses in Cerrada del Cóndor are migrants of rural origin. These migrants belonged to the poorest economic strata of the peasantry: disowned or landless farm workers, working seasonally on *ejidos*, for small wages. Fewer than 20 per cent were from towns of more than 25 000 inhabitants. Most migrants came from depressed areas in the neighboring states of Mexico and Guanajuato, and from rural areas within the Federal District. Many of the latter were "passive migrants" – peasants who lived in small rural communities surrounding the metropolitan area, and who were displaced by explosive urban growth. These people did not have to move from their villages to the city; rather, the city moved and engulfed their villages.

Up to 90 per cent of the migrants were assisted during and after migration by relatives already living in the city. Most migrants moved directly from their villages to Mexico City, without intermediate stops. Subsequent moves within the metropolitan area were likewise conditioned by the presence of relatives in other shanty-towns or marginal settlements. Most migrants tended to move within a given sector of the city (the southern area, in the case of Cerrada del Cóndor). A pattern of moving first to downtown slums and later on to the peripheral shanty-towns, as reported from other Latin American countries, was not observed.

The population of the shanty-town is comparatively young. Nearly 60 per cent of the heads of families and their wives are under 40. Illiteracy is high. Among the same group (heads of families and their wives), nearly 30 per cent are illiterate, and slightly over 2 per cent have schooling beyond the sixth grade. Nuclear families tend to be complete and relatively stable. In cases of marital desertion, most women seem to be able to find another man within a reasonably short time. Children of previous unions born out of wedlock are commonly accepted by the husbands on an equal footing with their own. In general, most heads of households are married both legally and through the Catholic religion; less than 18 per cent live in consensual unions. The average fertility is high. In spite of the predominance of young couples in the shanty-town, a majority of nuclear families have more than four live children. A high proportion of settlers lives in extended households comprising up to four generations. Depending on available vacancies and other peculiarities of the property system in the shanty-town, these households may either live under a single roof, in separate dwellings within a single plot, or in independent adjoining housing units.

The basic economic facts of shanty-town life revolve around the question of economic insecurity. Four economic levels may be distinguished, according to material possessions. Levels A and B may be described in a general way as *urban*; they include 16 per cent of the residential units in Cerrada del Cóndor. The remaining residential units feature rustic-type furniture and construction; thus, 60 per cent of all residential units belong to level D, which corresponds to the lowest rung in terms of material possessions. In terms of income, the average monthly earnings per residential unit in all four levels is less than $100. However, in terms of job security and occupational structure, the number of unskilled laborers and others subjected to chronic underemployment is significantly higher in level D than in level A. Also, the rate of incidence of alcoholism and illiteracy is significantly higher in level D. Most of the settlers in level A are owners of their housing units. More than half of the residential units lack any bathroom facilities. On the average there were about three residents per bed, but many settlers, especially children, slept on the floor.

The occupational structure of wage earners in the shanty-town (both men and women) is largely based on unskilled labor. The most frequent occupation among men is that of *peon*, i.e., manual laborer who may work at various trades according to demand. The highest demand for such labor is in the building trade, for bricklayers and construction workers in general. Among women the most frequent paid occupation is that of domestic servant. Industrial jobs account for about 10 per cent of the employment among male breadwinners; however, they represent jobs of the lowest category, namely janitors, doormen, watchmen, and the like. The common denominator of practically all shanty-town jobs, including commercial and service occupations, is the lack of a steady income or social and job security.

Life in Cerrada del Cóndor is organized around neighborhood networks. Because of rigidly defined sex roles, the emotional content of marital relations is generally low. A man's life revolves around his male friends (the *cuate* group) and a woman's affections are largely centered on her children and other kin. Men are supposed to be somewhat unreliable and irresponsible (this is an accepted trait of masculinity); women tend to develop a resilient, strong, and resourceful character. When women are allowed to work, their earning power is as high as that of their mates. In addition to their economic contribution, women play an important role in cementing the network of reciprocal exchange, because of their constant daily use of it through the borrowing of small quantities of money and food, and the exchange of kindnesses, services, and emergency assistance. The larger kinship networks are often held together by the authority of an elder matriarch.

Compadrazgo in the shanty-town has blossomed forth into a variety of hitherto unknown forms. Typically urban occasions, such as the opening of the barbershop, are consecrated through the use of *compadrazgo*. The frequent occurrence of *compadrazgo* among members of reciprocity networks suggests that this traditional institution is being used as a means of consolidating interpersonal relationships within these networks. Another traditional institution, *cuatismo*(the Mexican form of male friendship), is similarly utilized. The *tanda*, a typically urban form of rotating informal credit, was also found to exist predominantly among members of reciprocity networks.

The Future of Reciprocity

The secret of the survival of huge marginal populations in Latin American cities lies in the efficient use of their social resources. Some social scientists have claimed that reciprocity is an archaic form of economic exchange, well on its way to extinction. Perhaps so, though I have found it alive and well in Cerrada del Cóndor. The generalized use of reciprocal exchange occurs in human populations that exist under conditions of chronic economic insecurity. Under such conditions, co-operation has greater survival value than competition as found in market exchange. Reciprocal exchange in Cerrada del Cóndor is governed by a set of factors, including social and physical distance, equality of economic wants, plus a psychosocial variable I call *confianza*. As found in Latin American societies, *confianza* measures the readiness of two individuals to engage in reciprocal exchange of goods and services. *Confianza* between neighbors and members of a reciprocal exchange network fluctuates according to the flow of goods and services exchanged. It may be officially acknowledged by reducing the social distance between the partners through kinship, *compadrazgo*, *cuatismo*, and other forms existing in the culture.

Latin American marginality represents a successful evolutionary response of traditional populations to the stresses of rapid urbanization and industrialization. The marginals have carved out an ecological niche within the urban milieu, one that provides for their basic survival needs. How will they evolve? Will the shanty-towns gradually become absorbed by an increased demand for industrial labor, or will they continue to grow, feeding on the surplus population of the depressed countryside? Will they play an important role in the socio-political evolution of Latin America? If so, will their impact be on the side of tradition or on the side of revolution?

The challenge met by the settlers of Cerrada del Cóndor is the universal human predicament of survival. Their example may teach us a valuable lesson. Human societies have always been threatened; moreover, the experience of Cerrada del Cóndor is particularly relevant to the threats we are facing today. The economy of the marginals has proved to be efficient in two respects: (1) the utilization of social resources for economic ends, and (2) the recycling of surplus and waste materials toward their maximum utilization. There is an obvious contrast between the successful adaptation of the marginals to a situation of scarcity of resources, generating mechanisms of social solidarity and methods of intense utilization of waste, and the crisis of Western industrial societies attributed precisely to a lack of social solidarity and a wasteful utilization of dwindling resources. The reciprocity networks I have attempted to describe in the shanty-town of Cerrada del Cóndor may well prove to be a prototype for the social structures needed for the survival of mankind. Market exchange may still be the most efficient economic system as long as the resources of a society are abundant in terms of the population it supports. But as long as there are segments of humanity confronting a dwindling pool of natural resources or threatened by physical extinction, reciprocity as a system of socio-economic exchange will have a future.

Part VII

State and Society: Contemporary Perspectives

Introduction

There are two aspects to our selections on contemporary issues in Latin America. First of all, we focus on what has been the most significant social phenomenon in recent years: the experience of long-term military rule, and the emergence, under military rule, of popular opposition and resistance. Secondly, we draw attention to contemporary work in areas of substantial current research interest: gender relations, new forms of dependency and dependent development, and cultural studies.

Angell reflects upon the rise and fall of military regimes in the most advanced countries of Latin America in recent years. *Alves* traces, for Brazil, the emergence of popular resistance among the workers of São Paulo. The selection from *Moser* shows how popular resistance is organized at neighbourhood level, and reveals also the nature and significance of the leading role played by women in community politics in particular. In their account of the "Westernization" of the Bari, Buenaventura-Posso and Brown discuss the reshaping of gender and authority relations during two decades of incorporation into Colombian society. They provide a graphic reminder of the roots and the power of patriarchal values and relations in Latin America. *Jenkins* extends the dependency debate in two ways – first of all describing recent developments in the internationalization of capital, and secondly by drawing attention to the impact of the process upon domestic firms. *Martin*, in a wide-ranging article of a broadly cross-disciplinary nature, discusses recent Latin American fiction, relating it to social change over recent decades, and to changing perceptions of Latin American society in the twentieth century.

The debate on the nature of military rule in recent years is surveyed in O'Brien and Cammack (1985), which also provides case studies of the four Southern Cone countries. The nature of recent economic development and the role of multinationals are treated by Evans (1979), Fagen (1979), Jenkins (1977, 1984), the latter being the full-length study from which the summary conclusion below is drawn, Sigmund (1980) and Villamil (1979). Numbers of significant studies of gender relations have appeared over recent years. The most useful are Pescatello (1973), Wellesley Editorial Committee (1977), Nash and Safa (1980, 1986), and Nash and Fernandez-Kelly (1983). The latter is not focussed exclusively on Latin America, but adds a gender-related perspective to the studies of recent economic change listed above. This theme may be pursued further, for Brazil, in Humphrey (1984). For an examination of the political activity of women in Latin America see Chaney (1979), and the review articles by Aviel (1981) and Jaquette (1980). For the impact of contemporary social change on the family, see *Journal of Family History* (1978) and Chant (1984, 1985).

Military Rule and Popular Resistance

The Soldier as Politician

Alan Angell

Military intervention in the political life of Latin American nations has a long history, and almost certainly a long future. However, the late 1960s and early 1970s saw an apparently qualitative change in the type of regime that followed a successful *coup*. Moreover, the *coups* took place in the most developed Latin American countries, societies marked by complex social organizations and institutionalized political systems. On most indicators of modernity, Chile, Brazil, Uruguay and Argentina would score high, though Argentina had a poor record of political stability, and Peru has many of the features of backwardness associated with developing countries. The military no longer intervened to correct the political system; it intervened to govern. Explanations for this new development stressed a number of factors, including internal changes in the military itself, the need to press on with a particularly difficult stage of economic development, the need to suppress the agitated politics of the praetorian state, and the need to adjust national development to changes in the international economic and political system.

Yet the most striking feature to the outside observer was the brutality of the *coups* and the subsequent development of formidable agencies of repression and social control – and this in societies whose political life had been relatively tranquil, at least in comparison with many European countries in this century. The *coup* in Chile in 1973 shattered a long tradition of constitutional government; Uruguay in the same year saw the disappearance of a long history of rather indulgent political tolerance; in Argentina violence moved from the shadows of the political system into the limelight; Brazil after 1968 also found that repression was crucial to the maintenance of military rule; and even in Peru a reformist, though never liberal, military government was forced to abandon reform and adopt tough measures of censorship and suppression.

Was this state violence necessary for something other than dealing with opponents? Were military governments responding to new demands from the ruling class, from international capital, from the

USA? Was this the Bonapartist "state of exception", fascism revived, the last stand of the free world, corporatism renewed – or
whatever other convenient theory lay to hand? The theories all had
in common the feeling that a decisive break with the past had been
made. And there was evidence at least for that feeling, if not always
for the underlying theories. There were in these countries decisive
changes in the economy, in the role of the state as an agent of
economic and social control, in the exclusion of popular sectors from
political influence, and in the way that political life was regulated.
But how much further can we go with the comparison? How similar
were these Latin American regimes in their objectives, structure and
behaviour? Before discussing these questions it is necessary to
examine the theories offered to account for the new departure.

The Rise of the Bureaucratic Authoritarian State?

The term "bureaucratic authoritarian state" was developed by the
Argentine sociologist Guillermo O'Donnell. He argued (1977, p. 37)
that the new state was more

> comprehensive in the range of activities it controls or directly manages;
> dynamic in its rates of growth compared to those of society as a whole;
> penetrating, through its subordination of the various "private" areas of
> civil society; repressive in the extension and efficacy of the coercion it
> applies; bureaucratic in the formalization and differentiation of its own
> structures; technocratic in the growing weight of teams of *técnicos* . . .;
> and furthermore closely linked to international capital.

Many of these features were not new, and they have been well
described by earlier writers on the military in politics. But there
were differences. Not only was the working class and peasantry
excluded from politics, but elite groups that had formerly continued
to exert substantial influence under military governments – intellectuals, the church, politicians as a class, national entrepreneurs,
agrarian interests – were now pushed to the margins of political
influence. It was difficult to interpret the military as representatives
of any particular class or sectional interest. Nor was there any
attempt at political mobilization: the new regimes preferred political
apathy. Nationalistic rhetoric of an earlier generation of military
leaders was also muted.

Moreover, these coups were made by the armed forces acting as a
corporate institution. Apart from the rather special case of Pinochet
in Chile, personalism or *caudillismo* was discouraged. Indeed one
reason for the Argentine military's insistence on collective leader-

ship and a restricted executive is precisely to curb the ambition of any would-be imitator of Perón. Even in Chile, Pinochet's power lies in the close identification of his own fortunes with those of the army as a whole. Brazil has gone furthest in institutionalizing the principle of corporate rule and limited terms of office for the president, and unlike their Argentine equivalents, the Brazilian officer corps respects the rules of the game. This agreement surely helps to explain why the regime has enjoyed considerable stability.

Armies can and do act in unison to defend their corporate privileges. This can often explain the timing of a *coup*. But a military regime that subsequently attempts a dramatic restructuring of the social and political order and not just a restoration of the status quo, obviously has some other motive than sheer self-preservation.

One influential school of explanation located the rise of the new military regimes in the ideology developed by the military to deal with a threat that was seen as internal and subversive rather than external and belligerent. The "new professionalism" led to armies defining their duties largely in terms of combating internal subversion (widely defined) by a combination of repression and development. In Brazil, Stepan (1971, pp. 84–5) writes, "almost all military officers agreed that since agrarian, fiscal and educational problems were intrinsic to the security of the nation, it was legitimate and necessary for military men to concern themselves with these areas". And elsewhere (1976, p. 247), "the scope of military concern for and study of politics became unrestricted, so that the 'new professional' military man was highly politicized". Officer training schools came to resemble universities. Lectures on economic development complemented more orthodox military training. Peruvian generals, in particular, began to talk like sociologists.

These new concerns however did not mean any greater tolerance or liberalism on the part of the armed forces. On the contrary, since this new training gave greater confidence to would-be military politicians it made more, rather than less, likely military intervention, and it did not break down the caste-like nature of many Latin armies. The new professionalism was a technique to be used, not a way of modifying authoritarian structure. But what exactly did it amount to, in terms of the political vision of the military? The problem here is that of penetrating the military mind, of reconstructing the political thinking of the officer corps, of which we know very little. According to Jacobo Timerman (1981, p. 94), a journalist whose experiences of torture at the hands of the Argentine military gave him special authority in this murky area, "The world of the Argentine armed forces is a closed, hermetic structure. Most of the officers' wives are the sisters or daughters of men in the military. Nearly all are related and whenever there's a military regime, the civilians who participate are mostly relatives of the military or individuals who have frequented military circles . . . This pattern has separated the military from the most elemental currents of modern life."

One must not exaggerate the extent or importance of this "new professionalism". It may have improved the military's understanding of economic planning, but it did nothing towards increasing their political sophistication. Many of the issues treated in the Higher War Academies can be traced back to much earlier times. And some armies, like the Chilean, showed little evidence of interest in the issues debated in Brazil, before, or indeed after, 1973.

A more plausible explanation for the wave of *coups* that established military regimes lies in the crisis that was undoubtedly affecting civilian governments and the military's interpretation of the causes of that crisis. Countries in which military regimes replaced civilian ones were experiencing long-run problems of economic growth, and short-term fiscal crises. Superimposed on these, were problems of extensive and intensive political mobilization and polarization. Attempts to combine social reform and populist politics had gone disastrously wrong. Balance of payments deficits showed the failure to develop the export sector, and the failure to control the level of imports (too often of basic consumer goods to meet popular demands). High and accelerating rates of inflation demonstrated the inability of the executive power to control a multiplicity of social groups demanding satisfaction from the state. Low levels of investment reflected the anxieties of the entrepreneurial sector. Low agricultural productivity pointed to long-term neglect. Chile in 1973 was the most dramatic example of the breakdown of a democratic regime, but the other countries exhibited the same symptoms if in lesser degree (or, in the case of urban violence, greater degree).

The military saw this crisis as the failure of civilian politicians to live up to their national responsibilities and even more drastically, as the failure of the civil state to represent the national interest. It was not only politicians who had to be replaced, the whole state had to be restructured. The immediate post-*coup* tasks were the stabilization of the economy and the demobilization of an over-politicized society. This would create the conditions for the development of an alternative growth model that would avoid the excesses of the past.

Such a project could not, by its very nature be other than long-term and drastic. In the Southern cone countries, Argentina, Chile and Uruguay, monetarist economics provided the perfect blend of a reversal of economic policy, with the political need for authoritarian controls to eliminate the distortions brought about by populism and to create the right conditions in which market forces could operate. Reducing the size of the public sector would remove the basis for popular or sectional pressures for concessions from the government; redirecting the surplus to the private capital market would strengthen those forces supportive of the military's policies and penalize those who were likely to be against; opening the economy to free trade would provide the means for growth without having to give state support for uncompetitive sectors; allowing market forces to regulate wage rates would undermine the political bargaining strength of the labour movement. All of these would combine to eliminate the greatest propagator of social unrest – inflation. And the beauty of the solution was that the regulatory mechanism would be that most liberal of concepts, the operation of free market forces. At the same time the old forms of political allegiance would be eroded, and new forms, classless and national, would develop.

Monetarism offered a new panacea in contrast to the failures of the past, one which might "justify" the brutal suppression that followed military *coups*. According to Whitehead (1982) the new economic orthodoxy was attractive to the military because it offered coherence (an overall battle plan for the conquest of civil society), discipline, and the redistribution of resources from vanquished to victor. Once under way, the process was to be irreversible, and as necessary means for national salvation its premises were not to be questioned.

Many sectors, hitherto protected by populist governments, would find the new measures unpleasant. Interest rates, often negative to help the numerous small business sector, would rise. Devaluation, necessary for the exchange rate to find its market level, could lead to inflation unless there was strict control over wage rises and unless public sector expenditure was held back. Tariffs would come down, in spite of the opposition of industry. Nationalist opposition to foreign firms would be ignored; foreign capital had to be guaranteed the right economic incentives and political stability. In great need of foreign loans, aid and investment, these countries had to present themselves as models of economic orthodoxy, as more IMF than the IMF itself. Even the Peruvian military, which embarked on a social reform programme distinct from the other military regimes, still relied upon export-led economic growth, with all the restraints that that came to imply with the change in the international terms of trade in the 1970s.

The necessary political conditions for the experiment in monetarist economics were social stability, political tranquility and above all a powerful executive. These conditions could only be achieved in the first instance by repression and control, although in the long term it was assumed that the population would come to appreciate the benefits of the new order. This control was achieved in two stages. The first was massive repression. For obvious reasons estimates in this field are unreliable, but there is little doubt of the scale of repression. In Chile, estimates of those killed by the armed forces in the immediate aftermath of the 1973 *coup* range from five to thirty thousand; in the first six months there were an estimated eighty thousand political prisoners. Three years after the Argentine *coup* of 1976 an estimated five to fifteen thousand people had "disappeared". In Uruguay between 1973 and 1977 about seventy thousand people were arrested for alleged political offences, but though many were tortured, the number of deaths was far fewer than in Argentina or Chile.

The second stage was the development of massive counter intelligence and security agencies, often with US help and training. These agencies, in addition to those in the armed forces, also called for highly trained police and paramilitary forces "dispersed throughout the population to identify and neutralize dissidents without creating major disturbances" (Klare and Arnson, 1979, p. 156).

The Question of Legitimacy

How can a military government legitimize itself? Charismatic legitimacy is hardly possible for the grey men who rule in military dictatorships, especially if their economic policies impose considerable austerity. A corporatist state structure would invoke too many unflattering comparisons with fascism, would be opposed by the Church, and is hardly congruent with an economic model based on modern capitalism. An embracing one-party system cannot be manufactured to order, and anyhow a one-party or two-party system would dent the monopoly of political power held by the military; and parties have a habit of running out of control. So the military faces a paradox. The only long-term legitimacy it can claim employs the language of those whom it has overthrown and those who oppose it. The basic political discourse of Latin America, for all the times it has been violated, is still that of constitutional and representative government. And this is the tradition that the military claims it has come in to protect, perfect and eventually transfer to civilians. As Linz (1973) points out for Brazil, "the constant restatement of the intention to restore competitive liberal democracy was and still is a drawback for the legitimation of permanent authoritarian elitist rule". The fact that such countries form, or would like to form part of the Western political bloc adds international pressure to adhere, nominally at least, to the democratic tradition.

A military government has therefore to present itself as transitory. As Rouquié (1982) writes, "A permanent system of military rule is almost a contradiction in terms. The army cannot govern directly and durably without ceasing to be an army. And it is precisely the subsequent government, the successor regime that legitimates the prior military usurpation". When President Bordaberry of Uruguay proposed, in 1976, to introduce *de jure* as well as *de facto* a new authoritarian state in which the armed forces alone would have legitimacy, he was dismissed by the army high command. The form of the civilian state, a non-military president and executive, are traditions the Uruguayan military feels called upon to uphold in theory, in spite of the massive violations in practice.

Another problem that arises in the analysis of military regimes is the question of state power. Is there a ruling élite behind the military? In whose interest is the military governing? Most recent explanations have revolved around the concept of the relative autonomy of the state from civil society. The *coup* has destroyed most of the institutions that regulated political life. Civil society is disorganized to such an extent that the new government has relative freedom from social pressures. The military can choose its own allies and dictate the terms of alliance.

Military Government in Practice: A New Departure or Variations on an Old Theme?

There is nothing modest about the claims of the military governments when they take power. They promise to restore order, deal firmly with subversives, eliminate corruption and rule in the national interest. Their rule will be technocratic and just. Harmful political conflict will be eliminated. These conditions will allow for economic growth. When all this has been achieved and the nation re-educated, power can gradually be transferred to responsible politicians. These claims might have some plausibility if at the time of the *coup* the military were united not just in opposition to the civilian politicians, but also around a clear programme of government for the next few years. This claim assumes also that the military acted in the national interest and not out of any specific interests of its own. Neither of these claims can be sustained.

(a) *The intentions of the military*

It is certainly true that military *coups* enjoy considerable popular support. Indeed this support can persist over a long period of time even in the face of economic difficulty. The evidence, however, does not indicate that the military assumes power with any clear plan of government: it reacts to events rather than pursues objectives. The initial rhetoric of the Brazilian military, for example, was conservative-liberal: no one in 1964 would have foreseen the extent to which the state sector of the economy developed (nor the extent to which the security apparatus developed). To rebut accusations of lack of a coherent programme, the Peruvian military published its *Plan Inca*. But it was not published until 1974, six years after the military took over, and almost certainly was written in the year of its publication. The Chilean military adopted a whole range of political ideas in the initial period of power, mostly from the Catholic right. It was some time before the Chicago economists won over the ruling junta, and one can assume that many of their ideas were very new to the politically inexperienced men ruling after 1973. The Uruguayan military command had no real political experience. The background of the officer corps was mostly rural, lower middle-class, with very basic levels of education.

Most military officers are faced at the time of the *coup* with a new experience, for which they have had little preparation. Even those who had participated in previous *coups* were not expecting to assume the tasks of long-term government of the military regimes of recent years. It is an error to attribute to the armed forces either great knowledge of, or even particular interest in, the details of politics.

The organization of the military is hierarchical; its behaviour emphasizes discipline and obedience. These values obviously colour the general social outlook of the military, but do not transfer easily into the world of political choices. "The barracks becomes the world", wrote S. E. Finer (1962, p. 9), and he could equally well have added that the world becomes the barracks. Timerman (1981, p. 99) commented that "the incapacity of the Argentine military to formulate a structured ideology leads to their general acceptance of the phobias of reactionary groups with whom they feel more closely aligned than the democratic sectors". The Peruvian military was more open to a wide spectrum of ideas and doctrines than other armies in Latin America, but the problem was that it was too open, and the contradictory positions assumed by members of the officer corps reduced important areas of government policy to incoherence.

No military *coup* ever takes place without some, even substantial, civilian support. There are always civilian groups hoping to manipulate the military to its own ends. In every one of the six successful *coups* in Argentina between 1930 and 1976 substantial sectors of public opinion – political parties, trade unions, industrialists, landowners – have urged the military to intervene. Opposition forces often prefer a military *coup* rather than allow an elected government to serve out its term of office. The "propensity to intervene" seems stronger amongst civilians than it does amongst officers. Civilian groups are rarely satisfied with the military in power, but they lack the means to change its policies. The alternative is to conspire to bring about another *coup*, either to return power to civilians or to a more sympathetic group inside the military. This constant see-saw of public opinion helps to explain why Argentina has so many military governments, and why those governments are themselves unstable and prone to internal division. Military executives last no longer than civilian.

(b) Rule by technocrats?

Who, then, makes policy in military regimes? What is the role of the technocrat? Military officers in countries such as Brazil and Argentina do at least have some experience in the administration of public enterprises. In the other countries not only was this background rare, but as in Argentina and Brazil, it was felt that overall competence in managing the economy was the preserve of the civilian technocracy. But was this really rule by technocracy? In practice the military would not leave well alone. In the first place there is always an area of state expenditure that even the most daring technocrat must not touch – defence. Considerations of national security can lead to the military overruling the wishes of the technocrats; the Chilean military, for example, has always resisted plans to sell off the state copper mines. In Uruguay, residual populist ideas in the military led to the vetoing by the military of plans to dismiss large numbers of government employees. In Peru the military, perhaps more than else-where, sought to define itself as the government of the armed forces and kept civilian advisers at arm's length. Cabinet changes take place quite as regularly under military govern-ments as under civilian. Long-term planning is rarely im-plemented and technocrats are hired and fired with regularity as much vaunted plans for economic growth fail. Beliefs that policy-making under military rule becomes more technical, is removed from distorting pressures, and is made with a longer perspective are thus not borne out in reality. Some distortions are removed; but others are introduced.

Another claim which is equally ill-founded is the boast that political conflict and sectarian infighting has no place under the austere neutrality of military government. On the con-trary, political conflict is as intense as before, but now it takes place inside the armed forces. The one country where internal differences have not surfaced, or been allowed to surface, is Chile. The reasons for this may well have to do with the political inexperience of the armed forces in that country, and with the need for a strong executive to implement ruthless measures of repression and far-ranging plans of economic transformation.

The different branches of the armed forces have to be accommodated inside the governing coalition, even at the expense of weakening political unity. Military unity comes first. Different tendencies inside the armed forces have to be given their share of power. Inexperienced military officers can easily fall prey to the sectional interests they are supposed to control, especially where that interest is in collusion with the bureaucracy. Military hierarchy is a poor guide to policy-making, especially to dealing with political crises which can develop in any regime. Each ministry in Peru became a personal empire of the military man in charge, used to build up the political base of that officer, and military ministers behaved as selfishly when asked to accept reductions in budget or responsibilities, as any previous civilian minister.

(c) *The military and civil society*
The military are unsure about the generation and mainten-ance of support for the new regime. Initially the need was to demobilize, but that is a short-term solution. To establish their claim to rule they need to demonstrate some evidence of popular consent, if not enthusiasm. They cannot follow the

easy path of populism because it was precisely to end that style of politics that they took over.

This uncertainty is reflected in the attitude of military governments towards political parties. The Peruvian military went furthest in its rejection of the idea of a party system (even the Chileans envisaged parties operating in the rather distant future). They experimented with "national mobilization" agencies but these produced as little success, and as much confusion, as a party system would have done. The Brazilian military found equal difficulty in creating a managed two-party system. For the first few years the parties were allowed little autonomy and were useful neither in supporting the regime nor in providing more than a façade of democracy; given some autonomy and increasingly free elections the opposition party became a genuine expression of majority disapproval of the military, and undermined its authority. The Uruguayan military left a purged two-party system, and held a referendum in 1980 on a new constitution, confident that they would win. Unfortunately for the military the middle-level leaders of the parties mobilized opinion sufficiently to inflict a humiliating defeat on the military by 57 per cent votes against the proposal to 43 per cent in favour.

Perhaps more surprising than the failures to control the party system has been the inability to tame the labour movement. Trade unions had reached such levels of organization and support in many Latin American countries that permanent repression would be a mammoth undertaking. Moreover, as open economies depending upon trade with the West, they had to tread carefully: more than once North American unions had provided important defence of trade union rights in Chile. The very pattern of Brazilian growth led to the conditions for the development of a modern industrial proletariat, above all in the automobile plants, that weakened the Government by strikes from 1978 to 1980. Monetarist economists wanted the market to regulate wages, and they were prepared to allow for a minimal union organization to engage in limited bargaining. The Peruvian military created its own federation to rival the existing ones, but as real wages declined and the government began to repress labour organizations, even the government's own creation deserted it and joined the ranks of the opposition. Successive attempts by the Uruguayan military to win over workers from their previous allegiances have been dismal failures.

The military used to be able to count on the support of the Catholic church in the past, but no longer. Although the recent wave of military *coups* received support from most sectors of the Catholic church (the extent and influence of radical currents inside the church has often been exaggerated), that support has gradually turned to opposition. The reasons for opposition are to be found in the increasing repression of priests and active Catholic laity by the government, the desperation of oppressed groups turning to the church for help, active international encouragement, and a realization that the military governments regarded repression and control not as temporary expedients but as permanent features of political life. The reaction of the church has not been uniform, either inside the national church, or between countries. Although the Chilean church is very progressive, it has a number of bishops who support the military. Although the Uruguayan church has been relatively indifferent to the repression of the regime, there are some outspoken priests in that country. What is most interesting, however, is that opposition has evolved from defence of basic human rights to rejection of government policies *per se*. The Chilean church hierarchy reserve for the Chicago school of free market economics the kind of criticism they used to direct at communism. Moreover, the church plays a vital role in the protection of groups such as trade unions. By these criticisms and activities, the church refuses to legitimize military governments, in spite of the claims such governments make to be defending christian values against the marxist conspiracy.

(d) *Control through terror: the development of the intelligence agencies*
One undeniable common feature among the various military governments of Latin America has been the development of sophisticated agencies of control and repression. If opposition is defined as subversion, if politics is seen as war, if the army is convinced that the nation is under threat from the enemy, if there exists a powerful guerilla movement (which there was in Argentina and Uruguay) then it follows that all measures to defend the nation and the military are justified. If opposition grows, then it proves the point that the challenge is there and needs tough measures to counter it; if the opposition declines, then it shows that the tough measures were justified.

Yet there is an obvious contradiction between the stated political goals of the military – the eventual return to constitutional government, respect for law and order – and the activities of these intelligence agencies. Properly conducted legal trials are unacceptable to the military because they might not lead to convictions; trials based on the "revolutionary legality" of the communist systems are inappropriate given the lip service paid to liberalism; and so the adopted method is that of private violence, the development of paramilitary forces, assassinations and "disappearances".

This is the structure in which extreme beliefs and practices can flourish. The political isolation of many military officers produces a siege mentality in which they are prepared to accept excesses committed in the name of the state. Timerman (1981, p. 102) reported that his Argentine military interrogators believed that in fact the Third World War had already broken out, but not as a confrontation between democracies and communism but rather between the entire world and left-wing terrorism (synonymous for some with Zionism). Argentina, they believed, had been chosen as the initial battleground of the first phase of the war. Ludicrous as this is, one can understand why military officers would prefer a sinister plot to explain why they had been unable to erase the memory of Peronism from the working class, and why a powerful urban guerrilla movement had for a time run rings around them, rather than the more obvious explanation (in terms of the unpopularity of the military and the genuine popularity of Perón).

Such intelligence agencies become a state within the state, a method of surveillance over the military itself, with methods and structures which make it difficult for the executive to control. In Brazil the security forces began to conduct vendettas against senior members of the government. But following the death of a prominent Jewish journalist in 1975 (the Jewish marxist conspiracy fear existed in Brazil as well) President Geisel was able to carry out a purge in 1975, only to have to do so again in 1976 after another death under torture.

These agencies become involved in the economy, and establish dealings, often clandestine, with powerful economic groups. They are, after all, large establishments. At the height of DINA power in Chile, the head of the agency, General Contreras, commanded a small army of 9 300 agents and a network of paid and volunteer informants several times larger, honeycombing all walks of life inside Chile and abroad. Several important firms taken over by the state under the Allende government were passed secretly to the control of the DINA. Extortion and blackmail of victims is commonplace. In Brazil there is strong evidence of deals between members of the São Paulo business community, the intelligence agencies, and hardline civilian and military politicians, against the interests of the official government in Brasilia.

Important though these agencies are in consolidating the power of military governments, it is by no means certain that they continue to be an asset. Continued reliance upon such agencies undermines the already weak claims of the government to legitimacy. It underlines the fact that the basis of the government remains that of arbitrary power. In so far as these agencies seek to establish control over the armed forces themselves, they are seen as weakening the overall unity of the military and the authority of the executive. They arouse considerable international hostility towards the government, especially when they engage in activities abroad, as the Chilean DINA has with two assassinations, one in Buenos Aires of a former Commander-in-Chief of the Army unsympathetic to the government, and another, in Washington of a leading opposition politician. International criticism weakens the attractiveness of these regimes to potential foreign investors who fear that such criticisms could point to future political instability. The more important the role of these agencies, the more difficult is the return to the barracks. Victims will seek redress, the prestige of the armed forces will be further undermined, and the independence of the army may be called into question. In such circumstances it is not uncommon for hardliners to try to provoke artificial crises, and thus the continuance of military rule. These security agencies (and each important branch of the armed forces has its own) have a strong interest in the perpetuation of military rule, and with their links with the world of crime and with unscrupulous businesses, constitute a strong impediment to the return to constitutional rule.

(e) *Uniformities in economic policies?*
Most of the search for comparisons among the so-called bureaucratic regimes has concentrated on their economic policies. While it is true that the new economic orthodoxy is monetarism, the only country that made a really systematic effort to apply it was Chile; Argentina and Uruguay deviated in some unorthodox ways; it influenced economic policy-

making in Brazil only in the 1964 to 1967 period, and has influence during the present crisis; and assumed importance in Peru after 1975 when the first reformist phase of the military government was over. Rather than monetarism the characteristic of Peruvian and Brazilian development was an enormous development of the state sector. In both those countries the level of repression at the time of the *coup* was relatively slight, so the need to combine fierce measures of economic stabilization with political control was less intense than in the cases of Chile, Argentina or Uruguay. The Brazilian military in particular played an important role not simply in the formation but also in the control and administration of a number of important state enterprises. The air force for example controls Embraer, the state aviation industry which has an impressive export performance. The navy dominates nuclear research, and a part of the nuclear power industry. And the central role is occupied by the army which runs a whole series of industries from shipyards to communications, and electrical power to the arms industry. The financial sector is also an area of military activity: Brazil's biggest pension fund began as the army's own institution Capemi.

Even amongst the southern cone countries that proclaimed their loyalties to monetarism there were substantial differences. Argentine monetarists lacked the influence of their Chilean counterparts. Army officers controlled one of the biggest industrial complexes in the country, *Fabricaciones Militares*. The military-industrial complex interfered with many of the proposals of the economic team and contributed to the incoherence and failures of policy in that country. Similarly the Uruguayan military veered sharply away from monetarist orthodoxy. There were fairly strict controls over wages and even over prices; large fiscal deficits accumulated; exports were subsidized; and the real level of public investment increased.

In Chile the monetarist experiment went furthest, in part because those groups that might have opposed such measures had their powers eroded, because the tradition of military involvement with basic industry and public services was much less developed, and because a relatively inexperienced military was more inclined to place its trust in the plausible sounding remedies of the "Chicago Boys". But even here the state retained an impressive presence in the economy. The top eight firms in Chile in 1970 were state firms and they remained in state hands in 1980, even though they were being forced to operate as private firms and lost many of their traditional advantages. Further extensions of the monetarist experiment into areas hitherto safeguarded by the state were brought to an abrupt halt by the severe recession which hit Chile from 1981 onwards, discredited the monetarists, and forced the state to take into public ownership most of the private banking sector.

In two respects, however, one could point to considerable uniformities among the regimes: the way in which real wages declined, and the transfer of resources from the industrial to the financial sector. The reasons for the first are fairly obvious, both as a political and economic measure. The second was less consciously planned but resulted from opening relatively weak economies to international forces at a time of high levels of international liquidity, abolition or reduction of exchange controls and the general deregulation of banking activities. These factors, combined with high domestic interest rates aimed at reducing inflation, created the conditions for speculation.

Yet the military gained no long-term benefit from either of these measures. Lower living standards eventually led to an intensification of popular protest. A general strike in Peru in 1977 was of great importance in influencing the military to return to the barracks; strikes in Brazil in 1978 accelerated the programme of liberalization; and demonstrations against even the seemingly impregnable Pinochet forced the Government into panic measures in 1983. The banking sector, riding high in Chile in the boom of 1977 to 1980, crashed in spectacular fashion with the recession from 1981 onwards; and there were similar disturbances though on a lesser scale in the other countries. A great deal of the huge international debt accumulated by Latin American countries in recent years consists of short and medium-term loans from private banks to national private banks. The problem of severe indebtedness has made governments more concerned with state regulation of these activities and less with the free operation of market forces.

(f) *The failure to gain legitimacy through economic success*
The record of military governments in economic management is rarely bright, and that of the military regimes in Latin America is no exception. Argentina has not seen inflation fall

below 100 per cent for some years; real incomes fell by 20 per cent in 1982, and unemployment rose from 3 per cent in 1978 to 13 per cent in 1982. The Chilean economy suffered from two massive reductions in GDP of about 15 per cent in 1975 and again in 1982: unemployment in 1983 was over 30 per cent; and industrial production has fallen to levels current about twenty years ago. The Peruvian military left a legacy of high inflation, high unemployment and dismal growth rates. Even though Brazil has managed to grow at respectable rates since 1974, the turn to reliance upon the old style of import-substituting industrialization meant a return to balance of payments deficits. All these countries face huge external debts in the 1980s and in all income distribution has become increasingly unequal.

Why was there such a failure? Even if the economy had been managed with technical efficiency, Diaz Alejandro (1981, p. 128) has pointed to the caution that entrepreneurs show when faced with the possible uncertainties that attend dicta-torial governments. But the economies, apart to some extent from Brazil's, were not managed efficiently and flexibly. The most dogmatic team has produced, in Chile, the worst of the recessions. The monetarist gamble did not come off. Insensi-tivity to non-military opinion helped to produce badly planned decisions, badly executed. Targets were set without sufficient regard to real world factors. Continual interference by sectors of the armed forces for particular ends, disrupted the coher-ence of policy-making. Industrialists and landowners were alienated from governments that failed to consult them.

There were factors outside the control of national govern-ments. The oil price rises, high international interest rates and the world-wide recession were bound to undermine the basis of export-led growth economies. Not only military gov-ernments found the new international climate harsh and damaging. But governments that concentrate all power in their own hands, and do not in theory have to bow to sectional demands, should be able to respond more rapidly to the down turn in the economy. In practice their response was uncertain.

One factor that could have been controlled quite easily in theory to lessen the pressure on the balance of payments is defence expenditure. Apart from the special factor of the conflict in the South Atlantic, defence expenditure rose con-stantly, though accurate figures are difficult to establish as much defence-related expenditure is disguised. In Uruguay the armed forces' share of the national budget rose from 13.9 per cent in 1968 to 26.2 per cent in 1973 and in the mid-1970s to an estimated 40–50 per cent. In 1979 Chile was spending an estimated 9.4 per cent of its GDP on arms, and Peru 4 per cent. Much of this expenditure is for imports, which consumes scarce foreign exchange. In mid-1980 Brazil was running an annual balance of payments deficit of US$6 billion while at the same time US$2 billion was being spent on arms imports. In the ten-year period after 1970 the armed forces in Argentina grew by 35 per cent while military spending rose by 51 per cent. Chile doubled its military spending between 1977 and 1980. The days of easy US military aid to Latin America are now over. Arms are bought on the international market and paid for in scarce foreign exchange, even by Argentina and Brazil which are by now considerable producers and exporters of arms. The effect of such conspicuous expenditure is to distort economic policy, and to lay the military open to the charge of feathering their own nests to the detriment of everyone else (and the fact that a great deal of secrecy surrounds these transactions only fuels the unpopularity of the military).

The New Union Labour Movement in Brazil

Maria Helena Moreira Alves

The present structure of trade union organization was set prior to the military takeover by a labor code patterned on Mussolini's Carta del Lavoro and elaborated in 1943. After 1964, the military regime modified certain aspects and applied the controls with full severity. Labor legislation ensures absolute control of the national state over the activities of rural and urban labor unions. This forces unions to perform a welfare rather than a class-organization role. Finally, trade unions are corporatively organized in such a way as to eliminate the possibility of local horizontal union federations across sectors. Separate national confederations are established for industry, commerce, transport, and so on. Only at the confederation level may the various occupational groupings establish formal connections. The military regimes after 1964 implemented the right to intervene in trade unions with severity. Considering that by 1969 the government had intervened and removed from office the directors of a total of 999 unions, this amounted to a forced change of leadership in 50.2 per cent of the unions existent at that time. If one counted all the different acts of governmental interference (removal from office, intervention, interference in elections and dissolution) this figure is raised to 61.3 per cent of the 1 987 unions that existed in 1969. By that date, therefore, the expulsion of labor leaders who defied the regulations of control had been largely accomplished.

In spite of controls over trade union organizing, both rural and urban workers have worked within the existing structures to win control of the elected boards of directors of some unions. In fact, the rural trade union opposition leaders generally have been the most effective in winning control of regional federations and the confederation that unites all agricultural laborers. Urban unions are more likely to be the government-created artificial "ghost unions" – small membership unions which are created by the government to offset the strength of the large industrial unions which are generally more combative. The Ministry of Labor has final say in the formation and recognition of trade unions. In addition, each union has only one vote at the federation level; and it is the federations that choose the leadership of the confederation. This pyramidal structure of organization, corporative in nature, has been utilized by the military government to enforce control of the higher levels (federation and confederation) through the votes of the ghost unions. In the rural areas, however, most unions tend to be smaller and the effect of the ghost union vote to elect leadership of the federations and confederations is much weaker. Hence, the peasants are able to elect combative leaders for many of the federations and since 1968 to elect a radical top leadership of the *Confederação dos Trabalhadores na Agricultura* (CONTAG, Confederation of Workers in Agriculture).

The labor unions in Brazil may be politically divided into three distinct groups. The first comprises those trade unions whose leaders are connected to the official trade union structure and act as intermediaries between the working class and the federal government. They tend to demobilize the workers, discourage strikes, and adhere completely to the precepts of collaborative corporative union organizing. These have been called, in union language, the *pelegos*. A second group of trade union leaders have formed an informal network called *unidade sindical* (trade union unity). These are opposition union leaders who attempt to activate the labor unions in support of workers' rights. However, they often act in alliance with the pelego leadership when they feel that a broad-front alliance for a specific purpose is desirable. In addition, like the pelegos, they deemphasize rank-and-file participation and centralize decisions at the top leadership levels. A third group of union leaders have been called the *autênticos* (authentics) and are often interconnected with grassroots associations, members of the comunidades de base, and other Church-related organizations. The most prominent leaders of this current have come from the metalworker sector. One of the best-known union activists of this group is Luís Inácio da Silva, better known in Brazil as Lula.

The *unidade sindical* and the *autênticos* have some important joint programs. They are both part of the general opposition movement against the military government and consider it a priority to fight for a return to democracy; they both may be considered active organizers of the workers and fighters for better working conditions; they both strongly oppose the official union structure and defend the need to change the labor code so as to ensure trade union autonomy; they both search for political representation by working closely with political parties of the opposition. The *unidade sindical* current is prominent in the large *Partido do Movimento Democrático Brasileiro* (PMDB, Party of the Brazilian Democratic Movement), the *Partido Trabalhista Brasileiro* (PTB, Brazilian Labor Party) and to a smaller degree in the *Partido Democrático Trabalhista* (PDT, Democratic Labor Party). The autênticos tend to be active members or supporters of the *Partido dos Trabalhadores* (PT, Party of the Workers) of which Lula is the president.

Perhaps the biggest difference between the two opposition union currents is that unlike the *unidade sindical*, the *autêntico* leadership does not seek close alliances with the *pelegos*, maintaining a posture of strict opposition to the government and the mechanisms of social control imposed upon unions. In addition, the *autênticos* tend to emphasize strongly collective leadership and avoid on-the-spot arrangements between top leaders. The effort to create and foster intermediary levels of leadership and in-the-factory union representation through shopstewards and factory committees is one of the practical consequences of the emphasis on rank-and-file organization. While the *unidade sindical* has been influenced by the activities of the Communist Party, the labor unions of the *autêntico* current are closer to Catholic organizations and count on the active support of members of the *comunidades de base* and of the *pastoral operária*.

The two surface symbolic episodes that mark the political appearance of the "new trade union movement" in Brazil date back to 1977 and 1978. In August of 1977 the military government admitted the manipulation of the official figures used for the calculation of wage increases of Brazilian industrial workers for the years of 1973 and 1974. The manipulation of the statistics caused a 34.1 per cent loss in the real wages of the Brazilian workers during the period. The Metalworkers Union of São Bernardo do Campo and Diadema, led by Luís Inácio da Silva, organized a vast campaign to force the government to pay back to the workers the percentage lost in the manipulation of the official cost-of-living statistics. It was the "campaign of the 34.1 per cent" that began to shake workers out of their apathy and fear of the repression to seek redress and demand their rights.

However, in terms of overall interunion co-ordination, the most important episode marking the beginning of the "new trade union movement" took place at the *Confederação Nacional dos Trabalhadores na Indústria* (CNTI, National Confederation of Workers in Industry) in late 1978. Although the conference was organized by members of the *pelego* sectors, a group of more combative unions set up an alternate platform and gathered, for the first time, to co-ordinate the work of a network of leadership who openly voiced their opposition to the official controls over trade unions embedded in the labor code. While the events of 1977 helped to spur workers and rank-and-file members into action, the conference of the CNTI provided the opportunity for effective co-ordination between leadership from all states. It became the first step toward political action, establishing a network of contacts throughout the country. The opportunity to co-ordinate activities was important in a year that was marked by the resurgence of strike movements.

In May of 1978 without apparent prior notice, workers of the Saab-Scandia automobile factory in São Bernardo do Campo – the heart of the industrial belt of São Paulo – sat down in front of their machines, crossed their arms, and refused to work. Within a period of two weeks a total of 76 843 metalworkers had joined the strike. They demanded, among other things, a salary increase 20 per cent above the officially allowed increase based on the government's index. The force of their sitdown action within the major factories of the automobile and metalworking industries caught the military government by surprise. Strictly speaking, according to the legislation controlling strikes the workers were not on strike. They came to work daily, walked into the factories, turned on the machines and then sat down. The law defined a strike as "refusal to go to work" – a technicality that had been duly noticed by the leadership and upon which their strategy of action had been based. This complication temporarily stunned the government into inaction. The corporations, on the other hand, were pressed into direct negotiations with the Metalworkers' Union by their heavy daily losses. The workers inside the factories refused to negotiate without the mediation of their union. Soon a de facto collective bargaining process began and a settlement was reached. The metalworkers accepted a raise of 24.5 per cent above the official index, parcelled in different payments through the year, and voted to return to work. Two significant regulations of the repressive state had been broken: the anti-strike law and the government's automatic wage increase policy called the *arrocho salarial*.

The other industrial workers were quick to see the potential of the victory. By the end of July 1978, over 245 935 workers in São Paulo alone had participated in some form of strike action. From the metalworkers, the strike movement spread to other sectors and even to rural areas. From the working class it affected the professional and middle classes: these sectors also suffer the salary controls and are under considerable economic pressure. Even doctors, who in Brazil are primarily public workers in a growing health industry, received very low salaries in 1978 – the equivalent of between U.S.$125 and $200 per month. Public employees have further problems for they are prohibited from striking altogether and do not have some of the labor benefits granted to other workers. From the area of São Paulo as the year progressed the movement for wage increases and better working conditions spread to other states. By the end of 1978, a total of 539 037 workers had been on strike.

The demands of most labor groups centered on better salaries and working conditions. Clearly the chief concerns of workers in 1978 were with the low wages, poor working conditions, lack of health insurance, lack of safety standards, and long working hours of between 12 and 14 hours per day. Teachers, in addition, asked for regular legislation to be enacted by Congress to grant them specific benefits available to other professions. The strategy of strike action varied in 1978 from factory sitdowns to regular picket lines. Of course, under the Brazilian repressive regime all strikes were illegal; and picket lines increasingly became the target of direct police repression. The majority of the strikes in 1978 achieved some real economic gain or improvement in the working conditions through agreements between the strikers and employers.

The year 1979 was characterized by one of the largest strike movements in Brazil's labor history. A total of 3 207 994 workers participated in the strike actions throughout the year. Furthermore, the strikes spread throughout the nation and reached fifteen different states. In addition, an increased involvement of rural workers represented a fulfillment of the alliance between the networks of the comunidades de base and the rural unions. Most professions joined what in effect became a general strike that paralyzed the country for months. As the labor movement progressed in political conscious-ness and grew in organizational strength and bargaining power, it became clearer that the structure of the trade union legislation itself (which was embedded in the labor code) needed to be modified so as to free the unions from the direct control of the Ministry of Labor. Therefore, in addition to a real wage benefit (as measured by increases over the official government index) and better working conditions, demands in 1979 increasingly began to include the right to have on-the-job union representation, shopstewards with job security benefits, factory committees, and some form of job stability for all workers.

The reaction of the government to the spreading strike movement was predictable: increased repression. The military police of the various states targeted in particular the picket lines. The strategy of sitdown strikes inside the factories, utilized by the workers in 1978, was neutralized by an immediate lock up of the factories. If a strike was in the offing, workers were not allowed inside the buildings; they were forced out into the streets as pickets. As the National Security Law specifically prohibited demonstrations and assemblies, the government could then react by sending the military police to repress and arrest workers. The resulting conflicts at picket lines involved many arrests, caused bodily injuries, and led to the death of a major strike leader. In September of 1979 the metalworkers of São Paulo were on strike and a military policeman shot down one of the top Catholic union organizers in São Paulo. The death of Santo Dias da Silva increased the levels of tension. His funeral gathered to-gether an estimated 100 000 grieving workers, lay organizers, and priests. During the funeral mass São Paulo Cardinal Dom Paulo Evaristo Arns called upon workers to continue to act peacefully to avoid bloodshed but not to give up the struggle for human rights that had been the aim of Santos's life. His death became a symbol for the organization of Catholic workers in Brazil.

From the point of view of the state, the year 1979 clearly defined sectors of opposition that would not be tolerated – even during the period of political liberalization and *abertura*. From the standpoint of the opposition, two major conclusions were drawn from the events of 1979. The first was that although the strike movement was widespread, most actions were still to a large extent spontaneous revolts against extremely low wages and the plight of the salaried population. Many in fact took the form of revolts bordering on riots without the organized characteristic necessary for effective group pressure. The second major conclusion was that the actual organization at the base level was still weak and interconnections needed to be set up between the leadership and the rank and file. It was, perhaps, necessary to take a step back so as to deepen the organization inside the plants and companies. In addition, a careful analysis of the various strikes pointed to the need to set up a strike fund and, most particularly, to eliminate altogether the use of picket lines and stay off the streets so as to minimize the government's excuses for outright and direct repression. Workers increased their organizational efforts and, once again, the Metalworkers Union of São Bernardo do Campo and Diadema broke new ground. The metalworkers decided to deepen the base-level organization sector by sector in each factory and push for further changes and democratic reforms.

It should be highlighted at this point that it is wrong to assume that the autoworkers in Brazil have the consciousness that has been imputed to the "labor aristocracy". In fact, conversations among workers in São Bernardo at that time often centered upon the concern for other workers. There was a keen awareness of their own privileged position in the production line and their power to, as they put it, "stop the country". Brazilian industrial organization is so dependent upon the metal industry – linked to the automobile industry – that a longer strike would have had great repercussions throughout the economy. Hence, the metalworkers felt a responsibility to use their limited advantage for the benefit of others. Among the rank and file in São Bernardo there was a generalized perception that because of their particular importance in production they could take initiatives that would open the way for weaker unions.

In São Bernardo the year 1979 was filled with careful preparations of the intermediate levels of leadership, the training of the different kinds of strike command groups, and the raising of the workers' consciousness so as to allow the next phase to be conducted without the use of picket lines. The demand for tenure became one of the most important issues. Not only was it necessary to guarantee greater job security for all workers but, most important, it was necessary to guarantee that employers would not spur a sufficiently large labor turnover to break the organization and unity of the workers.

The Metalworkers' Union of São Bernardo do Campo organized meetings, assemblies, study sessions, and conferences for the discussion and debate of the major issues. From these experiences the consensus was reached and specific organizational strategies developed. Groups organized within each sector of each factory of the area and elected a representative of their sector to a factory committee. These, collectively, formed the intermediary *leadership* of the union – a body of 20–30 000 metalworkers. Meetings were then held in the factories to elect representative members with one representative per major factory. This, in turn, formed the Committee of the 450, which was responsible for the actual work of co-ordination. Finally, the workers chose by direct vote in a large open assembly a strike command composed of 16 workers who formed the Committee of Salary and Mobilization. It was an alternative command group of *base* directors who would work with the regularly elected union officials.

When in early 1980 negotiations broke down and the workers (in an assembly of more than 100 000) decided to strike, the alternative strategy and organization was ready. The government immediately intervened in the union, surrounded the physical premises with military troops, closed down the football stadium where the decisive assemblies were held and eventually arrested the 64 top leaders of the metalworkers including Lula and all the directors of the union. They remained in jail while the Committee of the 450 and the Committee of Salary and Mobilization proceeded to set up the necessary groundwork to resist. The intermediary leadership was crucial and virtually ran the strike and all the support work for the next 6 week period. These different levels of organization allowed the movement to continue in spite of new threats and brutal repression. As had been the case in 1979, the assemblies were first held daily in the local football stadium, the Estádio Vila Euclides, now an integral part of Brazilian labor history. There over 200 000 metalworkers from São Bernardo, Diadema, São Caetano, and Santo André met daily to discuss the ongoing strike and make collective decisions through open votes. When the federal government closed the stadium and surrounded it with armed troops, the Catholic Church came out openly in support of the strikers and offered the churches of the area for meetings. The union moved into the backyard of the Cathedral of São Bernardo, and the huge assemblies were held inside the church and in the surrounding park and streets. The Catholic Church also showed its support by helping to organize an effective strike fund and mobilizing the comunidades de base to grant neighborhood support to the striking workers.

The federal government moved in immediately with the full force of its repressive apparatus. The cities of São Bernardo, Santo André, and São Caetano, and even areas of the capital of São Paulo itself resembled an armed camp. Over 10 000 troops were moved into the area under the command of an army general, head of the Second Army Division. The streets were occupied by troops, army trucks, armored vehicles, jeeps, and helicopters in a joint military operation with the São Paulo military police. Workers were literally followed and beaten in the streets. The top leadership which remained out of jail were kidnapped from meetings in spite of the efforts of opposition congressmen and senators to protect them. Two of the top lawyers of the São Paulo Archdiocesan Justice and Peace Committee, Dalmo Dallari and José Carlos Dias, were unceremoniously kidnapped and arrested for a few hours until the direct intervention of São Paulo Cardinal Dom Paulo Evaristo Arns finally freed them. During one of the stadium assemblies, army helicopters, filled with heavily armed soldiers, hovered menacingly over the crowd. At the request of the leaders the crowd remained calm, fought panic, and waved to the helicopters small Brazilian flags which they carried hidden under their shirts.

In spite of the repression the strike continued. This was only possible because of the rank-and-file cohesion, the intermediary levels of leadership, and the absolutely decisive support of the neighborhood associations and the Church. Picket lines were not necessary, and workers avoided the streets by staying at home. All of the organizing work of the strike – including the raising of money and foodstuffs for distribution to the families of workers – was done within the neighborhoods. "Scabs" were stopped from going to the factory at their own doorstep by actively militant neighbors. It was through the interconnections between the secular grassroot neighborhood committees, the Catholic Church, and the *comunidades de base* all across the nation that the strike fund was able to distribute nearly six tones of food per week to the striking families in São Paulo. Long lines formed around the Cathedral of São Bernardo do Campo and, upon showing their metalworker card, the strikers collected wrapped packages calculated to support various sizes of families for the period of one week. Foodstuffs or the money to buy them were sent by grassroots organizations, Church support groups, student committees, opposition politicians, and trade unions from São Paulo as well as most other states. In the Igreja da Matriz, the Cathedral of São Bernardo, foodstuffs were wrapped and the actual distribution of the food was organized. Even though the strike fund in 1980 was able to take care of only approximately 30 000 of the total 120 000 striking families and proved insufficient, nonetheless the solidarity effort was significant and crucial to the maintenance of the strike. It was particularly important in building the interconnections between the trade unions, the grassroots organizations and the institutions of the Catholic church that would further strengthen the social movement in the next few years.

As 1980 progressed this network of support was cemented during the statewide strikes of primary and secondary teachers, particularly in the states of the Northeast and in Minas Gerais. Finally, at the end of the year, the power of the democratic grassroots alliance between secular organizations, unions, and the Church became clear in the strike of the sugarcane plantation workers of Pernambuco, the largest state in the Northeast. The difficulty in organizing such large numbers of rural workers, spread throughout hundreds of farms and completely vulnerable to threats of unemployment and repression, may well be surmised. Nonetheless, the strike started exactly at the day and hour planned in advance and ended also exactly as expected (see José Francisco da Silva, 1980). Approximately 250 000 sugarcane workers participated in the strike which had been carefully organized by a coalition of 42 rural unions and the Church's *pastoral da terra* and *comunidades de base* of the countryside. It was indeed an impressive collective action that resulted in a dramatic increase in the levels of rural organizing throughout the country through the joint efforts of Church groups and the rural unions coordinated by the CONTAG, which had over 6 million members.

During 1980 there was increased involvement, as well, of middle-class sectors that demanded better wages and a higher degree of participation in decisions of government. To a certain extent this increased involvement of middle-class professionals in strike actions reflects both their job instability and low wages and a higher level of awareness of the need to press for government-level reforms. On the one hand, doctors, earning some US$200 per month working in ill-equipped public hospitals, pressed for better working conditions and wages. On the other hand they knew that the final solution to the problems depended upon a government program to provide better health care through an increase in the overall budget spent on health. As the share of the national budget for health amounted to only 4 per cent of the governmental budget, one of the main demands reflected the generalized concern of doctors with the state of health of the population and the lack of proper facilities. The same may be said for secondary and primary level teachers and university professors. Like the doctors, they were aware that the solution for their problems of low wages, job instability, and poor educational facilities depended upon a modification of legislation and an increased national budget for education. The strike activities reflected this understanding of social and economic reality.

Gender

The Experience of Poor Women in Guayaquil

Caroline Moser

In Latin American cities low-income women work, not only in their homes and in the factories, but also in their neighbourhood communities. Along with men and children they are involved in residential level mobilization and struggle over issues of collective consumption. The inadequate provision by the state of housing and local services over past decades has resulted increasingly in open confrontation as ordinary people organize themselves to acquire land through invasion, or put direct pressure on the state to allocate resources for the basic infrastructure required for survival.

This case study is concerned with the experience of poor women in the Indio Guayas *barrio* level committee, situated in the low-income area of Guayaquil, Ecuador. Settlement in this peripheral zone, known as the *suburbios*, involves both the creation of solid land and the construction of incrementally built bamboo and timber houses linked by a complex system of catwalks. Indio Guayas is the name by which the local residents call an area of swampland about ten blocks in size. It has a population of some 3 000, most of whom belong to the *barrio* committee. Data from a household survey undertaken in 1978 showed a mean age of both men and women of 30 years, free unions (*compromisos*) the predominant form of relationship, most households male headed and a mean household size of 5.8. This is a low-income community, representative of the lower end of unskilled non-unionized labour surviving in highly competitive small-scale enterprises, underpaid and irregular "casual" work in a variety of marginal service sector activities – the men mechanics, construction workers, tailoring outworkers, unskilled factory workers and labourers, the women domestic servants, washerwomen, cooks, sellers and dressmakers. The motivation to "invade" this municipal floodland is primarily to own a home and avoid prohibitive rents. Community level mobilization in the *suburbios* is neither automatic nor immediate; plots are not always occupied immediately when acquired but are held as a future investment to be occupied when infrastructure has reached the area. The distance from the city centre, lack of electricity, running water, sewerage and above all roads deter families from living on a plot. Women are most reluctant to move because of the dangers to children from the perilous system of catwalks, the considerable additional burden of domestic labour under such primitive conditions, and the very real fear of loneliness. When they do move, women are forced very suddenly to rely on previously unknown neighbours and quickly develop complex interdependent mutual-aid linkages with each other, formalising them through *comadrasco* (god-parenthood) relationships at the birth of *suburbio*-born children. The unreliable nature of the labour market, which causes insecurity, and the high desertion rate in *compromiso* relationships (i.e. the fact that men desert women) are both factors which constantly reinforce support networks between women. Above all, however, it is the struggle for survival which forces women to develop and retain friendships with their neighbours, and gradually results in an increasing awareness among them of the need to try to improve the situation.

The existence of a widely known procedure for petitioning for services in return for votes by self-help committees proves an important external catalyst for instigating popular participation among newly settled communities.

The long history of *barrio* level committees in Guayaquil beginning in the 1940s was associated with a political system in which populist parties bought votes by providing infrastructure. Until the late 1960s committees were short-lived, formed prior to elections and disbanded soon afterwards. It was only in the late 1960s with the post-Guevara tremors which shook liberal Latin America that they took on a more "institutionalized" form. Along with the church, student, and middle-class women's organizations, which flooded the *suburbios* with dispensaries and clinics, came President Kennedy's Alliance for Progress programme. As a condition of a large USAID grant for squatter upgrading the Guayaquil Municipality was forced to create a Department of Community Development whose purpose was to assist poor communities to "fight for infrastructure" (*luchar para conseguir obras*). The 1972 Plan 240 to infill the mangrove swamps was organized around local *barrio* committees who formed by the hundred to ensure the arrival of infill. Although by 1976, when the project ceased for lack of funds, most committees had disbanded or existed only in name, nevertheless the experience of local organization gained during this period was an important one for the *suburbio* inhabitants.

The Role of Women in the Formation of barrio Committees

Barrio level committees in the *suburbios* of Guayaquil contain both women and men members. The *barrio* committee Indio Guayas was formed in 1975 as a splinter group of another committee because of discontent with the incumbent leadership. As Susana, who invented the name Indio Guayas, explained:

> The first committee here was terrible. All the president did was to steal the money. He was simply engaged in swindling the people. Many presidents of committees live off their members. They don't care if anyone dies or drowns. But to be a leader I think one must be truly human. And also to live here. Because otherwise how does one know what the needs are? I was experiencing that reality in the flesh living here. I made the people understand that we would not achieve anything if we stayed in that committee and that we should organize ourselves, whoever might be the President. But provided he really fought for the interests of this area. So one evening we met in my house, some thirty of us from this area and we organized the committee that I am directing. At that time I was not the president, my brother-in-law Julio was. But as he is lax, he does not like to fight if he meets any problem, he gives up saying, "I don't want to know anything about it". I would say to him, "Julio, you will only get things by fighting, get into the fight because otherwise we will not have anything". I was vice-president, so I became acting president and I went out into the streets to go after things. I would go with 10, 15 women to see what we could get. So I became President.

Although it is the women who urge their neighbours to form a committee they do not automatically see themselves as leaders. Susana, now President of Indio Guayas, started as a deputy in the first committee she joined. When she persuaded her neighbours to form a splinter group it was her brother-in-law, Julio, a white-collar worker in a brewery, her highest status male relative, who was considered most appropriate to become president. It was only 1 year later in 1976, by which time Julio had shown himself thoroughly inept that Susana had sufficient confidence to become president herself, a position she still holds today.

In the area of Cisne Dos, where Indio Guayas is located, four out of twenty committees were female-headed in 1976; by 1982 the number had increased to eight.

While women presidents constantly justify their decision in terms of their commitment to improve conditions for their children as the duty and obligation of a mother, the life histories of *suburbio* women show that those who experienced traumatic suffering in childhood or early adulthood are more likely to involve themselves in residential struggle, out of a determination that their own children, particularly their daughters, should not suffer in similar manner.

Two examples provide illustration of this: Susana, president of Indio Guayas, is the eldest daughter of a woman who had six children by five different men, most of them casual lovers. One was murdered in a fight, others simply walked out and the children were brought up in abject poverty. Susana, as the eldest, took the main responsibility for her brothers and sisters while her mother worked. She herself began working at twelve and when she married at fifteen it was to a much older man, with sufficient resources to allow her to train as a dressmaker. She still retains responsibility for her siblings while limiting her own family to two through birth control. Margarita, Susana's right-hand woman in *barrio* work, experienced a very traumatic first marriage. For fifteen years she lived with a taxi driver who locked her up whenever he went out. She only escaped at the cost of losing her seven children, becoming an itinerant market seller before settling in the *suburbios* in a second *compromiso*. Histories such as these are very common. Obviously for all women experiences such as these do not have similar repercussions. Nevertheless the evidence indicates that the experience of *internal* personal pain and suffering resulting from severe poverty are as important as *external* struggle (such as in the case of factory workers) in developing an awareness and recognition of the nature of oppression and a determination to confront it. In this case it is not a clear "class consciousness". As important is the gradual development of a consciousness of gender oppression and the subordinated position of women. As Susana, addressing an audience of both men and women in the weekly local-level meeting, said,

> We must fight. Above all I want the women, the housewives, to help us, to come with us where ever we go to get the services we need. Why? Because you are at the heart of your homes. You are the ones who suffer the actions of your husbands. The woman is a slave in the home. The woman has to make ends meet.

The Functions of the barrio Committee and the Role of Women

Local-level committees comprise up to fifteen elected officials, consisting of the president, four named officials and up to nine representatives.

The *barrio* committee performs a number of important functions, particularly in the early stages of settlement consolidation, and regardless of the composition of elected officials, it is the women members who take responsibility for much of the day-to-day work.

The most important "external" function of the *barrio* committee is to petition for infrastructure. This is a highly complex operation which can only be briefly mentioned here in terms of the particular role played by women. In common with low-income communities in cities throughout Latin America, the *barrio* committee mobilizes so as to influence the manner in which resources are allocated. Forms of mobilization are determined by the way in which the Municipality of Guayaquil allocates its limited resources on the basis of patron–client relationships. This requires local committees to allow themselves to be co-opted by political parties which exchange services in return for votes and political support. It also means, however, that the extent to which *barrio* level mobilization is successful is in large part determined by national political factors beyond their control.

The different stages of mobilization involve considerable time-consuming "voluntary" work. During the co-option process there are a succession of lengthy meetings (in addition to the regular Saturday neighbourhood meetings) within the *barrio*, as well as with party representatives and local government officials. The preparation and presentation of complex petition documentation is undertaken as well as the very rapid organization of "spontaneous" large-scale mobilizations to protest at the Mayor's office in City Hall at propitious moments. Since the provision of infrastructure is ultimately in direct exchange for votes, the *barrio* committee has particular responsibilities to the political parties at election time. These include attendance at party headquarter briefings, organization of busloads of supporters for political gatherings and extensive *barrio* level canvassing. Finally when infrastructure is provided, the committee must ensure that the community's plan of work is implemented and that neighbouring committees do not manage to divert the infrastructure through bribes to implementing agency officials. In local level committees it is the women, both *presidents* and *rank and file members* who bear the primary responsibility for this work, as the following detailed examination of Indio Guayas committee shows.

The History of Indio Guayas Committee

Indio Guayas committee was founded in 1975 during the 1972–7 period of military rule in Ecuador when few resources were allocated to low-income communities such as the *suburbios*. Until 1977 and the return to democratic government, Indio Guayas committee was effective primarily in its internal functions within the *barrio*. Political activity in the run-up to the 1978 national elections provided the opportunity for mobilization. The fact that Indio Guayas and the surrounding area had been settled since the previous elections, with *barrio* committees unco-opted, resulted in intense activity with the range of political parties (from extreme right to left) offering vote-catching promises. In a highly complicated process Indio Guayas together with twenty other local committees were formed into a Front (*Frente*) and co-opted by a newly formed centre-left political party, *Izquierda Democrática*. At the *barrio* level the critical decision concerning the choice of party to support was based less on its political line than on the perception of its capacity to deliver the promised infrastructure in return for election votes. In the 1978–82 period Indio Guayas, with the other members of the Front, retained its long-term commitment to the same political party as it mobilized, bitterly fought and finally acquired infill, electricity and water. Its success has been determined by events at both the national and the local level, where throughout, constant conflicts of committee fractionalization have occurred as infrastructure provision has continued to be allocated in a non-rational manner.

The Rank and File Members

All the women support the committee. In general when people are asked to help on something serious they will come. When we go to the City Hall, when we have a demonstration the women come and that's the base of the committee (Susana).

Since infrastructure is exchanged for votes the size and commitment of rank and file members is critical to the success and long-term survival of the *barrio* committee. Although in most families both the man and woman join as members of the committee, it is the women who regularly participate in the Saturday afternoon local meetings, the daytime "spontaneous" mass protests to the Mayor's office and the evening mass lobbies at political party meetings held in different locations in the city. While older children are left at school or locked up at home, younger children almost always accompany their mothers since even at night their men are generally reluctant to be involved in childminding activities. Where men do attend mobilizations, their participation is neither regular nor reliable and is often undertaken after considerable pressure has been put on them both by the committee and their women.

Political party leaders, administrative officials and working-class *barrio* men themselves, all see it as natural that most of the participatory work should be undertaken by women, "because women have free time, while men are out at work".

Although this may be true in some cases, particularily in relation to daytime mobilization, it is also a convenient myth that ignores reality. The majority of women, throughout their adult lives, are involved not only in domestic and childrearing work but also in a diversity of income-earning activities, even though these are more likely to be undertaken from home. Time spent in mobilization therefore is detrimental both to domestic and productive work, and women make considerable sacrifices, often risking their jobs as well as neglecting children, in order to make themselves available for mobilizations. The predominant attitude that community level politics, other than in leadership positions, is essentially womens' work is reinforced not only by men at all levels but also by the *barrio* women themselves. Just as it is natural for them to take full responsibility for domestic work in the home, women see it as their responsibility to improve the living conditions of their family through participation in *barrio* level mobilization.

It is the duty of a good mother and wife to improve the neighbourhood for her children (Maria).

In this way women justify their responsibilities in terms of their gender ascriptive roles. Equally they perceive themselves as benefiting most from, for instance, piped water, since the work of water collection and haulage is primarily undertaken by them. Thus the lack of reliable participation of men is lightly and often jokingly dismissed, as laziness, selfishness and irresponsibility, the predominant characteristics of male behaviour in the domestic arena. For their part, most men are willing to allow their women to participate, provided they can see the direct benefits to the family and ensure their own domestic comforts are not disturbed. Although mobilizations involve women travelling outside the *barrio*, and at night, the fact that it is a group activity, means that it is considered "safe".

In Indio Guayas the women have been involved in community level mobilizations for more than 8 years. Over time the experience and achievements of struggle has important consequences for their personal lives.

From the outset participation in protest meetings provides women with an opportunity to get out of their homes and meet their neighbours. For many it is their first experience of a group activity with non-kin. In the tedium and monotony of daily domestic work it provides excitement, if at times exposing them to hostility and violence, as the following mobilization account indicates:

> Susana said we must make a big demonstration, we must get all the people out. And Euclides [a man president] said "If they make any trouble for you, knock Pendola's [the Mayor] door down with your feet and you will see that they will give you something". And so it was. We came along the catwalks, José [a man president from the next door committee] along one side and Susana on the other side, going all around calling all the people to come to the City Hall. We went in seven buses packed with women and children; people full of mud, without shoes, because they had to go around like that, just like that the women went. We went around 10 in the morning. And we made a real big problem for Pendola. The mayor was real mad, he said that the police must evict us from there. And we didn't budge. "We want infill" everyone was shouting. We were happy because like that we could achieve something.

Popular mobilization involves endless waiting, in queues with petitions, in buses to reach destinations and at political meetings for the relevant politican to appear. This provides women with frequent small-group situations and the opportunity to discuss common problems and share intimate experiences: typical conflicts in their relationships with men, problems concerning their own sexuality and marital disputes over the use of birth control. As a group, women make consensual judgements about women who allow themselves to be sexually abused, and increase each other's confidence to return home and confront their men over issues such as sex or money. Group struggle provides catalytic situations for shared confidences which gives women the opportunity to examine and question their own lives.

In their personal lives most women moved very rapidly from the parental control of childhood, to the *compromiso* control of their children's father, and therefore have had limited previous experience of independence or recognition of their own power, even if in a limited arena. Group experience of shared problems and common successes produces an awareness of personal consciousness. The extent to which it gives women the confidence to question the subordinate nature of their personal relationships, cannot tangibly be measured. Nevertheless individual examples provide evidence of the manner in which the experience of group protest over time has assisted local *barrio* women in their decision to take greater responsibility for their lives. Both Anna and Josefina live in *compromiso* relationships with local artisans, a carpenter and a tailor. In their early years of living in Indio Guayas both brought up young children and provided unremunerated assistance to their men's work through a diversity of tasks. Neither had any economic independence and both endured the physical abuse of husbands who were heavy drinkers. Anna's situation was exacerbated by the fact that her husband openly, and with his mother's support, lived between two households in a bigamous arrangement. Four years later both had taken conscious steps to make themselves economically independent. Josefina returned to night school to complete her primary education, while intermittently selling cloth, travelling on her own, with her husband's reluctant consent, to retail it to rural family contacts. Anna was attending dressmaking classes and working as laundry woman. With her own income she had gained sufficient confidence to retaliate when attacked by her husband, and to prevent him access to the house for 3 months until he stopped both excessive drinking and beating her up. Both women clearly identified the community mobilization experience as critical in assisting them to recognize not only their need but also the possibility to get out of their homes and obtain some degree of economic independence.

The experience of protest exposes low-income women to the nature of the Ecuadorian political system, to the structure of local government and the function of political parties in the allocation of resources. In concrete terms, they see corruption in the way decisions are made, and exploitation in the manner in which the poor are constantly manipulated for political ends, resulting in increased cynicism about the political system. Despite the fact that literate women have had the vote in Ecuador since 1928, politics is still considered essentially a male world with women traditionally accustomed to vote in accordance with their father's or husband's view. In Guayaquil the low-income vote has predominantly supported populist leaders such as Velasco and then Bucaram. Popular participation provides women often with their first direct contact to a range of political views, which in the case of Indio Guayas from 1978 onwards, included the non-traditional new centre-left party, *Izquierda Democratica*. Obviously not all women are equally affected by this experience but as many begin to make their own decisions about political support they are no longer prepared to conform to family attitudes, resulting in many cases in splits between spouses in voting behaviour.

Although the experience of struggle affects the personal lives of the women involved it is important not to exaggerate the consequences particularly for rank and file members. Each mobilization by its very nature is a relatively short-term activity with the women returning home to continue their domestic and work responsibilities until the next occasion. Even during the protest period itself there are often strong pressures which prevent women from participating, and which make them frustrated and bitter. Women clearly identify the principal problem not their domestic commitments but the hostility of their men. As Margarita, a long-term activist expressed it:

> Many of the women got tired of going on because there was always trouble with the husbands, they are jealous, they don't want to let them, and one needs time for the business of politics, get up at dawn, leave the house early and come back late at night. You only survive if you can overcome that problem. But for a lot of them its too much. You know how men can bully and then they get frightened. What will the children live on?

However the history of mobilization in Indio Guayas throughout the 1978–82 period indicates that once women have participated the experience of struggle is not forgotten. Not only is it a bond which unites women, a frequent topic of discussion, recalled in retrospect as "a good time", but the same women can be called on, time and time again, whenever their support is required.

Women Leaders

For a very small number of women the experience of popular participation has fundamental consequences not only personally but also at the economic and political level. In the struggle for infra-structure women leaders emerge, presidents as well as prominent committee members, who in the process of co-option look towards political leadership roles. However, those women who try to move beyond the women's domestic arena into the men's world of politics do so at enormous personal cost and little reward. It is in the criticisms encountered and the conflicts confronted by women leaders that the powerful societal mechanisms to control women, and confine them to their domestic roles, are most blatantly manifested.

In their work within the community women leaders are viewed ambiguously, alternatively admired and criticized, subject to both verbal and physical abuse.

As women leaders become more powerful they are increasingly distanced from their women neighbours and friends. The fact that they have "got out", and that political leaders and important officials rush in and out of the area visiting their homes, is viewed with hostility and jealousy by women who feel "trapped" at home. Critical gossip of their roles as wives and mothers is the most powerful mechanism utilized by women to destroy their reputation and thereby control their behaviour.

The importance of conforming to the expected role of a woman as wife and mother fulfilling the required domestic obligations is also used by women to justify non-participation.

In fact, the most difficult personal problem faced by all women leaders is that of marital conflict. While their men are content, even proud, at the outset, a number of factors rapidly result in a deterioration in the marital relationship. Firstly the time-consuming nature of the work, particularly at time of national political activity; secondly the rampant gossip that assumes that because women are working with men they must be prostituting themselves; and thirdly that as women become public figures they achieve greater importance than their spouse, both inside and outside the *barrio*. Susana describes some of her feelings on the problem, and how, over the years, she has tried to cope.

> I have had problems for years, since I first went on the committee. Ever since then there has been lots of trouble. But I don't go around telling everyone about it, I just keep quiet. They come for me, I say fine and I get dressed and go. He says it's alright if I am fighting for our street only, but not for all those others. I tell him that's selfish. If I am a leader and people have trust in me I cannot let them down, I must go on until I get the works for them.

> It may be that he doesn't like it because I have to see a lot of men, because most of my work is with men. But if I don't want to do anything, nothing will happen to me, because that depends on oneself. I have been with him for 12 years and in all those years I have never failed him. It gets worse and worse. One week we are alright and the following week nothing but fights. But I don't care. I don't pay much attention to him. I don't suffer. I eat. If I stopped to think I would be miserable. I am not going to let him dominate me too much. He would like me to do nothing and let him do whatever he likes. Once he sees that I don't obey him, he'll have to decide whether he wants to go on or go to the devil. What does marriage do for us? I have always worked since I was a young girl. So I'll just have to work a little harder if he goes, to support myself and the children. Is that such a problem?

Susana, discussing the problem in 1978, when she stoically resigned herself to being locked into her home when her man decided she had done sufficient "running around with men", still saw the problem as a private affair. By 1982, however, the conflict had become public, and degenerated to such an extent that in a Front meeting Susana's husband Juan publicly, in front of twenty presidents and the regional party representative, forbade her to accept the presidency of the Front, moments after she had been elected in an open ballot. In the ensuing confrontation the women presidents attacked Juan as "macho", but added,

> The system is the critical problem. Even if we all vote for her, even if twenty of us democratically vote for her, in the end you, Juan, have the only vote that matters. It is you who has the final vote. It's the husband who decides everything.

When the male presidents interceded they explicitly praised Susana, explaining why the party could not survive without her, but without attacking Juan personally.

The problem was finally resolved by a compromise solution in which Juan agreed that his wife would remain president but only until the imminent elections were over.

Women leaders try in a number of ways to cope with marital criticism and local abuse. As McCourt (1977, p. 149) has commented:

> Active women may adhere even more strongly to the traditional female image and role, in order to make up for the ambivalence created by their participatory behaviour.

As women working in a "man's world" they are scrupulously "respectable" in their behaviour, always ensuring that they are accompanied by kin or a woman friend when travelling outside the *suburbios* and attending political meetings, dressing unprovocatively and consciously avoiding compromising situations. Publicly they constantly justify their active participation in terms of a common concern for the needs of their children rather than their personal ambition.

> I work for my children. In the future they will be able to say, "Our mother was loyal to us, let us help her" (Margarita).

Despite their efforts women leaders are faced with conflict on all sides and become painfully isolated. Their involvement in the world outside their community distances them from local women. They are used, but not accepted as equal by male leaders, and forced to rely on the friendships with other women leaders with whom they are often in conflict due to the competitive allocation of resources inherent in political patron–client relationships. A middle-class woman political leader summarized the problem in the following way:

> Women have a very difficult time. The patriarchal culture means that they are not helped at all, just used. If I was married I wouldn't be running all over the place. I would have to stay at home. Because of the

problem of *machismo*, women are not allowed out. But the competition between women is enormous. Women have to struggle against other women as well as against men.

Of all the low-income women involved in struggle it is the leaders who, through bitter experience, try to challenge conventional attitudes concerning the position of women. Thus Susana, while blatantly justifying her work to her husband in terms of her role as a mother caring for her children's needs, quite explicitly recognizes her own personal needs:

> I wasn't born to slave away at the sewing machine. I do believe that a woman has to do the cooking and cleaning, but not to be stuck at home all the time and nothing else. We must see something better, get some profession, do something for the community and also work. They probably think that I order my husband around, that I am very overbearing. But I am not overbearing, it's merely that the woman has the same rights as the man. Because if he wants to go out, so do I, although of course not to get drunk, but to have a good time.

The attempts by women leaders to change the nature of their marital relationships invariably, however, culminates in the breakdown of the *compromiso*. While Susana is in her early 30s, the life histories of older working-class women presidents in Guayaquil show a common pattern in which conflict over the woman's political work results in the couple separating. Although the woman frequently forms a second *compromiso* this is generally with a younger, often less aggressive man, on whom the woman is not financially dependent; indeed she may well support him. It is important to emphasize that although economic independence solves the immediate problem for the woman concerned, it does not result in any fundamental restructuring of the nature of interpersonal relationships between women and men.

The Co-optation of Women Leaders by Political Parties

In campaign speeches and political party slogans the virtues of working-class women are extolled with particular emphasis on their roles as mothers and wives, while their activities within the party are limited to women's affairs and they are prevented from gaining any real power. In *Izquierda Democrática* this policy reached a crisis in 1982 when the Party tried to organize *suburbio* women leaders into a Women's Front (*Frente Feminino*) under the leadership of the upper-class wives of national political leaders. The blanket refusal of leaders such as Susana, Margarita and Rosa to join the Women's

Front highlighted the impossible position of working-class women leaders caught in a conflict not only of gender but also of class. The assumption that as women they *a priori* have interests in common with other women, including the patronizing wives of upper-class politicans, fails to take account of the fact that both as political leaders and as members of the working class they feel they have more in common with other working-class leaders, male or female.

Although *barrio* women leaders are co-opted to obtain votes for political parties it is far more difficult for them, than for men, to achieve elected positions in Ecuadorian politics. Five different stages of political involvement can be identified: *barrio* level leader, activist in political party, elected representative within political party, elected municipal councillor, and finally elected national congress representative. Working-class men leaders quite frequently reach the fourth stage of elected municipal councillor. However lack of sufficient financial resources makes them unable to participate adequately in the complex system of political payoffs and they rarely survive more than one term in office. Women leaders, in contrast, rarely reach beyond the third stage, but are themselves far more ambivalent about their political ambitions.

Most women leaders show great reluctance about moving beyond the level of *barrio* level leader. As Susana, speaking in 1982, said:

> I don't know if I want to stand as a councillor. Politics just causes problems, problems in my home and problems with everyone here. Men like playing around, but I know what I can do well. I can get works [*obras*]. Look how many people have got water around here. I got the water not only in Indio Guayas but all over. I am a leader not because I am that capable, but because the people have confidence in me, because they see I will fight for what I believe in. That's why I know this is where my power is, here in the *suburbios*.

Susana's preference to stay at the level of community mobilization is the consequence of her situation. As a woman leader she has far greater commitment to the community than is the case with men who more frequently assume leadership responsibility in order to gain economic rewards or political advancement. However, the constant criticism she encounters in her work increases her personal guilt about neglecting her children and husband and reduces her self-confidence. Community level ambiguity about women leaders, combined with the fact that the political arena is effectively closed to women, ensures that leaders such as Susana limit their personal ambition, restricting it to short-term community gains rather than longer-term political goals.

Conclusion

This case study from the *suburbios* of Guayaquil illustrates the way in which, within one Latin American urban context, women's and men's spheres of work are clearly separated, and the implications of this in terms of community level popular mobilization. While the men's world lies outside the community in the productive work of factories and market places, and the power politics of City Hall and local government, the world within the community, identified as the arena of domestic responsibility and welfare provision is primarily organized by women. Thus popular participation over issues of collective consumption and community level politics is fundamentally seen as women's work, with men's involvement most frequently legitimized in clearly defined leadership positions.

However, the fact that women, supported by their men, mobilize in what is considered a natural extension of the domestic arena imposes limitations on such action. In the same way that women's domestic work, undertaken in their roles as mothers and wives, is not valued, so women's popular mobilization, undertaken in the same role, is not considered *real* work. This attitude is reflected throughout society: for it is not only men, but also the women themselves who consider it their duty to participate in mobilization as part of their domestic responsibilities. While women recognize that community level work is their most effective arena for action, the vast majority nevertheless fail to realize that in reality their only power lies in their gender ascriptive roles and that as people they have no power. Consequently after their success in achieving a change in the provision of items of collective consumption they are content to return to their homes without demanding any fundamental change at the ideological level concerning their role in society.

Those few women in leadership positions who do demand real power, by trying to move beyond the women's world of community level consumption provision into the men's world of power politics, become a threat to the prevailing gender divisions within society. Although they perceive of their struggle in *class* terms, and not in terms of *gender* struggle, which remains at the personalized level within the family, nevertheless in their attempts to achieve political power they are also, if unintentionally, challenging the gender subordinated role of women in Ecuadorian society. As a result they are caught between two struggles, of both class and gender, and alienated on all sides. They are viewed with hostility and jealousy by women of their own class and mistrusted by their spouses, but at the same time they are used but not accepted by men political leaders of all classes while instinctively rejecting alliances with women of other classes. In their struggle to survive without space for gender issues to be expressed their only recourse is either consciously to ensure that in their personal behaviour they conform to the traditional female role, or to avoid the worst marital hostility through economic independence. In neither case do the solutions openly confront the essential issue of gender struggle, thus demonstrating the lack of possibility under the prevailing conditions within Ecuadorian society for gender issues to move beyond the personal level and become formalized as a political issue.

In much of the recent literature on urban social movements the important role played by women is only mentioned descriptively in passing. Present in their gender ascriptive roles they have been effectively invisibilized to the extent that the dominant analytical issue concerns the nature of class struggle at the point of residence. Where the role of women in struggle is mentioned at the conceptual level it is in terms of the emergence of the women's liberation movement which "aims at overcoming the structural domination of one gender by the other" (Castells, 1983, p. 309). The evidence from this case study indicates the inappropriateness of evaluating the struggles of low-income women in a Third World city entirely in terms of their feminist consciousness, and consequently the limitations of assuming the universal commonality, both trans-class and trans-culturally of women's interests. At the same time it would suggest that any analysis concerned with establishing why residential level mobilization fails to create the same level of class consciousness as does mobilization at the point of production, needs to take account of the issue of gender subordination within "more realistic parameters for comprehending the underlying and persistent causes of gender inequality" (Molyneux, 1985, p. 2). Far too little recognition is still given to the fact that this is one of the most divisive mechanisms of social control, reinforced not only by the state but also, if unconsciously, by men of all classes. For this reason it is critical to identify the extent to which gender struggle and overcoming gender subordination may in the last analysis be one of the most important preconditions for popular movements (in which women play such a signifant role) to be effectively transformed into political movements. Only then will low-income urban movements combine both production and consumption but also involve both women and men equally.

Westernization and the Bari of Columbia

Elena Buenaventura-Posso and Susan Brown

When Western capitalistic systems expand upon egalitarian communal societies, their actions involve the introduction and imposition of features such as the structure for general male dominance over females based materially on preferential male access to strategic resources; private ownership of land and a money economy; overall inequality in the form of differential access to privileges and resources which lead to the formation of socio-economic classes; and an emphasis on the nuclear family, supported by a wage-earning male, as the ideal domestic unit. Wedded to their own experience of social and economic stratification, as well as to their concept of sex roles and statuses, such Western societies are unable to understand or accept the realities of a truly egalitarian society. Thus, outside contact with the Bari and their neighbors has been typically male-centered, élitist, and divisive.

Since the 1964 "truce," numerous transformations of Bari culture have occurred with particularly detrimental effects for women. In the political realm, other influences are working to create powerful, authoritative "chiefs" among the Bari, who do not themselves have even a word for "chief." Such newly appointed "chiefs" are, of course, all males. Changes in the economic realm have even more devastating effects for women. First, the forced breakup of the collective living unit and its replacement by the patriarchial nuclear family makes the female dependent upon a wage-earning male for subsistence items, which are now purchased with cash. Particularly important is the fact that males, and not females, are given access to the tools and skills necessary to acquire the newly desired cash. The introduction of male access to wage labor and cash cropping has brought with it a structure for male exploitation of female labor.

The breakdown of the collective living unit is also accompanied by the disintegration of communal subsistence activities such as double-dam fishing. In various ways, the collectivity is being destroyed in favor of a more individualistic mode of life. At the same time, many traditional female tasks are being eliminated through recent changes in Bari lifeways. Women's work is shifting from production tasks such as spinning, weaving, basket making, and food production to menial service tasks, such as washing clothes. In addition to these transformations, women's important traditional role in healing has been systematically usurped.

In the ritual-ceremonial realm we find that the characteristic sexual symmetry is being eroded to such an extent that, in those regions most influenced by colonial penetration, women no longer play a significant role in the only major ceremonial activity. Finally, all of these factors are almost inevitably creating a foreign and traditionally unheard of antagonism between the sexes.

In the following section we analyze these transformations of Bari society, and especially the impact of one aspect of intervention, the Motilon Development Plan. Begun in the mid-1960s this plan represents the most organized and successful attempt at absorbing the Bari into the contemporary industrial society, directly influencing a quarter, and perhaps up to one-third, of the Bari population. The plan has been well documented by its originator, a young North American missionary who made contact with the Bari in 1961 and, therefore, is an especially good focus for our analysis.

Our object is not to evaluate the overall value of the actual Bari Westernization plan, but rather to analyze in detail its effects on women's status and, in doing so, document the creation of a male-dominated hierarchy within this traditionally egalitarian society.

The Creation of Male Chiefs

In an attempt to organize hierarchically the Bari, the Motilon Development Plan has instituted a *cacique* within each of the seven indigenous Bari autonomous groups. These seven men, designated as "chiefs," have been given Colombian citizenship and officially instituted as the leaders and representatives of those people living within their assigned territories. In addition, seven young Bari males have been assigned as assistant leaders to these "chiefs." Together with the *caciques* of each zone they serve on the Board of Directors for the Motilon Development Plan (Olson and Neglia, 1974, pp. 117–20).

The attainment of Colombian citizenship papers for these fourteen privileged males means, legally, that they can become landholders and vote in Colombian elections.

As for the success of the Motilon Development Plan in creating viable Bari chiefs, all available data suggests that the mature Bari continue to resist such impositions. It does appear, however, that one mechanism has been elaborated which might allow for the successful creation of such chiefs and involves the intensive socialization of young Bari males: at times these boys have been adopted by the missionary; in other instances he only formally sponsors and guides their education. The total result, however, is that a small group of chosen males are being sent to urban centers for higher education and eventual professional training. Already, some of these boys have been classified as sons of *caciques* who will in time become chiefs of the Bari. Thus, we are now witnessing a dual transformation by which certain young males are being given access to a strategic new resource, education, while females are not given parallel opportunities. In addition, at least some of these male students are already being given the title of *cacique* – as if it were a real and even inheritable Bari leadership position.

The Ursurpation of Women's Traditional Role in Healing

Traditionally, women played very important roles in Bari medicinal practices. Recently, however, significant changes have taken place among the groups most influenced by the Motilon Development Plan. Attempts have been made to eliminate the roles played by women in the healing practices, which are connected with the plan's carefully planned introduction of new medicines. The manner in which the medicines were introduced not only bypassed women's role as collectors, preparers, and administrators of traditional medicines but also placed the administration of medicine solely in male hands. For example, the early use of Terramicyn for the treatment of eye infections was introduced through male healers, as were the vaccinations brought for the Bari. It was also the intention of the Motilon Development Plan to try to train the sons of these male healers to be more modern medical practitioners (Olson and Neglia, 1974, p. 120).

The Encouragement of Male Exploitation of Female Labor and Forced Economic Dependency of Women

A recent intervention involves the encouragement of Bari participation in the market economy through the production and sale of surplus crops. The plan worked to encourage surplus production of traditional foodstuffs such as manioc, and plantains. Never concerned with selling food, or even storing it for long periods, the Bari lacked the notion of surplus production. For this new production, each hearth group employed its usual communal-cultivation procedures with the one modification that the men received instruction and facilities for the selling of surpluses (Olson and Neglia, 1974, pp. 120–21). The result has been that individual males are now in control of the cash produced by the collective hearth group efforts. As unwittingly as it may or may not have been, this innovation provides the basis for male exploitation of female labor.

Bari entrance into and growing dependency upon the market

economy brings about various interactions. New goods are introduced and subsequently desired and/or required by the Bari. Therefore, a need arises for money with which to purchase these goods. At the same time the Bari males are sought as inexpensive agricultural laborers. Today, numerous Bari men work, if only sporadically, for missionaries, homesteaders, and others, and through this activity only males gain access to the important new resource, money. Money allows them to purchase manufactured goods such as machetes, shotguns, cotton hammocks, clothes, and the like. Without access to cash, women must depend on men for necessary and desired manufactured goods such as clothing, shoes and boots, metal cooking utensils, and foodstuffs. Also, male participation in wage labor weakens the traditional subsistence system and alters domestic patterns. Since the men are away working in another's fields for weeks to months at a time, they are no longer able to fulfill their traditional subsistence tasks. Not only does the level of general nutrition suffer but, beyond this, the man's former work must be picked up by the women who remain at home.

The Modification of Women's Roles in Subsistence Activities

Another revealing sign of Bari cultural disintegration is given by the changes being brought about in women's subsistence activities. The impact of these modifications can be clearly seen by focusing on collective activities in which both women and men traditionally participate, and subsistence activities carried out only by women.

A communal activity of major importance among the Bari is fishing. Fish are a major source of protein, and, unlike hunting, fishing involves a highly organized group effort in which all members of the dwelling participate. The double-dam fishing technique, for example, involved a close co-ordination of women's and men's labor. Through this collective effort large numbers of fish are obtained in one day. Current economic and cultural transformations, however, are eliminating this form of subsistence activity. On the one hand, as men are removed from the communal dwelling to work as wage laborers this collective fishing stops. On the other hand, with the introduction of new technology, the traditional double-dam technique is being replaced by individual male fishing with weighted nets and motorized boats. The introduction of these new fishing methods has excluded women from this most vital, once collective, subsistence activity.

A second important collective activity concerns the construction of the communal dwellings. Again, we see a highly organized task in which both females and males participate, each performing roles assigned by sex. This effort represents a highly complex and organized activity with numerous implications for Bari social organization. Neither sex can build the house alone, everyone's contribution is essential. Women, for example, collect and prepare the palm branches used for thatching while men gather and place the frame poles. A major goal of missionary intervention, past and present, has been the replacement of these collective living units with individual, nuclear-family dwellings. In the case of the Motilon Development Plan the large communal dwellings are being replaced by small concrete houses. These units are constructed by Colombian laborers with the help of Bari male "heads of households." The women are thus also excluded from dwelling construction.

In addition, those subsistence activities carried out exclusively by women, and associated with the woman's space within the dwelling, are extensively affected by the new type of housing. For example, in the zinc-roofed houses, women no longer spin and weave. These houses do not facilitate these tasks since they are unbearably hot during the day and because their concrete floors make it almost impossible to set up and operate there looms. The decline in weaving is also linked to the introduction of manufactured cloth and the strongly encouraged abandonment of traditional dress, consisting of a short skirt for women and a breechcloth for men. Along the same line, hammocks formerly made by the men from sisal spun by women have been increasingly replaced by those produced industrially. These changes in dress and hammock preference, in turn, have dual effects. On the one hand, they are associated with a reduction in the female contribution to group subsistence, and on the other hand, they intensify Bari dependence upon the external market economy. Such modifications in dress also create some unpleasant and time-consuming tasks for women. Women are instructed that it is their duty to regularly wash these clothes. For this task they must obtain commercially made soap which can only be purchased in distant centers with money. These imperatives, combined with the totally unadaptive nature of this new clothing to the tropical forest environment, contribute to the fact that today the Bari are often seen wearing dirty, tattered clothing.

The diminished importance of women's collecting activities represents another important development. As already described, the Bari had an extremely flexible and mobile lifestyle, but they are now being forced into a sedentary existence by the construction of permanent individual dwellings, the effects of male wage labor, the encouragement of cash cropping, and other influences. Sedentarization along with the introduction of money and manufactured foodstuffs has led to a minimization of women's collecting activities, once essential to the Bari economy. The subsequent deterioration of Bari nutritional standards is an important side effect. Traditionally, the Bari women collected some twenty-three species of plant food. Today the groups exposed to extensive contact consume considerably fewer wild vegetables and fruits. As Pinton and Jaulin suggest, the traditionally well-nourished Bari now suffer a decline in the quality of their food intake. There has been an increased dependency on starchy staples such as manioc and plantains as well as new use of wheat, oatmeal, and oil. One might well ascribe an excessive weight gain by many Bari women to these dietary changes. Thus, the decline of women's collecting activities not only signals a further deterioration of female contributions to the subsistence base; it also is associated with a degeneration of physical well-being among the Bari.

The Breakdown of the Communal Residential Unit

As described earlier, the fabric of Bari social organization is woven together by formalized relationships between what we might call kin, *sadodi*, and nonkin, *ojibara*. Alliances established upon the basis of the *sadodi-ojibara* division provided each Bari with special relations to various individuals within their own communal dwelling as well as with individuals of other dwellings; at the same time, the entire Bari society was held together through such pacts.

The move to nuclear-family residential units promoted by the Motilon Development Plan disrupts this highly organized and intricately balanced form of social organization. With the disappearance of the communal dwelling unit there is necessarily associated a breakdown of the society's interpersonal and intergroup relations. Women in particular suffer detrimental effects from this atomization. The move to individual houses causes the isolation of adult women from each other and the subsequent weakening of their co-operative systems of meal preparation, cultivation and child rearing. This co-operation was favored by matrilocality, a residence pattern in which closely related female kin are often found living within the same dwelling after marriage. On another level, the disruption of the communal living unit compounds the economic factors that destroy collective subsistence activities such as fishing and dwelling construction. Also, group communication and knowledge-sharing processes, important to the maintenance of such an egalitarian society, and facilitated by the traditional residence pattern, are eliminated or weakened by the transition to individual households.

Neglect of Women's Participation in the Ceremonial Cantos

The *Canto* celebrations represent an essential element in traditional Bari social organization. They offer the opportunity for communication and sharing between residential groups, and provide for the creation and maintenance of alliances and pacts with distant persons. For those groups most influenced by the Motilon Development Plan, the last decade has witnessed a significant shift in the structure and meaning of the *Cantos*. While traditionally both females and males participated in these celebrations, in recent years the *Cantos* have become known exclusively as male celebrations and are now called *El Canto de las Fechas*, which the development plan hopes to establish as the symbol of Bari cultural unity (Olson and Neglia, 1974, pp. 117; 120–21; see also Pinton 1973).

In a similar vein we can add that the only known musical instruments among the Bari are reed flutes. While little data is available on the ritual or social significance of these instruments, it is well documented that the flutes are manufactured and played by the women. Flute playing, however, like women's participation in the Cantos, is rapidly being lost with the present cultural transformations.

Incipient Alteration of Egalitarian Relations Between the Sexes

During our brief visit with the Bari we were impressed with the egalitarian and gentle relations between women and men. Voices were not raised, anger not witnessed; commands belonged to another reality. Such elements of our own society as men's domination of women, sexual objectivication of the female, an ideology of basic human inequality, and sexism still find no equivalent in Bari society.

The current impositions of the market economy, combined with the growing infringements of Colombian and Venezuelan nationals and international missionaries, are, however, beginning to affect relations between the sexes. These relations, unfortunately, are as vulnerable to the forces of ethnocide as other cultural components, and women are beginning to resent men's exploitation of their labor. They dislike their new dependency on individual men for money and the goods money can buy. Thus, we heard of women complaining that their husbands did not provide them with adequate manufactured cloth and clothing.

Also, we noticed that some Bari males who were in close contact with homesteaders have taken on their sexist behaviors. We witnessed, for example, two young Bari men referring in the presence of a potential marriage partner to her physical and sexual characteristics. Upon inquiring about the matter, we were told that such behavior is not socially acceptable among the Bari. In this case the young men were conversing with a male visitor from Bogota who they thought, no doubt, would appreciate their comments. While the Bari are very affable and sociable with each other, they do not impose themselves on others nor do they objectify individuals, sexually or otherwise.

In conclusion, traditional Bari society is fully egalitarian. Under the circumstances, however, it is doubtful that this system of social relations will survive. Like many other native groups, the Bari have been, since the earliest contact with Western society, continually threatened with usurpation and extinction. Most recently, they have been under attack from homesteaders and petroleum concerns. The intervention of the Motilon Development Plan has perhaps saved the Bari from outright genocide. In the long run, however, the price they must pay for their survival may well be near total destruction of their culture. For although the adult generation in contact with the whites seem to passively resist much of the change imposed upon them, the new generation, particularly the males, seem to be somewhat eager to try the Western way of life. On the other hand, some observers assert that those communities of Bari who still remain in the more isolated places of the territory view whites with the same mistrust as before the 1964 truce and might renew hostilities with them in the not too distant future (Jaulin, personal communication).

The future of those Bari groups or individuals who continue to be exposed extensively to the Western culture and economic system seems decided. Slowly, they will be absorbed into industrial society, mainly as peasants, while a few Bari males will enter into slightly more privileged positions. Today, this process is well under way and the sexual equality and individual autonomy characteristic of the Bari are already in the process of disintegration.

The Internationalization of Capital

TNCs, The State and Latin American Industrialization

Rhys Jenkins

The operations of TNCs should not be treated in isolation but seen as part of a wider process of internationalization of capital, of which they themselves are primary protagonists. The homogenization of production and consumption patterns is a characteristic of the internationalization of capital everywhere, but in the socio-economic context of Latin America, it has effects which are very different from those in the advanced capitalist countries. Most of the so-called "distortions" which are identified in Latin America are the result of the internationalization of capital interacting with the specific, local socio-economic structure to generate patterns which are in significant ways different from those found in the advanced capitalist countries.

Given their importance in the world economy today, it is not surprising that TNCs should play a leading role in the internationalization of capital. This should not lead to an excessive concern with the institutional form adopted, as opposed to the process of internationalization itself. Such an approach leads to a number of dangers. It underestimates the extent and significance of the internationalization of capital, identifying it only with that part of production which is under the direct control of TNCs. It also implies that local or foreign ownership is a crucial variable in determining the nature and behaviour of capital. However, large local firms, often operating with licences from abroad, behave in most respects in ways which are very similar to the TNCs. They employ similar capital-intensive production techniques, carry out very limited local R & D and modifications to production processes, have similar competitive strategies and are also overwhelmingly oriented towards the domestic market. In some cases, large Latin American firms have themselves begun to become TNCs.

Manufacturing TNCs in Latin America play a crucial role in the promotion of international patterns of production and consumption. They are able to do so because they occupy leadership positions within the most dynamic sectors of industry. Many local firms are then forced to adapt to the production norms and product standards set by TNCs. In order to compete successfully with TNC subsidiaries, local firms adopt imitative strategies, as in the case of the Argentinian pharmaceutical industry where the very successful local firms have based their strategy largely on heavy sales promotion, product differentiation and the introduction of new products, often produced under license from abroad. Also, the key positions occupied by TNCs within much broader systems of inter-industry relationships (industrial complexes) enable them to have a major influence on the production of a broader range of goods. The motor industry provides a classic illustration of this pattern, with the terminal sector being totally dominated by a handful of TNCs which can exercise considerable control over the parts industry, much of which is in local hands. As a result, major local part manufacturers produce international products to the terminals' specification.

The model of accumulation in Latin American manufacturing since the mid-1950s is characterized by a number of contradictions. The oligopolistic structure of industry and the relatively small scale of TNC operations in Latin America tend to limit the rate of capital accumulation. This is reinforced by the tendency of the balance of payments to deteriorate as a result of a growing outflow of profits, royalties and technical assistance payments, and of the import-intensive nature of TNC activities. A model which offers little or no benefit for the mass of the population, whose opportunities of employment are severely restricted, while at the same time concentrating the gains in the hands of TNCs and large local economic groups has major social and political implications. There is also a contradiction between the legitimacy of the *national* state and its objective role in promoting the internationalization of capital.

The question of the state is of central importance in this context because it plays a major role in revitalizing the accumulation process. The growth of the state sector and particularly the state productive sector has characterized a number of Latin American countries. The state also plays a role in attempting to attract new waves of foreign investment. It intervenes in order to loosen the balance of payments constraint, both by its general export promotion policies and specific measures aimed at reducing the trade deficit of TNCs. A further important way in which capital accumulation is maintained despite continuing balance of payments deficits is through growing external indebtedness.

The state is involved in a delicate balancing act. Expanding its role in production, it must not be seen to threaten the private sector. Attempting to attract new inflows of foreign capital, it must not be seen to threaten the position of local capital. While attempting to reduce the adverse balance of payments impact of TNCs it must not be seen as threatening the position of foreign capital, otherwise new foreign investment will dry up. Even in Brazil, the alliance between state, foreign and private local capital is subject to many strains.

Finally, the model of accumulation is affecting class structure in Latin America in a number of ways. The local bourgeoisie is becoming increasingly differentiated between those large local groups and other sectors of local capital which are closely involved in the internationalization of capital, and other sectors which find themselves restricted to low growth, low profit activities in the most competitive sectors of manufacturing. Both groups may find themselves in conflict with foreign capital over issues such as levels of royalty payments and export restrictions, or the spheres reserved for local capital. Nevertheless, such conflicts were relatively minor and do not extend to advocacy of the wholesale exclusion of foreign capital.

There is also a certain differentiation of the working class associated with the spread of Fordist labour processes and the accompanying bipolar skill structure. Politically, however, this is less important that the relatively slow growth of the industrial proletariat under the prevailing model of accumulation. The result is that the industrial working class remains a relatively small share of the labour force, and that with rapid population growth marginality increases. On the other hand, the effect of the internationalization of capital in agriculture is leading to proletarianization or semi-proletarianization of peasants in a number of Latin American countries, which is expanding the size of the rural working class and posing a new threat to political stability.

TNCs and Alternative Development Paths

Measures to restrict foreign capital and to give preference to local firms do not offer a significant alternative to the present model. Studies which show the superior performance of local firms in terms of certain development criteria, such as more labour-intensive production processes are often based on a fallacious methodology which does not compare like with like. When similar firms are compared, there is often little difference between foreign and local capital, and other variables such as firm size or industry are more important in explaining apparent differences. Thus, substituting local for foreign ownership may have very little effect on most aspects of firm behaviour. Measures for increasing local share ownership, far from being intended to alter the behaviour of firms as has sometimes been implied are, in fact, primarily a way of ensuring the local bourgeoisie's share of the fruits of economic growth.

Restricting the spheres of operation of TNCs is unlikely to alter the fundamental problems because these derive from the internationalization of capital rather than from the presence of TNCs *per se*. Is there, then, an alternative in the shape of national capitalist development of the kind which historically characterized Japan, independent of the internationalization of capital? To sustain such a thesis it would be necessary to abstract from the specific historical and geo-political characteristics of the development of Japanese capital. In particular, the internationalization of capital, and the development of the forces of production in transport and communications which have made it possible, were much less advanced in the late nineteenth century. It should also not be forgotten that imperial expansion played an important part in the development of Japanese capitalism, while it is highly unlikely that this could be repeated in Latin America in the late twentieth century.

A more active role for the state in production and in the control of foreign capital is unlikely to alter the pattern of accumulation significantly. The capitalist state is not an independent agent able to construct a socially more rational development strategy, but itself reproduces in its interior the conflicts and contradictions of the capitalist mode of production. The role of the state in production is restricted by the prime objective of promoting capital accumulation. Moreover, state capital itself tends to reproduce the patterns of behaviour of private capital as individual state firms seek to free themselves from their obligation as *state* capital and realize their nature as *capital*.

The fundamental problem with all these alternatives is that they do not question the capitalist nature of production relations. The internationalization of capital is a social process involving the extension and strengthening of capitalist relations of production. It is not surprising that a model of accumulation based on the valorization of capital does not lead to the full utilization of human resources. It is only by changing the main purpose of production and adopting different criteria that the latter objective can be fulfilled. Thus, ultimately, human needs must be the purpose of production. It is the failure of the internationalization of capital to fulfil these needs that is its major indictment. The success of Cuba in this respect shows the possibilities which a socialist transformation offers.

Can and should TNCs have a part to play in a socialist development strategy in Latin America? A socialist strategy will undoubtedly reduce the scope for TNC operations, as for example public transport replaces private transport or preventive health care increases relative to intensive promotion of drugs. Similarly, those areas in which the competitive advantage of TNCs lies in the creation of demand through advertising branded products could be substituted by undifferentiated basic products. Nevertheless, the TNCs do make a real technological contribution in many branches and local alternative technologies may not exist. It is, therefore, likely that even socialist regimes in Latin America could resort to the TNCs for technological inputs. There would, however, have to be a major effort at local adaptation not simply to the different local conditions in Latin America, but also to the socialist nature of the new relations of production. Clearly, such a strategy is by no means free from problems, but the solution is not to refuse to maintain any relations with TNCs. The crucial question is whether TNCs are involved as leading elements in the internationalization of capital, which determines a particular model of accumulation, as occurs at present, or whether the model of accumulation is directed towards fulfilling the needs of the mass of the population, and the TNCs are permitted a certain degree of involvement in fulfilling these needs.

Latin American Fiction

Boom, Yes; Novel, No

Gerald Martin

No cultural phenomenon of the 1960s did more than the apparent explosion of creativity in the Spanish American novel to bring Latin America to international attention. It is no exaggeration to state that if the Southern continent was known for two things above all others in the 1960s, these were, first and foremost, the Cuban Revolution and its impact both on Latin America and the Third World generally, and secondly, the boom in Latin American fiction, whose rise and fall coincided with the rise and fall of liberal perceptions of Cuba between 1959 and 1971. At a moment when such creativity was in short supply internationally, when the French *nouveau roman* was antagonizing ordinary readers and academics everywhere and critics repeatedly asked themselves whether the novel, in the age of the mass media, was now moribund, a succession of Latin American writers – above all, Cortázar, Fuentes, Vargas Llosa and García Márquez – rose to international prominence, others from an earlier generation, like Borges and Carpentier, consolidated their status, and Asturias became the first Latin American novelist to win the Nobel Prize, in 1967. At the same time Vallejo and Neruda were increasingly recognized, albeit belatedly, as two of the world's great poets of the twentieth century. Moreover, although the rhythm of Brazilian cultural development has always been different to that of the larger Spanish American countries, the movement for the first time incorporated Brazil, retrospectively appropriating such works as João Guimarães Rosas' classic *Grande sertão, veredas* (1956).

The impact of these writers was immediate and overwhelming. For the first time Latin American authors saw their novels published in large quantities, and were soon able to conceive of living off the proceeds of their writing and its commercial by-products. Latin American middle-class readers, a rapidly expanding group whom the writers in many ways represented, flattered both by the literary reflection of their own image and by world attention focused on the new fiction, began at last to prefer works by writers from their own continent to those from Europe, and waited eagerly for the next book by Cortázar, García Márquez or Vargas Llosa, encouraged all the way by a complex and contradictory network of communications, from the popular press and television to university journals and symposia, in which for a time it was almost impossible to disentangle advertising from criticism, cosmopolitan forms from Americanist themes, the reverberations of capitalist modernization from those of the Cuban Revolution. The astonishing result of all this was that the boom writers became household names in Latin America, like film or pop stars, sportsmen or politicians. What really confused the issue was that at the same time these profoundly ambitious men were also evidently serious – as well as highly "professional" – writers, who managed both to achieve critical recognition and to become bestsellers (*Cien años de soledad* is the classic example of this). The wholesale conversion of literary production into a commodity process has made it impossible in practice to separate the aesthetic from the political – if such an enterprise were ever possible, in Latin America or elsewhere. On the whole, though, it is also true to say – though few critics have actually recognized this distinction – that in the case of most of the boom writers the early successes remain the outstanding achievements, and the works written for the suddenly emerging market soon showed marked evidence of decline and even decay. Since my own view, reluctantly arrived at, is that all these famous works had a relationship of ambiguity and equivocation towards the ideological alternatives of the decade which was extraordinarily fruitful in terms of narrative form, it would not then be surprising if those outstanding achievements also coincided – before success was assured, before the new movement became the "boom" – with the moment of greatest ambiguity in the face of the alternative between the lure of the Market and the vocation of Art. Certainly Cortázar never improved upon *Rayuela* (1963), nor Fuentes upon *La muerte de Artemio Cruz* (1962: a view of the Mexican Revolution from the temporarily assumed perspective of the Cuban Revolution), nor Cabrera Infante on *Tres tristes tigres* (1963: a novel about Cuba that was not yet counter-revolutionary), nor Vargas Llosa on *La Casa Verde* (1966), nor García Márquez on the incomparable *Cien años de soledad* (1967), which marked the apotheosis of the movement and, as it transpired, heralded its decline.

There was, in reality, no sudden explosion of the new novel (as, in justice, wise heads like Cortázar admitted at the time) the boom was in readership, publishing, university and newspaper criticism, and – above all – in propaganda. It was that, quite simply, that was new. This requires three comments, among others: firstly, the continuity of Latin American fiction, carefully examined, is unmistakable, and goes back almost half a century to Azuela; secondly, despite all the just and unjust things that may be said about the new novel as the encoded petty-bourgeois response to a consumer boom and a new cosmopolitanism disguised as a new internationalism (thus doubly repeating the experience of Modernismo), the movement also appeared to continue that dominant Latin American artistic tradition which considers social concern a minimum and political commitment a maximum requirement; and thirdly the new novel was the material product of Latin America's own literary and economic history, and was therefore "Joycean" not only because it imitated Joyce, which to some extent it did, but because Latin America was now fully ready for the "Joycean" moment of consciousness, which is conjunctural and which in Latin America had much to do with the contradictory complexity of that time and the assimilation and focusing of the history of colonialism and neocolonialism.

The picture can only be sketched in here in its most general outlines, but is roughly as expounded below. My point of departure is that the 1960s, an age of energy and optimism in Latin America as elsewhere, cannot be fully understood either in politics or literature, without particular recourse to the decade with which it is in any case most profitably compared, the 1920s. Between 1918 and 1929 Latin America truly entered the twentieth century and this period was identified at the time as the decade of the "new" and of "modernization", or retrospectively, as one marked by the economics of integration and the politics of incorporation. In the next period of accelerated political, economic and cultural change, between 1958 and 1969, Latin America became, through Cuba (not forgetting Guatemala, 1954), a direct protagonist of the Cold War; and, once again, in a second age of pluralist politics and easy money, newness, modernization and development became key concepts, but now with one crucial difference: whereas in the 1920s the world's first communist revolution had only just occurred, leaving intellectuals, including artists, free to choose, without definitive commitment, either the still untried communist path – as many in Latin America did – or some other – usually populist road (PRI in Mexico, APRA in Peru), in the 1960s such pluralist illusions, although generated anew, were quicker to dissolve; and whereas in the 1920s the principal revolutionary model for Latin Americans, inevitably, was not the distant Soviet one but the equally complex and more ambiguous Mexican experience (Recabarren, Mella, Mariátegui, Prestes, F. Martí and other Marxist intellectuals notwithstanding), in the 1960s it was Cuba's "Third World" communist revolution which provided the intellectual motor, whilst the populist, multi-class alliances which had united so many artists and intellectuals since the 1920s and allowed unbroken dialogue among them, rapidly disintegrated as both sides were forced explicitly to commit themselves – all the more so because the United States, looming ever larger with each passing decade, had now become the principal economic, political and ideological antagonist of that same Soviet Union on which Cuba, in the face of the imperialist blockade, had been forced to depend.

The young Arielist students of the 1918 Córdoba movement had quickly put most of Rodó's philosophical idealism and Darío's literary posturing behind them, identifying themselves, in the wake of the First World War, Mexico and the October Revolution, with the material world of the Latin American peasantry and its incipient worker movements, on the lines envisaged by the great Peruvian intellectual González Prada. Sometimes missionaries (on the Vasconcelos model), sometimes revolutionaries, invariably educators and propagandists among the people (the muralists, the popular universities organized by Haya, Mella and others), that generation, born with the twentieth century, originated a link between students and workers and a practice of student political activism, which would henceforth characterize Latin American social life and would reach one of its great crescendoes in the 1960s, another great age of student revolt world-wide, when in Mexico of all places, exactly half a century after the Córdoba movement, the aspirations of another generation of student rebels came to a bitter end at Tlatelolco, as authoritarianism again became generalized in Latin America, a year after the death of Guevara and a few months after the frustration of the Parisian May.

In the 1920s many young Latin American students yearned to be poets, usually at first on the model of a Darío whom they know only too well to be outmoded (even though he had called his movement "Modernist"): like him they wanted to travel to the "City of Light", there to undergo aesthetic, erotic and political adventures; like him, most of them turned to journalism as a means of earning a living, travelling the world ("from our correspondent in Paris . . ."), and engaging in writing as a profession; although, unlike him, in that decade in which the aesthetic and ideological attractions of France intermingled inextricably with the speed, dash, variety and sheer athleticism of the American Way of Life, they embraced the role of reporter "enthusiastically", if not wholeheartedly, for their inner soul still yearned for Art. The period of Spanish American literary Modernismo was over, and the period of Vanguardismo (that is –

confusingly – what in Britain, North America and Brazil is known as Modernism) had begun (and still – presumably – continues). One of the striking features of Latin American literature at that time, we can now perceive, was the contrast between the image of poetry and that of fiction. In poetry at least, the continent was already fully modern, in the sense that numbers of poets – Huidobro, Borges, M. de Andrade, Bandeira, Vallejo, Neruda – were writing poetry fully as "up to date", innovative and recognizably twentieth-century as anything being produced in Europe, the Soviet Union or the United States. (Moreover, poets like Luis Carlos López, Baldomero Fernández Moreno and, above all and again, Vallejo, were initiating a line of deliberately prosaic, conversational poetry which remains fertile and relevant today.) The novel, however, is always slower to mature (in the end it is always a *historical*, retrospective genre, whose best achievements seem to take at least 30 years to find focus), and in the 1920s, the age of both Mexican muralism and the cosmopolitan avant-garde, we see in literature a contrast – broadly speaking – between a poetic expression whose dominant mode was cosmopolitan, produced by international experience and orientated in the same direction; and a nativist fiction – regionalist, creolist, telluric, indigenist, etc. – somewhere between realism and naturalism, whose impetus had been both accelerated and shaped by the Mexican Revolution, which in the 1930s would turn increasingly towards Soviet-style socialist realism, and which at that time, not entirely paradoxically, was thought to be the most innovative current in Latin American literature. Superficially this looks like a divorce between the genres in terms of the approach to form and content. Yet the novelists who were closest to the poets (and who were usually also poets themselves) were young avant-garde writers like the Guatemalan Asturias, author of the brilliant quasi-ethnological *Leyendas de Guatemala* (1930), the Argentinian Borges, who was already intermingling literature with criticism in quite new ways, the Cuban Carpentier, with his Afro-American *Ecué-Yamba-O* (1933), and the incomparable Brazilian Mário de Andrade with his pathbreaking novel about the Brazilian culture-hero *Macunaíma* (1928). It was to these writers that the future belonged. In the case of the Spanish American trio, the full dimensions of their talents would not become apparent until the 1930s and – due to the nature of the 1930s and the intervention of the Second World War – would only become visible after 1945; and even then only relatively so, because not until the 1960s, as we have noted, did the complex Latin American and international conditions of education, readership and publishing combine to produce a situation in which the achievements of Latin American art could be relatively quickly and generally recognized, both in Latin America and further afield.

Because that same period, the 1960s, also saw a remarkable intensification and flowering of Latin American fiction – what has been called the boom – it is not surprising, in retrospect, that the achievements of that earlier generation of writers – Asturias, Borges, Carpentier, Marechal (author of one of the great Joycean novels, *Adán Buenosayres* (1948) – and even of a later generation – Rulfo, Onetti, Roa Bastos, Arguedas – should for a long time have been eclipsed or, when recognized, radically differentiated from the boom which, if some promoters of megaphone criticism has been believed, must either have been the product of a virgin birth or of some newly discovered island, like Columbus's America. Yet that 1960s fiction – to repeat – was not only very largely the product of the fiction which had gone before, just as all literature is produced by varying combinations of real history and literary history, but it was also the climax and consummation of Latin American Modernism in the Anglo-American and Brazilian sense. In short, the development of Modernist fiction, which in Europe had really begun in Flaubert's day and reached its climax with Joyce (followed, as I see it, by a long decline, which still continues), took longer to complete in Latin America, where it began in the 1920s (though even here, critics beware: Brazil had a Machado de Assis in the last quarter of the nineteenth century), partly because it took that long for conditions in Latin America to reach an equivalence, however inexact in the neocolonial context, to what they had been in Europe in the 1920s, and partly because it takes that long for influences in fiction to work their way through – particularly in this case, because, as I shall now attempt to indicate, the new Latin American novel of the 1960s was a very specific kind of fiction, unequalled since Joyce himself in its structurally implicit claims and ambitions. At the same time, and in the light of these claims and ambitions, it is essential to understand that although a part of the explanation is based on concepts of cultural lag, dependency and one-way influences, it is by no means as simple as this, since, as we have seen, there were on the one hand many Latin American writers and artists, above all those resident in Europe, who in the 1920s were already producing avant-garde, "modernist" works; and on the other hand, there are many conventionally bourgeois or provincial artists in Europe and North America, as well as in Latin America itself, who have still not assimilated the impact and implications of 1920s Modernism and thus continue to produce what in style and ideology we could almost call nineteenth-century works. Moreover, there have been few Kafkas, Picassos, Joyces, Prousts, Stravinskys or Einsteins anywhere since the 1920s, and even the cinema can hardly be said to have made "progress" as an art form since the days of Griffith or Einstein. In other words, if we are to look for progress in recent art, it is not to "high" art that we should look.

Turning, then, to the Latin American novels of the 1960s, they were essentially, in my opinion, "Ulyssean" works. Although Joycean novels continued to be published in the West, no achievement ever matched his. *Ulysses* was the supreme literary product of a peculiarly fertile, highly charged *conjuncture*, at the moment where the old European regime really was – or so it seemed – finally to be laid to rest, and when some new modern world – which might be either communist or capitalist – was imposing itself with a speed and vigour which the mind could barely encompass. Suddenly, writers of the period, above all in the 1920s, were able to take a step back, gain perspective and write works which were no longer, in their one-dimensional "realist" historicity, secret metaphors for their own terminal lifespan, but metaphors for the whole of human experience since the earliest times. It was of course the development of the social sciences, especially ethnology, which had made such a development possible, viewed from the standpoint of a western civilization whose own belief systems were in a state of disarray, at once underlining the relativity of culture and making mythology and mystification ever more alluring to the – reluctantly – profane mind of capitalist consciousness.

The key features of the Ulyssean novel (rather than of the later *Finnegans Wake*, which, overflowing, inaugurates post-modernism) were the following:

(1) The quest for totality
(2) The use of mythology, whether to fashion and unify history or to negate it
(3) A heightened, and indeed insuperable awareness and exploration of language
(4) A preoccupation with "consciousness" as it streams and flows from language to myth and back again
(5) The coincidence between, and even the superimposition of, the human mind and the image of the city as site and subject of the novel over the course of time: a perspective from modernity on the roads leading to it
(6) A preoccupation with the relation between urban and rural,

high and popular, written and oral culture (seen most clearly
not in the boom writers but in their forerunners: Andrade,
Asturias, Borges and Carpentier)
(7) Flowing from all this, a twin concern with both artistry and
craftmanship.

This Ulyssean model, whose labyrinthine passage through everyday life was emulated by Woolf and Faulkner, was in fact peculiarly
apposite for Latin America, where the challenge of uneven development was even more complex than in Joyce's Ireland. But in the
1920s, unsurprisingly, Latin Americans were not fully ready for
these innovations (nor, come to that, were most Europeans nor are
they still), sensing, no doubt, that such a climax of bourgeois
consciousness was the ultimate moment of balance and focus before
a great many other things finally became clear, the result being a
choice between a totally consumerist art or its total politicization. In
any case, and ironically, Latin American writers had first to travel
through the avant-garde and the consciousness of modernity before
they could then turn again and conduct their own quest for identity,
had first to understand the world before they could understand
themselves. But this quest, for the Third World intellectual, involves
more mirages and illusory reflections than even Alice had to negotiate, as soon as he tries to move beyond the culture and the aesthetics
of hunger. At any rate, it was the Parisian generation of Latin
Americans of the 1920s who began this quest, which they completed
some time after the Second World War (when Asturias completed
Hombres de maíz and Marechal completed *Adán Buenosayres*) – significantly enough, at the time when Paz's *The Labyrinth of Solitude*
concluded that Latin Americans were now "the contemporaries of
all men", a historic statement which contained both a striking truth
and a great falsehood: and it was the next Parisian generation (some
of whom also resided in London and Barcelona) – Cortázar, García
Márquez, Fuentes, Vargas Llosa, etc. who brought this literary-
historical phenomenon to a climax and a close in the 1960s, with
works like Cortázar's *Rayuela* (1963), Cabrera Infante's *Tres tristes
tigres* (1963), Vargas Llosa's *La Casa Verde* (1966), Lezama Lima's
Paradiso (1966), García Márquez' *Cien años de soledad* (1967) and
Fuentes' *Terra nostra* (1975).

Each of these novels was about a quest or quests; each was also
about the nature of Latin American identity; each also provided a
metaphor or metaphors for the course of Latin American history –
since the creation, the conquest, independence, the birth of the
author, etc. Each was linguistically exploratory and structurally

mythological, pre-occupied with consciousness, obsessed with the woman both as muse and materiality: in short they were Joycean, Ulyssean works, products of patriarchal idealism inspired by and dedicated (though not addressed) to Penelope, the Other, the world of matter, the female, the people, the nation, Mother America. Their writers had come to see, explicitly or implicitly, largely thanks to the Cuban Revolution that no writer could produce the Great Latin American Novel without a consciousness of colonialism as the determining structural fact of Latin American history, and without integrating this consciousness into the very structure of his fiction. This was not entirely new, however: it was just that a new genera- tion had to learn again what had been known in the 1920s, and writers like Andrade, Asturias, Carpentier, Rulfo had already shown the way to a fiction which would make the Latin American Oedipal quest for historical self-knowledge and identity its central structur- ing motif. The real story of the new novel, then, is of a moment in Latin American history when the Joycean novel became both gener- ally writable and unavoidable. That process was demonstrably complete when, in 1976, Jorge Adoum's novel *Entre Marx y una mujer desnuda*, lamented not only the impossibility of writing "after Joyce" but also, much more definitively, "after Cortázar".

To begin to sum up, then, the major optical illusions of the period in narrative literature among writers, critics and the public in Latin America and abroad, were:

(1) The implicit assumption that anti-imperialism was the same as anti-capitalism, and hence revolutionary, exemplified in the particular interest shown by both Cortázar and Fuentes in the Parisian May of the 1968, the inverted logic of Vargas Llosa's belief that 'a great flowering of the novel always foreshadows great historic transformations of society', and the euphoric conclusion of *Cien años de soledad*. It was, para- doxically, just this confusion, this fertility of contradiction, which allowed both the growth and the publicizing of the new novel.

(2) The idea that the New Novel was genuinely and overwhelm- ingly new, rather than the intensification and consummation of a process, thereby confusing a publishing and advertising event (the boom) with a literary phenomenon (the allegedly new novel).

One demonstration of this is the remarkable rapidity with which the boom novel was followed by the post-boom novel and its accompanying post-structuralist criticism whose main characteristic has been its complete surrender to the free play of language and the loss of a historical perspective. For what must be conceded, despite all that I have said, as rather more than a quantitative difference between the writers of the late 1950s and 1960s and their predecessors, was that the former had developed not only a focused historical perspective on Latin American "development" as a whole from the vantage point of a critical juncture within neo-colonialism, but also, in particular, on the regionalist literature of the 1920s, which Fuentes cruelly parodied in his *La nueva novela latinoamericana* (1969) and Vargas Llosa contemptuously called "pre-literature". Arrogant or not, it was this historical-metaphorical-mythological framing device (a Joycean procedure), since lost to Latin American fiction as to that of the developed capitalist nations, which allowed those works to appear both local and "universal" (acceptable to liberal Europeans) in perhaps the only way possible for a Third-World writer. Now, however, at a moment when that particular bubble has unquestionably burst, we are left to wonder whether Latin American literary culture has finally caught up with that of the "First World" – thereby explaining its relative sterility at the moment – or whether we can look forward, as I suspect, to another burst of creativity, in the age of moon voyages and galactic exploration, around the five hundredth anniversary of Columbus's first landing, where the story of "Latin" America began. What we can already say is that in some of their early novels the greatest of the writers caught up, to their cost, in the boom (Cortázar, Fuentes, García Márquez, Vargas Llosa), undoubtedly emulated the achievements of the earlier – and equally great – writers in producing global metaphors for Latin American history which will still seem entirely appropriate when Colombus's anniversary is celebrated.

Bibliography

Abel, C. and Lewis, C., eds, 1984. *Latin America, Economic Imperialism and the State: the Political Economy of the External Connexion from Independence to the Present Day*. London: Athlone Press.

Albert, B. 1983. *South America and the World Economy from Independence to 1930*. London: Macmillan.

– – 1984. "The Creation of a Proletariat on Peru's Coastal Sugar Plantations: 1880–1920", in Finch, M. H. J. and Munslow, B., eds, 1984.

Alejandro, C. D. 1981. "Southern Cone Stabilization Plans", in Kline, W. and Weintraub, S., eds, 1981.

Alves, M. H. M. 1984. "Grassroots Organizations, Trade Unions and the Church: A Challenge to the Controlled Abertura in Brazil". *Latin American Perspectives*, 11, 1.

– –. 1985. *State and Opposition in Military Brazil*. Austin: University of Texas Press.

Anderson, R. D. 1976. *Outcasts in Their Own Land: Mexican Industrial Workers, 1906–1911*. De Kalb: Northern Illinois University Press.

Anglade, C. and Fortin, C., eds, 1985. *State and Capital Accumulation in Latin America*, vol. 1. London: Macmillan.

Archetti, E. and Stolen, K. A. 1980. "Burgesia rural y campesinado en la Sierra ecuatoriana", *Caravelle*, 34.

Ashby, J. 1967. *Organised Labor and the Mexican Revolution under Cardenas*. Chapel Hill: University of North Carolina Press.

Assadourian, C. S. 1982. *El sistema de la economia colonial*. Lima: IEP.

Aviel, J. 1981. "Political Participation of Women in Latin America", *Western Political Quarterly*, 34, 1.

Baily, S. 1967. *Labor, Nationalism and Politics in Argentina*. New Brunswick: Rutgers University Press.

Balan, J. 1969. "Migrant Native Socio-economic Differences in Latin American Cities: A Structural Analysis", *Latin American Research Review*, 4, 1, 3–29.

Baraona, R. 1977. "Una tipología de haciendas en la Sierra ecuatoriana", in CIDA, 1977.

Barraclough, S. 1973. *Agrarian Structure in Latin America*. Massachusetts: D. C. Heath.

Barsky, O. 1978. "Iniciativa terrateniente en la reestructuración de las relaciones sociales en la Sierra ecuatoriana: 1959–1964", *Revista Ciencias Sociales*, II, 5, 74–126.

Bauer, A. 1975. *Chilean Rural Society: From the Spanish Conquest to 1930*. Cambridge: Cambridge University Press.

– –. 1979. "Rural Workers in Spanish America: Problems of Peonage and Oppression", *Hispanic American Historical Review*, 59, 1.

Bazant, J. 1973. "Peones, arrendatarios y aparceros en México: 1851–1853", *Historia Mexicana*, 23.

– –. 1974. "Peones, arrendatarios y aparceros: 1868–1904", *Historia Mexicana*, 24.

– –. 1975. *Cinco haciendas mexicanas: tres siglos de vida rural en San Luis Potosí.* Mexico: Siglo XXI.

Becker, D. 1983. *The New Bourgeoisie and the Limits of Dependency: Mining, Class and Power in 'Revolutionary' Peru.* Princeton: Princeton University Press.

– –. 1984. "Development, Democracy, and Dependency in Latin America: a post-imperialist view", *Third World Quarterly*, 6, 2.

Bethell, L., ed. 1984. *et seq. Cambridge History of Latin America.* vols I–V. Cambridge: Cambridge University Press.

Birkbeck, C. 1978. "Self-employed Proletarians in an Informal Factory: The Case of Cali's Garbage Dump", *World Development*, 6, 1173–85.

Blanchard, P. 1982. *The Origins of the Peruvian Labor Movement, 1883–1919.* Pittsburgh: Pittsburgh University Press.

Bonardelli, E. 1916. *Lo stato di Sao Paulo de Brasile e l'emigrazione italiana.* Turin.

Boron, A. 1979. "New Forms of Capitalist State in Latin America: An Exploration", *Race and Class*, 20, 3.

– –. 1982. "Latin America: Between Hobbes and Friedman", *New Left Review*, 133.

Boserup, E. 1970. *Women's Role in Economic Development.* New York: St Martin's Press.

Boxer, C. 1969. *The Golden Age of Brazil, 1695–1750.* Berkeley: University of California Press.

Brading, D. 1975. "Estructura de la producción agrícola en el Bajío, 1700–1850", in Florescano, E., ed. 1975.

– –, ed. 1980. *Caudillo and Peasant in the Mexican Revolution.* Cambridge: Cambridge University Press.

Brown, J. 1979. *A Socio-Economic History of Argentina, 1776–1860.* Cambridge: Cambridge University Press.

Buenaventura-Posso, E. and Brown, S. 1977. "Westernization and the Bari", in Etienne, M. and Leacock, E., eds. 1977.

Butterworth, D. and Chance, J. 1981. *Latin American Urbanization.* Cambridge: Cambridge University Press.

Buve, R. T. J. 1975. "Peasant Movements, Caudillos and Land Reform during the Revolution (1910–1917) in Tlaxcala, Mexico", *Boletín de Estudios Latinoamericanos y del Caribe*, 18.

Caballero, J. 1976. "Agrarian Reform and the Transformation of the Peruvian Countryside". Unpublished manuscript. University of Cambridge.

Carbo, L. A. 1953. *Historia monetaria y cambiaria del Ecuador.* Quito: Imprensa del Banco Central.

Cardoso, F. H. 1972. "Dependency and Development in Latin America", *New Left Review*, 74.

– –. 1977. "The Consumption of Dependency Theory in the United States", *Latin American Research Review*, 12, 3.

– – and Faletto, E. 1969. *Dependencia y Desarrollo en América Latina*. Mexico: Siglo XXI.

– – and Faletto, E. 1979. *Dependency and Development in Latin America*. Berkeley: University of California Press.

Carr, B. 1979. "The Casa del Obrero Mundial, Constitutionalism and the Pact of February 1915", in Frost, E. C. *et. al.*, eds. 1979.

Carvalho, J. M. de. 1975. "Elites and State Building in Imperial Brazil", PhD. dissertation, University of Stanford.

– –. 1982. "Political Elites and State Building: the Case of Nineteenth Century Brazil", *Comparative Studies in Society and History*, 24, 3.

Castells, M. 1983. *The City and the Grassroots*. London: Edward Arnold.

CEPAL-FAO. 1978. "Reforma agraria y modernización agrícola en América Latina", *Comercio Exterior*, 28, 11, 1393–1406.

Chaney, E. 1979. *Supermadre: Women and Politics in Latin America*. Austin: University of Texas Press.

Chant, S. 1985a. "Family Formation and Female Roles in Queretaro, Mexico", *Bulletin of Latin American Research*, 4, 1.

– –. 1985b. "Single Parent Families: Choice or Constraint? The Formation of Female-Headed Households in Mexican Shanty Towns", *Development and Change*, 16, 4.

CIDA. 1977. *Monografía sobre algunos aspectos de la tenencia de la tierra y el desarrollo rural en América Latina*. Washington: OAS.

Coletti, S. 1908. "Lo stato di Sao Paulo e l'emigrazione italiana", *Bolletino dell'Emigrazione*, 14.

Conniff, M, ed. 1982. *Latin American Populism in Comparative Perspective*. Albuquerque: University of New Mexico Press.

Cornelius, W. 1975. *Politics and the Migrant Poor in Mexico City*. Stanford: Stanford University Press.

– – and Kemper, R. 1978. *Metropolitan Latin America*, 6 vols. Beverly Hills: Sage.

Cortén, A. 1965. "Como vive la otra mitad de Santo Domingo: estudio de dualismo estructural", *Caribbean Studies*, 4, 3–19.

Cueva, A. 1982. *The Process of Political Domination in Ecuador*, London: Transaction Books.

Davatz, T. 1972. *Memorias de um colono no Brasil*. Sao Paulo: Livraria Martins.

Dean, W. 1969. *The Industrialization of Sao Paulo*. Austin: University of Texas Press.

– –. 1976. *Rio Claro: A Brazilian Plantation System, 1820–1920*. Stanford: Stanford University Press.

Deas, M. 1977. "A Colombian Coffee Estate: Santa Barbara, Cundinamarca, 1870–1912", in Duncan, K. and Rutledge, I., eds, 1977.

Deere, C. D. 1978. "The Development of Capitalism in Agriculture and the Division of Labour by Sex: A Study of the Northern Peruvian Sierra", PhD. dissertation, University of California.

– –. 1982. "The Division of Labour by Sex in Agriculture: A Peruvian

Case Study", *Economic Development and Cultural Change*, 30, 4, 795–811.

– – and de Janvry, A. 1979. "A Conceptual Framework for the Empirical Analysis of Peasants", *American Journal of Agricultural Economics*, 61, 601–11.

De Janvry, A. 1981. *The Agrarian Question and Reformism in Latin America*. Baltimore: Johns Hopkins University Press.

Denis, P. 1911. *Brazil*. London.

DeShazo, P. 1979. "The Valparaiso Maritime Strike of 1903 and the Development of a Revolutionary Labour Movement in Chile", *Journal of Latin American Studies*, 11, 1.

– –. 1983. *Urban Workers and Labor Unions in Chile 1902–1927*. Madison: University of Wisconsin Press.

Drake, P. 1978. *Socialism and Populism in Chile, 1932–1952*. Urbana: University of Illinois Press.

Duncan, K. and Rutledge, I., eds, 1977. *Land and Labour in Latin ·America*. Cambridge: Cambridge University Press.

Einaudi, L. and Stepan, A. 1971. *Latin American Institutional Development: Changing Military Perspectives in Peru and Brazil*. Santa Monica: Rand Corporation.

Elhuyar, H. 1825. *Memoria sobre el influjo de la minería en la nueva España*. Madrid.

Erickson, K. 1977. *The Brazilian Corporative State and the Working Class*. Berkeley: University of California Press.

Etienne, M. and Leacock, E., eds, 1977. *Women and Colonization*. New York: Praeger.

Evans, P. 1981. *Dependent Development: The Alliance of Multinational, State and Local Capital in Brazil*. Princeton: Princeton University Press.

Fagen, R., ed. 1979. *Capitalism and the State in US–Latin-American Relations*. Stanford: Stanford University Press.

Fernandez, M. "British Nitrate Companies and the Emergence of Chile's Proletariat, 1880–1914", in Finch, M. H. J. and Munslow, B., eds, 1984.

Finch, M. H. J. and Munslow, B., eds, 1984. *Proletarianisation in the Third World*. London: Croom Helm.

Finer, S. E. 1962. *The Man on Horseback: the Role of the Military in Politics*. Harmondsworth: Penguin.

Fitzgerald, V. 1979. *The Political Economy of Peru 1956–78: Economic Development and the Restructuring of Capital*. Cambridge: Cambridge University Press.

Florescano, E., ed. 1975. *Haciendas, latifundios y plantaciones en América Latina*. Mexico: Siglo XXI.

Frank, A. G. 1969. *Capitalism and Underdevelopment in Latin America*. New York: Monthly Review Press.

Frost, E. C. *et al.*, eds, 1979. *El trabajo y los trabajadores en la historia de Mexico*. Mexico: Colegio de Mexico.

Geertz, C. 1971. *Agricultural Involution*. Berkeley: University of California Press.

Gibson, C. 1964. *The Aztecs under Spanish Rule*. Stanford: Stanford University Press.
– –. 1966. *Spain in America*. New York: Harper & Row.
Gilbert, A. 1983. "The Tenants of Self-help Housing: Choice and Constraint in the Housing Markets of Less Developed Countries", *Development and Change*, 14, 449–77.
– – *et al.*, eds, 1982. *Urbanization in Contemporary Latin America*. London: John Wiley
– – and Ward, P. 1985. *Housing, the State and the Poor*. Cambridge: Cambridge University Press.
Goodman, D. and Redclift, M. 1981. *Peasant to Proletarian: Capitalist Development and Agrarian Transitions*. Oxford: Blackwell.
Grabois, G. P. 1973. *Em busca da integração. a política de remoção de favelas no Rio de Janeiro*, M. A. thesis, Social Anthropology Programme, National Museum, Rio de Janeiro.
Graham, R. and Smith, P., eds, 1974. *New Approaches to Latin American History*. Austin: University of Texas Press.
Grindle, M. 1986. *State and Countryside: Development Policy and Agrarian Politics in Latin America*. Baltimore: Johns Hopkins University Press.
Guerra, F–X. 1981. "La révolution mexicaine: d'abord une révolution minière?", *Annales ESC*, 36.
Guerrero, A. 1977. "Renta diferencial y vias de disolución de la hacienda precapitalista en el Ecuador", *Caravelle*, 28.
Halperin-Donghi, T. 1973. *The Aftermath of Revolution in Latin America*. New York: Harper & Row.
Hamilton, N. 1982. *The Limits of State Autonomy: Post-Revolutionary Mexico*. Princeton: Princeton University Press.
Harding, C. 1975. "Land Reform and Social Conflict in Peru", in Lowenthal, A., ed. 1975.
Hemming, J. 1978. *Red Gold: The Conquest of the Brazilian Indians, 1500–1760*. London: Macmillan.
Henfrey, C. 1981. "Dependency, Modes of Production and the Class Analysis of Latin America", *Latin American Perspectives*, 8, 3–4.
Hobsbawm, E. J. 1959. *Primitive Rebels*. Manchester: Manchester University Press.
Holloway, T. 1980. *Immigrants on the Land: Coffee and Society in Sao Paulo, 1886–1934*. Chapel Hill: University of North Carolina Press.
Horowitz, J. 1983. "The Impact of Pre-1943 Labour Union Traditions on Peronism", *Journal of Latin American Studies*, 15, 1.
Humphrey, J. 1984. "The Growth of Female Employment in Brazilian Manufacturing Industry in the 1970s", *Journal of Development Studies*, 20, 4.
Ionescu, G. and Gellner, E., eds, 1969. *Populism*. London: Weidenfeld & Nicolson.
Jacobs, I. 1982. *Ranchero Revolt: The Mexican Revolution in Guerrero*. Austin: University of Texas Press.
Jaguaribe Filho, D. 1877. *Algumas palavras sobre a emigração*. São Paulo.

Jaquette, J. "Female Political Participation in Latin America", in Nash, J. and Safa, H., eds, 1980.

Jaulin, R. 1973. *Gens de soi, gens de l'autre*. Paris: Union Général d'Editions.

Jenkins, R. 1977. *Dependent Industrialization in Latin America: the Automotive Industry in Argentina, Chile and Mexico*, New York: Praeger.

— —. 1984. *Transnational Corporations and Industrial Transformation in Latin America*. London: Macmillan.

Joly, L. 1981. "One is None and Two is One: Development from Above and Below in North Central Panama", PhD thesis, University of Florida.

Journal of Family History 1978. Special Issue: *The Family in Latin America*. vol. 3, no. 4.

— —. 1985. Special Issue: *The Latin American Family in the Nineteenth Century*. vol. 10, no. 3.

Katz, F. 1974. "Labor Conditions on Haciendas in Porfirian Mexico: Some Trends and Tendencies", *Hispanic American Historical Review*, 54.

Kavanagh, D. and Peele, G., eds, 1984. *Comparative Government and Politics: Essays in Honour of S. E. Finer*. London: Heinemann.

Kay, C. 1977. "The Development of the Chilean Hacienda System, 1850–1973", in Duncan, K. and Rutledge, I., eds, 1977.

— —. 1982. "Achievements and Contradictions of the Peruvian Land Reform", *Journal of Development Studies*, 18, 2.

Keith, R., ed. 1977. *Haciendas and Plantations in Latin American History*. New York: Holmes & Meier.

Kirsch, H. 1977. *Industrial Development in a Traditional Society*. Gainsville: University of Florida Press.

Klare, M. and Arnson, C. 1979. "Exporting Repression: US Support for Authoritarianism in Latin America", in Fagen, R., ed. 1979.

Kline, W. and Weintraub, S. 1981. *Economic Stabilization in Developing Countries*. Washington.

Knight, A. 1980. "Peasant and Caudillo in the Mexican Revolution", in Brading, D., ed. 1980.

— —. 1984. "The Working Class and the Mexican Revolution c. 1900–1920", *Journal of Latin American Studies*, 16, 1.

— —. 1986. *The Mexican Revolution, 1908–1920*. 2 vols. Cambridge: Cambridge University Press.

Kowarick, L. 1977. "The Logic of Disorder", Discussion Paper 102, Institute of Development Studies, University of Sussex.

Laclau, E. 1969. "Modos de producción, sistemas económicos y población excedente: aproximación histórica a los casos argentino y chileno", *Revista Latinoamericana de Sociologia*, 2.

— —. 1977. "Towards a Theory of Populism", in *Politics and Ideology in Marxist Theory*, London: Verso.

Latin American Perspectives 1974. Special Issue: *Dependency Theory: A Reassessment*, vol. 1, no. 1.

— —. 1976. Special Issue: *Dependency Theory and Dimensions of Imperialism*, vol. 3, no. 4.

Lavrin, A., ed. 1978. *Latin American Women: Historical Perspectives*. Westport: Greenwood Press.

Leeds, E. 1972. "Forms of 'Squatment' Political Organization: The Politics of Control in Brazil", M.A. thesis, Department of Political Science, University of Texas at Austin.

Lehmann D., ed. 1974. *Agrarian Reform and Agrarian Reformism*. London: Faber & Faber.

– –, ed. 1982. *Ecology and Exchange in the Andes*. Cambridge: Cambridge University Press.

Leon-Portilla, M. 1962. *The Broken Spears*. London: Constable.

Lewis, O. 1961. *The Children of Sanchez*. New York: Random House.

Linz, J. 1973. "The Future of an Authoritarian Situation or the Institutionalisation of an Authoritarian Regime: the Case of Brazil", in Stepan, A., ed. 1973.

Lipton, M. 1974. "Towards a Theory of Land Reform", in Lehmann, D., ed. 1974.

Little, W. 1975. "The Popular Origins of Peronism", in Rock, D., ed. 1975.

Lockhart, J. 1968. *Spanish Peru (1532–60): A Colonial Society*. Wisconsin: University of Wisconsin Press.

– – and Schwartz, S. 1983. *Early Latin America: A History of Colonial Spanish America and Brazil*. Cambridge: Cambridge University Press.

Lomnitz, L. 1976. "Migration and Networks in Latin America", in Portes, A. and Browning, H., eds, 1976.

– –. 1977. *Networks and Marginality*. New York: Academic Press.

Long, N. and Roberts, B., eds, 1978. *Peasant Co-operation and Capitalist Expansion in Central Peru*. Austin: University of Texas Press.

– –. (1984). *Miners, Peasants and Entrepreneurs*. Cambridge: Cambridge University Press.

Lopes, J. R. B. 1978. "Capitalist Development and Agrarian Structure in Brazil", *International Journal of Urban and Regional Research*, 2. 1.

Lowenthal, A., ed. 1976. *Armies and Politics in Latin America*. New York: Holmes & Meier.

McCourt, K. 1977. *Working-Class Women and Grassroots Politics*. Bloomington: Indiana University Press.

Machado Nunes, S. 1860. "Colonias na provincia de S. Paulo", in Brazil, *Relatorio de 1860*. Rio de Janeiro: Ministerio do Imperio.

Macpherson, C. B. 1975. *The Real World of Democracy*. Oxford: Oxford University Press.

Madero, F. 1908. *La sucesión presidencial en 1910*. San Pedro, Mexico.

Maistrello, G. 1923. "Fazendas de cafe – costumes (São Paulo)", in Ramos, A. 1923.

Mallon, F. 1983. *The Defence of Community in Peru's Central Highlands*. Princeton: Princeton University Press.

Malloy, J. 1977 "Authoritarianism and Corporatism in Latin America: The Modal Pattern", in Malloy, J., ed. 1977.

– –, ed. 1977. *Authoritarianism and Corporatism in Latin America*. Pittsburgh: University of Pittsburgh Press.

Mangin, W. 1967. "Latin American Squatter Settlements", *Latin American Research Review*, 2, 65–98.

Martin, G. 1984. "Boom, Yes; 'New Novel', No: Further Reflections on the

Optical Illusions of the 1960s in Latin America", *Bulletin of Latin American Research*, 3, 2.

Martinez-Alier, J. 1977. *Haciendas, Plantations and Collective Farms*. London: Frank Cass.

Martz, J. and Myers, D. 1983. "Understanding Latin American Politics: Analytic Models and Intellectual Traditions", *Polity*, 16, 2.

Mencher, J. P., ed. 1983. *Social Anthropology of Peasantry*. Bombay: Somaiya Publications.

Moises, J. A. and Stolcke, V. 1980. "Urban Transport and Popular Violence in Brazil", *Past and Present*, 86.

Molyneux, M. 1985. "Mobilization without Emancipation? Women's Interests, State and Revolution in Nicaragua", *Feminist Studies*, 11.

Moore, B., Jr. 1978. *Injustice: The Social Bases of Obedience and Revolt*. London: Macmillan.

Moser, C. 1985. "Residential Struggle and Consciousness: the Experiences of Poor Women in Guayaquil, Ecuador", DPU Gender and Planning Working Paper No. 1, Development Planning Unit, London.

Mouzelis, N. 1978. "Ideology and Class Politics", *New Left Review*, 112.

Munck, R. 1984. *Politics and Dependency in the Third World: The Case of Latin America*. London: Zed Books.

– –. 1984a. "The Formation and Development of the Working Class in Argentina, 1857–1919", in Finch, M. H. J. and Munslow, B., eds, 1984.

Murmis, M. 1978. "Sobre la emergencia de una burguesía terrateniente capitalista en la Sierra ecuatoriana como condicionamiento de la acción estatal", *Revista Ciencias Sociales*, II, 5, 145–56.

– – and Portantiero, J. C., eds, 1971. *Estudios sobre los orígenes del peronismo*, vol. 1. Buenos Aires: Siglo XXI.

Murra, J. V. 1975. "El control vertical de un máximo de pisos ecológicos en la economía de las sociedades andinas", in *Formaciones económicas y políticas del mundo andino*. Lima: IEP.

Nash, J. and Fernandez-Kelly, M. P., eds, 1983. *Women, Men and the International Division of Labour*. Albany: State University of New York Press.

Nash, J. and Safa, H., eds, 1980. *Sex and Class in Latin America*. South Hadley: J. F. Bergin.

– – and – –, 1986. *Women and Change in Latin America*. South Hadley: Bergin & Garvey.

Nelson, J. 1979. *Access to Power: Politics and the Urban Poor in Developing Nations*. Princeton: Princeton University Press.

O'Brien, P. 1975. "A Critique of Latin American Theories of Dependency", in Oxaal, I. Barnett, T. and Booth, D., eds, 1975.

– –. 1984. "Dependency Revisited", in Abel, C. and Lewis, C., eds, 1984.

– – and Cammack, P., eds, 1985. *Generals in Retreat: The Crisis of Military Rule in Latin America*. Manchester: Manchester University Press.

O'Donnell, G. 1977. "Corporatism and the Question of the State", in Malloy, J., ed. 1977.

Olson, B. and Neglia, A. 1974. *Una Raza Bravia: Estudio Socio-antropológico de los indios Motilones*. Bogotá: Instituto de Desarrollo de la Comunidad.
Oxaal, I., Barnett, T. and Booth, D., eds, 1975. *Beyond the Sociology of Development*. London: Routledge & Kegan Paul.
Palma, G. 1978. "Dependency: A Formal Theory of Underdevelopment or a Methodology for the Analysis of Concrete Situations?", *World Development*, 6, 3–4.
Peattie, L. 1968. *The View from the Barrio*. Michigan: University of Michigan Press.
Peña, M. 1972. *El peronismo: selección de documentos*. Buenos Aires.
Perlman, J. 1976. *The Myth of Marginality*. Berkeley: University of California Press.
Pescatello, A., ed. 1973. *Female and Male in Latin America*. Pittsburgh: University of Pittsburgh Press.
Pinton, S. 1973. "Les travaux et les jours", in Jaulin, R., ed. 1973.
Portes, A. 1972. "Rationality in the Slum: an Essay on Comparative Sociology", *Comparative Studies in Society and History*, 14, 268–86.
– – and Browning, H., eds, 1976. *Current Perspectives in Latin American Urban Research*. Austin: University of Texas Press.
– – and Walton, J. 1976. *Urban Latin America*. Austin: University of Texas Press.
– – – –. 1981. *Labor, Class and the Industrial System*. New York: Academic Press.
Preston, D., ed. 1979. *Environment, Society and Rural Change in Latin America*. London: John Wiley.
– – and Redclift, M. 1979. "Agrarian Reform and Rural Change in Ecuador", in Preston, D., ed. 1979.
Ramos, A. 1923. *O café no Brasil e no estrangeiro*. Rio de Janeiro.
Ray, T. F. 1969. *The Politics of the Barrios in Venezuela*. Berkeley: University of California Press.
Redclift, M. 1978. *Agrarian Reform and Peasant Organizations on the Ecuadorian Coast*. London: Athlone Press.
Roberts, B. R. 1973. *Organizing Strangers*. Austin: University of Texas.
– –. 1974. "Small Scale Activity and Development: the Case of Peru" Unpublished paper, University of Manchester.
– –. 1976. "The Provincial Urban System and the Process of Dependency", in Portes, A. and Browning, H., eds, 1976.
– –. 1978. *Cities of Peasants*. London: Edward Arnold.
Rock, D., ed. 1975. *Argentina in the Twentieth Century*. London: Duckworth.
Rouquié, A. 1982. "Demilitarization and the Institutionalization of Military-Dominated Politics in Latin America", Working Paper 110, Latin American Program, Washington: Wilson Center.
Roxborough, I. 1984. "Historical Unity and Diversity in Latin America", *Journal of Latin American Studies*, 16, 1.
Safford, F. 1974. "Bases of Political Alignment in Early Republican Spanish America", in Graham, R. and Smith, P., eds, 1974.

Schwartz, S. *Sovereignty and Society in Colonial Brazil*. Berkeley: University of California Press.

Scobie, J. 1964. *Revolution on the Pampas: A Social History of Argentine Wheat, 1860–1910*. Austin: University of Texas Press.

Sharp, W. F. 1974. "Manumission, Libres and Black Resistance: The Colombian Choco, 1680–1810", in Toplin, R., ed. 1974.

– –. 1976. *Slavery on the Spanish Frontier: the Colombian Choco, 1680–1810*. Norman: University of Oklahoma Press.

Sigmund, P. 1980. *Multinationals in Latin America: The Politics of Nationalization*. Madison: University of Wisconsin Press.

Silva, J. F. da. 1980. *As lutas camponesas no Brasil, 1980*. Rio de Janeiro: Editora Marco Zero.

Skidmore, T. and Smith, P. 1984. *Modern Latin America*. Oxford: Oxford University Press.

Smith, G. A. 1984. "Confederations of Households: Extended Domestic Enterprises in City and Country", in Long, N. and Roberts, B., eds, 1984.

– – and Cano, P. H. 1978. "Some Factors Contributing to Peasant Land Occupations in Peru: the Example of Huasicancha, 1963–8", in Long, N. and Roberts, B., eds, 1978.

Smith, P. 1969. *Politics and Beef in Argentina*. New York: Columbia University Press.

Smith, T. 1985. "Requiem or New Agenda for Third World Studies", *World Politics*, 37, 4.

Spalding, H., Jr. 1977. *Organized Labor in Latin America*. New York: Harper & Row.

Spalding, K. 1983. *Huarochiri: An Andean Society under Inca and Spanish Rule*. Stanford: Stanford University Press.

Stein, Stanley and Stein, B. 1970. *The Colonial Heritage of Latin America*. New York: Oxford University Press.

Stein, Steve, 1980. *Populism in Peru*. Madison: University of Wisconsin Press.

Stepan, A. 1976. "The New Professionalism of Internal Warfare", in Lowenthal, A., ed. 1976.

– –, ed. 1973. *Authoritarian Brazil*. New Haven: Yale University Press.

Stern, S. J. 1979. "The Challenge of Conquest: The Indian Peoples of Huamanga, Peru and the Foundation of a Colonial Society, 1532–1640", PhD thesis, Yale University.

– –. 1982. *Peru's Indian Peoples and the Challenge of the Spanish Conquest: Huamanga to 1640*. Madison: University of Wisconsin Press.

– –. 1983. "The Struggle for Solidarity: Class, Culture and Community in Highland Latin America", *Radical History Review*, 27, 21–45.

Stolcke, V. and Hall, M. 1983. "The Introduction of Free Labour on Sao Paulo Coffee Plantations", *Journal of Peasant Studies*, 10, 2–3.

Tandeter, E. 1981. "Forced and Free Labour in Late Colonial Potosi", *Past and Present*, 93.

Tella, T. di. 1981. "Working Class Organization and Politics in Argentina", *Latin American Research Review*, 16, 2.

Therborn, G. 1979. "The Travail of Latin American Democracy", *New Left Review*, 113–14.

Thompson, E. P. 1971. "The Moral Economy of the English Crowd in the Eighteenth Century", *Past and Present*, 50, 76–136.

– –. 1978. "The Peculiarities of the English", in *The Poverty of Theory and Other Essays*. London: Merlin.

Timerman, J. 1981. *Prisoner Without a Name, Cell Without a Number*. Harmondsworth: Penguin.

Toplin, R., ed. 1974. *Slavery and Race Relations in Latin America*. Westport: Greenwood Press.

Torre, J. C. 1976. "Sobre as origens do peronismo", *Estudos CEBRAP*, 16.

Tutino, J. 1975. "Hacienda Social Relations in Mexico: The Chalco Region in the Era of Independence", *Hispanic American Historical Review*, 55.

Valdetaro, M. J. 1858. "Colonias de S. Paulo", in Brazil, *Relatorio da repartição geral das terras públicas, apresentado em 31 de março 1858*. Rio de Janeiro.

Villamil, J., ed. 1979. *Transnational Capitalism and National Development: New Perspectives on Dependence*. Hassocks: Harvester Press.

Wachtel, N. 1977. *The Vision of the Vanquished*. Hassocks: Harvester Press.

Warman, A. 1980. *"We Come to Object": The Peasants of Morelos and the National State*. Baltimore: Johns Hopkins University Press.

– –. 1983. "Peasant Production and Population in Mexico", in Mencher, J. P., ed. 1983.

Wellesley Editorial Committee, 1977. *Women and National Development: The Complexities of Change*. Chicago: University of Chicago Press.

Whitehead, L. 1982. "Whatever Became of the Southern Cone Model?", Institute of Latin American Studies, Occasional Papers Series, 5, Melbourne, La Trobe University.

Wolf, E. 1969. *Peasant Wars of the Twentieth Century*. New York: Harper & Row.

Womack, J. 1968. *Zapata and the Mexican Revolution*. New York: Alfred A. Knopf.

Zamosc, L. 1986. *The Agrarian Question and the Peasant Movement in Colombia*. Cambridge: Cambridge University Press.

Zeitlin, M. *et al.* 1976. "Class Segments, Agrarian Property and Political Leadership in the Capitalist Class of Chile", *American Sociological Review*, 41, 6.

– – and Ratcliff, R. 1975. "Research Methods for the Analysis of the Internal Structure of the Dominant Classes", *Latin American Research Review* 10, 3.

Index

agrarian reform 167–9, 186, 186–96
agrarian structure: in colony 23–6;
    in nineteenth century 73–8,
    79–95; in Brazil 171–7; in
    Peru 186–96
agriculture: capitalization of 175;
    export 172; peasant 213–16;
    role of women in 196–212,
    323–6
Alessandri, J. President of Chile
    (1921–4) 110–11, 113
anarchism: in Chile 112
Argentina: politics of 137–44
authoritarianism: political 126,
    146, 235
Ayllu (community land tenure) 39

black population 49–54
Brazil: agrarian structure of
    169–70, 171–7; colonial 55–64;
    politics in 234, 294–303; urban
    conditions in 221–8, 229–40
bureaucracy: in colony 62

capitalism: and urban life, 228;
    internationalization of,
    329–33; state, 196
Cardenas, L., President of Mexico
    (1934–40) 121–3, 132
Cardoso, F. H. 3–12
Chile: labor movement in,
    109–15; military intervention
    in, 282, 291–3
cities: and class formation 97–9;
    and living conditions 221–8,
    229–31; and politics 148, 320
class 247–8: and culture, 335; and
    gender 320; and politics
    66–70, 99–101, 150–6; and

populism 119–123, 130–1,
    141–5; ideology of 140–3; in
    colony 44–7, 58–63; in rural
    areas 177–86; working 97–109,
    141–2, 226–7, 234, 241–4, 157,
    300, 305
coffee *see* plantation, coffee
Colombia: colonial 49–54
community: village 39, 46, 190,
    321–2; urban 256–8, 258–61,
    305–20
conservatives, 65–70
Cuba: influence on literature 335–8

dependency 8–18, 158
differentiation, social, in colony,
    35–41, 50–4

Economic Commission for Latin
    America (ECLA) 11
Ecuador: agrarian structure of
    177–86; politics of 147–59
education: in colony 56–7;
    significance for jobs 251–2
enclave, economic, 3
enganche (debt peonage) 77–8
export economy 3; and politics
    67–8, 140–1, 147

Faletto, E., 3–12
Frank, A. G., 9, 14

hacienda, 73–6, 177–80, 186–91, 199
household: rural 92, 323–7; urban
    259–66
housing: and informal sector,
    244–7, 269–71; and politics
    305–20; in Brazil, 221–6